Seeing Around Corners

Powerful Lessons of Perseverance, Grit, and Luck

ALAN B. LEVAN

CHAIRMAN & CEO:

BBX Capital (NYSE)

Bluegreen Vacations (NYSE)

BankAtlantic Bancorp (NYSE)

Levitt Corporation (NYSE)

with Beth Herman

Library of Congress has cataloged the hardcover edition as follows:
Names: Levan, Alan B., author with Beth Herman.
Title: Seeing Around Corners: Powerful Lessons of Perseverance, Grit, and Luck
Description: First (edition) Florida: Bee Hive Publishing, 2022
Identifiers: ISBN 978-1-956470-48-2 (Hardcover), ISBN 978-1-952106-88-0 (Paperback), ISBN 978-1-956470-64-2 (e-book), LCCN 2022921548
Subjects: Biography & Autobiography, Memoir, Business & Economics: Success

Published by Bee Hive Publishing (Fort Lauderdale, Florida) Manufactured and printed in the United States
First Edition
Jacket Design by Graphique Designs, LLC
Front Cover Photo: Tiffany Photographic Studio

DEDICATION

*I*n loving memory
of my parents,
Zit and Pearl Levan

---

*T*o my incredible wife and partner, Susie

---

*T*o my five exceptional children and their spouses,
who are like my own:

Gina and Mario De Varona
Don and Judy Levan
Shelley and Jeff Margolis
Jarett and Dara Levan
Lauren Perlstein and fiancé, Travis Acker

---

*T*o my twelve fabulous grandchildren

---

*A*nd to my wonderful brother Jay and his wife, Lori

TABLE OF CONTENTS

FOREWORD

I tend to take my successes and failures, gains and losses, in stride. People who know me say I'm a very private person. I decided to write this book for no other reason than that my five children and twelve grandchildren would get to know me better, though the deeper I got into the story, the more I understood there may be something here for others as well.

In my life and in business, my mantra has always been "next" and "move on," significant lessons I learned very early on from my father. We don't spend too much time stewing in our losses or even celebrating our wins. There is always more to do, experience, and accomplish. In the realm of experience, my own children—all of whom I love, respect, and am very close to—don't know some of these stories and it is time to share them.

I have always been saddened by not really knowing my grandparents. Just imagine what the story of my grandparents would have been, coming from Russia and Poland in the early 1900s, tales of their lives there, arriving by boat, through Ellis Island without any money, finding work, creating a family. I mean, what incredible stories that would be, and yet we have nothing. We know absolutely nothing.

I was even more saddened when my father and mother died, and their legacy and memory were left in picture frames and photograph albums we rarely spend time reviewing. We do not tell their stories.

Sure, we remember them as wonderful people and honorable and courageous parents and grandparents, but the glorious, humorous, and colorful stories of their lives fade over time. My father has been deceased only sixteen years and some of his great grandchildren (my grandchildren) are already inquiring about his name and who he was. Most weren't born when he died. I do my best to pay homage to him in this book because though we had little materially, he and my mother provided the kind of childhood most kids only dream about.

Maybe it's an age thing: I wanted to tell my story so that generations to come would at least have a better understanding of who I am inside and how I achieved what I did. I wanted to offer a perspective on my inner life…my thought processes and why I took the actions I did…hoping others will derive some benefit from it all.

Seeing Around Corners

I've been blessed with the unique desire to try to see around corners. Said another way, it's a continual "what if" scenario. Anticipating different scenarios of outcome is an important discipline that I've trained myself to expect from myself. Most people don't ask enough questions to form a contrary opinion. Many would prefer to just accept conventional wisdom or take the position, "how was I to know that would happen." Instead, I firmly believe we are responsible for our own destiny. The fact that others made the same mistake or everyone else suffered the same ultimate outcome is not a satisfactory resolve. I see it as an excuse. My desire to see around corners and act on my intuition is what the judge in the Security Class Action case incorrectly and pejoratively referred to as "truth by hindsight." (More about that in chapter 20.)

Lucky Levan?

I've realized as I have focused on writing this book that there have been certain themes in my life. People have called me "lucky" since I can remember. My friends, family, people in the community, and my colleagues have all assigned that moniker to me. We sometimes reflect on the most complicated, seemingly insurmountable challenges that turned out in my favor. We laugh about it in the form of somebody's watching over me, I come from the lucky sperm club, it's my lucky charm or my lucky day, it's amazing or it's unbelievable. But luck can be all around if you're ready for it, looking for it, and waiting for it. I've often wondered when you come upon opportunities, are they just proverbial once-in-a-lifetime opportunities? Do only certain people get these kinds of opportunities all the time—or do we all actually get them? Perhaps we all do but it's just that some people are truly open to them. They are willing to absorb them. "Luck" for me comes from reading, listening, and watching the news; it comes from talking to people; it comes from being a lifelong student of everything. My ears and mind are always open to ideas and opportunities that others don't see or are not prepared to execute or take the risk. I am prepared to act on my concerns or seize the opportunities when they present themselves—that's what makes me lucky. In the final analysis, Luck Is Earned. The adage my wife, Susie, uses all the time is: "When the student is ready, the teacher appears."

If the truth be told, no life or business progresses in a straight line or continuously up and to the right. The perfect life graph doesn't exist, and in that way mine has followed suit.

There is no question I always look on the bright side. Clearly I believe to a large extent I have enjoyed a charmed life, but it wasn't until I "finished" writing this book that I was able to reflect on what all this means. Was it really a lifetime of luck or is it instead a prevailing attitude of finding the best in people and situations, being optimistic no matter what the challenges, and taking care of the business of life?

The Tactful Naysayer

I have always kept close and encouraged at least one person in my inner circle to disagree with me. Every leader needs supporters to get to the goal. But it is also healthy to have a tactful and discrete naysayer, someone who is not intimidated or afraid to speak their mind. For me, this has kept me out of trouble because it forces me to step back and constantly evaluate what I am doing. There's a great quote by Napoleon Bonaparte that illustrates this point:

"Those who failed to oppose me, who readily agreed with me, accepted all my views, and yielded easily to my opinions were those who did me the most injury, and were my worst enemies, because by surrendering to me so easily, they encouraged me to go too far... ."

Litigation

Because I am able and willing to seize opportunities or act definitively on matters that others could have thought of and similarly acted, but didn't, it often subjects me to significant criticism. As a consequence, frivolous criticism or litigation often results from others in an attempt to slow us down or take away our opportunity. As long as I know and believe that what we are doing is ethically, morally, and legally correct, I can take the litigation in stride, as a cost and consequence of doing business. This litigation is always where we are a defendant. We never use litigation as a business strategy of intimidation and rarely do we ever file a lawsuit as a plaintiff, except for the normal collection of defaulted unpaid bank loans where we are due the money.

Outwork Everyone

To a large degree, my success is from outworking the competition. Most often, I work hard for my own self-satisfaction and desire for self-accomplishment. It was never about the money—it has always been about the challenge. When I was younger, up to the age of sixty-five, my daily routine was to work until midnight or 1:00 a.m., after having dinner with the children and putting them to bed. I did this to catch up on the day's work and prepare for tomorrow. I've always had multiple projects going on at the same time.

When I travel on vacation, I take large amounts of projects and reading with me. I maintain my work schedule of calls and conferences while on the road.

That is who I am. I outwork most people. Aside from being with my family, working is my hobby. I work all the time and I love it.

The Glass Is Always Half Full

I live by the mantra "I am healthy, happy, and terrific." If you say it often enough you will believe it, even if you are not. I truly believe that a positive state of mind and mood is something you can train yourself to adopt. I have always tried not to give in to adversity. As simple as it sounds (it isn't always), my life is structured around optimism. Sitting on my desk for years has been a quote by William Arthur Ward, whose maxims have inspired many, especially me:

"Deep optimism is aware of problems but recognizes the solution,
knows about difficulties but believes they can be overcome,
sees the negative but accentuates the positive,
is exposed to the worst but expects the best,
has reason to complain but prefers to smile."

Persistence and Determination

My favorite quote is on persistence—a significant component of any success I've had and a key trait instilled and cultivated by my parents. Calvin Coolidge said persistence and determination are omnipotent. I am certain of that. Coolidge's full quote entitled "Persistence" has also been a plaque on my desk for forty-five years:

"Nothing in the world can take the place of persistence.
Talent will not; nothing is more common than unsuccessful men
with talent.
Genius will not; unrewarding genius is almost a proverb.
Education will not; the world is full of educated derelicts.
Persistence and determination alone are omnipotent."

Compartmentalize

I've trained myself to compartmentalize the "noise" so I can focus on one task at a time even though I am multitasking projects simultaneously. This allows me to focus intently on the project at hand without being distracted by an unsolved issue. Most often the solution to an unrelated issue will pop into my head and I will capture it by writing it down to deal with at the appropriate time.

Consider the Downside

I always consider the downside in every situation, which I believe is more important than the upside. The downside can wipe you out financially. Perhaps, even worse, the fear of an unknown downside can create constant stress, volatility, and illness. Conversely, the upside is easy to visualize and accept. Once I understand the worst case in each situation and reconcile that I can accept it—I can then focus on doing better than the worst case, and work like hell to achieve the best case. This can relate to personal or business situations such as health issues, family illnesses, recessions, bad investments, or almost every conceivable situation. Throughout my life, I have been tested on this resolve many times relating to raising children, cash flow, our kidnapping, *20/20*, SEC litigation, and more.

I've been told I sometimes appear unemotional, unconcerned, or robotic in serious situations. Nothing could be further from the truth. My perceived demeanor is because I have analyzed the worst case scenario, sometimes in seconds, particularly if I have no control over it. I always make my peace with the worst case scenario. That doesn't mean I am happy about it, in fact just the opposite: If I recognize the worst case in every situation and accept it, I can move forward without a lot of stress.

Accordingly, there is nothing left to chance...rarely any surprise for which I am unprepared. I like to believe this personality trait has made me a survivor of everything from the prospect of losing my business, more than once, to the kidnapping of my wife, my child, and me. It is this level of calm that has served me well over the years, however it often gets me into trouble. Many people view my calmness as uncaring or oblivious to a current crisis.

For me, it's a natural mindset. I am always sorry when I give off this impression but it allows me to function at my best in the worst of situations.

Lifestyle

At the age of fifty, I became a vegetarian. It's quite ironic, since prior to that time, I never enjoyed fruits or vegetables. I have forced myself to do this because I believe it leads to a healthier lifestyle and keeps my weight in check. Dr. Joel Fuhrman encourages the daily eating of G-BOMBS—Greens, Beans, Onions, Mushrooms, Berries, and Seeds (and nuts). Additionally, he recommends reducing your intake of salt, sugar, and alcohol. The salt and alcohol pieces are easy for me since I have never consumed alcohol and I started reducing my salt intake in college. Sugar, on the other hand, is a regular challenge. I try to follow this routine daily. I am not fanatical about it and do not evangelize about it. It just works for me and I have followed it for fifteen years. Also exercise—I'm not much of an athlete but I've had a trainer every morning at 6:00 a.m. for thirty-five years.

Success, Challenges, Disappointments, Failures, and Tragedy

I've had my share of successes and adversity in my life. Some would say I've experienced more than most. I force myself to not dwell on the past, but to look forward. There is so much more to experience, share, and contribute.

It turns out it's not only about luck, seeing around corners, and hard work. For me, it's the consistency of adhering to certain core values and following tenets that work for me. I've read hundreds of biographies of successful people and businesses—even dozens of books on dieting! One of the things I've learned is that there is no one magic bullet. No one size or thing that fits all. For all people this book is no different. What works for me may not work for you, but my intention is that if you choose what you believe can work for you, this book can be a reference to help you live a fuller, happier, and successful life.

To you!

Alan B. Levan
Fort Lauderdale, Florida
May 2019

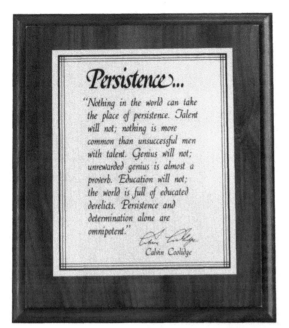

Persistence...

"Nothing in the world can take the place of persistence. Talent will not; nothing is more common than unsuccessful men with talent. Genius will not; unrewarded genius is almost a proverb. Education will not; the world is full of educated derelicts. Persistence and determination alone are omnipotent."

Calvin Coolidge

Optimism...

"Deep optimism is aware of problems but recognizes the solution, knows about difficulties but believes they can be overcome, sees the negative but accentuates the positive, is exposed to the worst but expects the best, has reason to complain but prefers to smile."

Dr. William Arthur Ward

Edward, my maternal grandfather. I spent limited time with my maternal grandfather and I know very little about his life. I also never met my maternal grandmother Miriam and have no photographs of her.

Daniel, my paternal grandfather, and my paternal grandmother, Anna. I never met my grandmother.

My paternal great-grandmother and her son Daniel, my grandfather. I never met my great-grandmother.

Daniel, my grandfather, and his three sisters. I met my great aunts a few times but know nothing about their lives. (L to R): Lena, Grandfather Daniel, Rose, and Fanny

Daniel, my grandfather. I spent limited time with my grandfather and know very little about his life.

OF TRIALS
AND TRIBULATIONS

"Our greatest weakness lies in giving up. The most certain way to succeed is always to try just one more time."
—**Thomas Edison**

I am angry as we walk back into the courthouse. I have to remind myself to breathe. It's May 2017 and I am seventy-two years old, at the end of my third six-week trial in ten years for the same inconceivable issue. I've been accused of deliberately making false statements to shareholders about the health of certain loans and failing to disclose concerns about the bank's portfolio. I've been further accused of using accounting tricks to conceal recession-related losses that, when revealed, led to an instant 37 percent drop in share price. In short, I've been accused of investor fraud.

"BankAtlantic and Levan used accounting gimmicks to conceal from investors the losses in a critical loan portfolio," Robert Khuzami, director of the SEC's Division of Enforcement, said in a public statement at the time of the suit. "This is exactly the type of information that is important

to investors, and corporate executives who fail to make that required disclosure will face severe consequences."

It's been years of false accusations, trumped-up charges, negative press, and acrimonious legal arguments. While I'm tired of it all, tired doesn't begin to describe the way I really feel.

In this third installation of the lawsuits, and though this is a civil and not a criminal case, the Securities and Exchange Commission is trying to prohibit me from ever running a public company again. I've successfully created and run public companies for forty-five years as CEO of four NYSE-listed companies, and have steered our bank through a global financial crisis, all to the letter of the law.

What am I doing here?

The company for which I've been on trial for nearly ten years is BankAtlantic, and my vice chairman and business partner of thirty-three years, Jack Abdo, is staunchly by my side as he has been since we got together in 1984. My indefatigable attorney, Eugene (Gene) Stearns, an association of four decades, stands before the judge. I am simultaneously cringing and deeply saddened that we are being dragged through the mud again.

I was exonerated after appealing the outcome of the first trial, a frivolous civil class-action shareholder lawsuit filed by ambulance-chasing class-action lawyers, claiming that BankAtlantic and I had misled investors during the 2008 financial crisis. They were hoping for a quick settlement. I refused to settle. It was a matter of integrity. We were alleged to have soft-pedaled the extent of troubled loans, fraudulently understating the losses. The claim was bogus—the lawyers concocting information and actually inventing confidential

---

* "SEC Charges Florida Bank Holding Company and CEO with Misleading Investors about Loan Risks During Financial Crisis." U.S. Securities and Exchange Commission. January 18, 2012. Redacted December 22, 2018. https://www.sec.gov/news/press-release/2012-2012-13htm.

witnesses in order to get past the dismissal stage of the litigation. After five years of discovery, the production of millions of pages of documents, and a six-week trial, we won the case. The class-action law firm was fined for fabricating the affidavits of confidential witnesses.

Much to our surprise, a few days after the class-action trial's verdict was announced in 2007, the SEC filed a civil lawsuit of its own against BankAtlantic and me for exactly the same claims. Why would they do that? We had already proven my actions were perfectly appropriate and commendable. Worse yet, this time the requested penalty by the SEC was a lifetime ban from ever serving as an officer or director of a publicly traded company!

The case was assigned to a different federal judge than the one who presided over the class-action suit. During this trial, the judge made two outrageously absurd rulings. One based on three obscure sentences I uttered in a July 2007 conference call (explained in detail as my story unfolds). Secondly, our national accounting firm was prohibited from testifying that our accounting was correct, making it difficult for us to win. Both of these issues should have been left for a jury to decide. Still I remained optimistic. Another six-week trial ensued and, despite these bogus rulings from the judge, which the jury had no choice but to accept, it found in our favor on all counts the judge hadn't already (outrageously) decided. For all intents and purposes we'd won again, but the SEC inappropriately took the position with the court that *it had won* on all counts, asking the judge to assess maximum monetary damages against us, also penalizing me with the lifetime ban. The judge agreed. We were fined accordingly and I was banned from running a public company—specifically the company I had founded forty-five years earlier.

We appealed. The 11th Circuit Court of Appeals eventually ruled that the two rulings the judge had made were clearly judicial error. I took back my leadership position at BankAtlantic, the $5.85 million dollar fine we'd paid was reimbursed (a little over $4 million to the bank; the rest to me), and my life appeared to be returning to normal.

But in continuing its witch hunt to affix blame to someone (anyone!) for the 2008 global financial crisis, the intellectually and morally bankrupt SEC tackled us again in 2016, essentially finding a way to retry the case on the points they had won, but now had been reversed by the appellate court.

So here I am, back in a dark, intimidating, all-too-familiar courtroom with an unpredictable cast of characters: judge and jury. Beginning with the first SEC trial, the SEC lawyers had proven themselves to be unethical. They'd been masters of misinformation, prepared to use the respected name of the highest securities agency in the country in an inappropriate way. Now they were at it again. But I was holding fast to my principles and integrity, no matter what.

Twenty feet away from me a jury of my peers will again decide my fate. I can't help but think that with all the things I believe in—and practice—my ethics, optimism, resolve, and persistence—this is yet another extreme test of my mettle.

Freedom takes many forms in this country, including the freedom to choose what we do in life. I can say now from firsthand experience that until that option is taken away, as it was for me, you cannot begin to imagine how frustrated, helpless, betrayed, and bereft it leaves you feeling. Sure I was optimistic—confident I was in the right and we could again win and all of this would be behind us. Still I checked my thoughts at the door. Sadly, what I have observed during my lifetime is that when your fate is in the hands of a judge or jury, the outcome is no longer predictable. The phrase "jury of your peers" is problematic. Oftentimes, justice is truly random.

LIFE LESSONS LEARNED

- Analyze the worst case scenario and make peace with it. Once you establish the worst case, and can live with it, work like crazy to achieve better than worst case. And don't give up.

CHAPTER 1

EARLY DAYS: ROOTS AND WINGS

"Life is a great big canvas. Throw all the paint on it you can."
–Danny Thomas

A few years before my mother's death at age ninety-eight, she and I were on a trip to visit Manhattan, from Florida, to which we'd moved in 1959. My parents, who I'd always known were madly in love, had been born in the United States to Eastern European immigrants who'd come to this country just after the turn of the twentieth century. There wasn't a lot of family history talked about in the days when I was growing up and my grandparents lived an hour away, which made long, probing conversations in their stilted English even more difficult. I never presumed either one of my parents had known any semblance of wealth, but I was about to find out differently.

"Turn here," my mother said suddenly as we drove north. We were just about at 80th Street as it crossed Broadway.

I was curious about the request but followed her directions. In a moment we came to an apartment building to which she pointed.

"I lived in that building," she said.

I looked at her and then at the building with its crisply pressed doorman.

"Wow," I chuckled. "Times really have changed!"

"I lived there with my parents, sister, and brother when I was eight or nine years old," my mother continued, impervious to my comment. Parts of her were wearing out as they do in most people her age, but her mind was sharp. Still I wondered what she was talking about.

I persisted. "Clearly you didn't live in a building in the 1920s when you were eight or nine years old with a doorman." She nodded emphatically that she did, explaining that her father, a jewelry designer who'd appropriately named her Pearl, had come home one afternoon in 1929 announcing the family of five was moving out that same day. It was Black Tuesday. They abruptly took up residence in a single hotel room in Brooklyn, victims of the stock market crash.

Years later, when my mother was grown and married and we had moved to Miami, I remember passing a downtown jewelry/flea market-style establishment. There in the storefront window was a charm you'd put on a bracelet. Apparently my grandfather had designed it decades ago in New York. My mother recognized it, pulling us into the store to show it to us. You'd turn something on the charm and pictures would appear in a tiny window—something like a locket. My older brother Jay's and my baby pictures were still in that window, much to our surprise, used as they were at the time as samples—just as today's photos are of anonymous model-type babies when you purchase a picture frame.

Not that my brother and I were model babies...or children. In fact we weren't anything close. I was no shrinking violet. I was loud, rambunctious, and could run like the wind. Brooklyn was home to my family until I was eight years old, so much so that I was born in Presbyterian Hospital in 1944 just as my mother had been, though for a few years she'd apparently moved away, living in some form of Manhattan luxury.

We lived in a small apartment near Coney Island and Brighton Beach. In the same independent, resourceful way my mother's family had survived the stock market crash and ensuing Great

Depression, as had my father's family, strong qualities were very important to my parents. They wanted to instill them in us. Both of them worked and Jay and I were encouraged to rely on ourselves to get to elementary school.

Actually the walk to school was an adventure, fueled by the fact that our parents didn't want us to cross a lot of busy streets. We had to figure out workarounds (or more specifically walk arounds). We thought we were Brooklyn's answer to Tom Sawyer and Huck Finn as we deftly cut through what seemed like a zillion backyards to reach our destination. Our journey was punctuated with fence-hopping, dog-dodging, ducking under low-hanging clotheslines without soiling anything, and outrunning threats about such from fiery residents.

If I were caught doing anything wrong, both of which I tried not to do (that is, *do* anything wrong or *get caught* if I did—though things like broken lamps and mud on the floor mysteriously appeared), I always got into trouble. Actually I got into trouble no matter what. I was always deemed guilty because of a kind of silly grin I've always had. It was typically perceived as a guilty grin, but frankly it was more of an expression of embarrassment and defensiveness that I could not help no matter how I tried—guilty or not guilty.

If my brother and I were made to own up to our offenses, punishments were meted out differently in my family, that is, different from what I came to know of other families. Though my parents were not exceedingly educated, both the first in their families to graduate from high school, nor was there a preponderance of child psychology books out or at least that they read at the time, instinctively my parents knew how to punish the deed without damaging the child. They were disciplinarians but not in a draconian sense. Certainly no one is without flaws, but to this day when I think about how my parents raised us I am astonished by their unrelenting optimism and fairness, something I hope I've reflected and passed along to my own children. They were wise beyond their age and education.

My parents never flew off the handle, never punished us impulsively or in a fit of anger. Randomness was never part of the equation; punishments were not reckless. A spanking was done in a controlled way if that makes sense. My father, Zit, was on the road most of the week as an independent jewelry rep, and depending on the severity of the crime, sometimes we were told by my mother he'd deal with us when he got back. If we were spanked by either one of them, which was not uncommon for children in the 1940s and '50s, we were told immediately after that they loved us and punishment was for the deed we'd done, not who we were. They knew we were capable of doing better and they always told us so. We knew we could believe them, which was probably the most important part.

If sent to our room, we were not sent to bed without dinner, as was a common practice at the time. Dinner was either brought to us, or we would be allowed out for a time to eat but then had to return to the confines of our punishment. To this day I recall very little of the bad times in my childhood because they were suffused with positive lessons. Both the punishment and the love that followed were equally important components of the learning process.

With my father away so much, when my mother returned each day from her dental office bookkeeping job, she and I would spend hours around the kitchen table. We had long talks about the importance of virtue, channeling energy into pursuits that were important to us, smiling, being a kind, honorable human being, doing the right thing, and working hard. She always encouraged us to bring our friends around and based on what she observed in them, would identify who would ultimately be successful and who would not. My mother was highly intuitive and able to see a lot in people—perhaps even see around corners, which is something I've also been able to do and which has impacted my career and the decisions I've made more times than not. My mother and father never missed an opportunity to tell me how much they trusted me, which motivated me to rise to the occasion. Even though they were both incredibly busy, they were never too busy for us.

My mother actually wore a lot of hats. She worked—something not all that common for women of her generation—and with her propensity for numbers she was in charge of balancing the family checkbook and managing our finances. And she did more than that, being quite active in our Brooklyn school and maintaining a high level of involvement later on when we would move to Long Island. She was like the Energizer Bunny, always full of energy.

She was incredibly organized and did everything efficiently. I recall multiple PTA membership mailings where she recruited us to help her insert letters into envelopes—hundreds of them! Apparently my production line prowess—struggle to fold the letter in some random fashion; force into envelope; seal; lick stamp and apply one at a time—was as yet undeveloped at the age of nine but I was surely about to learn. And it was a lesson in efficiency I was able to share with employees, and teach my children, each of whom worked in my company mailroom at one point in their lives.

"If you're going to do it, do it right—not one letter, one envelope, and one stamp at a time," my mother told us in a kind but boot camp-ish kind of directive.

Her modus operandi involved folding letters uniformly until there was nothing in the pile; opening the flaps of all the envelopes at once; placing all letters in envelopes; sealing them simultaneously; tearing off an entire strip of stamps instead of licking them in the process (in the pre-self-adhering stamp days), using a damp sponge to swipe across the strip and then affixing. Sir, yes, sir! (I wondered if there'd be any shore leave that weekend.)

The Gatekeepers

The entry to our Brooklyn apartment building was flanked by fortress-like wrought iron gates at least six feet tall. Talk about forms of freedom! I *lived* to climb and play on those gates. I could not imagine a day without swinging on them. They became like air, food, and water to me. My brother and I would hang on them for hours and for dear life as they swung open and closed; open and closed. Sometimes we'd make them move by jerking our bodies for momentum. We were always admonished by neighbors—a lot of whom were elderly—saying we'd get hurt or break the gates. But swinging on those magical metal missiles was like flying by my own hand. It was the same feeling that would manifest later on when I started to work, even at my first menial jobs as a young boy, and felt the jolt of self-reliance work would bring.

The whole time Jay and I were growing up, my dad would regale us with long conversations about business. He was a great salesman and negotiator and quite self-assured, but not in an arrogant way. You knew when he walked into a room. He was always proud of whatever job he had, no matter what it was. He was an entrepreneur with a twinkle in his eye—a real presence. My dad, who wore a coat and tie every business day, never missed an opportunity to impress upon us the value of hard work and that being in business for ourselves would give us freedom, lead to more opportunity, and provide a better quality of life. He showed us how work could be fun and exciting—it was all up to us. His glass was always half full. His attitude and optimism toward life made a huge impression on me and still does to this day.

My father was wildly resourceful and would call us long distance from the road. In those days long distance calls were expensive and operator-assisted. So that he didn't actually have to pay for the call, he'd do things like make a collect, person-to-person call to John Madison, which of course we would not accept, but which would reveal to us he was in Madison, Wisconsin. One time he placed a person-to-person call to Joe "Nokey," meaning he was on his way back and had left his key at home.

In sharp contrast to the business side of my father, he was, as my mother would say, a hopeless romantic. He read poetry to her the whole time they were dating and it didn't stop when they married. Perhaps the funniest story was of his reading her poetry on a rowboat in Central Park. The boat capsized and they both went in, but the story became more and more embellished over the long telling of it throughout their many years together.

Dad read poetry to our entire family. My mother, brother, and I would pass many an evening listening to him. As I grew older it became abundantly clear to me that poetry fed him, and nourishing his family with the source of his joy was paramount. In the sixth grade my elementary school had a poetry reciting contest I decided to enter. My choice was Joyce Kilmer's "The House with Nobody in It." I recall asking my father for help, whereupon he told me it had always been among his favorites. I didn't win the contest but it brought me even closer to my dad.

Among dad's romantic tendencies was his propensity for singing to my mother, particularly "Summertime" from the George and Ira Gershwin/DuBose Heyward musical *Porgy and Bess*. Years into the future he'd sing it to my children, whereupon they'd carry on the tradition at family events such as weddings and bar mitzvahs. My children—and their children—still do. We all still sing it when we're together. My father singing that song the way he did is a powerful memory I have to this day. At large family events, he would relish holding the microphone and asking, "What is the secret to a happy marriage?" With a big smile he would answer the question with the words, "Yes, dear."

Pails in Comparison

One of my earliest childhood memories of my father and work has to do with the beach at Coney Island. Dad saw an opportunity for his young sons to sell sand pails to the parents of children on the beach who'd forgotten their pails, thinking it would be fun and educational for us. He was able to buy pails at a discount from a contact in NYC. When I think, today, about a five- and seven-year-old, hawking stacks of metal pails for twenty-five cents apiece up and down a scorching beach teeming with boisterous Brooklyn families, I wonder how we did it. Sometimes it was pandemonium. But with dad's faith in us, we made it work.

I distinctly remember calling out, "Pails! Pails! Anybody want to buy a pail? Don't your children want pails? Look—they're using their hands! You can fill the pails with sand, turn them over, make a mountain, make a castle!" It worked. Fortunately my dad's sales genes hadn't skipped a generation.

We hustled like there was no tomorrow and had a lot of takers, selling out repeatedly—just like the vendors who traversed the beach, selling popsicles and soda. I loved asking for the money. It was achingly hard physical work in the heat yet I couldn't get enough. My dad trusted me and that's what mattered most. From an early age he would tell us any problems we may encounter are just challenges and opportunities and I would always remember that. He instilled the importance of a firm handshake, looking people in the eye, exuding confidence, and letting negativity roll off your back. I wanted to be just like him in *every* way. I always knew how proud he was of me and though he is gone, I continue to strive to meet and exceed his standards.

Years later I would do the same thing with my own children. In lieu of pails at Coney Island, they would take advance Sunday bagel orders in our Florida neighborhood using a form we'd created that people would fill out. We'd go to the bagel store at 6:00 a.m., purchase and put the designated bagels in brown paper bags with cream cheese. Then we would travel the route we'd mapped out, and along with orange juice, deliver them to the neighbors. What was left we'd take to the local marina to try and sell as people were boarding their boats for the day. It was a wonderful lesson in entrepreneurship if we didn't eat the inventory.

Soaring in Suburbia

The summer just before I turned nine, my parents told us we were moving out of Brooklyn to Freeport, Long Island. Two of the three families in our building with whom my parents were the closest had exited Brooklyn, moving out there in much the same way. I would miss everyone and everything, including the Sunday night tradition where half the building would gather on the roof to watch fireworks racing across the sky from a barge in the Atlantic Ocean. But it was 1950s post-war America and suburbia was the rage. Everybody was doing it. The 1950s were a time of change. Rosa Parks, drive-in restaurants, fins on cars, *I Love Lucy* (the first two-camera show), and of course Elvis Presley. The change applied to us as well. Planned communities, such as the one to which we were about to move, were the American dream set to a tract house tempo.

Tract house developments, perhaps with Levittown the most famous as the prototype for post-war suburbs (interestingly, at one point in my career we would actually acquire Levitt & Sons, which had developed Levittown), provided mass affordable housing options for the middle class. The war was over and these were burgeoning communities that reflected the preferred lifestyle of post-war parents, a way of life that featured time-saving modern conveniences and freedom from the cramped confines of city living.

Located in Nassau County, Levittown was considered the grand-daddy of planned communities, but we were moving to Freeport, twenty minutes from Levittown. Regardless of where it was, it was a move to a house instead of the apartment building with the iconic (at least to me) wrought iron gates I'd known all eight years of my life. The new house was not large by any standards, and by design was indistinguishable from the one to the right and the one to the left, but it would be our house and a brand new one at that. We'd have a larger living room than the tiny space in Brooklyn. Where Jay and I had shared a room in Brooklyn, in Freeport we'd each have our own, albeit in the attic under the eaves. But that only added to the adventure.

With ceilings at a 45-degree roof angle, my father would bring back pennants with the names of the cities to which he'd traveled on his sales trips. Today you might bring back a T-shirt or baseball cap, but in the '50s pennants were the fad. The thing about the angled ceilings is that we could tack up the pennant at the wide end and let it hang down naturally. I remember having fifteen or twenty at a time suspended from the ceiling in my room. I was surrounded, which made me feel closer to my dad no matter where he was in the country. I was still very young and never really thought about traveling outside of New York, but in time another family move out of state and later my career would take me to some of the cities displayed in my faraway pennant compendium.

Walking home from school one day just after our move to Freeport, a man rolled down his car window to ask if I wanted to deliver newspapers. It would be a *Newsday* route and now, having just turned nine, I was elated to have been asked. I'd be taking over an established route from someone who was no longer delivering the paper. I ran all the way home to ask permission. My mother said yes in a heartbeat, believing it would teach me responsibility, accountability, and perseverance. I was given the money to pay for my first week's worth of papers, as the *Newsday* rules were they had to be purchased in advance, and I never looked back. Once again, as with the sand pails a few years earlier, I thrived on work.

A week after I'd started my route an interesting thing happened, which I remember to this day. I received a form letter from the company. The letter said I'd been chosen to be a *Newsday* paper boy because of my "work ethic, high integrity, and ambition." This was quite amusing to me because I was keenly aware they knew absolutely nothing about me. How could they? I'd only been selected off the street, and on the job a week, and there had been no inquiry into my character: good, bad, or otherwise. While I think most people would have disregarded the letter, I used it as a springboard to work hard enough to be the person they'd so eloquently described. I figured I had a lot to live up to.

I delivered newspapers, rain or shine (or worse), seven days a week. My job was to ride my bike to the dispatcher's warehouse each day after school and on weekends to pick up my bundle. I had to fold the papers individually and place them in plastic bags so I could toss them onto customer's lawns. I filled my bike basket and started delivering. I also had to memorize my ever-evolving route and no matter how it changed, was still able to deliver my papers in an hour. If I didn't memorize and organize the route, it could take me twice as long. My tips—I learned early on—were directly proportional to my dependability, service, and smile. Aha! I was learning that to some degree income hinged on attitude.

My father showed me how to knock on doors and make the collections on Saturdays and Sundays. Most customers were prompt in their payments and included a tip. Dad then taught me to keep a record of my collections. He helped me put together a notebook that facilitated keeping track of each customer's name, address, telephone number, what they owed, dates, the amount I collected, and how much tip I received. With this tool and some discipline I was able to budget: to project how much money I would have and when in the month I would have it. I could then figure out how much would have to go toward purchasing the newspapers and what I got to keep. It was a classic historical ledger and my first real step toward the responsibilities of adulthood. Later in college in the 1960s I would have many jobs, which I talk about in chapter 3, and creating a similar budget book helped me organize my finances.

On inclement weather days, my mother drove me around as opposed to my using a bike as it was either too slippery, or maybe snow was too deep, and low visibility made my route quite dangerous. It looked like kindness on the surface but in fact she was also instilling a strong work ethic. She would tell me the papers needed to get to their destinations because customers expected them. I received many awards from *Newsday* for my good service, based on customer feedback to the company, which made my family very proud. And I'll say once more that the feeling of freedom that came from self-reliance was indescribable. Though they were miles away, I was swinging on the wrought iron gates all over again. I was flying.

On one occasion I was almost run over on my bike. I'd ridden through a stop sign, which scared the living daylights out of me—and the driver! I returned home white as a ghost and told my mother. Instead of confining me to my room and forbidding me to ride my bike, or making me give up my paper route, she thanked me for being honest enough to share what had happened. She asked me to be more careful and trusted that I would. My parents and I had a unique relationship that became more and more apparent to me the older I got, and the more I got to observe what life was like for others my age.

Delivering *Newsday* was truly the foundation of learning how to be in business. This was something that would manifest in a larger way when I went away to college and undertook various jobs to help finance my education; my parents had two sons in college at the same time. Though I was initially an employee at my first professional job after graduation and could count on a paycheck, knowing how to work for myself would serve me in the years that followed when I had to depend solely on myself to keep the doors of my businesses open. At the age of nine I had begun to learn important lessons of consistency, reliability, customer service, keeping accurate financial records, and what a real work ethic was. And my parents continued to trust me, which was probably the most significant outcome of all. The depths of their love and all that came from it fueled me like nothing else. Interestingly, my parents never bragged about us to others so as not to create a false sense of accomplishment and achievement in us.

Many years later, well into my business career, Wayne Huizenga, founder of Blockbuster Video, AutoNation, Extended Stay America, Waste Management, and owner of the Miami Dolphins, Florida Panthers, and Miami Marlins, would call my business partner and close friend, Jack Abdo. He told Jack he wanted to nominate me for the Horatio Alger Award. Wayne was on the selection committee for the award, given to Americans who demonstrated the virtues of hard work, perseverance, and achievement, and apparently he'd had his eye on me.

Wayne explained to Jack that candidates had to have overcome great adversity, coming from humble or economically challenged environments or deeply dysfunctional families, etc. After I told Jack to tell Wayne I'd come from none of that, I was removed from the list. The fact is I'd actually met some of the criteria, which Jack was aware of, but my parents had always been proud and resourceful people—never seeing things through a dark lens, so I didn't have the heart to encourage the application. I loved them.

LIFE LESSONS LEARNED

- Any problems we encounter are opportunities.
- Put all your energy into everything you do.
- Work hard; be completely reliable at all times.
- Have a firm handshake, a genuine smile, exude confidence, and look people in the eye.
- If you are going to take the time to do something, do it efficiently.

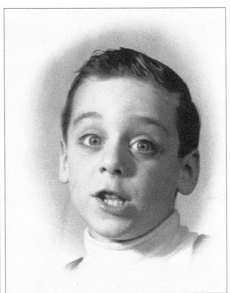

Alan   *Alan*

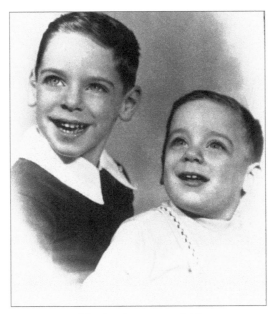

Older brother Jay and Alan

*Jay and Alan take a break
from selling pails.*

Alan and the "famous" gates

Alan and Jay playing with our father

Jay and Alan

*Ruth and Norman Horowitz in front of
our Brooklyn apartment building. My
good friends then and I'm still good friends
with them and their spouses today.*

Our house in Freeport, Long Island

My parent's wedding

Very much in love

My parents frolicking at the public pool.

My Dad, Central Park

My Mother, at another birthday party.

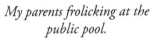

My Dad, always smiling

My Dad, super traveling salesman

*My Dad selling diamonds
to jewelry stores.*

*My Dad's company, Jayal Co,
named for Jay and Alan.*

*My Dad, amateur artist,
Emmett Kelly Clown, 1950*

*Samples of dozens of other paintings
by my Dad.*

CHAPTER 2

MOVE TO FLORIDA: GETTING THE BUGS OUT

"At a young age, winning is not the most important thing…the important thing is to develop creative and skilled players with good confidence."
—Arsène Wenger

I was in New York heaven. I had unbelievable parents, great friends, a girlfriend, and my life was just fine the way it was. I was fifteen, it was summer, and I was about to enter ninth grade.

Though in retrospect it may have been odd for a kid my age to have had these observations, I really loved the formality of New York—everything it represented. So when my parents announced we were moving to Miami it didn't exactly sit well with me. It wasn't that I had a lot of misgivings about where I was going as I'd always had a good attitude toward change; the concern was about what I was leaving behind.

One of the many things I've always admired about my father is that he never agonized over decisions. He was definitive, optimistic, and trusted his instincts. Later in his life, he'd be faced with open heart surgery and its potential downside, which the cardiologist painstakingly laid out. He immediately decided to have it done, not wavering on his choice for a single moment.

The fact is I didn't know my father had been invited numerous times by a Florida friend to work with him in his exterminating business. He had apparently resisted, but ultimately negotiated a partnership as the lure of sunny Florida represented an opportunity to get off the road five days a week. He wanted to spend more time with us and have a reliable income instead of commissions. As always, he was confident and optimistic.

It seemed strange to me that my father could go from wearing a coat and tie in a white collar job to a blue collar exterminator's uniform, driving a truck from house to house to spray bugs. But he didn't think twice about that kind of transition. He was always motivated, loved to work, and preferred self-employment to the alternative. I strongly recall him saying many times, "Everything's a business." Clearly he meant it, and those words would influence what I did later on when it came to the trajectory of my own career.

At one point after college I would return to New York to work for JP Morgan, but two years later would leave its hallowed halls to join my dad back in Florida as we targeted insects (please see chapter 5). I had learned by his example not to view this move as a step down in any sense of the word. Dad took things as they came. Again everything was a business.

Because of my *Newsday* experience in New York, when we arrived in Florida I immediately called the *Miami Daily News* in pursuit of a route for the afternoon paper, which I was lucky to get as a summer job.

When fall came, the reality of a new school with its protocols and personalities set in, starting with the realization that unlike the class structure in Freeport, I would not be low man on the totem pole. Could this really be happening? In my old combined junior-senior high school, ninth grade was considered the first year of high school and I'd have been drowned by upperclassmen, considered a bottom feeder at best—much like an Army private in a sea of generals.

In Miami, however, ninth grade was the final year of the seventh-eighth-ninth grade structure commonly known as junior high school. I understood I'd be functioning in a different realm—a junior high school upperclassman, so to speak—which would garner respect.

Over time I began to look at myself differently, developing a newfound maturity, sense of empowerment, and self-confidence. Suddenly there was a stride—a swagger—not only coming from me but from my fellow ninth grade Miami classmates. I could feel the change in my bones.

When I really think about it, in all my years as a student in New York it had felt as though I was just kind of going through the motions. I was happy but there was predictability to everything. We'd go to class, go home, and play in the streets. I still recall stickball games in Freeport and swimming in the community pool. I had the best parents. I had the right girlfriend. I had the paper route and didn't want for anything. But I was just like everybody else. Now I found myself in Florida at the top of my junior high school (instead of the bottom rung of high school as it was in New York), a little on fire about that!

Mrs. Burroughs, my ninth grade English teacher and advisor, suggested I give speech and debate a try. It was an extracurricular activity held in high regard by many and I was all for it. Learning significant communications skills and speaking in front of groups would become defining moments for me. I began to believe I could stand out a little. I was never good at athletics. Granted I was a good runner—fast—and I had very big calves! Because of my calves (thank you, in part, to my genetics), people assumed I was a serious athlete. But I could not compete in group sports. I didn't like Little League because I was never chosen. I didn't like football for the same reason. And I certainly wasn't tall enough for basketball. Excelling where I could was important to me but I never felt I had to win every single time, which is the idea in group sports. I believe you have to pick your battles. And you have to figure out what's important. To some people, everything is important. They have to win every single time. There's no oxygen left in the room when they're done.

I was motivated but I never felt I had to win and everyone else had to lose—that it was the only way. There was room for achievement all around. Somewhere in my growing up years, I recall reading Dale Carnegie's *How to Win Friends & Influence People.* The content would impact me from the moment I read it to this very day. There were few times in my life when I didn't think that in some way, it was possible for people to function in win-win situations.

Later, when I would go into business, we'd hire consultants to conduct a standard Myers-Briggs test. This was to ascertain what the different personalities were on our executive team and how we could play well together in the sandbox. Though most individuals on executive teams are type-A personalities, and I am no different, I learned at the same time I was categorized as an introvert, apparently despite tearing through every yard in Brooklyn at yahoo warp speed on my way to school and swinging 'til the cows came home on the iron gates of our apartment building—defying anyone who didn't approve.

While one may think of a CEO as characteristically hard charging, there are apparently people who exhibit introverted tendencies though they are in leadership roles—like me. Left to my own devices, I may be a little more intuitive and circumspect than many CEOs, retreating to a quieter space to study and analyze things, though I can be extroverted when I need to be: meeting and greeting; selling; giving speeches; motivating people.

I prefer information consisting of documents, other data, and recommendations be given to me in advance, not on the fly or at the eleventh hour; and these had better be strong, fact-based concepts. When someone is going to make a presentation to me it needs to be well thought out. These are some of the components that make up my leadership style, allowing me to be hard charging when I need to be. It worked for me growing up and continues to, and I will say that the boot camp kind of rigor I went through in preparing for speech and debate in junior high and high school gave me the artillery I needed to stand before a room of people and make it count.

* * *

Little did Mrs. Burroughs know how much her suggestion about speech and debate would change my life. With this newfound confidence and mounting achievements, school and homework came more easily. They were less of a struggle. In New York I was a C student with the occasional D; in Florida I'd quickly become a B student with the occasional A. My parents had always put more emphasis on competency and independence than things like grades—or cleaning my room. I got away with a lot more than most of my friends because my mother and father turned a blind eye to clutter and piles, channeling their time and energy into helping me develop a strong character and making sure I associated with people of equal character. So grades had not been a priority to them or me, but now, with higher marks, it felt quite good and I started to grasp their importance.

In a matter of time I began to embrace who I was—and who I wasn't. I was definitely not one of the cool kids and it ultimately didn't matter. But for a time I more or less tried it on, joining the cool kids for Cokes and fries at a local restaurant called Corky's. On a Saturday night there may be twenty or thirty kids standing around the parking lot, gabbing about nothing. I would understand I was not one of them, though people would give me advice about how to join their legions.

"You can't wear this and you can't wear that."

"You've got to do this and not that."

"Stop wearing that tie. Loosen up. Relax."

I was accepted among members of their group (which was something in its own right, as there was a lot of talk in that parking lot about who they would let in and who they wouldn't), but I really wasn't one of them and didn't care about that. Status didn't mean much. Being a cool kid just didn't seem like the best use of my time.

My father had suggested I dress for my newfound success by wearing a white shirt and tie to school. I thought this was an outstanding idea as again I was not a cool kid, but neither was I one of the smart kids. I needed to quietly project who and what I was. Cuirassed in that way, and with a briefcase instead of a book bag, I would stand out as a *serious* kid. Actually I stood out so well that way, classmates assumed I was smart and come graduation time asked if I were to be the class valedictorian! Though my intention was never to deceive anyone, these were lessons in perception that would serve me well into my professional life. Everything was a lesson and while I may not have understood it as such on the spot, I would find myself reaching back to apply things, often hearing my parents' voices in the decisions I made—including dressing for success, which would come up time and time again.

The Difference Between

Speech and debate were like caffeine to me. They made me feel alive, energized, sometimes even invincible. I wore them like a badge. I just couldn't get enough.

While they were grouped together as an activity, it's important to distinguish one from the other. Debate is as it sounds: the opportunity to parley a topic back and forth, usually as part of a team, against another team that will take the opposing argument. It catapulted me into new worlds of challenging subjects I'd research to fully comprehend, then organize my thoughts and arguments to present in tournaments. I learned about strenuous preparation. In

1960 Cuba was a hot topic as Castro had ended Batista's rule and come to power the year before. The Cuban Missile Crisis loomed ahead and we never lacked for material.

In speech, as opposed to debate, the idea is to impart information to a group. Sounds simple enough but there is a method that any accomplished public speaker will tell you. First you tell an audience what you are going to tell them; then you tell them; then you summarize by telling them what you told them. The best public speakers do it and who was I to argue? Presenting ideas this way taught me powerful organizational skills I'd not otherwise have had.

I was presenting legacy speeches (the "Gettysburg Address" and others), dramatic speeches from the theater, poetry (Edgar Allen Poe was a favorite of mine), but I especially coveted speaking extemporaneously about a topic, finding I was at my best without notes. In all instances I had to make eye contact, project, and in the case of extemporaneous exercises, really think on my feet. The process involved randomly picking a subject out of a hat, mulling it over for a whole thirty seconds, and delivering a cohesive speech before other students and possibly judges for five or ten minutes. And talk about developing powers of persuasion—important both in debate and the speeches I delivered. I needed to enroll my audience in what I had to say. It's impossible to fully describe how this speech and debate would serve me later in business. Mastering any and all of it was exhilarating. My purpose and success gave me a new identity.

The National Forensic League, an academic organization providing leadership at the national level for speech and debate, had programs offering a number of points for each speech delivered by a high school student before a group. At the time I became a member in high school, I was working to qualify for a two hundred fifty-dollar college scholarship—which frankly I wasn't sure was a lot of money or a little when it came to my perspective on college. I only knew I wanted to win it.

So as a teenager, I often found myself on the glittering chicken à la king circuit at Miami's business clubs. These included Kiwanis, Knights of Pythias, Lions Club, Optimists Club, and any community organization that would allow me to speak before it. I was excused from class to be a lunchtime speaker and yes, I won that scholarship. At this point you may wonder what, of interest, an adolescent has to say to groups of businesspeople. Not to undermine my appearances, but these groups cast a wide net for free speakers and I fit right in. Using a little creativity and my ever-evolving public speaking preparation methods and skills, I might talk about school and school sporting events, the state of education in Florida, perhaps something inspirational such as becoming more active in one's community and why, or getting out the vote so the right candidates can be elected. There were dozens and dozens (did I say dozens?) of subjects—there for the taking—a virtual cornucopia of commentary and I couldn't get enough.

In high school I continued to soar. My achievements and initiative resulted in being honored as a North Miami Senior High School "Pioneer," something bestowed upon only eight out of twelve hundred students. I found myself in the *Miami Herald* as "Top Teen of the Week." I was also winner of the prestigious *Miami Herald* Silver Knight in Citizenship award while in high school—my award, a two-foot statue of a silver knight. In fact my father had helped me create an extensive album of my awards and activities in order to help me garner this recognition. I was patrol leader for the Boy Scouts and was president of my temple youth group. Being in charge was intoxicating. I became a columnist for the school newspaper and wrote for a local teen magazine. I was a parliamentarian of the Key Club. I had perfect attendance all three years and was occasionally on the honor roll. I joined the National Thespian Society though was never comfortable acting—and it showed! I participated in Junior Achievement and was elected president of the company (Junior Achievement Company or JACO) we were tasked with forming, with the objective to learn how to start a business. My company made a startling fifteen dollar profit designing, making, and selling ceramic ashtrays. Years later I would pay the experience forward when my company, BankAtlantic, agreed to be the first storefront tenant in a large JA World complex for fifth through eighth graders in Broward County schools. When our company, BankAtlantic, signed up, other large businesses immediately followed our lead.

The Nemesis Here; the Nemesis There

We met in ninth grade. In one way or another, his achievements and in fact his very presence would plague me well into my early business years. The sometimes tacit, sometimes bristling competition ramped up considerably when we entered North Miami Senior High School. It was always there.

"Nick" was a pedigreed bully. Big bucks and browbeating. Major money and menacing. He was in most of my classes and participated in many of the same activities I did. He took no prisoners and always seemed to be one step ahead of me. I realized early on I was never much good at responding to bullies. I didn't think that way and never had the quick wit to respond effectively. He was on the debate team and I can recall him essentially strong-arming Mrs. Burroughs and our high school speech coach into giving him the choice topics. And it just kept happening. I became a reporter for a local radio station, WFUN; he became a commentator with his very own show. I was always one step behind.

His mother worked for or was friendly with prominent liberal Claude Pepper, who, during a long career, would end up serving in the Florida House of Representatives, the US Senate, and US House of Representatives. One summer, while Pepper was in the US House, Nick's mother arranged for him to work as a page—a highly coveted position often reserved for the offspring of the inner circle, which he clearly was. Where most students would come away from an opportunity like that with good references, Nick returned to Miami with references and a gaggle of Washington elected and appointed officials, including members of JFK's cabinet, squarely in his quiver. He could call upon them to address our meager student assemblies—for which they'd promptly board a plane and appear. Whenever he got on stage in all his glory to introduce them, I pulled my hair out. While I disliked him intensely and stayed out of his way as much as possible, people thought we were good friends because thanks to the kind of person my parents were raising me to be, I was always cordial and even friendly toward him.

The lesson here would come shining through when I understood there's always going to be someone bigger, better, wealthier, brighter, and more connected than I was...no matter how they got there. It just made me get up earlier, work harder, and strive for higher levels of achievement. (Besides, let's face it, sometimes people who achieve things with a less than honorable operating code don't quite make it to the finish line!) Regardless it's kind of like a runner, running all by himself, thinking he's out there at top speed. Suddenly someone steps onto the track and they're way ahead of him. He realizes just how far behind he is and does everything he can to become better at his craft. Though I didn't actively seek it, and "Nick" creeping into my head at inopportune times (which they always were) could conjure up unsavory thoughts, I learned competition could help me develop inner strength and resiliency. In a strange way I would come to be grateful for "Nick," at least in hindsight.

As luck would have it, one of the debate tournaments in which we took part occurred in New Orleans on the Tulane University campus. The school made an impression on me and in a serious effort to ultimately escape my high school nemesis, I would make sure to apply there when I learned he was applying only to Florida schools. It worked. I was accepted. I finally got free of him—though only for a time (more on that in chapter 4).

Where the Boys Are

The faculty of my high school selected me to be its representative to American Legion Boys State in Florida, a program run on the campus of Florida State University in Tallahassee. It was the summer between my junior and senior years, and every school in the state sent a candidate: one candidate only. Being chosen was a kind of exhilaration I can still feel and it was my first experience in a dorm—also a treat. The purpose of this week-long program was to teach us how government works. We were divided up into citizens of fictitious cities, each electing city councilmen, a mayor, congressmen, senators, and a governor.

I learned how to lobby for the office I wanted, making campaign speeches and asking others for their votes. The final session was held in the Florida Senate chambers—for ambience and a lot more. The powers of persuasion I'd had to develop to be effective in speech and debate were powerful allies during my time at Boys State; I brandished them all the way to winning the mayoral race as well as becoming a senator!

In many ways the victory assuaged the sting I'd felt when, just a couple of months before leaving for the week at Boys State, I'd run for senior class president. At North Miami High School, you ran at the end of your junior year because if you won, there was work to be done prior to the actual year in office. I lost. I'd had the encouragement of the faculty and the endorsement of most of the student leaders and campaigned vigorously by handing out brochures and putting up posters. With all the awards and other achievements I'd racked up since junior high school, I still lost out to someone with no honors and no extracurricular activities. His credentials? He was one of the cool kids. I was disappointed but had learned from my father not to spend a lot of time stewing in it. Disappointment and negativity had to roll off my back. As it turned out, the student who won was a stand-up kind of guy and would end up doing a good job as president of the senior class. From the defeat I'd gone on to Boys State anyway, learned a lot, and was elected to the two offices. So I got past my previous defeat in a nanosecond!

Where the Boys Are—For Real (the movie)!

As busy as I was at school, the idea of making money was never out of my mind. I loved to work for the sense of freedom and independence it gave me. Aside from my summer paper route, I worked at Richard's department store where I sold housewares earning minimum wage (one dollar and ten cents an hour). As an usher at the local movie theater, I shined a flashlight for patrons to find their seats and got to see snippets of movies like *Where the Boys Are* starring Connie Francis and George Hamilton. By the end of the run, I'd probably seen these random clips fifty times without ever seeing the entire movie.

Probably one of the most enterprising and fun jobs I ever had was hawking Cokes at Dolphins games on weekends. There'd be dozens of us boys and we'd start by purchasing a case of twenty-four Cokes in cups with ice. We'd cap the filled cups so they wouldn't spill and fit them into a giant rectangular kind of wooden box carried by a strap around our necks. We'd spend the day traipsing up and down the bleachers until we sold out, returning to the staging place to start all over again. This could be done fifteen or twenty times. It was hot, sweaty, tiring work but with tips I could make fifty dollars' profit in a day—more than I'd make in an entire week at my one dollar and ten cents an hour department store job.

My dad taught me another invaluable lesson in standing up for myself one summer when I got a job at a beach hotel.

In those days, hitchhiking was a safe and acceptable mode of transportation for a teenager of which I availed myself to get over to Route A1A: the beach. It was about twenty minutes from our house in North Miami Beach. I had gotten a job as a cabana boy, which entailed bringing out lounge chairs to guests who asked for them and putting on a pad to protect people from the hard surface of the chair.

As many jobs as I'd had in my life by that time, this was all new to me and when I asked the manager how much I'd be paid, he replied my "pay" would be in the form of tips. I was pretty excited about this and hustled as hard as I could on my first day—a Sunday—working from 8:00 a.m. to about 6:00 or 7:00 p.m. And almost nobody tipped me! It appeared that the tipping was going on with the cabana manager as he was the one approached by the guests, whereupon he'd motion to one of us worker bees to get the chairs.

When I returned home and told my father about my day, and my take, in his inimitable style he explained to me that it just couldn't go on like that.

"You need to have self-respect. Earning what you did is just not right. Go back tomorrow and tell the cabana manager you need a salary or guarantee of how much you are going to make," he'd said. That's why my father was all that he was.

I loved him. I knew he was right but I was scared to death.

First thing the next day I asked the cabana manager if I could talk with him. He responded that now wasn't the time and I needed to set up some chairs. He was brusque because he wanted me just to get to work. I heard my father in my head, called up some courage, and insisted. When I explained the situation as best I could, he told me I didn't have the right attitude and fired me on the spot. That was the end of that summer job, but my father was right. While money was not the most important part of a new job—any job—no one should take advantage of you. There's a freedom that comes from knowing and applying that.

I started knocking on other doors and got another job as a cabana boy at a different hotel. This time they were going to pay me a real salary—plus tips.

My first day of work I happened to get into a conversation with one of the other, more senior pool boys who, upon learning my last name, informed me he knew another Levan. It turned out to be my brother Jay. He asked what Jay was doing for the summer and when I responded he was looking for work, I was told to have him call. When Jay did, he was told they'd hired me but would prefer to have him, being two years older. So I got the boot and Jay was hired. A week or so later, Jay broke his ankle so the job became mine again.

While all this had been going on I don't recall any animosity between us. I may have been disappointed but didn't feel resentful. My dad always said "move on." Sure, I'd spent a week in limbo knocking on doors again, but I was going to find work because that's who my parents were raising me to be. And as fate would have it, except for hitchhiking twenty minutes to the beach, I didn't have to look far when the hotel welcomed me back.

Florida was the place my family had moved to so my father could get into the bug business, but living there had heartened me to shake the bugs from my own life as well. I had grown up. I was ready for college.

LIFE LESSONS LEARNED

- While competition may be uncomfortable, it is actually a good thing. It establishes a goal, creates a sense of urgency, and makes you think and work harder.
- There will always be someone out there better than you so don't waste your time and energy comparing yourself. Make it a goal to learn to be comfortable in your own skin. It will make a difference in how well you function and succeed in the world.
- Be definitive in your decision-making.
- Everyone should read Dale Carnegie's *How to Win Friends and Influence People*. Written in 1936, it continues to be one of the bestselling books of all time for a reason.
- Being cool doesn't matter.
- Learning how to speak in front of a group or run a meeting will change your life.

Silver Knight Awards presentation

North Miami Senior High School

800 N.E. 137 STREET NORTH MIAMI, FLORIDA

" A COMPREHENSIVE AND FRIENDLY SCHOOL "

W. E. RICE   PRINCIPAL   PHONE PL 4 - 4651

DR. JOE HALL   SUPERINTENDENT   PHONE PR 7 - 4311

March 5, 1962

Silver Knight Committee
Miami, Florida

Dear Members:

Alan Levan, a student of this school, is entering the
Silver Knight competition in the category of " citizenship ". It is a genuine pleasure for me to recommend
this student to you.

Few students in the history of North Miami Senior High
School have been involved in as many worthwhile activities as this student. Being a good citizen indicates
that one has expended his mental, physical, emotional,
and spiritual energies in functions that center around
the home, school, place of worship, and community. Alan
scores a high " A " in this evaluation.

In another section of his application you will note that
he has listed the specific activities in which he has
been engaged during the past three years. In scholastic
achievement he has achieved on a high level. In service
to his school he has attained the highest possible score.
You will note that he has been involved in functions of
varied interests; this indicates his talents and abilities
have been utilized in many ways.

When a job needs to be done, we can always count on this
young man to attack it with deliberation and enthusiasm.
Alan is conscientious and loyal, perseverant and helpful,
friendly and personable.

It is my sincere belief that Alan will work diligently to
deserve any consideration that you give to him. My prediction is that he will succeed in life because of the pattern
of life that he has created for himself in his relationships
with others.

Sincerely yours,

W.E. Rice, Principal

Silver Knight Presentation Album

Page one of Silver Knight Album
(Drawing by my dad)

Degree of Distinction

Takes Honors In District Contest

Allen Levan, son of Mr. and Mrs. Z. Levan, 1180 NE 179 St., a student at Miami Senior High, took first honors in a public speaking contest representing North Miami Beach Knights of Pythias Lodge. He competed against contestants from eleven lodges in the district.

Alan Levan Cops Oratory Honors

Alan Levan, a junior at North Miami Senior High School, was awarded the the first prize prize to Emanuele Club oratory contest held March 20 with an original oratory on Amer-icanism.

ALAN

Eleven Students Win First Place at State Discussion

Keith Barish, Ronald Werner, Harold Dadosh, Howard Bredin, Michael Solomon, Richard Erick-son, Alan Levan, Malcolm Manning, and Ronnie Reddwick all attend-ed this two-day conference at Gainesville, Florida.

On FSU Campus
Boys State Cranks Off Machinery for Elections

Alan Levan Attends Boy's State Meeting

Alan Levan To Talk

Allen Levan, the North Shore Kiwanis Club's representative to Boy's State, will talk at tomor-row's meeting of the North Shore Kiwanis Club, at 12:15, at the Bal-moural Hotel. Allan remained in Tallahassee extra time, after Boys' State, to take additional courses offered to the delegates.

Eight Students Attend Girls And Boys State; Five Make Offices

Honors Bestowed On Debate Team

Many honors have been bestowed on North Miami High by the mem-bers of our debate team during the past few weeks.

Alan Levan Wins 1st in Speech Contest

"The Constitution, Defend it Now!", "Americanism and Wake Up America" were the award win-ning speeches of the Buena Vista Exchange Contest.

MINIATURE CONGRESS INSTRUCTS STUDENTS; RESOLUTIONS PASSED

LOCAL STUDENT WINS CONTEST

Allen Levan, a student of North Miami Senior High School, re-ceived an award of a $25 Bond from the Knights of Pythias Lodge #195.

Mayors Attend Boys' State

Barish, Levan Win Trophies
For Best Presiding Officers

THURSDAY, SEPTEMBER 21, 1961

Cavanaugh Post Honors Boy And Girl Starters

At Boys State Jay Beskind was elect-ed mayor, and Alan Levan was elect-ed mayor, and Dennis Wightman was nomi-nated for the Supreme Court.

Students attending Girls and Boys State

Today's Teen

Alan Levan Readies Talk
... North Miami debater

Alan Has Sights On Law Career

Alan Levan likes to argue — for his debating team. The 17-year-old North Miami High senior is preparing well for his hopes of becoming a lawyer.

"I hold my 'Degree of Distinction in debate,'" says the blue-eyed 138-pounder. "This summer I hope to work in a law office."

Alan rates high in scholarship. Maintaining an "A" average, he has been on the Dean's List.

In the field of leadership, Alan is secretary of publicity of Student Council, Silver Knight Nominee in citizenship, and he has participated in over six plays in the past three years.

"English and debate are my favorite subjects," he says, "and I study about one and a half hours a night."

Spare time is spent water skiing or playing baseball. Son of Mr. and Mrs. Zel Levan, 1180 NE 179 St., Alan was chosen as the Miami Herald Top Teen by a committee of faculty and student leaders.

TOP TEENS of the week

ALAN LEVAN

The North Miami High senior twice is one of South Florida's better young speakers. He list of awards is enough to set any-one talking.

He recently placed second in the state level of the Knights of Pythias Oratory Contest. Pre-viously, he took first place at local and county levels.

He also also placed first and second, respectively, in the lo-cal and state levels of the Amer-ican Legion Oratory Contest. And, he placed second in the state level of the Key Club Ora-tory Contest.

The son of Mr. and Mrs. Zel Levan, of 1180 NE 179th St., North Miami Beach, has just re-turned from the select facility of Speech Institute of Florida state University.

The National Forensic League "member of distinction" esti-mates that he speaks before an every class each year.

"Through speech," he said, "I've found myself involved in so many other activities." Each year Democratic Youth of Flor-ida, Key Club, National Foren-sic League, National Thespian Society and Student Council.

After all his speaking experi-ence, does he still get nervous when he's on the podium? "Yes he I do ... well, at least for the first few words, any-way."

Miami Herald   *Miami Herald*

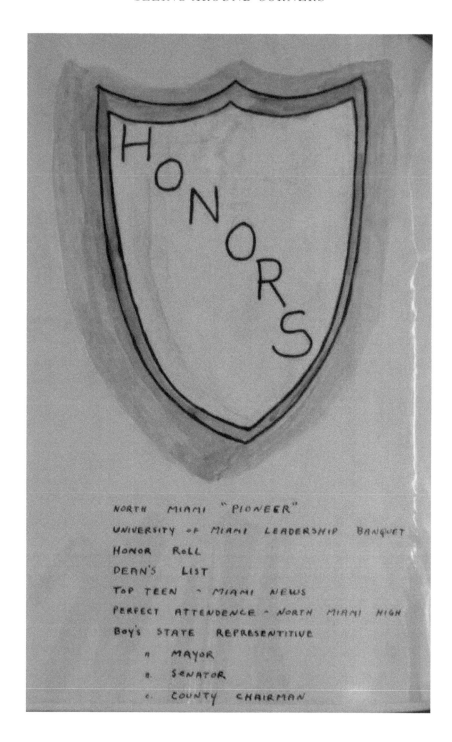

NORTH MIAMI "PIONEER"

UNIVERSITY OF MIAMI LEADERSHIP BANQUET

HONOR ROLL

DEAN'S LIST

TOP TEEN ~ MIAMI NEWS

PERFECT ATTENDENCE ~ NORTH MIAMI HIGH

BOY'S STATE REPRESENTITIVE

    A   MAYOR

    B. SENATOR

    C. COUNTY CHAIRMAN

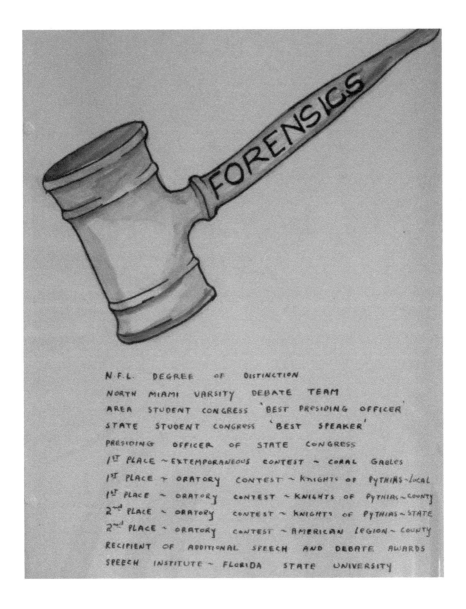

Dividers in my Silver Knight Album (Artwork by my Dad)

Off to a debate tournament.

Alan working as a pool boy.

*Alan —
high school photo*

Pearl and Zit

Pearl

*Zit's mighty fleet
of pest control trucks*

*Manual-mechanic, lawn sprayer,
all around loyal employee*

*Zit – maybe the fleet
wasn't so mighty*

CHAPTER 3

COLLEGE DAYS:
MOSTLY EASY IN THE BIG EASY

"Success is never final, failure is not fatal:
it is the courage to continue that counts."
—Winston Churchill

With my nemesis, "Nick," squared away at the University of Miami, I boarded a train from Miami to New Orleans late in the summer of 1962.

I had clipped the handcuffs; snipped the shackles. I was free of "Nick." This would last until our paths crossed again when I went to work for Morgan Guaranty in New York and he masterminded nothing less than a mammoth European-based real estate venture with international investors. But that was well into the future. For now—yeehaw!—I was swinging on the wrought iron gates again.

The Tulane University campus had been the setting of a pivotal debate tournament three years earlier—pivotal in the sense that while my high school team's winning or losing was important at the time, it was ultimately inconsequential. The school and its imposing campus had made enough of an impression on me that I'd set my sights on matriculating. I had been accepted, I believe, largely because of my extracurricular activities.

Rush week on campus began the first week of school but my soon-to-be Alpha Epsilon Pi fraternity brothers didn't let an obstacle like that get in their way. They and their compatriots from other fraternities routinely canvassed trains known to be ferrying freshmen to Tulane for the last one hundred miles of the trip. They were jockeying for position and seizing the time to regale prospective members with the merits of joining their ranks. As freshmen on those trains, we were a captive audience, but I can think of worse places to be. It was a heady experience being pursued.

Once in New Orleans, random fraternity boys carried my luggage from the train, drove me to campus, and helped set up my dorm room. If you joined a fraternity or sorority, per the rules you couldn't move into the house until sophomore year, so it was nice to have the help and early camaraderie in unfamiliar surroundings.

Incoming freshmen went through a whirlwind courtship that included nightly parties at all the houses. If a particular brotherhood liked you, you were asked back to a party the next night, with additional parties on your agenda if you continued to make the cut. New Orleans was famous for its home-grown bands and the parties were loud, wild, with lots of beer and hard liquor flowing fast. It didn't take long for me to hear the stories of many a Tulane student succumbing to the lure of Bourbon Street, seduced by Lorelei's siren song: four fingers' worth over ice. Some flunked out in their freshman year. I don't drink so was confident it was not going to happen to me.

The fact that I didn't drink became somewhat of an inconvenience at rush parties. I kept refusing what was offered so then someone else, followed by an unwitting someone else, and then still maybe someone else, would come along every five minutes asking if I wanted a beer. An enterprising soon-to-be fraternity brother eventually suggested that I simply hold a can of beer. This was good advice except that by the end of each evening the contents of my can were disgustingly flat and warm—even to smell and look at—cooked by the hours in my sweaty palms.

I joined the pledge class of Alpha Epsilon Pi while holding true to myself about not drinking though I went through typical pledge class rituals—the hazing. It all seemed pointless and dangerous, the insanity of rush, but I was getting to know and like certain members of the fraternity that I believed shared my values. So I held my breath and dove in.

For the most part these boys from different parts of the country seemed to be a serious bunch, not like others at the so-called party fraternities. They were also not wealthy boys like members of ZBT—Zeta Beta Tau—or Zillions, Billions, and Trillions as they came to be known. I cared little about status and was certainly not wealthy so AEPi seemed a good fit for me. A little investigation after I got there revealed the fraternity as a whole had one of the best academic records on campus, so I knew these were serious, like-minded people. It was a good thing I joined because another pledge, Norm Silber, would quickly become a good friend, trusted confidant, coworker in at least one on-campus job, an innovative campaign manager when I ran for office, and so much more. Norm would later go on to work with me in my business career and impact my life in so many ways (more on that later).

* * *

Both my older brother Jay and I were in college at the same time when I entered my freshman year, with Jay at the University of Florida. It's hard enough putting one child through college, let alone two. Because my parents had paid for my freshman year tuition, housing, and meal plan, I was determined to limit the amount of money I would ask of them for incidentals. Just as my father had taught me during my time delivering *Newsday*, I went to the local

39

drugstore and bought a ledger notebook with lined paper. The cover said "cash." The goal, which I uncompromisingly met, was to keep track of every penny I spent that year to hold incidental expenditures to a minimum. In fact I was able to get through my first year of college never exceeding $1.25 a day; I still have that budget book as proof! And I was able to finance the balance of my college years—tuition; room; and board—with student loans and money earned from maybe a dozen college jobs—including one that took me into the wilds of New Orleans. I liked to work and while others may have chosen to spend their spare time imbibing New Orleans' famous Hurricanes at Pat O'Brien's, that way of life just wasn't for me.

Jobs I held on campus included washing test tubes in the chemistry lab and working shifts at the switchboard, the latter of which in many ways was the heartbeat of the university. I got to know who was calling whom, though I was always discreet. Norm Silber, who worked alongside me, took the same vow of discretion I did as we spent hours plugging and unplugging a web of fifty or seventy-five wires to the various offices and departments. Lily Tomlin, as quirky switchboard operator "Ernestine" in her TV comedy routines, had nothing on us.

I also worked restacking books students and professors had checked out of the university library. Learning the Dewey Decimal System, which I had to essentially master to make the way I did my job more efficient, would impact how I organize paper files in my office to this day. No experience is wasted.

At the end of my freshman year, a senior fraternity brother who had been advertising manager for the university student directory recommended I take over his position as he was graduating. I had developed a reputation as someone who gets things done. The publication board approved me and I jumped in with both feet.

I told my parents I needed a car in order to sell advertising as I was going to have to cover the city of New Orleans. Entering my sophomore year, I was now allowed to keep a car on campus. My mother wasted no time in giving hers to me. She managed by sharing my father's exterminating truck for getting to the pest control office, where she was the company bookkeeper, and anything else she needed to do.

The student directory was a large, bound, yellow pages-style book with student and faculty names, phone numbers, and addresses. In order to break even, the directory needed thirty-five full and partial page ads from local businesses. I started by putting together a presentation book (today it might be called a media kit) from scratch. I took the previous year's student directory and cut it up to show the different size ads, with the inside front and back covers costing the most because of the exposure.

Scouting my territory, I'd start at one end of Canal Street and work my way everywhere. I had to learn how to pitch the owner or manager of a business when he or she was trying to wait on customers. I couldn't get in their way, and I didn't want to bother them to the point that they'd ask me to leave and look the other way when they saw me coming the next time. Often getting them on board was a lesson in persistence, among the many lessons learned from my parents, though I had to figure out how to maintain a low profile in front of customers while applying it.

I enjoyed the work, going from door to door, and in addition to an hourly rate the sweetener was I earned a commission for any ads I sold. That year the student directory had more ads than it'd had in all of its history. It was my forte. My track record paved the way for the publications board to approve my request to appoint me business manager for all publications going into my junior year: the Student Directory; *Hullabaloo*—the school newspaper; *Jambalaya*—the school yearbook; and WTUL—the Tulane University radio station. These entities had had separate business managers in the past, but by giving me the group, I was able to bundle them together, cross sell, and offer volume discounts to advertisers.

41

Norm Silber had a propensity for technology—in as nascent a stage as it was in the early 1960s—and suggested I carry a beeper (of course, this was decades before cell phones). I created a business card that said "Alan B. Levan, business manager, Tulane Student Publications and Radio Station. Call me." Merchants I was pursuing could call the number. The caller's name and number would go to a national answering service that would relay it to a screen on my beeper. In this way I was not tied to the fraternity house phone where if I were lucky enough to get a message, it could be a day or more before I could get a hold of and visit the merchant. There was relatively good money to be made from selling ads and I wanted to be able to strike while the iron was hot. Sometimes the beeper would go off in a social setting such as a frat party. I'd excuse myself to go call the merchant back and make the sale. I wasn't about to miss a single opportunity.

Upstairs Downstairs

As a sophomore I would move into the AEPi fraternity house, a three-story structure with ample underground parking. The second floor was the living, dining, and kitchen area, with the president's suite: a large bedroom with three beds, a private bathroom, and an adjoining office for studying and fraternity business.

The third floor was the dormitory, consisting of fifteen rooms, two beds to a room, and a large, communal bathroom. As fate would have it, going into my sophomore year the fraternity president asked me to be one of his two roommates—the other being my friend Norm Silber. Turns out Norm had been invited first, whereby he'd immediately suggested I be the third occupant. This was most fortunate for me because I was not looking forward to moving into the raucous third floor of a frat house. When you get that many boys together, though AEPi was not known for hard partying, the results have to be a little bit crazy. I was relieved I didn't have to live that way or opt not to live in the house at all (which may have offended some), enjoying the relative peace and comfort of the president's space.

In my junior and senior years I became president of Alpha Epsilon Pi, so I never had to leave that suite. In fact it was Norm Silber who helped me get elected having established friendlier relationships than I with members of our brotherhood. Like me, Norm was serious with high energy, so the symbiotic relationship we formed for generations with its roots in college served both of us.

Whenever rush week came around during my tenure, Norm got to work. With his knack for cutting-edge technology, Norm brought his ideas to Tulane University rush week, at least to those of us at Alpha Epsilon Pi. In fact his methodology singlehandedly streamlined the recruitment process.

Canvassing trains was one thing, but Norm put us way out ahead of that when he purchased IBM punch cards. When the school sent each fraternity the list of incoming students, we'd put that information on the punch cards whereby Norm would secure use of a machine that printed off mailing labels from the cards. In turn we were able to send multiple mailings to incoming freshmen all summer, introducing ourselves long before they'd ever board a train or plane, or set foot on campus. Norm was a first-rate logistics, advance, and administrative person and would aid me accordingly when I ran for student body president (more on that later), becoming my campaign manager. He'd go on to graduate from Tulane University Law School, landing a job with Fiduciary Trust Company in New York. In 1971, after my return to Florida, I would later call upon Norm to move down and join me in a real estate investment business I was forming, I.R.E Properties, Inc.: Investors (Tax Sheltered) Real Estate (please see chapter 6). I also asked another good friend, Stan Linnick, to subsequently join me in the formation of I.R.E. Properties but Stan was now within the management ranks of Exxon Oil, where he stayed for thirty-five years before joining me in Florida.

Cashing In

Possibly the most invaluable lesson I learned from serving as fraternity president had to do with cash flow. It was an exercise etched indelibly in my mind to this day.

In my junior year—my first year as AEPi president—I instructed my fraternity brothers to invite only freshmen candidates that would make outstanding fraternity brothers. I wanted the crème de la crème: boys that we earnestly wanted and who really wanted us.

Historically our pledge classes were comprised of thirty boys. I mandated that we accept only the top fifteen on our list. I hadn't understood that dues from the additional fifteen candidates were necessary to pay the overhead of the fraternity house and go toward activities. This was a wake-up call as I almost singlehandedly bankrupted the Tulane chapter of AEPi. Fortunately we scraped by and were able to find some transfer students and others at midterm. It was a significant business lesson at the tender age of twenty. Many people never grasp that cash flow is the most important element in running a business. In fact cash flow was one of the themes of a commencement speech I would make in 2019 at the H. Wayne Huizenga College of Business and Entrepreneurship at Nova Southeastern University, of which I was to become chairman of the Board of Trustees.

There's a marked difference between sales and cash flow. In some businesses sales can be strong—they can continue to increase—but you run out of money. You can have a deficit because you're spending a fortune on marketing, for example, to generate sales so despite a great product that's doing well, you're not profitable. That's a cash flow issue. Or maybe your overhead is too expensive, so you have a certain level of sales achieved but your rent, salaries, and other elements exceed what is right for you.

I learned in college that I was looking at these prospective pledges at face value as pledges—fraternity brothers. I was never considering them as money in the form of a product or commodity. Alpha Epsilon Pi owned a house. It had a mortgage. We had telephone and electric bills. We had to pay the house mother and a house boy. We had to buy our food and pay other expenses. I'd been thinking only quality, not quantity. But while that kind of thinking is nice, it's not practical and can surely get you into trouble. Actually, in running a business, you need both quality and quantity.

Math-itis

While a misuse of logic steered me down the wrong path on the necessary size of our pledge class, with a little tweaking the use of logic would come to define me. So what does that mean? Sometimes we fall into a vat of something with a life-changing effect, as I did.

I'd always had difficulty with math, going back to high school. I could add, subtract, multiply, and divide, but by the time I got to geometry, algebra II, and calculus, I sank like a stone. I'd go to my father for help, quickly recognizing that as sharp as he was he also lacked this skillset. I managed to claw my way through it but math was never a good grade for me. The idea of eventually applying to graduate school for business, getting an MBA—something I'd always considered—became more and more a remote possibility because of the math issue. I knew I couldn't handle it as an under-grad and met with my freshman advisor when having to take math loomed large before me in a paralyzing kind of way.

"There are several required courses," the advisor had explained, "math being one of them."

I panicked. "Is there an alternative to the math?" I'd asked my advisor, not expecting much but seeking a kind of workaround.

He said advanced logic would totally satisfy my math requirement, and the prerequisites for the course were courses in philosophy and ethics.

I never looked back, signing up for philosophy and later logic as quickly as the opportunities were made available to me. I studied Plato's *Republic* in my freshman year, along with Socrates, Aristotle, and all the philosophers over time. I found an abundance of life's lessons in their work. Sitting in these classrooms discussing philosophy, ethics, logic, and morality was my idea of Bourbon Street. I got drunk on it. I couldn't get enough. It spoke to me and I was good at it. Eventually, I selected philosophy and English as a double major.

In my professional life, logic defines everything. I can get to the finish line quickly in a business plan someone has created, based on complicated math calculations (which I clearly do not do), and say, "This math makes no sense whatsoever. Something's wrong here. You've got the zeroes wrong."

The writer of the plan will invariably ask, "What do you mean? It proves out in the math!" I find myself responding that it may prove out in the math, but reasoning tells me you're supposed to be in the millions, not hundreds of thousands—or vice versa. They don't realize the error because there was no logic to what they did. Perhaps they started with the wrong premise: what you put in is what you'll get out.

Immersing myself in logic back in college gave me the ability to analyze and write. Logic provided a strong foundation for problem-solving and interacting with people in an ethical way. It was also about the constant Socratic questioning of "why." "Why" has served me well. In time I would have a son, Jarett, who lived in the land of "why," which could drive my wife and me crazy, but I embraced it and him because I knew where it was coming from. I wasn't comfortable with advanced math, wasn't competent in it, but really wanted to be in business. I paid attention to what my advisor offered and found another way to reach my goals: a workaround. It was another lesson in persistence—internal, if nothing else.

During my years at Tulane, I became a voracious reader of dozens of biographies of successful people. I was hungry to understand the elements of their achievements and what morsels of style I could embrace for myself.

Shortly after I became president of AEPi, the social committee planned a Saturday night hayride for the brothers and our dates. We used two flatbed trucks with siding and a requisite amount of hay to provide the ambiance of a hayride, while riding on the streets of New Orleans. Unfortunately, one of the brothers tossed a beer can across trucks, hitting a date in the forehead and drawing a small amount of blood. As luck would have it there was a motorcycle cop right behind us and he pulled both trucks over and demanded to speak to who was in charge. That would be me. He hauled all eighty of us, including dates, to jail. Our booking with charges of reckless behavior made the 10:00 news. Unbelievably, my parents in Miami were watching the 10:00 news. Fortunately, I was able to reach our fraternity advisor in the middle of the night. He was a lawyer and he was able to get us all released from jail by 6:00 a.m. but we still had to appear in court thirty days later. The judge was somewhat amused by the situation and after admonishing me and the others, with a smile, he acquitted us without the incident appearing on our permanent record. So much for being in charge.

Trying Harder

In college I also served on the student honor board, in time being elected its president. The honor board, which investigated and presided over allegations of cheating, was one of those activities people didn't know a lot about. It wasn't part of the vernacular. The work was sensitive and confidential and being a part of it wasn't for everyone. There were ethics involved and the potential of serious consequences that could impact the accused's future in a very big way. I took this very seriously, honing my interpersonal skills in exploring awkward, uncomfortable situations with an accused student. These are the skills people in business and particularly

CEOs need to have, and I was fortunate to have had the opportunity to develop them so early.

Perpetuating the practice I'd begun at North Miami High School, I spent a lot of time in Tulane's student activities office. From that vantage point I was able to keep my finger on the pulse of so many university goings-on and, at the end of my junior year, decided to run for student body president. I diligently put together a ticket with candidates for vice president, secretary, and treasurer. We called ourselves the V.O.TE. ticket: Voice of the Electorate.

School elections rules stipulated a twenty-five dollar campaign spending limit. Accidentally, I figured out a creative way of marketing without any cost. At the time, Avis was rolling out a national advertising campaign against market leader Hertz. Avis adopted the slogan, "We're #2. We Try Harder." It was everywhere: on TV; radio; in newspapers and magazines.

I wrote to Avis about our election, requesting any slogan materials we might have for free. Ten days later, to my surprise, boxes filled to the brim with posters and snap-on pocket pins appeared at my door with the "We Try Harder" slogan. What was particularly interesting is that the product name appeared nowhere on the collateral. I imagine they'd figured out their slogan had caught fire enough to be recognized without the Avis name. Our election was a form of campus marketing to them. We could use the materials as we saw fit. So we easily adopted their slogan, combining their posters with our V.O.T.E. posters. The campaign was off to a running start.

It appeared the election was in the bag for our V.O.T.E ticket, but a scant few days before voting day I was called before the director of student activities. Apparently there'd been a complaint filed that the V.O.T.E. ticket's campaign expenditures exceeded the twenty-five dollar limit and no amount of explaining I did to the contrary would change this erroneous thinking. I pleaded hard, explaining the Avis materials were available to anyone who'd asked the company for them, just as I had. It wasn't as though I'd had my parents purchase something and send it to me so that technically I had not paid for it. Nothing like that had occurred. It was not a question of ethics or anything close.

Nevertheless the director made the decision to purge the V.O.T.E. ticket from the ballot, leaving the opposing party uncontested— automatic winners of the election by default. While I strenuously disagreed with his actions and received a measurable amount of support in the student newspaper, on the radio station, and from arbiters around campus, I could not dissuade the director. Never one to give up, at the eleventh hour I was able to convince him to leave the V.O. T. E. ticket intact, eliminating my name. He agreed, and when the ballots were printed our ticket won in a landslide. Without a presidential candidate, however, the opposition candidate automatically won though the rest of his ticket lost.

Though I was entirely incredulous and distraught over the issue, I had decided to take one for the team—another lesson learned early on—as there was more to the election than one person's success. It was a very early lesson that failure is a result of the CEO and success is a result of the team.

Several weeks later, the election for president of the College of Arts and Sciences came up. Dad had always told me to move on.

I ran. I won.

Forty-one years later, Tulane University honored me with their Distinguished Alumnus Award, 2007. Each year, only one alumnus receives this award.

The Award Criteria:

"The Distinguished Alumni Award recognizes alumni who, through their remarkable attainments in professional and civic life, have brought honor to themselves and Tulane University, and whose accomplishments and contributions have had a broad impact and positive effect on others. Recipients of this award are celebrated for going beyond their successful vocation and bringing benefit to the greater community."

I was so impressed with the Avis marketing campaign that I looked up who their advertising agency was. It was Doyle Dane Bernbach, whose clients were Avis, Volkswagen (the beetle bug), Braniff Airways (started painting their planes colors other than the traditional silver), and others. They were said to be the hottest and most creative agency of the time. I ordered a subscription to *Advertising Age* and every time DDB announced a new client, I bought a modest amount of stock in that company. It was my first foray into the stock market.

LIFE LESSONS LEARNED

- Cash flow is everything.
- Look for workarounds—such as substituting logic for math.
- Math is important; logic is more important.
- Learn to "move on"—quickly.
- Failure is a result of the CEO. Success is a result of the team.
- Become a voracious reader of biographies of successful people.

TULANE

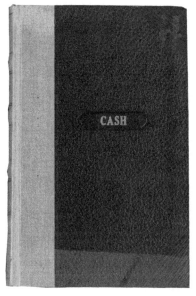

My college budget book

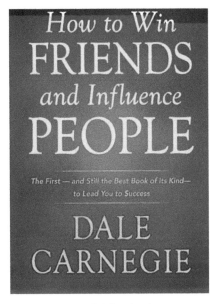

A must read. This book got me through the rest of my life.

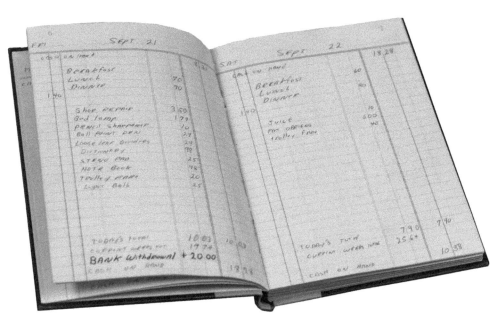

Watching every penny

Alpha Epsilon Pi

Alan Norman Silber Stan Linnick

*Norman would become my Chief Administrative
Officer at IRE Financial; Stan would work for Levitt
and BankAtlantic and today is the Executive Director of
the Susie and Alan B. Levan NSU Ambassadors Board.*

Campaign poster　　　　　*Campaign slogan, thanks to Avis*

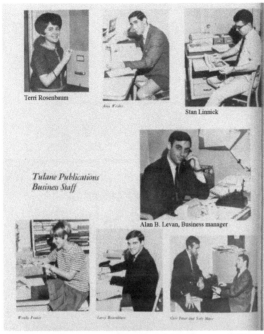

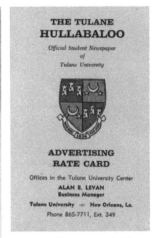

My advertising bible

Three years of Student Directories

Three years of Tulane newspapers

Sample Hullaballoo page

Three years of Tulane yearbooks

Graduation – Zit, Alan, Pearl

Graduation – Alan and Stan Linnick

Alan – Graduation

Senior Photo

Terri Rosenbaum would become my wife.

Hall of Fame, yearbook recognition

CHAPTER 4

RETURN TO NEW YORK: COUNTING THE CARS ON THE NEW JERSEY TURNPIKE

"The future belongs to those
who believe the beauty of their dreams."
—Eleanor Roosevelt

I called her the Blue Bomb—the 1950s Dodge something-or-other I'd purchased in college about a year after my mother had lent me her car. The Blue Bomb had gone through Hurricane Betsy in New Orleans and lived to tell the tale. As mentioned earlier, my mother had selflessly shared my father's exterminator truck for a year to get to work, the grocery store, and run all their other errands, just to make it possible for me to drive around New Orleans in her car, selling ads while at Tulane. The French Quarter alone was seventy-eight square blocks, and I'd not have had one-tenth the success I'd had were it not for my parents' generosity in forfeiting that car. Purchasing one of my own had been a top priority.

The Blue Bomb was about to steer me all the way to my next mission: the wilds of New York. I was going back to the land of opportunity, and to all the formality I'd regretted leaving when I'd first moved away at age fifteen. Life in Florida and later at Tulane had exceeded my dreams and expectations, but it was time to be exactly where I'd always felt I'd belonged.

To prepare for the more than twelve hundred-mile trip, I got a TripTik from the Miami AAA branch, as my father was a member. He was not in favor of my living in New York, but much to his credit did not try to discourage me knowing I had to figure it out for myself.

I got to work packing the Blue Bomb. Family mementos, my old Smith Corona college typewriter, which would come in handy for resumes, a navy-colored suit, sport coat, some ties, pair of black dress tie oxfords, white shirts (a nod to my high school days), casual shirts, Weejuns loafers, and jeans. I didn't yet have a job and would be staying with my mother's sister and her family in Brooklyn, so any household items were unnecessary.

There I was—a newly minted soon-to-be professional, about to be unleashed in full force on the New Jersey turnpike. I could feel New York in my bones and can actually say I was pumped! It was the iron gates all over again, this time at 60 mph—or whatever the turnpike speed limit was in 1966. As I got closer to New York City I'm sure I exceeded it. But fast or slow, I was flying. It was summer; the heat was scorching as I drove through the Holland Tunnel. Regardless, I remember the feeling of exhilaration with all the windows rolled down, breathing in the New York air as deeply as I could, belting out, "New York, here I come! Here I come!" I was surely home.

In my aunt's Brooklyn home, I pored over help wanted ads in the *New York Post* and *New York Daily News*. I had no idea what I was going to do for a living though I was sure I wanted to take whatever business skills I'd picked up in college to the next level. It had to be about business. I'd applied to law school and had not gotten in. My grades were pretty good and my student activities and achievements were exceptional, but apparently pretty good grades were not good enough to be accepted to law school. The fact is I'd never wanted to practice law—only use it as a foundation for business. So I had to find another way to learn what I believed I needed to learn.

Banks were advertising heavily for employees that summer in New York, looking to fill a variety of positions, and I figured working in one was an efficient way to learn about business. Applying to Chase Manhattan, Manufacturers Hanover, First National City Bank (now Citibank), Chemical Bank, and Bankers Trust, I waited for interviews, feeling nervous.

I'd had ample opportunity to perfect my public speaking skills in speech and debate at North Miami High School, and addressing lunchtime business and community organizations in those years, and certainly while campaigning for office at Boys State and Tulane. But a one-on-one formal employment interview was another thing entirely. Any jobs I'd had in the past were not at this level and I was understandably concerned about what to say and how to act. Time after time I'd hear my father's voice telling me to use a firm handshake, make eye contact, and be genuinely focused on what someone was telling me. The first impression is the best impression, he'd say. *It will matter.*

My interviews would invariably start out with, "Why did you apply here?" I knew it wouldn't serve me well to say I was there because I wanted to learn about business so I could end up leaving the bank. I needed a storyline and crafted one that went something along the lines of how intrigued I was with banking, that it would make a good, stable, interesting career. I was also confident about my past achievements and work ethic. Whatever I said in the end, I must have impressed the interviewers because I received offers from four out of the five banks.

Around the time I'd made up my mind to accept the offer from Bankers Trust, a fraternity brother living in New York invited me to join him at Roosevelt Raceway. His father and some of his father's friends would be there, and it looked to be a nice evening. I found myself seated in the VIP dining room, taking in the races in an unobstructed view through giant open windows. In a sense, and it only came to me in retrospect, it was as though there was nothing in my way.

This was my first dinner with a group of adults, other than family and my parents' friends. These men were in big business—high finance. I felt privileged, definitely out of my depth, maybe a little nervous because this world was something to which I aspired. I didn't care so much about personal wealth but cared deeply about immersing myself in business. I was prepared for whatever came my way, dressing up in my sport coat and looking every part the young, hopeful professional. The man sitting next to me knew I'd just graduated from college and asked about my career plans.

"I've been interviewing at different banks and am about to accept an offer from Bankers Trust," I told him, answering still more of his questions. He seemed interested in what I had to say. It was a relaxed environment, conducive to easy conversation.

I'm not sure he knew these banks were only offering me entry-level positions, and I'd likely be working as a teller and nothing more. But apparently it didn't matter. He wanted to know more about me. I'd always presented myself as genuine and serious, and perhaps dressing up in a sport coat that night (the others were more casual) helped me project the right image though the fact is I wasn't out to impress anyone in particular. I just wanted to put my best foot forward—always—something I'd learned from my parents.

As it turned out this man was a vice president at Morgan Guaranty, which was steeped in history. Founded by J.P. Morgan in 1871, it was one of the largest, most prestigious banks in the world known in its early years as The House of Morgan. After the stock market crash of 1929 and the Great Depression that followed, the 1933 provisions of the Glass-Steagall Act forced J.P. Morgan to separate its investment banking from its commercial banking operations, spinning out Morgan Stanley. In 1959, J.P. Morgan merged with The

Guaranty Trust Company of New York to form the Morgan Guaranty Trust Company. Other events would result in a name change back to J.P Morgan in 1969, but when the vice president and I were dinner partners that fateful evening, it was still Morgan Guaranty.

He asked me to consider his company, promising to arrange an interview the very next day. He also requested I hold off on accepting a job at another bank. I felt there was no harm in my agreeing to one more interview, believing I could practically write the book on how to interview by that time!

Paradise Found

The opening credits to the iconic 1970s *The Mary Tyler Moore Show* feature an inspired Mary Richards, on the town in bustling Minneapolis, tossing a knit beret into the air to celebrate her independence. She had arrived and was starting a brand-new life.

Though it was a few years before Mary Richards's time, I, too, had arrived and was on the brink of entering a hugely important phase of my life. I didn't have a hat to toss that day but stood in awe at the entrance to Morgan Guaranty—at the intersection of 23 Wall Street and Broad Street, with the New York Stock Exchange and Federal Hall, the United States Sub-Treasury building across the street. It was right here that George Washington was inaugurated as our first president on April 30, 1789. I walked into the Morgan Guaranty interview in my blue suit, white shirt, and red tie; briefcase, hopes, and dreams firmly in tow. Talk about lost (or found!) in paradise. Though I'd been instructed to enter through the customer entrance at 23 Wall Street, I would learn that the employees' entrance was at 15 Broad Street—an equally potent experience—"employees" being the operative word here. Was it possible my professional life, almost as I'd envisioned it, would begin that day?

Navigating a breathtaking two-story atrium with a shower of chandeliers and large, exquisitely carved wooden desks, someone at the other end escorted me to my interview. The process was totally different from any of the other interviews I'd had in New York, as the interviewer spent a long time with me, essentially selling me on why Morgan was a great place to work. At the other banks I was nothing more than the average applicant, made to feel I was really lucky to be sitting in a room with them in the first place. My experience at Morgan felt as though the tables had turned: They were the pursuers and I was the one being sought after. It was as though I were interviewing them—and about a future, not a mere job. Two days later I received a letter with an offer of employment that I immediately accepted.

On my first day I knew I was not an ordinary employee, I found myself in an elite training class with a group of fifteen others, all young men, and all from Ivy League schools like Harvard and Yale. They were scions of the captains of industry who did business with Morgan, raised by nannies and polished by boarding school head-masters. I now understood the royal treatment I'd received during my interview, thanks to the vice president who'd recommended me. My fellow trainees asked where I'd gone to school.

"Tulane," I replied proudly.

They paused, asking me where it was.

I was stunned. The wind had been knocked out of me. When I caught myself again I remembered Tulane was known as "the Harvard of the South," at least that's what I'd always been told. How could they *not* know that? It was supremely evident I wasn't one of them. They were pleasant but arrogant and cocky—the building blocks of blueblood DNA. The training class was designed to give them the experience they needed to return to work in their fathers' empires, taking over when their elders retired. I found it curious that Morgan would invest all this effort and expense only to lose these young men after a few years. Though I had no intention of sticking around either, it was clear I was going to have to outwork troop trust fund while I was there. I thought of "Nick," my junior high and high school nemesis, and the realization it'd taken me a long time to come to that in this world there is always going to be someone bigger, better, brighter, stronger, wealthier, better connected—even all of the above. Once again I'd just have to get up earlier and work like there was no tomorrow. For my coworkers, the training class was nothing special. It was an expected component of their trajectory. But to me it meant everything. I felt I was the privileged one, and certainly not because I came from money.

My living situation at my aunt's large two-story house in Manhattan Beach, a residential neighborhood in Brooklyn, was awkward at best. As a young boy, I was always intimidated by this side of the family. My aunt was pleasant enough but none of the other family members ever gave me the time of day—then or now. My two cousins were raised with total emphasis on achievement and success, at the expense of any sense of humanity. The environment in which they lived had always felt devoid of love, feeling, empathy—any semblance of emotion—and without my parents and brother I felt it even more acutely.

When my uncle came home from work, he would grunt something that sounded like a hello but he never looked at me. We would eat dinner together with no conversation whatsoever. At our house, the din at the dinner table could be deafening (well, almost)—all of us trying to talk about what we did all day. Being with my aunt and uncle was a very strange experience—like another world. It was hard to believe we were related.

After dinner my uncle would plop himself down in the den. He'd light a big cigar and smoke it all evening. The TV would be broadcasting the news with the volume so low it was practically inaudible, strictly as background noise. He wasn't watching. He'd read several newspapers—including *The New York Times* and *The Wall Street Journal*—and a variety of books with which he'd surround himself. My aunt would be in the kitchen or somewhere else in the house. At 9:00 p.m. my cousin Eric (née Ricky—which I innocently called him one night and which elicited a sharp reproach; I guess it wasn't professional enough) would come home, newspaper and briefcase in hand. My older cousin, Eric's brother, was married and out of the house. Just like his father, Eric would barely (or not at all) greet me. If he said anything at all to his parents, it was in passing as he made his way to his room, never emerging until he left for work the next morning.

Eric was four years older than I, treating me now the same way he did when I was six and he was ten, or when I was thirteen and he was seventeen. It had always been the same way. I knew little about him. He and my uncle wore suits to work each day (that much I knew), and I'd been told my uncle worked for Bulova Watch Company and my cousin for Goldman Sachs.

Eric worked a couple of minutes away from where I did and would drive to work every day, never once offering me a lift—in any kind of weather. I'd brought the Blue Bomb to New York but it was more efficient, when you took parking constraints and expense into account, to take the subway. I considered this living arrangement completely dysfunctional, coming from a warm, loving, expressive household where we couldn't get enough of each other. I dreaded coming home to this environment each night, saving my paychecks until I could rent a studio apartment in the basement of a brownstone in the Park Slope section of Brooklyn. It was only four houses away from Prospect Park. In the '60s, Prospect Park and Central Park were dangerous places and I never ventured into either place, but having a place of my own was far more comfortable than where I'd been staying, no matter what it looked like or where it was.

It was clear I'd grown up in a different socioeconomic class than my Brooklyn relatives and certainly from everyone in my training class. Members of the class had more spending power and would do things together in the evenings and on weekends that I couldn't afford to do. I was making one hundred fifteen dollars a week—sixty-five hundred dollars a year—not bad for a first job in 1966, but not enough to accompany them to dinner, the theater, or on their weekend getaways to the Hamptons, as they were not dependent on their income.

While cliques and the upper class may bother some people who are not part of them, the fact is I didn't spend a lot of time thinking about these things. Just as in high school, I couldn't have cared less about fitting in with the cool kids. I was focused. I had a goal to learn everything I could at Morgan and a self-styled short timeframe in which to do it. But I wasn't in New York for more than two or three weeks when I called my father, telling him he was right.

"You can't really live in a place like this," I conceded. I knew it was too crowded, no matter how much money or importance or the kind of position someone would have. I said I would return to Florida, just not right away. I would have to be disciplined. I'd end up spending two years in New York, functioning like a sponge at Morgan Guaranty. I didn't know it at the time, but having Morgan on my resume would have cachet that would serve me well as I built my career. However more than just the name value, I was going to make it count.

Feeding My Soul

My initial job was credit underwriting by spreading financial statements. This meant using percentages to forecast future financial statements. Morgan viewed its name as a credit reference and only wanted customers who had a reason to do business with the bank, not those whose sole intent was to trade on its name. My job was to call other banks and references to determine who these potential customers and businesses were. I had to research why they needed a New York bank and whether they were worthy of having a Morgan checking or savings account. Minimum checking account balance requirement for an individual was five thousand dollars; twenty-five thousand dollars for a business. I was earning one hundred twenty-five dollars a week, so I didn't even qualify for an account at the bank where I worked. I had to open one across the street at Chase Manhattan!

I loved being on Wall Street: the people; the energy; the history. Everyone wore a suit. At lunchtime I'd go to the brokerage houses and watch the tickertape. Being able to do that fed me more than anything else. I also loved being in cold weather again and actually decided not to buy a heavy coat, saving the money. The subway was hot and wearing a coat made it feel even hotter. I went through two winters in New York without a coat, reading *The New York Times* and *The Wall Street Journal* en route to work with other businessmen on the steamy train. It would be unthinkable to show up at work having missed some important piece of news or other information someone wanted to talk about.

I was extremely inquisitive, curious about everything, constantly asking questions. One time I was asked to do a rush credit report on a business. My initial research did not reveal anything promising. I asked my boss why there was such a rush for such an unimpressive company. He explained the owner had an appointment with Morgan Guaranty's president with a request to borrow one hundred million dollars for an acquisition he wanted. It appears large sums turn heads—a lesson I carry with me to this day. Had the request been for a much smaller amount, such as one hundred thousand, for which my research showed he wasn't even qualified, he'd have met with a regular loan officer or no one at all.

On another occasion I had an unpleasant exchange with an employee who was a vice president. He was somewhat aggressive toward me, quite brusque in fact. I asked my boss who he was.

"That's one of the Guaranty guys," my boss had replied. "He came over with the merger and was unhappy Morgan bought his bank."

The merger had occurred ten years earlier, and the lesson I'd eventually figure out and apply to my own businesses is that mergers are complicated and difficult—just as much about people as they are about numbers. They need to be orchestrated carefully so that everyone is well integrated into the new structure.

Another time I learned of a vice president who was retiring after a long, "successful" career at Morgan. He'd been there thirty years. I asked my boss how much he earned after three decades at Morgan and was told the figure was fifteen thousand dollars a year. I was incredulous because it was only a little more than double what I was earning as a trainee. My boss must have noted my dismay, adding that Morgan was a great place to work with tremendous job security—a place that didn't lay anyone off during the Great Depression. That was a defining moment for me, underscoring my plans to learn as much as I could in the short window I'd designated for myself. In the next thirty years, I was not going to succumb to low pay (and the feelings that go with it) in the interest of some kind of job security.

My feelings about leaving were reinforced when I was tasked with researching a company called Gramco that was buying a high-rise apartment building in Atlanta. Gramco was a large company raising funds throughout Europe to buy US real estate. My eyes bugged out when I saw that the president and CEO was none other than Nick, my junior high and high school nemesis. *What?* I was crazed! My heart sank. I could not believe he'd created a company to provide a safe haven for foreign money to invest in US properties. His board of directors (no surprise) consisted of luminaries including two former John F. Kennedy ambassadors, two former Kennedy staff assistants, a former Kennedy undersecretary of Health, Education, and Welfare, a former Kennedy Assistant Secretary of Commerce, and former Kennedy press secretary Pierre Salinger. I just knew he'd met those people during that summer he'd spent as an intern in Washington.

By this time Gramco had raised hundreds of millions of dollars owning prime real estate all over the US. Here I was earning sixty-five hundred dollars a year. I was so far behind "Nick" in my career, I felt I would never catch up. I'd been in New York a year at that point and called home, reiterating I'd be back in Miami soon. I knew I needed another year at Morgan though. I had to keep learning.

Gramco would ultimately go broke. When the European nations saw how much money Gramco was raising and was leaving their countries by investing in US real estate, they halted Gramco's sales. As redemptions increased, without new investor money, there was not enough cash to pay back investors.

* * *

Morgan had a significant fringe benefit. If you worked late, there was a floor with a dining room where you could grab dinner at no charge. This was perfect for me, especially after I moved out of my aunt's house because I could save money. I was accustomed to working hard and late, whatever jobs I'd held, so I'd head for the dining room and then straight for the Morgan library.

A large area with extensive files was maintained by the company librarian, and the library was a candy store to me. There were mountains of customer files, industry files, and others—all there for the reading. Whatever I wanted to know, even if I didn't yet know that I wanted to know it, was there in those files. Bank officers were instructed that if they saw anything interesting in a newspaper, magazine, or book—anything from a personal profile to an interview or any one of thousands of trend or news stories—they should send it through intercompany mail and the librarian would create the files. None of my coworkers would stay after work and do this, but I would burn the midnight oil reading about thought leaders and dozens and dozens of industries—everything from car washes to communications—to determine what I wanted to do with my life. I learned how to start a business, which businesses were more profitable than others, and which might suit someone like me. Not only would I read about them, I would make copies of my own to build a personal library I imagined I'd use for years. Ultimately I found myself drawn to real estate, requesting a transfer to that area of Morgan Guaranty.

Under Morgan's employee benefits policy, I'd had the opportunity to take an accounting class and a contracts class at City College of New York, adding these to my experience with financial statements and cash flow knowledge. And I'd certainly learned a valuable lesson about cash flow in that unfortunate, ultimately beneficial fraternity pledges matter at Tulane. I knew all of this would serve me well in real estate.

Working in the commercial real estate realm of banking was an exceptional fit for me. I had access to developers' annual reports and financial statements. In the 1960s these were not the kind of massive-scale developers that are common today. They were individuals building high-rises in Manhattan and all over the country. After being introduced to the real estate industry, I would walk the streets of Manhattan, my neck craned, looking up at all the skyscrapers, imagining I would own these kinds of buildings one day.

Requests for commercial real estate loans came into the bank. I was on the underwriting team where I got to see how much these buildings cost and how financing was obtained—either from a bank or another entity. I learned what kind of profitability was generated from these projects, relishing every second of it.

One of the things I discovered in doing credit research on various companies was that real estate developers tended to build larger and larger projects as their careers went on. I came to the conclusion that most of the time it was ego that was driving them. They were never satisfied with the size and scope of their last project, which often was their great financial undoing—a lesson I would take to heart.

By My Calculations

At one point the bank made an amortizing loan on a large building. The duration of the loan was to be twenty years, and we needed to give the borrower an amortization schedule reflecting what their payment would be, specifically how much their principle and interest payment would be every month for the duration of the loan.

In those days there was no such thing as an amortization book or table so I had to build one from scratch, an effort that would take many hours. It was to be a schedule of two hundred forty months of payments. Theoretically the loan balance needed to come out to zero at the end of the two hundred fortieth month and if it didn't, it would mean I did something wrong and would have to start all over again.

The process was tedious and painstaking, doing a month-by-month addition, subtraction, and multiplication process. The Friden calculator I was given looked something like a typewriter, maybe a foot long and six inches high. There was a giant handle. I'd have to add and use the handle, multiply and use the handle, and subtract and use the handle. It would come out on a tape to be put on the schedule. It took days and fortunately I did it right the first time—a process that today can essentially be done in a few seconds on an iPhone.

One night toward the end of my two-year stint at Morgan, I decided to look up my uncle and cousins in the library purely out of curiosity. I learned my uncle was not only with Bulova Watch Company, he was its treasurer. My cousin Eric was one of Goldman Sachs youngest partners—having graduated from Wharton—earning an incredible eight million dollars a year in 1968. His older brother, who had gone to Harvard, was CFO of Shearson Hammill & Co., a major brokerage company later becoming Shearson/American Express and Shearson Lehman Brothers, going through many other incarnations as financial entities tend to do. I was truly impressed and wished more than ever they'd made time for an earnest family member who could have used a little guidance.

At the end of 1968 I decided my time at Morgan Guaranty was over. I'd absorbed all I could and needed to get to it—the rest of it—whatever form that would take. When I gave notice, my supervisor asked what I was going to do. I told him I was headed home to Miami to join the family exterminating business. (It was going to be a stop for me so I could survey the real estate industry in Florida, but I didn't go into any detail.) He was quite disappointed—incredulous, in fact—saying he questioned his own judgment in having been my supervisor. All he knew was that I was leaving the hallowed halls of the House of Morgan to kill bugs.

LIFE LESSONS LEARNED

- Outwork them all.
- Always dress for success.
- Large sums and big ideas turn heads.
- Ego should not drive business decisions.
- In mergers, people's well-being is very important.
- You only have one opportunity to make a good "first impression."
- There's always someone bigger, better, brighter, stronger, wealthier, and better connected.

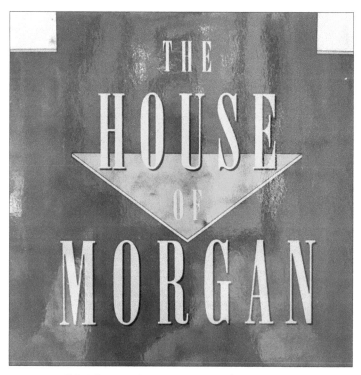

J.P. Morgan: An American Banking Dynasty

CHAPTER 5

RETURN TO FLORIDA: AND SO IT BEGINS

"A journey of a thousand miles begins with a single step."
—**Lao Tzu**

I was married on June 18, 1968. Terri and I had met at Tulane while she was at H. Sophie Newcomb College, Tulane's counterpart women's college at the time. Two years younger, she joined me in New York after the summer, transferring to NYU and then to the University of Miami for her final year of college when we married. We were moving to Florida so I could enter my father's pest control business, canvass the area for my foray into real estate, and because I'd decided that New York was not a place I wanted to raise a family.

As they'd planned, a few weeks before the wedding my father and his partner split, amicably dividing the pest control business. It had been in the works for a while. His partner's son-in-law was coming aboard, as were my brother Jay and I. It was about to get crowded. There was enough business to go around, thanks largely to my father's entrepreneurial skills and work ethic, so it seemed like a good time for the partners to go their separate ways.

Jay had obtained a degree from the University of Florida in entomology: the study of insects. He would be a lifer in the family pest control business; I saw it as an opportunity for a paycheck and some security—a placeholder—on the road to other pursuits. I would work hard and appreciated the opportunity I was given, especially getting to work alongside my mother, father, and brother, but my heart was elsewhere. I made it clear to everyone about being a short timer as there was no reason to deceive them. We'd always enjoyed open communication and this occasion was no different. When I eventually left, however, my mother, who worked as our bookkeeper, kept an open desk for me for years in the event I decided to return. Jay and I had spent the second half of our childhoods growing up around the business and it was her dream that the family would end up in it, permanently together.

We renamed my father's half of the company—now a whole business of which he generously gave my brother and me one-third each—Vanguard Pest Control. It was the heyday of space travel and Vanguard 1, the first solar-powered satellite, had launched from Cape Canaveral in 1958 (interestingly it is still orbiting the Earth, the oldest manmade object to do so). Of course vanguard means forefront, leading, or cutting edge, and we liked the association.

Cutting edge or otherwise, we needed an economical place in which to deposit our new name, typewriters, telephones, office supplies, chemicals, and other accoutrements of the business. Terri and I had rented a house, so we allocated the Florida room—a screened-in patio common in the state—for the route men to congregate and get their daily assignments, and a second bedroom for the office. It was a less than ideal situation for newlyweds but, as I'd done before, we took one for the team. The arrangements lasted about a year, whereupon I was able to find a commercial building for sale. My resourceful father negotiated the purchase with the entire amount in the form of a purchase-money mortgage, or a seller's mortgage. No cash down! I have often thought that had he gone to college, there would have been no limit to his success.

The building he bought was a former tourist stop three blocks off the Florida turnpike exit on 163rd Street—a main east-west artery in North Miami Beach on the way to Miami Beach. The building had large neon signs screaming "tourist information," "hotels-motels," and "free directions." Cars would end up at our location, park, and go inside to ask directions to AIA—the beach route. This was the same road along which I'd hitchhiked for my first jobs as a cabana boy. As we set up the pest control office, tourists would continue to drive up, thinking it was the old tourist stop and ask us to arrange reservations for the motels on the beach.

"Wow!" my dad had exclaimed in another genius business moment. "Let's not take down the signs. Let's also go into the travel business. We'll just use the back for pest control."

I got the idea to add another sign saying we provided fresh-squeezed Florida orange juice to entice even more cars to stop. It worked. I went to all the hotels and motels along AIA and got contracts for them to pay us a referral fee when we sent them guests.

Later on, with a toe dipped in local tourism, my father decided to create an actual full service travel agency, which he named Vanguard Travel. This enterprise was not limited to featuring information about Florida hotspots, but one that booked cruises and wrote airline tickets. Unfortunately he could not obtain airline ticket stock as stock was controlled by the IATA (International Association of Travel Agents). One of the requisites for airline ticket stock was cash liquidity of $5,000, which he could not yet produce. We went to County National Bank for a $5,000 loan but were declined. I would soon be engaged in real estate with a dozen employees traveling all over the country, every single day, raising money and buying properties. The commission for him would be significant if he could write our tickets and any others. Somehow through my father's due diligence, he discovered Icelandic Airlines was not exclusive with IATA. In those days, when you showed up at the airline ticket counter with a ticket, it was okay for it to be written on any airline's ticket stock despite the fact that you may be flying on a different airline. For example a Delta or United or Pan Am flight from Miami to New York could be written on Icelandic ticket stock. Tickets were interchangeable because before deregulation, all pricing was uniform. One would think it was strange showing up for a domestic flight with an Icelandic-issued ticket, but the agent would accept it. Delta (or other airlines) would process the ticket through their system, the transaction ultimately making its way to Icelandic, which would reimburse the respective airline for the flight. Dad became the travel agent for all of our business trips, using Icelandic stock.

After two years of operating this way, Icelandic Airlines confronted my father.

"Mr. Levan, I'm not sure we understand what's been happening here," the Icelandic sales representative began. "You've written $150,000 worth of tickets and not a single one of them was for an Icelandic flight. That's a lot of back office processing for us." With no profit.

My dad apologized and because enough time had passed, Vanguard Travel's financial statement indicated to IATA it was now qualified for all ticket stock. Dad was then able to write tickets precisely on the ticket stock for the airline on which the bearer was flying. My father always inspired me. This episode was another example of his creativity and resourcefulness, and the kind of workarounds I'd learned and continued to learn from him for many years.

With the arrival of the Internet, my father asked his grandson, my older son Donny, to explain it to him. Well into his seventies and then his eighties, the wheels were turning. He got one of my lawyers to incorporate a business name: Discountcruises.com, and promptly started advertising on the Internet. With Miami known as the cruise capital of the world, it came as no surprise that once again dad was seizing the day. He sold a lot of cruises and he and mom ended up leading many group trips. They became world travelers, journeying to China, Israel, Europe, and other locales thanks to perks from his travel business. In time the website was getting twenty thousand hits a month but it wasn't enough: he was always improving. When he got to forty and fifty thousand hits a month, I asked him what he was doing, seeing it was getting too big and he didn't have employees to keep up with the volume.

"Don't worry. I'm just increasing the leads," he'd replied. I learned his ultimate goal was to sell the name and website, which he did for $75,000—more than the pest control company would make in an entire year. Even with that kind of profit for practically a zero initial investment, it wasn't about the money for dad. He loved the work and creativity. He loved the action. He loved the fun.

Hialeah, Here I Come!

Prior to dad's conquering cyberspace, our family was working extremely hard maintaining and expanding Vanguard Travel and Vanguard Pest Control, catering to the Florida tourist trade along 163rd Street as well. I always had an ear to the ground for my transition to real estate. One day a real estate broker introduced me to a piece of land west of Miami in Hialeah. It was zoned and there were architectural drawings in place for a two-story apartment building. I was able to sign a contract, telling the seller I didn't have the capital but would immediately pursue financing.

"When I get the financing, I'll buy the land and build the apartments," I'd said confidently. I thought I was really on my way.

What I didn't know was the reason the seller hadn't built anything and was willing to give me the time is he couldn't get financing himself. An aggregate of eyesore master utility poles and lines went right through and over the property. I went all over town, to every

73

bank, denied at every turn. I had to drop the contract because I'd extended it several times to no avail.

In addition to the big lesson here, which was to sharpen my assessment skills when looking to acquire property, I'd gotten tremendous experience visiting all the community banks with my set of plans and projections of how much money there was to be made. I was able to apply my Morgan experience to my quest. At one bank in particular I got to meet with the president, who promptly called in his partner, the chairman. They grilled me for two hours about how things worked at Morgan. It finally dawned on me they had absolutely no interest in my project. They were small town bankers intrigued by the formidable J.P. Morgan. It didn't matter to them that I'd been a lowly trainee. Information was information.

Granted, the property with the master utility poles and lines was a bad bet for any bank, enamored of Morgan or not, but another teachable moment was when, in hindsight, I realized each bank had had a different suggestion on what the building should look like. This ranged from the size and layout of the apartments to the building's exterior and type of landscaping.

In my inexperience, I wasn't strong enough to say no. I tried to accommodate everyone by agreeing to change this and consider that, and then there'd be a request for more of this and less of that, and so on and so forth. In the end I understood I just couldn't accommodate everyone because their suggestions were conflicting. Nobody offered me financing anyway, even contingent on changes in the design. Later I'd form I.R.E., soliciting investment bankers in the process. Each of them had a different idea of how to structure the company. Based on the experience in Hialeah, I decided I was going to take into account their suggestions but do what I thought was best.

"This is what I have to sell," I would tell them. "This is my plan." If they were willing to support it, fine. If not, I'd keep going until I found people who did.

If You Build It…

I was really frustrated by the Hialeah episode. I was still in the pest control business, spending my days driving the truck up and down our customer routes and spraying houses. Sometimes Jay and I would have to climb up on top of a house to drape a vinyl-coated nylon tent over the roof and down the sides, enveloping it completely in order to fumigate the property for termites. It was a massive feat in the searing Miami sun, 95-degree temperatures, and unrelenting humidity. I was learning a lot but again, this was not the reason I'd returned to Florida.

My dad suggested I see a good friend of his by the name of Charlie Weissman who worked for Midwest Mortgage Company. The thinking was that Charlie would introduce me to his boss, David Harris, who might give me some advice on real estate. Dad had actually met David Harris at Miami Dolphins games. Charlie was quite gregarious, coordinating the purchase of tickets where a group of friends—all Dolphins fans like my dad, would end up sitting together at games.

David Harris—Midwest Mortgage Company president—was just a few years older than I. His father, A.J. Harris, was chairman of the company, occupying a formidable corner office of this highly successful company. It had a net worth of $5 million.

A.J. was legendary as one of about half a dozen fabled Miami pioneers who'd built the region into the glamorous, wildly profitable destination it became in the '30s, '40s, '50s, and throughout the '60s. One of his contemporaries owned a racetrack. Another had built glittering hotels on the beach. Yet another owned a bank, and as the gods would have it, I was about to grab hold of those swinging wrought iron gates once again, gaining entry into this world.

"Why don't we become real estate partners?" David said to me during our first meeting. I wasn't sure I understood. *Partners?* What had he seen in me?

"I don't have any money," I'd replied, wondering if I'd missed something.

He said that was not a concern, offering to finance things through his father's mortgage company.

After that, my father's friend Charlie was quite helpful in introducing me to a bevy of commercial real estate brokers. I found a piece of land in North Miami Beach and brought it to David.

"Get a contract and we'll build apartments," he immediately said. Charlie then introduced me to a law firm to get everything tied up, and then to an architect named Barry Sugarman who'd just hung out a shingle.

The architect drew up plans for a forty-two-unit, three-story building. I'd not done this before and had to know everything. I was there every day from dawn to dusk, watching him, learning from him, asking millions of questions, participating in the building's design process not just from an architectural standpoint but just trying to comprehend how things were done. Just out of architecture school himself, it was Barry's first large commercial project. He was eager for it to be a resounding success and pleased to have me along each day for the ride.

When the drawings were complete I told David we were ready to go and needed to find a builder. He told *me* to build it.

"How can I build it?" I recall asking dubiously. "I don't know the difference between a roof truss and a door frame." At least I knew the words, as they were in the plans, but that was the extent of what I knew about construction.

I took David's words to heart anyway. I interviewed many general contractors but decided not to hire one. Instead, I hired a labor contractor and asked him to pull the permits. I hired all the subcontractors myself, interviewing dozens along the way. I decided I wanted the direct experience of building and if I hired a general contractor I'd miss out. So I didn't. I took David's words quite literally. It was interesting to find out there was an actual science to the process, for example certain subs had to finish their work before other subs could begin theirs. It made sense. All the logic classes I'd taken at Tulane came rushing back. I may also have been a proverbial babe in the woods but I was accustomed to outworking anyone, figured it out, and was never entirely lost. No breadcrumbs necessary for me.

I developed detailed flowcharts of what the order of the trades would be along with highly detailed budgets. I was at the jobsite every single day, revising budget and flowcharts daily, based on new information that would come in. I actually finished the building within budget, something I'd come to find out was a rarity, the inspectors signing off with few, if any, problems.

Construction is a rough and tumble industry, brimming with maverick tradesmen. I yelled. I cajoled. I fired. I encouraged people as much as I could, bringing in soft drinks, lunch, and ice cream to keep them working.

When all was said and done, my job was to build the apartment building and David's job was to obtain the permanent mortgage to pay off Midwest Mortgage's construction loan. Unfortunately he was unable to get permanent financing as markets characteristically open and close, and at that moment in time the permanent loan market had closed where apartment buildings were concerned due to a weak market.

Faced with the challenge of paying off David's construction loan from his mortgage company, I was aware of a relatively new concept in 1960s Florida: condominiums. My parents had purchased one for themselves in 1962 just after I'd left for Tulane. Theirs was one of the very first condo buildings that went up in those years.

I went back to the lawyers and asked if they'd be able to convert rental apartment documents into condo documents. They were able to comply and I secured permanent loans for the individual home buyers through Chase Federal Savings & Loan. I renamed the project

Sevilla Plaza Condominium—and started selling them myself to learn what I could about that aspect of the business. One-bedroom units went for $8,500 and two-bedroom units for $10,500. I was able to pay down the construction loan as we sold each unit, and the project sold out. I was also ecstatic because just as my father had made Jay and me partners in the pest control company, I had done the same by making each of them partners in my real estate ventures. If there was a profit to be made, I was going to share it with my family.

At twenty-five years old, I now had experience finding land, in construction, financing, documentation, architecture, apartments, condominiums, and sales. Pleased with what I'd accomplished, David suggested I look for other opportunities.

Of Squatters and Stewardesses

It was a Sunday morning when I first saw the ad in the *Miami Herald*: forty-eight unit apartment building at a steal price in the Kendall area—South Miami. I drove to look at it, noting it was, in a word, dilapidated. I called the phone number in the ad, reaching someone out of state who said he was the estate's trustee. The owner had died months ago, nobody was paying their rent, and he was eager to unload it. While mostly vacant, I would learn there were a few college students, including University of Miami law students, and a handful of vagrants living there—squatters. There were perhaps a dozen occupants in total. I flew to Philadelphia and signed a contract to buy it with Midwest Mortgage financing the acquisition. David Harris and I were off and running again.

My first challenge was in getting tenants out of the building. Florida law is strong on proper eviction procedures. Tenants cannot be forced out without following a strict protocol. An eviction process would take a long time and I didn't want to wait. Besides, none of these tenants had leases—they were all squatters. Knowing all I did about the extermination business, I got an idea that if we fumigated the building (though I had no idea if there were termites or not!), everybody would have to leave for a few days. As soon as they were out, we'd go in and change the locks. I'm not sure if it was legal or not, and I had some trepidation because there were law school students living there who I thought might challenge me, but I took a chance.

When occupants returned following the fumigation, they went right to the office proclaiming they could not get in to their apartments. I told them they were not paying rent so they could not stay. We allowed them to remove personal belongings from their units and no one took issue with it. As I was in the habit of thoroughly exploring the downside of a situation before embarking on it, I knew the worst that could happen was I may be sued for improper eviction. I'd have to let them back in and go through the process, but it was definitely worth a shot.

With tenants permanently out of the building, I hired subcontractors to renovate and repair. We cleaned it up, painted, and changed the carpeting. We also decided to furnish each unit so I contracted with a company for the purchase of the furniture. We leased the apartments to actual paying tenants and sold the building at a profit. A month later, the furniture company vendor, Bob Henderson, came to me saying he'd really enjoyed working with me. He wondered if I planned to buy any more buildings. I said sure, though really having no idea if my partner would agree to finance anything else like this.

"I put furniture into a couple of apartment buildings in Miami Springs and I'm not getting paid," Bob told me. Miami Springs is a part of Miami with a street called South Royal Poinciana. "I think they're in foreclosure," he explained.

Some investigation on my part revealed the property was near the airport and comprised of very popular residences catering to pilots and stewardesses (not yet called flight attendants). In those days, stewardesses had to be strikingly attractive and of a certain height and proportional weight. When you have buildings populated by this demographic, everyone wants to live there. Turns out they were in foreclosure with the mortgage held by First National Bank of Miami. A.J. Harris had relationships at the bank so he introduced me to the loan officer. The lender suggested that we talk with the owners, saying the bank would release them from liability if they sold us the property. It would be a good deal for the bank because they could restructure their loan with us, resulting in a new loan that was paying.

The owners sold us the property by just giving us the deed to get released from liability. The bank financed it at 100 percent as we bought it for the amount of the balance outstanding on the mortgage.

Bob Henderson got paid, whereupon he came back to me with two more properties for which he'd supplied furniture and for which he was not being paid.

These were mammoth projects, one a 448-unit building on the golf course of the Doral Country Club. The Doral Country Club was built and owned by the Kaskel family and in fact in addition to the country club, the family had built the beachfront Doral Hotel and Doral Golf Course. The individual who owned this building was a Kaskel brother, however operating independently of the group. The Kaskel brother and his company had gotten into trouble on the 448-unit building so the mortgage was in default.

Interestingly, this apartment building also catered to airline personnel and was an incredible property. It was considered a party apartment building due to its size, massive clubhouse with an entertainment center inside, and a huge patio that could hold one thousand people at an event. The other property was a 172-unit building also near the airport over which the Kaskel brother and his company had similarly gotten into trouble.

The two buildings were financed by an REIT (real estate investment trust) out of Atlanta by the name of Great American Mortgage Company (GAMC). I flew to meet with them, explaining that we wanted to purchase the buildings in that they were in foreclosure.

They readily agreed and I was able to cut a deal, similar to the one we'd done with First National Bank of Miami.

In retrospect I believe the reason the property went into foreclosure may have stemmed from the fact that the owner had not been able to rent the building as quickly as he should have. When I took over, we had lots of parties on the patio and I purchased a 4COP liquor license. In Florida, as in some other states, liquor licenses are restricted—just as taxi medallions are in New York. There are only so many issued so if you want one you have to buy it from an existing owner. The 4COP license allowed us to serve hard liquor, which we did at an open bar. We hosted hundreds and hundreds of tenants, friends, and prospective tenants at open houses every weekend. We filled the building quickly. At this point we owned nearly one thousand apartment units. I had sourced, negotiated, and acquired all of them for our partnership.

Another project I did with David was building a large commercial warehouse facility on Tigertail Boulevard off I-95 in Broward County. Ultimately we built fifteen or twenty warehouses measuring ten thousand square feet apiece, subdivided into 1,000-foot bays. They weren't much to look at, but the cash flow was strong.

On another occasion, I had signed a contract to buy land near the Golden Glades Interchange in North Miami Beach. Apparently, the adjacent property owner learned of my contract and wanted to talk to me. (I didn't know why—maybe joint venture or purchase?) Turns out the adjacent owner was Daniel Lifter, a very successful, well-known Miami real estate entrepreneur. He had built the Marco Polo and Waikiki and other hotels on Miami Beach.

His son, Bennett Lifter, called me and asked me to come to their office and meet him and his father. The Lifters were known as the "biggest hotel men in Miami." I was nervous about meeting such successful men so I showed up fifteen minutes early. The receptionist asked me to sit down and wait. I could hear the Lifters talking behind the receptionist wall. Since I could hear them gabbing, at five minutes past the appointment time, I asked how long they would be. I also asked at ten minutes past the scheduled time.

I started thinking about my cabana boy experience as a teenager, setting up beach chairs. My father taught me to have self-respect. It was obvious that the Lifters did not think I was all that important. At fifteen minutes after the scheduled time, I got up and left. That afternoon, an incredulous Bennett called me and asked what happened. I told him I thought it was rude of him and his father to make me wait. Subsequently, I did sell them the property, but on my terms. My father was so wise!

Though firmly ensconced in the corner office, A.J. Harris was for all intents and purposes retired at this point with David running the company. Midwest Mortgage was not a home mortgage company: it was financing home builders with multiple projects and also large commercial properties, making million dollar construction loans. They borrowed their money from local banks, including City National Bank. So our ventures were providing financing opportunities for their general mortgage business. Since David was also my partner in these side projects, based on my ingenuity, energy, and output, he was profiting separately from the work I was doing.

David had people in and out of his office every five minutes asking him to sign off on this and sign off on that. He was running a mortgage company with several hundred employees in a very large one-story building, and working separately with me as a partner. But it turned out he had other people like me with whom he had partnered, and who ended up being part of our deals and thereby profiting. So I determined that in order to get myself into everybody else's deals much in the same way, I needed to be front and center when the deals were brought to him.

The only way to do that was to sit on the couch in his office for long periods of time, between projects, shooting the breeze. This was the bane of my existence as I had absolutely no patience for it. I hated wasting time and was never big on small talk. But David was king of the hill, plopped in a chair in his office all day. If I were shooting the breeze with him and one of his other partners happened to come in saying "let's build warehouses," I was considered a part of it as David divvied up the percentages among us. I thought perhaps he'd seen something special in me the day Charlie Wiseman had brought me to meet him, but in fact it had nothing to do with me. He had no idea what I was or was not capable of accomplishing.

David was not interested in doing the legwork for the deals and sent me out the door to do my thing. Fortunately for him I worked hard at it. Many of the others with whom he'd made the same arrangements did not equal my success. In fact, most of them had dismal performance as a result of carelessness, lack of planning, or downright fraud. David had done no due diligence on any of them—or me—for that matter. As a result, several years later, during the 1970's recession, Midwest Mortgage had to foreclose on many of these other deals, putting the mortgage company liquidity at risk. It was an extremely stressful time for David.

About the same time our partnership had just received our first big payday from the sale of a building. Previously, all our profits had been reinvested back into our partnership. I was ecstatic—my first cash distribution. My partnership share was $150,000. Of those proceeds, I gave $50,000 to my father for his share and $50,000 to my brother for his share. I offered to lend all $50,00 of my share to David because of his desperate situation. He accepted. I felt he had put his trust in me and had given me my first real taste at being an entrepreneur and it was the least I could do.

Ultimately, Midwest Mortgage went under—David's father's business was destroyed. Sadly, amidst all the controversy, the prolific A.J. Harris became persona non grata among his contemporaries, losing his fortune as well.

It had been an exciting and challenging three years since I'd returned to Miami. I was earning multiples of the $6,500 I'd been earning at Morgan. I was crazy busy and couldn't get enough of what I was doing. Our first son, Donny, was born in 1970. In 1971 I attended a seminar on real estate investing presented at a local hotel. Both events would change my life.

LIFE LESSONS LEARNED

- There comes a time when you have to stop listening to suggestions, reflect, and make your own decision by doing what you believe is best.
- Passion for what you do is everything!
- Evaluate the downside. If you can live with the worst case scenario, move forward, working hard to achieve the best.

Alan and Terri's Wedding

Alan and Terri

*Time off, Alan trying
to look very sophisticated.*

*We now have a conglomerate,
my dad enters the travel business.*

*I'm learning the pest control business.
Clearly, I know nothing about trucks.*

*Jay and Alan putting up a termite
tent. Boy, it was hot.*

CHAPTER 6

FORMATION OF I.R.E.: THE LAW OF LARGE NUMBERS

"Do not attempt to do a thing unless you are sure of yourself; but do not relinquish it simply because someone else is not sure of you."
—Stewart E. White

As hotels go, the Four Ambassadors Hotel in Miami was a nice enough place. I made my way down the hall toward a function room, pondering what may lie ahead. I really had no idea. The sight that greeted me stopped me in my tracks. I was struck by what must have been five hundred people in the ballroom. I was there because I'd seen an advertisement for a seminar on how to invest in real estate through limited partnerships. This was a brand-new concept. The ad said prospective investors were encouraged to attend. The packed premises, which I'd come to find out consisted of real estate brokers, financial planners, broker dealers who typically focused on mutual funds, and people involved in the stock market, led me to believe there might be more to this than I'd realized.

Two speakers emerged, Seth Werner and Richard Wollack, vice presidents of California-based Pacific American Real Estate Fund. They used slides of shopping centers, apartment complexes, office buildings, and warehouses to illustrate their succinct, 45-minute message, after which they took audience questions from a clearly motivated crowd. Seth and Richard were excellent speakers. In the not-too-distant future they would factor into my formation of a company—in fact becoming executives of that company—that would become a virtual money machine, impacting not only my life but the lives of thousands of others.

The premise of the seminar was that because US tax laws had recently changed, investors, called limited partners, could now invest small amounts of money—as little as $5,000—into a real estate fund to buy multimillion-dollar properties for the tax write-off. In short there could now be hundreds or thousands of investors in a single property or group of properties. The wealthy had been doing this for years, only with fewer individuals and much larger sums of money. Previous tax laws had allowed only a limited number of high net worth individuals, or what's called a general partnership, to band together for the purposes of buying real estate for the tax credit. Now the door was wide open.

The limited partnership pitched at the seminar would be managed by a corporate general partner whose job (for a fee) would be to find the real estate, make decisions, and assume liability. In this case it was Pacific American Real Estate Fund. Seth and Richard explained that one of the true ways to create wealth was through real estate (they didn't have to twist my arm about that), in order to take advantage of tax benefits from depreciation and at the same time enjoy the increasing value of real estate. Pacific American's first offering, Series I, had raised $10 million and the goal for Series II, which is why we were all there, was $25 million.

Because these limited partnerships could now have hundreds and thousands of investors, the fund had to be registered with the SEC and the offering documents had to be filed and cleared by the same before the offering could be made. We'd all been given an SEC-registered prospectus and a folder of glossy material for our perusal. It was an excellent presentation and the interest in the room was intense—increasing by the minute.

My adrenalin was pumping. The two vice presidents were about my age and it didn't appear to me they had any real estate experience. On the other hand I had bought and renovated apartment buildings, built and sold condominiums, and built and rented warehouses. With the chutzpah that comes from youthful confidence, I sat there asking myself what they were doing that I couldn't do. Frankly, why would I invest in their fund when I could also start one of my own?

I raced home to read the prospectus and accompanying materials, immediately calling my friend, attorney Steve Arky. Steve and his wife, Marlin, were contemporaries of ours—a great couple with whom we often socialized. My wife, Terri, had attended her last year of college at the University of Miami with Marlin. Steve exuded confidence and had spent a few years working at the SEC before setting up his own law firm. I was over the moon about what I'd heard in that room, the interest shown by attendees, and by the material I was reading. I asked Steve how to file an SEC registration statement and in fact if he could do it for me. He said it wouldn't be a problem.

My mind was going a million miles a minute. I would need to create a general partner, be it corporate like Pacific American Real Estate Fund, or an individual (more later on Steve Arky's direction about that), put together a board of directors, raise about $75,000 to cover start-up expenses, hire people to sell the limited partnership interests, buy the real estate, secure office space, and figure out administrative support. It also reminded me of what my old nemesis Nick was doing on an international scale. Maybe this was my way to catch up!

Though the thought of it was daunting, it all sounded doable except for one "small" obstacle. The new tax code required the general partner to have a substantial net worth of at least one million dollars. I went to my partner at the time, David Harris, and asked if he had any ideas about where we could get that kind of money. He suggested we ask his father, A.J., for the money.

A.J. was usually sequestered away in the corner office at Midwest Mortgage though I'd occasionally interacted with him in the few years David and I had been partners. He was a decent man but like many persons of great wealth, he had his share of idiosyncrasies—frugality among them. In more than one instance he'd recommended I not put stamps on local letters that could just as well be hand delivered.

David and I met with him to explain the opportunity.

"What? Are you *crazy*?" he'd responded, incensed, practically jumping out of his chair. He wielded his words like a machete. "I would *never* put a million dollars into something like that!" In the next breath, he sent us to his friend, Leonard Abess, Sr., owner and chairman of City National Bank and a compatriot in the growth and development of Miami.

Though I had some obvious trepidation, not knowing what to expect or even what to say, David and Leonard Abess were more relaxed, exchanging brief pleasantries after which the very friendly Abess asked what he could do for us boys.

Before I could speak, David asked to borrow a million dollars. Point blank.

"Are you boys going to guarantee it?" Abess asked, matter-of-factly. I glanced at David. I was clearly out of my depth again.

"Yes," David answered immediately. I also choked out a "yes," knowing I had absolutely no net worth but that this venture was all my idea and I was following his lead.

"All right. Go downstairs and see the bank president, Dan Gill, and he'll do the paperwork," Abess replied. That was that.

I sat there in awe of what had just transpired, but this affirmed exactly what I had seen at Morgan: It's much easier to do business at high levels of finance than it is around smaller sums of money. Of course there was also a long professional history between the

Harrises and the Abesses, whose families had also socialized together, but the whole thing was quite dizzying to me. Still, I insisted we tell Mr. Abess about my idea. He listened politely and wished us luck. Again, that was that.

My plan for the million dollars was that it would sit in a bank account. It wasn't cash we would use. It was a placeholder, checking the right IRS box. It would be on the company balance sheet, giving its corporate general partner a million-dollar net worth. The City National Bank loan would be to us personally and we would capitalize the company with the necessary $1 million. The interest we would pay on the loan would be offset by the earned interest in the bank account, minus perhaps a 1 or 2 percent difference. So at a cost of maybe 2 percent a year, we got the net worth that was needed.

Unbeknownst to David, who was not inquisitive, I made sure I had the only signature control over the bank account because I was concerned about some of David's other deals and partners in the other ventures. I was protecting both of us. I needed control over the million dollars so I could be sure City National Bank would be paid back. Even if I went broke in creating the business—or if David went broke—if we raised inadequate money for the operations or the fund—that million dollars would still be there. In spite of David's subsequent financial woes, I was able to repay the million-dollar loan to City National Bank.

Stacking the Deck

The company would be called I.R.E. Properties, Inc., standing for Investor's (Tax Sheltered) Real Estate. In order for a limited partnership to qualify under the new tax code, it needed the aforementioned general partner. Again the general partner could be either an individual or corporation. Steve steered me away from doing it as an individual because of the amount of liability the general partner must take on. All the limited partners are passive: They invest their money

91

in the fund but have no liability if things go south. Their only "job" is to enjoy the tax break and the increase in value of the real estate. The general partner buys and manages the real estate. Steve made it clear the general partner should be a corporation.

Next I needed a board of directors. I was twenty-seven years old so I wanted directors with age and credibility. I would be president. I asked David to be chairman but made sure A.J. was on the board as well.

I asked Steve Arky if he would help me recruit the board. Among his many outstanding qualities was his immense self-confidence, extreme competence, and his charisma—an ability to attract people significantly older than we were and in the upper echelons of business and industry to do business with him. In fact Speaker of the Florida House of Representatives Richard (Dick) Pettigrew was one of the law partners Steve had brought to his firm. Pettigrew asked me if I'd be interested in talking to former Florida governor LeRoy Collins. Dick and I traveled to Tallahassee to meet with him, whereupon he became a member of our board. I had always known Dick Pettigrew as low-key and easygoing. When we walked the hallway in the statehouse, it became obvious he was a kingpin. Steve introduced me to Lee Ruwitch, owner and publisher of the *Daily Business Review*, a legal publication, who also joined the board. We managed to attract a few more high-profile individuals and of course I sat on the board.

At this point, I asked Steve to introduce me to the SEC. Since we were required to file formal registration statements with the SEC for review, and then subsequently be responsible to the SEC for compliance, I wanted to meet someone so it wouldn't be nameless and faceless. Steve said we would meet with his prior boss. We traveled to Washington, DC, and had a wonderful hour-long meeting with Stanley Sporkin, an SEC staff lawyer. Interestingly, Stanley became director of the Enforcement Division two years later.

We were on a roll. Midwest Mortgage, with approximately two hundred employees, was located in an expansive one-story building.

A.J. and David gave me office space in the back to start I.R.E. The unintended good fortune of that arrangement was when people walked through the front door to meet with me and my team, they made their way through a labyrinth of desks and personnel and activity that had nothing to do with our operation. Midwest Mortgage was a large and credible operation, and visitors assumed it was all about us. Once again it was all about perception. It appeared from the starting gate we were a highly viable and substantial enterprise. I always felt a little disingenuous when our visitors entered the building. However, because A.J. and David were on the I.R.E. board, that made the show okay.

Liftoff

Among the many things I learned from my parents was self-discipline. I learned from my mother that when I had the paper route, I had to make sure the newspaper was delivered no matter what. I learned how to stuff envelopes quickly and efficiently so the job was done on time and properly. I learned powerful lessons about organization and preparation from both my parents. Most of all I learned that when you have all your proverbial ducks in a row, you don't lose sleep over things as it's much easier to focus on the work. But when it came to the formation of I.R.E., getting my ducks in a row became a whole other matter.

One of the first things I did in launching the business was to contact my old fraternity brother Norm Silber and another, Stan Linnick. After college, Stan had taken a job at what is now Exxon Mobil Corporation and would remain there thirty-five or more years before retiring, later joining me in another of my companies: Levitt Corporation, but he could not leave at that time for I.R.E. Norm was working at Fiduciary Trust Company in New York. He jumped at the opportunity for us to be together again, quickly moving to Miami to oversee all administrative operations. He attracted Mickey Cohen, yet another fraternity brother with a deep Southern accent who was working in Macon, Georgia, to be our chief financial officer. Norman's second hire was Susie Corredera to be my secretary. Susie was bright, ambitious, and a hard worker. Seventeen years later, Susie would become my wife.

I took a shot at calling Seth Werner and Richard Wollack from the seminar to see if they had any interest in heading up our sales operation. I was delighted when they said yes.

What remained at that point was the working capital necessary to fund the operation. The million dollars in the City National Bank account was to demonstrate the general partner's net worth. It had to remain there intact and could not be used for operations. But I needed $75,000 to start the business. This would include hiring eight product wholesalers who'd need to travel nationally and extensively, signing up broker dealers and financial planners to bring investors into the fund. We'd require secretaries and other administrative personnel, and a national accounting firm. Midwest Mortgage provided the office space and desks. Steve Arky would help me raise the $75,000 operating capital we needed for all this from local businessmen—who'd be known as stock investors—becoming investors in the overhead and corporate profits. These investors were separate from participants in the limited partnership, who would invest in the fund to buy real estate.

I carefully worked on budgeting and forecasting and just as I'd done with my paper route and the apartment building I'd constructed, I set up models such as detailed flowcharts and spreadsheets to determine daily expenditures. I calculated that the $75,000 would last us one hundred ten days of paying all the expenses before we ran out of money. I thought about my pledge class cash flow experience for every one of those one hundred ten days.

The securities requirement was that we could not use the real estate fund money for operating expenses no matter how much we needed it, that is, until the real estate fund raised at least $500,000.

Until that time, all monies went into escrow. After achieving $500,000, the escrow would be released and could be used for reimbursing expenses.

I decided to call the limited partnership fund Investors Tax Sheltered Real Estate, Ltd., Series I. It provided for total subscriptions of $10 million. With financing of 75 percent, we could buy $40 million worth of real estate. I.R.E. Properties would be the corporate general partner. We were all set. Now we just had to raise the $10 million in one hundred ten days, before the $75,000 for operating expenses ran out!

* * *

In order to create the documentation of the offering prospectus, I reviewed and dissected Pacific American Real Estate Fund and several other prototypes in the market. Armed with that information, I created the I.R.E. Fund with the best features of each.

When I first started soliciting the securities brokerage houses, they all gave me suggestions on how the structure should look, often conflicting. I wasn't about to make the same mistake I had made with the Hialeah apartment building. I noted their suggestions, made some modifications, and then created my own final document. I was optimistic that even though I didn't take all their suggestions, I had designed a quality product that would have wide appeal. Actually, firms like Merrill Lynch and the other major brokerage houses with thousands of brokers had lots of suggestions but because we were a start-up with limited financial backing, they ultimately passed. In a manner of speaking we were just getting out of the car.

While it wasn't 100 percent of what each wanted, I did find active interest within the financial planner market. Ultimately, most agreed to do business with us.

In the 1970s, a lone financial planner or broker dealer (or a small group of them) would get a license and hang out a shingle, independent of the powerhouse Wall Street firms. They generally did not sell stocks; instead they largely sold mutual funds. The product we were introducing to them was a new platform—a real estate investment—a departure from their bread and butter. Now they could add one more egg to their basket.

I had been successful in attracting Seth Werner and Dick Wollack to become marketing executives with I.R.E.. Their responsibility was to set up a national sales organization to market our funds.

Seth was a super salesman and also kept us laughing with his quick wit and endless analogies of sales strategies. Two of his stories have stuck in the culture for decades:

The Steep Driveway

When Seth was selling residential real estate in California, he had a particularly difficult listing because of a very steep driveway on a hill leading up to the house. Prospective buyers would be disturbed by the dramatic uphill slant. So he changed his sales pitch.

After convincing a buyer that this was a great house for them, he suggested maybe it wouldn't work because of how steep the incline was. On the drive to the house with the buyer Seth continued to excite the prospective buyer about this fabulous house and price and then throw in that they probably will think the driveway is too steep. He actually made it seem much worse than it was. As they approached the driveway, the buyer was expecting a hill at a severe 45-degree angle, but was pleasantly surprised and delighted it wasn't that bad.

Mother on the Roof

One brother was off for six weeks to Europe and asked his stay behind brother to watch his cat. He was extremely fond of his cat and asked the brother to take good care of it. When he returned from his trip he asked where the cat was. The brother said the cat had died.

The returning brother could not believe it and had an emotional breakdown. When he came back to see his brother he explained that this was no way to give someone bad news. First you should call to say the cat had climbed up a tree. On the next call you should have said the firemen were trying to get him down. On the next call you should describe that the cat jumped to the roof. And then finally that the cat had fallen off the roof and died. That's the way to break bad new gently.

Since the brother had been in Europe and then recovering from the news of the cat, he hadn't talked to any of his other members of his family. To catch up, he then asked, "how's mom?" The brother replied that mom was on the roof!

Seth Werner and Dick Wollack hired eight wholesalers with individual territories throughout the country. They talked to stock brokers, financial planners, life insurance agents, and prospective investors every day. They would give seminars, similar to the one I'd seen in Miami, to explain the new tax law, the 8 percent commission (a generous amount at that time) that could be earned by professionals selling the investment. All of us traveled, giving seminars, including Seth, Dick, and me. We crisscrossed the country, courting small shops, pounding the pavement over and over again. My speech training from high school really came in handy here.

Following one particular presentation I conducted in Terre Haute, Indiana, the first question I got was, "How can this be a real company if the president comes all the way from Florida to talk to just ten of us?" He was right, as it certainly wasn't the way most companies did business, but we had a different business model. We had to do things the way we did because no one knew us or our product, and our sustainability beyond the next few months depended on talking to every last person who would listen, even ten or fewer at a time.

The National Association of Securities Dealers (NASD) published the Red Book, which listed every licensed broker dealer and financial planner in every city. Each of our eight wholesalers would take a geographic territory, call the names in the book, and send letters about the investment opportunity with its tax benefits and broker commission along with the seminar date in their area. At the seminar, we made sure to teach these people precisely how to explain the fund to their clients as it was a novel concept previously available only to the wealthy. We were dealing with many hundreds of brokers all over the country. Following the seminar, the plan was for them to send a prospectus and brochure to each of their clients.

One of the unanticipated problems we found was with the marketing brochure itself. Because David, Norm, and I were so young, we almost looked as though we were in high school and this was a Junior Achievement project. I figured out if we used a reverse negative photo, putting us in shadow, it'd be difficult to determine our ages, along with which we emphasized our esteemed gray-haired members of the board and my track record in acquiring properties over the past few years.

As incentive to the broker dealers and financial planners, we provided a gift catalogue so they could choose something after their first sale and multiple sales, in addition to their commissions. Selections included a pocket transistor radio, world globe, and other fifty-dollar gifts. We preordered the gifts and piled them in the corner of my office, always telling people they were on back order and delivery would take three weeks. Three days after a broker's first sale, though, we promptly mailed them out so it would appear they arrived a week or two early. The concept was to "under promise and over deliver." When brokers and planners got their gifts "early," they thought we were the greatest company on Earth, many telling us they treated them so much better than other product originators. They were highly motivated to sell more of our fund.

As if that weren't enough, we offered higher-tier gifts for sales volume, such as qualifying for an all-inclusive sales conference at prestigious destinations such as Nassau, Bahamas, at the Atlantis, Colorado Springs at the exquisite Broadmoor Hotel, and Miami. We had outstanding speakers, like Lou Holtz, the great American football coach. This also gave us an opportunity to spend vital face-to-face time with our top one hundred producers, creating strong personal relationships about which they could tell their clients. Of course, my dad handled all the airline tickets and hotel accommodations.

"I know the managers of this fund personally," the broker dealers and financial planners would say to their clients as a result of these face-to-face opportunities. "I can vouch for them. You need to invest." This would turn up the volume on the next series and the next, which would occur. But in getting our first series to fly, we left no stone unturned.

Sale Ends at Midnight

We've all heard it: Time is running out! Sale ends tomorrow. A two-day special. Call in the next ten minutes to take advantage of this special offer—and get free shipping! Today the airwaves are rife with urgent, ephemeral, life-and-death deals that have us tripping over our own feet to find our misplaced cell phones.

But while we were out there in the first few months of I.R.E., time really was a life-and-death matter for the company. We were burning through our $75,000.

Since most investors take the idea of investing $5,000 or $10,000 quite seriously and want to think about it, they don't want to write the check until the last possible minute. Money was only trickling in. We had determined that if we didn't meet our $10 million goal for this fund in one hundred ten days, we would not be viable. Our operating funds would be exhausted. We'd not be able to sustain ourselves. Everything was costing us money: office operations; airline travel, hotels, and meals for the wholesalers; event rooms for seminars; printing costs for thousands of prospectuses and brochures; massive mailings. We were burning through thousands and thousands and thousands of dollars of upfront costs like there was no tomorrow—and at that rate, for us there would not be.

We had to figure a way to induce prospective investors to take faster action, creating a real sense of urgency, so I developed a mailer to be sent to the broker dealers and financial planners with whom we had touched base. The mailers screamed "urgency"—that there were only sixty days remaining to invest. This was followed by another mailer saying only fifty days to close, then forty, thirty (we're almost sold out, we'd say, though we'd barely raised a million dollars), then twenty, ten, and finally five days remaining. Each day we'd hightail it to the lobby to greet the mailman, scrambling to open envelopes that might have our checks. With each mailer subscriptions spiked.

While the 8 percent commission was indeed high in those days, it became apparent that on its own that wasn't going to be enough to get us to the finish line. We had to find a way to make it so they encouraged their clients to act now. We reached out to them saying they didn't want to get lost in the shuffle, collecting the checks from their clients, mailing them to us, only to find out the deadline had passed and the fund had closed. We created a reservation system so once they ascertained their client was on board, they should reserve a spot to ensure that client would be counted in. After all (we said), they wouldn't want to disappoint clients and not get their commission with I.R.E. having to return their money because we were "oversubscribed." (If only that had been the case!) This step eliminated the madness around ambushing the mailman and waiting for checks as we knew exactly what was going to come in. It allowed us to plan more effectively and breathe a little easier.

Despite the fever pitch and all the risk, my gut told me we were going to be successful. It's the law of large numbers. What I'd seen at the seminar in Miami and the kind of attendance we'd had throughout the country at our own I.R.E. seminars told me we had an outstanding idea. It was just a matter of taking it to the finish line. The last few days were magical and euphoric. Literally 75 percent of the money came in between the one hundred fifth and one hundred tenth day. By that final day, near exhaustion, we had raised the $10 million. We celebrated and high-fived briefly and then moved on. "Next," as my father had taught me. You can't dwell too long on your successes and failures. We quickly followed with a second fund, Investors Tax Sheltered Real Estate, Ltd., Series II for $25 million, just as Seth Werner and Richard Wollack of California-based Pacific American Real Estate Fund—now executives with I.R.E.—had done with their fund, and the reason I'd found myself at that Miami seminar. Series III and others raised over $70 million. Between 1972 and 1974 we raised more than $100 million and had tens of thousands of investors. I was not yet thirty years old.

Each of our funds was a separate public partnership. Each partnership had to file its own quarterly 10-Q and annual 10-K disclosure reports, mandated for publicly traded companies, with the SEC. We actually had four public entities by 1974 and this was the beginning of my long history meticulously dealing with regular disclosure reports to the SEC—all the more reason what happened when the SEC sued me twice was inconceivable, on which I elaborate in chapters 20 and 22. My track record with them had been lengthy and completely unblemished.

Winner Doesn't Take All

As the money came in, a real estate acquisitions team we'd put in place when we were sure we had money coming in (which was almost instantaneous after the first series offering) would travel all over the country with real estate lawyers contracting for properties. I wanted to personally see every piece of real estate and would go with them to negotiate. I had become far more competitive than I'd been in school, where I'd eschewed sports largely because I never felt I had to win and everyone else had to lose.

In my early business negotiation style, I had to win every single point and the seller had to lose every point. I became pretty good at it though I did ruffle more than a few feathers.

At one point in Dallas, I negotiated so hard for a seller to pay all the closing costs and adjustments that he excused himself to go to the men's room and never came back. Another time in Cape Gerardo, outside of St. Louis, we had negotiated until 5:00 a.m. and I won every point. We then recessed until his secretary could type all the changes, deciding to reconvene at 8:00 a.m. As the seller read the final draft, he realized he'd lost every point and his face got redder and redder. He finally stood up, declaring he'd never do business with people like us again, throwing us out of his office. I had won all the battles but lost the war. It wasn't the first time my negotiations had ended badly because of my winner-takes-all behavior.

In time I realized that a negotiation had to be fair and beneficial to both parties. It didn't have to be about ego. Business is based on relationships, credibility, and integrity. A few dollars either way on a million-dollar transaction didn't make that much of a difference. Getting the last dollar in a deal didn't determine whether it was a good or poor investment. I took a step back, was honest with myself, maybe grew up a little, and modified my negotiating style to ensure sellers would speak well of I.R.E. and me after a closing.

This is best illustrated by my subsequent relationship with Dr. Robert Cornfeld. I met Bob in 1974. A dentist by training and profession, he loved the real estate business. Ultimately he gave up practicing dentistry and gravitated to being a full-time owner and operator of real estate. He became an extremely astute investor. Pretty much every real estate investment he made turned to gold.

As the 1970s recession kicked in, I sold Bob an apartment building in Tampa from Series 1 to raise cash for the partnership. I used my modified approach to negotiating with Bob and much to my pleasant surprise we both came out winners. This was the beginning of an extraordinary forty-five-year personal and business relationship. I sold Bob more buildings, I purchased some from him, and both I.R.E. and BankAtlantic financed some of his acquisitions. We engaged in dozens of transactions and in each case it was a win-win. He has also been one of my most ardent supporters and a major shareholder of our companies.

We both learned and honored that our word is our bond. We never needed a written contract or a lawyer. A handshake cemented the deal though we ultimately needed a lawyer to document the transactions because real estate transfers require legal documentation. He's a wonderful friend and a true class act.

My observation of his negotiating style and kindness had an incredibly positive impact on my business career. I am truly indebted to him.

I.R.E. had great success in purchasing real estate. We found terrific opportunities we could value enhance for our investors. One of scores of examples was a 100,000 square foot shopping center we bought which had a 30,000 square foot A&P grocery store as a tenant. The rent was a $1.00 a square foot. We decided not to renew the lease and instead subdivided the space for six other tenants at $6.00 a square foot, increasing the value by 500 percent. Our investors were very pleased.

All in all we purchased dozens of apartment buildings, office complexes, warehouses, and shopping centers in Dallas, San Antonio, and College Station, Texas; North Carolina; South Carolina; Georgia; Alabama; Orlando, Tampa, and Jacksonville, Florida; and dozens of other venues. It was early 1974 and the money was flowing in at an incomprehensible rate. We had thousands of brokers and financial planners raising dollars for our funds with commissions providing an excellent source of income for them.

Somehow, though, I had a feeling at that point things were just too easy. Series after series, we had a well-oiled machine going where it became almost cookie cutter. But when you see yourself as a fiduciary, which I did, you want to make sure you can properly and appropriately invest people's hard-earned money. You're a trusted guardian of such. I was concerned about our ability to invest the money at the rate it was coming in. I wondered how long the boom economy in which we found ourselves would continue, knowing it couldn't.

I considered slowing the fund down, which created a small riot of brokers and financial planners threatening never to do business with us again. The money train had surely given many of them access to a kind of lifestyle they'd not had before. Our employees didn't think it was a good idea either as it would affect their job security. Our investors anticipated the returns they got and wanted nothing but to continue investing in subsequent funds. Still, performance is the key to long-term success and I was increasingly worried. My knack for seeing around corners was being put to the test and I didn't like what I was seeing—or maybe envisioning was a better word at that point.

I decided to shut down I.R.E.'s fundraising machine cold turkey. Brokers and planners were mutinous. Investors were disappointed. We had to lay off employees. Nobody was happy with me, and I didn't like it either, but the willingness to make unpopular decisions is where leadership comes in. Time would tell if my decision was the right one.

LIFE LESSONS LEARNED

- Under promise and over deliver.
- In a negotiation, both parties should walk away winners.
- Leaders must be able to make tough decisions even if no one else agrees.
- Big ideas turn heads and open doors—it's the law of large numbers.

I.R.E. Building

Alan, IRE early portrait

IRE in the News

Alan, IRE early portrait

Norman Silber

Steve Arky

Susie Corredera

Dr. Robert Cornfeld

FORMATION OF I.R.E.: THE LAW OF LARGE NUMBERS

IRE Capital Raises $225 Million

Covers of IRE marketing brochures

Samples of IRE properties

Samples of IRE properties

I.R.E. Real Estate Fund, Ltd.-Series 24

SUMMARY OF THE SALE OF
PROPERTIES BY PRIOR I.R.E. SEC REGISTERED NATIONAL PARTNERSHIPS

While none of the prior I.R.E. SEC registered national partnerships have, as yet, disposed of their entire portfolio of properties, the following table sets forth a summary of results which have been achieved thus far in the sale of properties held by these partnerships.

This summary is prepared from the information contained in Table VI of the Prospectus of I.R.E. Real Estate Fund, Ltd. — Series 24. Investors should review the complete table carefully.

PARTNERSHIP/PROPERTY	PARTNERSHIP CAPITAL INVESTED (1)	NET REALIZABLE PROCEEDS FROM SALE AND REFINANCING (2)	NET PROCEEDS AS A PERCENTAGE OF PARTNERSHIP'S CAPITAL INVESTED	HOLDING PERIOD
Investors Tax Sheltered Real Estate, Ltd.				
El Presidente/Roman Gardens Apartments	537,500	1,625,025	302%	6.0 Yrs.
Monaco I Apartments	95,020	644,950	679%	6.0 Yrs.
Monaco II Apartments	80,025	443,192	554%	6.0 Yrs.
Cordova Apartments	530,177	603,111	114%	4.5 Yrs.
Windjammer Apartments	700,000	(11,877)	(N/A)	2.7 Yrs.
Posada Del Rey Apartments	30,961	329,894	1066%	6.0 Yrs.
Tanglewood South Apartments	307,342	1,809,778	589%	6.0 Yrs.
Homestead Plaza Shopping Center	1,384,747	1,665,826	120%	1.7 Yrs.
Gateway Shopping Center	491,955	1,679,379	341%	5.7 Yrs.
Aegean Apartments	1,012,802	1,793,163	177%	7.9 Yrs.
Investors Tax Sheltered Real Estate, Ltd.—Series II				
Brittany/French Colony Apts.	149,441	515,196	345%	4.6 Yrs.
Posada Del Norte Apartments	89,786	328,665	366%	4.6 Yrs.
Westchester Apartments	628,461	827,196	132%	4.8 Yrs.
Bennettsville Shopping Center	150,094	288,083	192%	2.9 Yrs.
Boulevard Apartments	88,326	119,299	135%	4.1 Yrs.
Westgate Shopping Center	371,091	1,377,989	371%	3.6 Yrs.
Westcourt Apartments	160,770	519,645	323%	6.8 Yrs.
North Lake Apartments	665,489	2,799,621	421%	6.0 Yrs.
I.R.E. Real Estate Partners, Ltd.—Series III				
Executive House Apartments	690,690	1,485,674	215%	4.5 Yrs.
Warrington Plaza Shopping Center	513,663	1,105,143	215%	4.0 Yrs.
Kingsway Plaza Shopping Center	281,020	931,034	331%	4.3 Yrs.

1) Down payment and the cash costs of investment. These amounts do not account for all of the Limited Partners' capital contribution to the Partnerships.

2) Cash payments received from buyer; less expenses of sale; plus the amount of any excess of principal balance of secured notes received on sale over principal balance of the underlying mortgage indebtedness. Any potential interest or equity buildup on the secured notes is not included.

CHAPTER 7

ACORNS: RAISING A FAMILY

"Life affords no greater responsibility, no greater privilege,
than the raising of the next generation."
—C. Everett Koop

I t had been a heart-pounding time, first forming and then disman-
tling I.R.E. In many ways the process had changed my life, but
the birth of my children while all this was going on would change
it profoundly.

Donald (Donny), born in 1970, Rachelle (Shelley), born in 1972,
and Jarett, born in 1973, lightened whatever load I was carrying and
the feeling is always there, no matter how old they are. While I may
not have been conscious of it every moment, I was trying to replicate
my extraordinary childhood in the way I raised my children. I was
fortunate to have the parents I did, parents on whom I could always
rely and who'd get to play a significant role in helping my wife and
me raise the next generation. I loved being a father.

My objective in raising my children was to help them grow to be
self-sufficient and competent at whatever they chose to do. Applying
the same thinking as my parents, I didn't care as much about grades as
the fact that they worked hard—to the very best of their ability—in
all things. On the other hand I was intensely focused on their ability
to smile, converse with adults, use a firm handshake, and look people

in the eye—just as I had been brought up to do. My children were always present at business and nonprofit organization parties in our home because they were well-spoken and knew how to act around adults. As a result, we felt they deserved to be there.

When they were very young their strengths and talents began to emerge. You might say Shelley was in training for a black belt in organizing. Today, as a busy mother of three, her lists have lists—just as they always did. As a little girl she loved cleaning and organizing her closet (we thought of renting her out to the neighbors). She had a walk-in closet and in the middle of a rigorous cleaning effort, she'd fall asleep on the carpet beneath the racks and shelves. I would find her there, pick her up, and gently carry her to bed.

Donny's reason for getting out of bed in the morning was to take things apart. He needed to figure out how things worked. Whatever the toy or mechanical item, Donny would dismantle it, study it, and put it back together—sometimes with a piece left on the table. Nevertheless it would work without the orphaned component. Donny was also extremely sensitive and compassionate—qualities that reinforced his first profession as a photojournalist. He had tremendous empathy. He was given a camera as a child (something else taken apart and thankfully put back together). He carried that camera wherever he went, capturing the soul of his subjects as he probed deeply for their stories.

There were times in raising my children—especially Jarett—when I'd think back to that pivotal day at Tulane when an advisor told me I could get around compulsory math—my Achilles heel—by taking freshman courses in philosophy and then moving on to logic. Advanced logic would satisfy the math requirement. I lived for Plato's *Republic*, existentialism, and all the philosophers.

It was and is the constant Socratic questioning of "why" that influences the way I conduct business and my son Jarett caught the bug at a very early age. Whether I passed it on to him or not, it has always been a part of who he is. While Donny and Shelley appeared to hang on my every word, Jarett did not. His questions were unrelenting. If I said he couldn't do something, he'd challenge it in an intense search for the meaning behind it.

"That makes no sense," he'd say. "Tell me why."

"Because I'm your father and that's what I want you to do," I'd respond.

"This is unbelievable," was his classic retort. "You have to give me a better reason why I can't do this!" "Why can't I do that?" "Why can't I play with that?" His constant questioning became the soundtrack of his life.

After a while I realized he was absolutely right. It wasn't enough to give my children an order about what they could and could not do. They were not babies, and if I wanted them to grow into independent adults with strong enough reasoning powers to be able to make informed decisions, I had to substitute "because I said so" with an explanation. In order to do that, I also had to question exactly why I was telling my children to do something. It really did make sense.

We all have different parenting styles. I refuse to read the kinds of business books that put forth the premise that operating a business is a one-size-fits-all proposition. Parenting books can be the same way and I never read them while raising my family. There are so many examples out there of children who went off-course though raised by wonderful parents, and children who excelled despite coming from unconscionable family situations. In some cases it's the luck of the draw, and I never take for granted the way my children turned out.

On the Road Again

When Donny, Shelley, and Jarett were growing up, in my efforts to give them some alone time with Dad I would take them, individually, on business trips. These were some of the trips described in chapter

6 where I'd be on the road, in lengthy real estate negotiating sessions that may go all day. It's a long time for a child to sit in a meeting, or a series of meetings, and I certainly never made them sit through overnight sessions, but it was exciting for them to be a part of my world. They were always happy to be with me. At times my wife and I agreed that I would take them, one at a time, out of school for a couple of days to go on the road, which made each feel even more special.

Though we'd always top a long day with a trip to a carnival, sightseeing, or another fun activity, these were not the kinds of meetings where my children were allowed to sit there in jeans with toys, games, and coloring books. They knew if they came they had to dress up, just as the adults did, and pay attention. They had to follow whoever was speaking with their eyes so they would be sure to focus on what was going on, taking notes on a legal pad about anything they didn't understand. In this way I could answer their questions when we were alone together in the evenings.

If my business trips and their activity schedules conflicted, there was always the possibility that I'd miss an important school event. I would rectify that by arranging to fly back in from wherever I was for the event, resuming my trip the next morning.

I tended to go back to work until midnight or 1:00 a.m. to prepare for the following day, no matter where I am, and when in town I made it a practice to have dinner with my family and attend whatever events were important to them because they were also important to me. Then I'd go back to work.

My life, other than family, was all about business. I was away so much on these trips it was crucial that my family understand what the reasons behind them were. With three young children, it was vital that each one got to know how much I loved him or her as an individual, and the extent to which I enjoyed their company. One-on-one travel with Daddy was the best way I could think of to show them how I felt. Each child knew he or she was special and their memories of this time with me are something they talk about to this day.

When they were very young, someone gave Jarett a Day-Timer—perhaps it was a holiday or birthday gift—which became an appendage. He never put it down, diligently filling it with schedules and activities. Every hour he'd ask, "Okay, what's the next activity? What are we doing tomorrow?" He didn't want to miss an opportunity to organize his life and ours. As an adult, he received a BBA at Emory University and a law degree at the University of Miami. He would join me when I bought BankAtlantic, which I talk about in chapters 12 and 23, and he's currently president of BBX Capital, successor to BankAtlantic.

Shelley's propensity for the arts manifested in her study of dance and art. She later obtained a degree in communications at Syracuse University and her MBA at Nova Southeastern University. Applying her prodigious organizational skills, she became director of the BankAtlantic Foundation, a nonprofit that supported local charities, having started out as an assistant. Today, she is a full-time mother.

In the late 1970s, I.R.E. listed on the American Stock Exchange. I have a wonderful photograph of Donny, Shelley, and Jarett holding the tape on the floor of the AMEX for the first trade. But my decision to include them in my world had nothing to do with an agenda. I'd had no preconceived notions that any of my children would go into business—mine or anyone else's. I gave them all the latitude they wanted to make up their own minds about what they would do with their lives and the impact they could make on this world.

I insisted upon driving them to school every morning—even at one point when they went to three separate schools—deeply anticipating that time with them. Over time they came to accept me as one of them (is that just a dad talking?)—or maybe more realistically they forgot I was in the car—when their conversations, sometimes with friends along, drifted to the kinds of things children talk about when their parents aren't present. I like to think they were just comfortable enough with me to do that.

A Kiss by Any Other Name

My father always shook my hand when we greeted, no matter how young I was. I'm certain that was the way he'd been raised. He was affectionate—his handshake warm and loving—but rarely did we hug or kiss. On the other hand I opted to kiss on the cheek and hug my children when they were little and as they grew, to this day, without reservation. If they were in the company of friends I tried to do it in a way that would not embarrass them. I always gave them a kiss when dropping them off at school.

On Jarett's first day of junior high school he asked me to let him out a block before the building. Clearly he felt awkward about the kids seeing my show of affection. I accommodated him without issue. The next day, when I stopped the car in the same place, he said it was all right to let him out in front of the school, kiss and all.

"It's really okay, Dad," he said. "Drive right up to the door."

I remember sitting there with tears in my eyes. Even at thirteen, when most kids can't get far enough away from their parents, apparently he had enough maturity and self-confidence to know who he was and be grateful for his family. I think the saying is he was comfortable in his own skin. To this day we still greet with a kiss and hug even in a business setting. In fact my father jumped on the warm and fuzzy bandwagon soon after he saw me interact with my own children in the way I do, trading the handshake he'd used with me for so many years with a big embrace and an even bigger kiss!

I Love You; I Love You; I Love You

I was a strict disciplinarian, but much in the same loving way my parents had been when I was growing up. I'd lived with my aunt and her family in Brooklyn after college when I moved back to New

York—a challenging experience at best and one that showed me in no uncertain terms what I didn't want for my family: an existence devoid of love, warmth, and compassion. My aunt and uncle's children had been raised to be superstars in business but they weren't nice people.

With my children, if warranted, spanking was a part of the equation but only in the privacy of their rooms—not in public or in front of the rest of the family. Just as my parents had done with my brother and me, my focus was on what they did or didn't do—not on who they were. Any punishment in this way was followed by a hug and an "I love you." If one of them misbehaved in a restaurant, we'd go outside and have a conversation about the matter. I would not yell and scream, and our interaction would be followed by the same hug and an "I love you." With three young children in a car things can get rough. Again, I'd not stoop to yelling and screaming because matching tone for tone only exacerbates the situation. I'd pull off the road, take the instigator outside the car, and we'd have a conversation. This was followed by a hug and an "I love you."

We'd take Donny, Shelley, and Jarett everywhere with us. We never needed a break from them the way other parents talk about needing time away. They had plenty of time to run around, have fun, and just be kids (sometimes with their dad the biggest kid of all—joining the boys in carpet wrestling matches) as long as they listened when it was time to move on to something else. If they didn't pay attention, and I was angry, I'd quietly lower my voice but be very stern. They knew immediately I didn't want to have to tell them something again. My children were not saints and neither was I. Each and every one of us on the planet is a human being, not a machine. The last thing I wish to do in this book is paint a perfect portrait of how I raised my children. But somehow, whatever the challenges, what my wife and I did worked.

Because I believed strongly in independence, our kids were the first in the neighborhood to get to walk to their friends' houses or ride their bikes around the block. I'd always follow behind them, at a safe distance, so they could not see me. They were the youngest of their friends to go to summer camp—never because we wanted to get rid of them, but because we wanted them to know from an early age what it was like to learn self-reliance.

We also encouraged them to use our house as the gathering place so we could meet and regularly see their friends. As they got older, our house became the party house and Terri and I were always invited to attend or at least make an appearance. They were just as happy to show us off to their friends as we were to show them off to ours.

Early Entrepreneurs (with a side of cream cheese)

Just as my parents had done with me, I was always looking for opportunities for my children to earn money. I wanted them to feel proud of the work they would do in the pursuit. At one point we took some steps in an entrepreneurial direction by figuring out a bagel route. Seeing a need and filling it, we decided warm, fresh-from-the-bagel store bagels when people rolled out of bed on a Sunday morning would satisfy a lot of people, so we went for it.

The children would take orders from the neighborhood during the week. Sunday at 6:00 a.m. we'd head for the bagel store, taking what was normally a huge (discounted—so my children could earn a profit) cache of twenty dozen bagels back to the house, where we'd fill each neighbor's order. The bagels would be transferred to smaller bags, with cream cheese and lox if the order specified such, the invoice stapled to each bag. We delivered them to the various houses and if there was inventory left over, we'd go over to the local marina where people were boarding their boats and sell what remained. Just as my father had taught me, my children had to take care of collections and maintain a record book. Bagels weren't the pails my brother Jay and I had hawked on a stiflingly hot and crowded Coney Island beach, and they weren't the newspapers I'd had to deliver in rain, snow, or otherwise, but I like to think Donny, Shelley, and Jarett learned something about business and responsibility from our Sunday morning bagel beat.

When we weren't delivering bagels I took the utmost pleasure in cooking breakfast for my children and their friends. My specialty, then and now, was cinnamon French toast, matzah brie, and egg in the basket. The more friends who came over for breakfast, the better I liked it.

* * *

In the late 1970s, the five of us moved to Gables Estates in Coral Gables. Gables Estates was prime real estate. We bought a 6,000-square-foot home with a large circular driveway and waterway behind it leading to Biscayne Bay. I was able to negotiate a seller's mortgage much in the way my father had for the building that would house our pest control business and the travel agency. We got a twenty-four-foot Aquasport speed boat that we docked behind the house, and on which the family had some of the best times ever.

My challenge was for our children to enjoy my financial success without spoiling them into thinking that as a result, they were special, or entitled to more than their friends who may not have as much. We'd take drives around the neighborhood so I could point out more expensive homes and boats. The lesson for them was the same I'd learned in junior high school: there is always going to be someone who has more. But that doesn't make you less. Our spending habits were very much in check as Terri and I made sure our children didn't have better clothes, toys, and more spending money than their friends. In addition to our efforts to instill a sense of self-worth and self-confidence in them, we agreed they needed to be raised with a strong sense of humility and decency toward other people.

One of our favorite activities was reading poetry. I'd learned to love poetry as a boy, something that my father had instilled in me. I tried to cultivate the same interest in my children, lulling them to sleep at night with favorites that included "The Road Not Taken" and "Stopping by Woods on a Snowy Evening" by Robert Frost, "If" by Rudyard Kipling, "O Captain! My Captain!" by Walt Whitman, and Ernest Thayer's "Casey at the Bat." We read a lot from the 670-page *The Best Loved Poems of the American People*, taking great pleasure in an offbeat poem, "I Had But Fifty Cents," by Sam Devere. Years later, Shelley's son, Jordan, would memorize this poem for a competition, bringing nothing short of extreme delight to the rest of the family!

Sometimes we'd get together with the children's grandparents— my parents—and read poetry by the fire (yes, the occasional cozy fire—even in sweltering Florida!), a practice I maintain to this day with my twelve grandchildren. My father, always a romantic with a mellifluous voice to boot, had sung Porgy and Bess' "Summertime" to my mother the whole time Jay and I were growing up. This was another tradition I was sure to perpetuate in my family. We would sing it all the time, led by my father when he visited, until his death in 2003. I can barely get through a rendition of it today, without tearing up, when my children and grandchildren join in to sing and remember him.

Terri was an exceptional mother and our children loved, cherished, and respected her. We enjoyed many wonderful years but were not destined to stay together, separating and divorcing after eighteen years of marriage. She would die years later in a freak accident while on vacation in Aspen with her second husband and some friends. She was well known and admired in the community. A thousand people showed up to honor her at the funeral.

The divorce was extremely hard on Donny, Shelley, and Jarett. They were young and we'd spared them from all of our disagreements, so they didn't see it coming. I moved close by so I could continue to drive them to school, seeing them every day. Because of the kinds of young people they were, each did an incredible job managing not to take sides and staying close to both of us. When they went off to college I didn't want them to have to choose which parent to spend their breaks with, so I remained living in the vicinity, commuting three hours a day round trip to and from Fort Lauderdale where my business had taken me. It was more important that my children have both of us until they were solidly on their own.

In the months following the divorce, Donny and I took a walk one day. He was about fifteen years old. "Dad," he said softly, revealing the same empathy and compassion I'd heard in his voice a million times, "if there's anything you ever want to talk about, you know you can talk to me."

He went on to graduate from the University of Florida College of Journalism and Communications. Donny clearly had heart but had never been a great student. In fact he'd gone to a less desirable college out of state for a year before his chosen school, the University of Florida, would accept him as a transfer student. He always worked hard but academics were not his strong suit, so it came as an enormous surprise when, after four years as a photojournalist, he decided to go back to school.

"I want to get a master's degree in psychology," Donny announced one day.

I was in disbelief, knowing how he'd struggled all his life in school. When he asked if I'd pay for it, I reluctantly agreed with the stipulation that if he didn't do well in his first semester, I'd get to choose what I thought would be a suitable profession for him. He agreed, and I imagine there was some kind of a "knowing" in his soul about the direction his life needed to take because he achieved a 4.0 grade point average every semester. When I asked him how he was achieving this academic success, he looked directly at me and simply said, "This is something 'I' want to do for myself."

Donny went on to receive a Doctor of Psychology degree (PsyD) from Nova Southeastern University. Today, Donny—now known professionally as Don—works as a technical product manager, helping companies develop rough product concepts into the best possible customer and user experiences. He has done work for Apple, ADP, and other large companies. He uses his background in psychology—something clearly rooted in his overarching sense of empathy and compassion—to design products and services geared toward the people who actually have to use these systems in their jobs and their lives. In other words, there's a psychology behind user-friendly solutions and Donny has found it.

I still think back to that walk he and I took at one of the most difficult times in all of our lives, when he was still young, the one where he told me I could talk to him about anything. Though my life was all about being available to my children, Donny made it clear he was also there for me.

LIFE LESSONS LEARNED

- Every parent wants their children to love them. If you add discipline and encourage competency, you will have a better chance at gaining their love and respect. You will also raise well-behaved and independent children.
- The unique and complex relationship between you and your child is known only by you. Don't substitute someone else's recipe for raising their child for your own judgment about raising yours.

L to R, Jay, Lori, Alan, Terri, Donny, Jarett, Shelley, Pearl, Zit

Alan, Pearl, Zit, Donny, Shelley, Terri, Jarett

Alan, Terri, Shelley, Jarett, Donny

Alan and Zit

Alan and Pearl

Donny   *Shelley*   *Jarett*

Jarett, Donny, Shelley   *Jarett, Shelley, Donny*

Jarett, Donny   *Shelley*

American Stock Exchange Listing Ceremony
Alan, Jarett, Shelley, Donny

I.R.E. Financial Group granted listing on Amex

Coral Gables-based I.R.E. Financial Corp., a national real estate and financial services firm, has been approved for original listing on the American Stock Exchange, with trading scheduled to begin March 5 under the ticker symbol IF.WI, according to Alan B. Levan, I.R.E. president and chief executive officer.

Alan B. Levan

for new I.R.E. stock certificates, have been mailed to current shareholders.

March 4 will mark I.R.E.'s final day on the NASDAQ over-the-counter exchange, where it has been listed and actively traded since 1980.

Since its founding in 1972, I.R.E.'s primary activity has been the sponsorship, marketing and management of publicly registered real estate limited partnerships.

Today, I.R.E. owns 9.9 percent of all Atlantic outstanding common stock, and has acquired options which, when exercised, will increase I.R.E.'s stock ownership to approximately 35 percent of the thrift's outstanding common stock, and has acquired options which, when exercised, will increase I.R.E.'s stock ownership to approximately 35 percent of the thrift's outstanding shares. An I.R.E. application for approval to assume control of Atlantic Federal is pending with the Federal Home Loan Bank Board.

I.R.E. also owns 193,000 shares of Heritage Federal Savings and Loan in Daytona Beach, which represents 9.9 percent of all its outstanding common stock. The company purchased its holdings for $9.12 per share, and anticipates selling them pursuant to a proposed $23 per share buyout and merger play by American Pioneer Savings Bank of Orlando.

Currently, I.R.E.-sponsored real estate partnerships own income-producing properties totaling approximately 4.6 million square feet. ∎

MAR-6 -86

I.R.E. Financial
410 Moves To AMEX

IRE Lists on AMEX

CHAPTER 8

THE RECESSION OF 1974: PERSEVERANCE IS MY CURRENCY

"Even the darkest night will end and the sun will rise."
—Victor Hugo, *Les Misérables*

In 1973 we had pulled the plug on I.R.E.'s fundraising momentum. The goal was to focus on cash flow from operations by prudently investing the funds we'd accumulated in real estate and beefing up our property management team. I had learned a crucial lesson at Alpha Epsilon Pi about cash flow. Sure, it's a cliché, but cash really is king.

I'd made a lot of people angry with me—largely brokers and financial planners, who ended up selling for our competitors. Most people couldn't understand why I'd stopped the gravy train. There didn't appear to be any slowdown in the market. Our competitors were raising record amounts and our once loyal brokers quickly switched over. It was not a comfortable place for anyone, and certainly not for me, but I was not looking for agreement. Granted, no one has a crystal ball and neither do I, but I had an uneasy feeling and was fortunate to have it a full nine months before the economy completely collapsed.

We'd been incredibly successful in the real estate market, raising vast amounts of investment money from limited partners, but

I believed the market was overheating. It had become too easy. While I sometimes questioned whether I had done the right thing, I continued to have the courage of my convictions that we were on the correct side of that decision. Prices were rising. There were cranes on every corner, from South Beach to Miami Beach to the north beaches, all along route A1A—my old hitchhiking route to summer jobs from my North Miami High School days. The cranes peppered the landscape up and down the Florida coast all the way to Jacksonville like shiny, towering, gangly birds. It was a feeding frenzy—a bona fide condominium binge-building effort.

South Florida is also an international region. Due to their unstable political and economic climates, people from Central and South America wanted to get their money out of their own countries and into US vacation homes. They were plunking cash down on what Florida was putting up.

Even my dad was making money on the real estate boom. He didn't have a business degree, much less a college education, and he'd never invested in the stock market before. Other than a couple of homes (including a condo) in which he'd lived and the office he'd purchased for Vanguard, he'd never bought real estate. But a friend of his who had become a condominium developer suggested a surefire way he could make money. He'd ask my dad to sign a contract to buy a pre-construction condo in a new project and put up a $5,000 deposit. The developer would get enough of these pre-construction contracts to qualify for the construction loan from the bank. As the building neared completion and the sales center reported strong sales, the developer would release my dad from the unit he'd bought, replacing it with a real buyer at a higher price. The developer would then give my dad $10,000 to $15,000 for helping him out. My father did this a number of times; it seemed too easy, and for a while it was. Fortunately, he made his money before the real estate market bottomed out.

When the stock market crashed in 1929, my mother's family was forced to move from a deluxe Upper West Side Manhattan building with a doorman to a single hotel room in Brooklyn. When people start panicking, as they did then and as they did again in 1970s, they no longer buy discretionary items. If they're not buying discretionary items, everything slows down; company earnings soon plummet. People lose their jobs as a result. The months between late 1973 and early 1974 were the bellwether of a spiraling downward economy.

Many years later, in 2007, when everybody was saying how robust the economy was, I didn't like what I was seeing. It was the same feeling I'd had more than thirty years earlier. And what happened during the 1974 recession was part of an enormous learning process that permanently affected the way I did business. It made me hyperaware and hypervigilant. The fact that the SEC sought to punish me in 2008 for the prudent and responsible steps I'd taken on behalf of my bank depositors and public shareholders, in light of what I'd seen coming, confounds me to this day. I'd been proactive and called the market as I saw it, but they made me the scapegoat for their own failure to see it.

In 1974 inflation became rampant. The cost of food, automobiles, houses, and just about everything else went through the roof, and consumers felt the pinch. The building boom was teetering. I didn't have an extensive background in business—I hadn't gone to Harvard or Yale—but I had good instincts. By July of 1974, there were 28,000 unsold condominium units along the South Florida beaches. Developers found themselves stuck with vast quantities of inventory. Real estate values were in free fall. Contracted buyers refused to close at the original price, which further increased the surplus. If you have a contract to buy a condo for $250,000, and you realize there's a ton of unsold inventory, why would you continue to buy it for $250,000 when you can buy the one next door or next door to that for $175,000 or less? It became obvious that the unsold condominium inventory would take years to be absorbed by buyers.

It's said that when real estate sneezes, the Florida economy catches a cold. The construction industry in Florida is a major employer, and when construction slows, thousands of ancillary workers—architects, plumbers, electricians, carpenters, painters, etc.—lose their jobs. There's less individual buying power, and non-real estate businesses—retailers, manufacturers, service companies, and many others—begin to suffer and are forced to reduce their workforces.

This recession was brutal by any standards, undisputedly the harshest since World War II. Interest rates and unemployment rose: The unemployment rate nationally jumped from 5 percent in the third quarter of 1973 to nearly 9 percent in the third quarter of 1975. During that same period the rate of inflation went from 7.4 percent to 12.2 percent, and the prime interest rate rose to more than 11 percent. Long-term mortgage rates in the home buying market went as high as 18 percent. Foreclosures were everywhere. The "see-through" condominium buildings—no curtains; no furniture; sometimes even no glass in the windows—stayed vacant for years.

It had not been an easy decision. I had been right, but I certainly was not gloating. I'm not afraid to make decisions that may be unpopular. Elsewhere in this book I've used the expression "seeing around corners"; you have to be able not only to look ahead, but also to the left and right to anticipate events that can knock you out. In retrospect this may have been the first time I recognized that I was seeing around corners. The future had started to look quite bleak to me, and I'd acted on my instincts.

When we decided to ramp up our property management efforts, we were short staffed. We had raised so much money so quickly that our systems and people were lagging behind, and we had no property management professionals in our stable. Because of the way we'd budgeted our cash, I'd elected not to staff up with property managers too early, for fear we wouldn't actually raise enough money to need them. But we were extraordinarily successful with Series I, followed shortly thereafter with Series II, Series III, and a local Florida offering. Now we had to launch ourselves headlong into property management; I even had my dad flying around the country visiting our properties to provide property management oversight.

Property management requires extensive administrative acumen; you have to be able to lease and collect rent, whether it's for an apartment building, a shopping center, or an office building. Financial statements on these properties must be produced so you can see exactly how you're doing. You need maintenance people to fix pipes and paint, clean the carpets, mow the grass, and repair air conditioning. All these day-to-day minutiae need to be attended to when you're managing a property of any sort. We started behind the eight ball because we'd bought a tremendous amount of real estate, and were not traveling all over the country dealing with our properties in a true property management capacity. However because I'd predicted the collapse of the real-estate market nine months in advance, it was not too late. We had that time to gear up and prepare. By the time it was obvious that the nation was in a recession, we'd already developed the expertise we needed to stay alive.

Nationally, commercial real estate values plummeted to 25 to 40 percent of what they'd been. Florida's real estate declines were even worse. We suffered through four years of real estate declines in our own portfolios. Fortunately, we managed not to have any foreclosures: Property management was our saving grace. The adage about real estate and recessions is that you have to stay alive long enough to get to the other side, where you can benefit from the recovery.

Eenie, Meenie, Miney, Moe

I had cut off the largest source of our revenue. We earned substantial fees from raising money and investing in real estate. Property management fees were but a fraction of the other revenue. We were very tight for cash.

Mickey Cohen, our CFO and a former AEPi fraternity brother, spent a great deal of his time from 1975 to 1977 separating the bills that had to be paid, determining which we could partially pay this week, and cajoling and negotiating with vendors to pay them more next week or the week after. Then this week's recipients had to wait another two to three weeks to be paid again. We wanted things to keep flowing because if we didn't pay anything to a vendor, they'd stop supplying a necessary product, or an entity like Florida Power & Light would shut the lights off. It was an endless juggling act. Our company executives (myself included, of course) went without regular salaries. We operated in a bunker mentality. I also started personally signing every check for the partnerships and I.R.E. There were thousands of checks but I wanted to personally oversee every expenditure before it was made, instead of on a financial report after the payment was made. Frequently, I would kick the unsigned check back to the authorizing executive for an explanation and further documentation.

On a personal level, I did the same thing I'd done for the business, which was to cut off all discretionary spending. I'd never been prone to spending sprees, but when I saw what was coming Terri and I reduced our spending dramatically and made saving money a priority. We needed to keep enough money on hand to get through the unknown. Just like the business, my wife and I adopted a bunker mentality. Fortunately we had not yet moved into the large house in Coral Gables, and although the children were babies and toddlers with all the usual expenses, our needs and wants were modest. Still, on many occasions I thought we could go bankrupt personally. With no salary coming in, three children, a house, and mortgage, things looked bleak. I took a loan from my life insurance policy, ran up my credit cards, and borrowed from my retirement account. I actually started to dictate cassette tapes daily covering the events we were experiencing and the fires we were putting out each day. I talked about how I felt about everything. I thought I might use all this to write a book that would be my only source of income. I still have those four dozen tapes but have never been able to bring myself to listen to them, or have them transcribed, because the period was so painful.

The early public limited partnerships were skinny on cash because we'd invested all the money before 1974, and the latter partnerships were flush with cash because we'd slowed down the investment cycle as we assessed the economy. It's important to note we were a separate fiduciary to each of these partnerships: We could not comingle cash or borrow cash from one partnership to help another partnership. We also could not lend ourselves money from one account to make our corporate payroll just because we were the managers of these funds. Lots of people got into trouble when they breached these divides, moving funds from one account to another—which theoretically was only a temporary fix for deeply entrenched problems. In light of the sinking economy, great discipline and resolve were required for us to resist the overwhelming temptation of this "method" of conducting business, and many competitors who gave in to that were accused of fraud and embezzlement, ending up incarcerated.

We didn't know when the recession would be over so we had to take it one day at a time. Whatever we had to do, we had to do honorably. When you looked out the window, the world was coming to an end. People were losing their jobs and businesses; their real estate was being foreclosed upon. Inflation was raging. The recession seemed endless with no light at the end of the tunnel. At the bottom of a recession, it always feels as though it will last forever.

Fortunately, all of our partnerships survived, albeit injured and devalued. We made it to the other side of the recession. An experience like that can destroy you, but if you can somehow hold your own, you can come back stronger once it's over.

Net Game

While the recession was officially over in 1975, the effects of the recession continued to be felt for several more years. Unemployment, however, did not fall to 6 percent (still a high number) until June 1978.

By 1978 the market had begun to stabilize, and we decided to start offering private investments to our existing and new investors. During the next two to three years, we would buy large, net-leased properties and syndicate each of them to twenty to twenty-five investors. Instead of the legions of small $5,000 investors we'd had, we now worked with high-net worth investors who might put in $100,000 apiece or more. The lease could be a Burger King or Wendy's, a Kmart or a bank. We would buy the real estate on which the business was situated and lease it to the operator. In some cases, we were able to buy buildings leased to Fortune 500 companies. The operator or company paid us rent and took care of all the bills: taxes, electricity, repairs, etc. For all intents and purposes it was the same kind of business we were in before. We were raising money and getting fees. We bought real estate, but we didn't have to do any property management because that was in the domain of the operator.

Because these were smaller offerings with fewer investors, we did not need to file with the SEC, which was always expensive and time-consuming. We did fifteen of these private offerings during this period of time, raising about $50 million, and the success we had with them allowed us to energize the team, solve our cash flow problems, and move our business forward.

It's important to note that during this time we were still filing quarterly 10-Qs and annual 10-Ks on each of our public partnerships. The filings had to be detailed and accurate, reporting all activity including prospects, risks, and opportunities for the business. Full disclosure. We did everything by the book. In fact, we continued this practice for nearly forty years, probably filing 750 reports in that time for the many public partnerships and public companies we managed—and yet the SEC came after us in 2007 for failure to disclose! We were model citizens; we certainly were not perfect, but we were an honest company boasting expert management and stellar employees. That the SEC was suddenly accusing us of violating securities laws was mystifying.

During the recession we had to focus on survival, strategizing to figure out *how* to survive, sometimes on a moment-by-moment basis. In that situation, knowing we could lose everything, we had to keep our wits about us in order to channel our energy into the creative pursuits that would save us—or at least stall for time.

I've always been able to compartmentalize things in my life, both on a personal and professional level. Some people regard me as stoic—even to a fault—in the face of crushing circumstances. But that's just because I've explored the downside; I've made myself go there in my head and imagine the worst that could possibly happen. Once I'm aware of that worst-case scenario, and recognize I can live with it, I'm calm and completely prepared and that helps me work more effectively to achieve the best upside. When I have all the pieces of the puzzle, it's easier for me to work with one situation and then put it away while I work on another, and then subordinate what I've just done to the next task at hand. I don't succumb to worry and fear; I just get on with what needs to be done today. It's the voice of my dad again, telling me not to let worry, failure, or disappointment get in the way of living my life. It's in me (as it is in all of us) to keep going. Persistence is the best currency.

LIFE LESSONS LEARNED

- Train yourself to see around corners.
- Have the courage of your conviction.
- Be calm and understand the downside. Once I'm aware of the worst case scenario, and recognize I can live with it, I'm calm and completely prepared to work more effectively to achieve the best upside.
- Leadership is not a popularity contest.
- Cash is king, again.
- Persistence and determination are omnipotent.

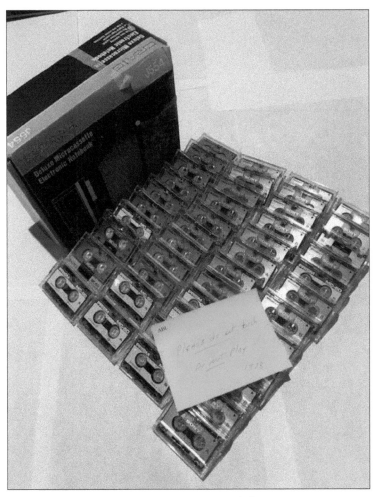

Cassette tapes I recorded
but were too painful to listen to.

CHAPTER 9

AMERICAN SAVINGS AND LOAN ASSOCIATION: ANY PORT IN A STORM

"I find that a great part of the information I have was acquired by looking up something and finding something else on the way."
—**Franklin P. Adams**

It was now three years since the recession had begun and one year since it was officially over. In order to protect the assets of Series I, Series II, and Series III during that time, we'd asked the investors to convert their partnerships into independent public corporations instead of limited partnerships. The conversion would provide immediate liquidity to those who wanted to cash out and sell their shares on an exchange, and an opportunity for those who elected to stay in to ride their investment back to profitability. We had thousands of investors and this proposal required an SEC-registered proxy to present to the investors for a vote. We engaged Donna Ackerly of Georgeson & Co. to assist us in doing the proxy solicitation. Donna would play a major role during the next thirty years in soliciting proxy votes for us on numerous transactions.

Our proposal met with success with investors voting in favor of turning the partnerships into independent public corporations, or

C corporations. This worked out extremely well as these corporate entities could now also borrow money and purchase other real estate, both of which had been restricted by the limited partnership documents. Using this ability, the entities were beginning to grow out of the recession-created devaluation.

In 1979, we went to all the investors who'd stayed with us, asking them to vote to approve the consolidation of I.R.E. Series I, Series II, and Series III, into I.R.E. Financial Corporation. The vote went through, and we listed I.R.E. Financial Corporation on the American Stock Exchange. Donny, Shelley, and Jarett joined me on the AMEX floor to celebrate the first trade. Because I.R.E. was now a significant single entity, it provided additional liquidity for the investors and shareholders and created the opportunity for increased growth for everyone.

By 1981, I thought it was time to make some bold moves to accelerate growth. I assessed the viability of going back into the national syndication business. This time, I.R.E. Financial would be the general partner. Because its net worth far exceeded $1 million, I did not have to go through the complexity of infusing the $1 million as I did previously with Leonard Abess, Sr. at City National Bank.

We were feeling strong and energetic again, just like the economy, and because we were going to be raising money from large numbers of investors, we needed to file SEC registration statements again.

We decided to go back to our original model: the proverbial gravy train. Between the original SEC-registered public partnerships and private offerings over the years, we had done twenty limited partnership offerings. So I decided our next SEC-registered program would appropriately be called I.R.E. Real Estate—Series 21. Most of our former competitors were knocked out of business from the recession and the financial planners and broker dealers that had raised money for us were also gone. They'd not paid attention to what was on the horizon the way I had, rushing off to work with competitors to perpetuate the gravy train and eventually dying off. We had to rehire a sales organization to raise money for new funds and acquisition specialists to go out and buy the real estate. We needed an administrative operation, and fortunately my fraternity brother, Norm Silber, and Susie Corredera from early I.R.E. days, were still aboard. Frank Grieco, formerly a partner with our national accounting firm, Peat Marwick, joined as CFO, after Mickey Cohen left to start his own accounting practice.

Guns blazing, we hit the market in the summer of 1981. We closed the fund in September of that year having raised $11,775,000. We were back, and it was as though we'd never left the business! Between 1981 and 1985 we completed Series 21 through Series 28, raising more than $200 million in our funds. In present-day currency that would equal just under $460 million. We were now investing the money raised in real estate and managing the funds' properties in addition to our own. We acquired more than $500 million worth of real estate all over the country. Our portfolio consisted of apartments, shopping centers and malls, office buildings and warehouses. Our parent company, I.R.E. Financial, was now a strong publicly traded company because of earlier consolidations.

Then one day the palace door stretched open a bit more—or so I thought.

Broad Reach

In 1981 I was approached by Norman Broad, an acquaintance of mine with a law firm with which we did business from time to time. Norman was the nephew of Shepard Broad, a kind of Miami royalty in his 80s, of the same vintage as Florida pioneers A.J. Harris and Leonard Abess, Sr. He was chairman of American Savings and Loan Association: a $3 billion bank.

A larger-than-life character, in 1945 the elder Broad had met with twenty-one Jewish men in a New York City apartment to help create a homeland for the world's Jews. It would be known as Palestine and later Israel.

Broad, a lawyer, had founded and developed the community of Bay Harbor Islands, an exclusive enclave between North Miami and Miami Beach, in addition to getting into the banking business. The Broad Causeway, connecting the North Miami mainland to Miami Beach, was his namesake. He'd turned the savings and loan he'd founded with just one branch into an empire, and I was about to be invited into his lair.

When Norman approached me I was flattered though suspicious. By reputation Shepard Broad was a master manipulator—someone with whom, when you left a meeting, you had to count your fingers and toes.

"How'd you like to meet my uncle," Norman asked one day, almost matter-of-factly. I agreed to go but asked why. It was an honor to be invited, but something had to be up.

"Well, he'd really like to meet *you*," Norman had responded, adding his uncle wanted to know if I wanted to buy American Savings and Loan Association! That was it. *Shepard Broad wanted to sell me his $3 billion institution.*

I asked myself (and Norman) if he was kidding. I was all of thirty-seven years old with a very good business. We'd raised money, and my background had been in real estate, but I knew nothing about banking or the S&L industry—especially not a $3 billion business. In my time just out of college at Morgan Guaranty, I'd basically been today's equivalent of an intern—a trainee. What I knew about the banking business could fill a shot glass, and I don't even drink. Maybe paramount to that, I.R.E. Financial, which I believed to be substantial, did not have the money to buy Shepard Broad's large and decades old S&L.

I sat in his office thinking about a wolf in sheep's clothing. The man was forty years my senior, courting me to buy his business. It really was true. So something was up. The thing is he was gentle, grandfatherly and easy to talk to, maybe deliberately throwing me off balance in that respect. He told me he was thinking about retirement.

Oh sure, I thought to myself. Men like that never retire. It's not in their DNA. They go on negotiating and manipulating until they die, usually face down at their desks.

"I don't know whether or not you know Morris, my son," he said, probably trying to cover all the bases as my suspicions about the situation mounted. "Well he's just not up to the task of running a bank. So I want to merge American Savings and Loan Association into I.R.E."

I told him, as I had Norman, that I knew nothing about running a bank, to which he replied he'd show me. The money I'd need to find to acquire it also did not seem to present a problem for him. "It's all fine," he said. "We'll work it out and teach you how to be president of this institution," implying running a $3 billion institution was easy and the process would be quick. *Quick?* He continued, "I've read a lot about you. I know you're a really smart guy. We should do this," he concluded, almost as though it were a done deal.

When I left the meeting my head was spinning. I called Steve Arky, my friend and attorney, and told him about the meeting. He concluded I was crazy!

In the days that followed, I did some research and discovered American Savings and Loan was a NYSE company. Its fifty branches were losing money to the tune of $4 million per quarter: a $16 million a year loss! Historically, the government required the S&Ls to make thirty-year fixed rate home mortgages. It also regulated the rates that could be paid on savings accounts. When the government deregulated the interest rates on deposits, the S&Ls had to pay a higher competitive rate to prevent the deposits from leaving to another higher paying bank. As a result, the S&Ls were now paying more for their deposits than they were receiving on low fixed rate loans, hence the losses.

Deregulation was the death knell for the savings and loan business, and in time most would go under. If American Savings and Loan Association continued to lose money without new capital, it would fail within twelve months. Shepard Broad needed a merger partner with at least $15 or $16 million in capital to support his own waning capital. If I.R.E. Financial merged with American Savings and Loan Association, I.R.E.'s $16 million worth of capital would become part of American Savings' capital. Shepard Broad undoubtedly hoped that after twelve months on life support, the rules or maybe something else would change to solve his problem. I was his port in a storm. All the S&Ls in the country were bleeding, and of course Shepard Broad had failed to disclose his plan to me. In mulling it over the way I did, I didn't think the wolf was looking to pull the wool over my eyes—not entirely. He wasn't going anywhere and would still be chairman of the bank. He wasn't looking to steal whatever money I.R.E. had (or could raise) and dupe us. He just needed capital and a strong lieutenant who could get things done—maybe move a mountain or two. Again, I was really flattered.

I'd learned to always look at the downside of anything, in my business or personal life, in fact to put more effort and energy into exploring the downside than anything else. In that way, the fear of failure is gone, or at least mitigated, because you know what can happen—what to expect. There are no unknowns. I took a good, hard look at the worst that could happen if I entered into this deal with him and what I'd found didn't outweigh the advantages of the whole experience. Despite identifying all of this, I was still interested. I actually thought the banking business could be fun. With my energy, I believed I could make this a successful venture. I called Shepard back telling him we should continue our conversation.

Shepard and I had dozens of meetings with our attorneys and others, in his office, at lunch, over coffee. We toured the massive computer room and I.R.E. received many dozens of documents, books, and records reflecting the past and present of American Savings and Loan Association. There was a great deal of work to get to the point where I could fully evaluate the risk and reward.

As a side note, Shepard Broad was quite a character. One time we were having lunch at the Standard Club in downtown Miami. He looked at his watch and abruptly announced we had to go. He asked if I would drive him somewhere. I said yes, and while we were driving he explained we were going to a funeral in Coral Gables. This was for a former employee of his and he thought it would blow the family's minds if he showed up. When we walked into the funeral home, someone who knew me approached us, questioningly.

"Hi, Alan," he said, "I had no idea you knew the deceased."

Not only did I not know the deceased, I didn't even know his name! I was somewhat embarrassed, muttered about the passing being so sad, and Shepard and I sat through the funeral. I drove the two of us back to the Standard Club to finish our meeting as though it'd never been interrupted. Anything to make a deal!

Steve Arky walked around shaking his head, acknowledging it was a tremendous opportunity but in disbelief that I'd somehow secured it. It was truly a David and Goliath story: Our small company was acquiring a behemoth. As the weeks and months leading up to the contract signing approached, I was increasingly euphoric, anticipating the future—even a future so significant I could *not* imagine it as a result of this deal! Here was an opportunity to control a $3 billion well-known, highly respected institution and to diversify our business into banking. Once again, maybe more than ever, I was swinging on the wrought iron gates.

During this time, I.R.E. Financial stock had started to run, meaning there was a huge volume in trading every day. Our stock price was rising fast in a way that was not proportionate to our average daily volume and day-to-day business. It appeared there'd been a leak somewhere that I.R.E. was about to do something highly beneficial, pending a big announcement. I ultimately found out Shepard Broad was behind the leak, though probably inadvertently. In his own kind of due diligence, he'd been checking up on me among presumably dozens of his peers, inquiring of them if they thought a merger with I.R.E. was a good idea. Hence the rumor mill had started to turn.

Because both American Savings and Loan Association and I.R.E. Financial Corporation were public companies, the SEC rules required us to put out a joint press release. The release announced the merger—specifically that American Savings and Loan Association, a NYSE company, was merging with I.R.E. Financial Corporation and that Alan Levan would be president. The sense of accomplishment was indescribable. The euphoria continued.

The next day I got a call from Morris Broad, Shepard's son, the one allegedly unworthy to run the bank. He said he needed to see me immediately. This was quite strange because all of my dealings had been with his father. He came to my office, somewhat nervously telling me American Savings could not go forward with the merger. Stunned doesn't begin to describe the way I felt. Run over by a Mack truck may have been more accurate. Morris explained that when the investment bankers and shareholders learned the bank was being sold to such a small company, they rebelled, saying there were much more suitable buyers. Had they known the bank was for sale, they'd have stepped in to facilitate a deal to what they would consider a more acceptable organization. The deal was off almost as quickly as it had been on. Shepard had sent Morris as an errand boy to break the news, and he never even ended up calling me himself. I was truly disappointed.

In the end, given the amount of time, effort, energy, and money we'd put into this deal, not to mention the publicity when it fell through, I could have moved forward with litigation. I've been on the receiving end of lawsuits many times, and maybe because of that or more likely because I don't believe it's the most constructive kind of recourse one can take, I didn't sue. We don't do business in the courthouse; we don't use litigation as a business strategy. It was awkward. It was embarrassing. But he was the one who'd come to us. I couldn't let my ego tell me what to do. My father's voice was in my head, telling me not to stew in this. Just move on.

Years later when my son, Jarett, joined our company BankAtlantic, which eventually became BBX Capital, I asked him if he'd like to meet Shepard Broad. I never burned bridges because what was the point? In fact I owed him a debt of gratitude for allowing me to immerse myself in the world of banking, which is how I looked at the situation. I called Shepard and he agreed to meet us for lunch if we would pick him up at his home. He was now in his nineties and frequented a restaurant in an old hotel on Miami Beach. The maître d' led us to his usual table.

Shepard congratulated me on the success BankAtlantic was having and expressed regret that our deal never worked out. He told me he wished he had a son like me, and I asked if he'd share with Jarett a little bit of his history and how he'd achieved all his success in real estate development and banking. I knew Jarett would be interested as he'd gone to law school and was also starting his career in banking.

Shepard began slowly, explaining he was born in Pinsk, Belarus. His parents had put him on a boat to Canada at the age of eleven, and when he stepped off the boat, a nice woman in a red dress befriended him. He lived with her for several years before migrating to the United States. At that point in the story, we'd been listening to Shepard's detailed account of his life for four hours and he'd only gotten from birth to age eleven. His total recall of minute details was extraordinary. I was eager for Jarett to hear about how he'd built his businesses but it was late and we had to go. I apologized for having to leave, asking to continue the conversation another time. Unfortunately, he died soon after. At his funeral, his family showed a twenty-minute video of his life that he'd produced before his death as a kind of self-eulogy. He wasn't about to take chances knowing what others might say about him.

By the time the American Savings and Loan Association merger was called off, I had become knowledgeable enough about the savings and loan industry. The effort had not been for nothing. I knew I wanted to be in the banking business so we looked for a bite-sized bank that we could afford.

Sunrise on Sunset

Sunset Commercial Bank was a $200 million local bank with seven branches. Its main branch was in South Miami. I got myself introduced to the bank president and asked if it might be for sale. He said he'd consider the idea, arriving at a price for us, which I then negotiated.

When buying a bank, you're paying for its capital, and perhaps a premium for its assets and liabilities. Sunset Commercial's capital was $16 million dollars. This is not a small amount of money no matter how you look at it, but we were a substantial company at that point and in a position to do it. We signed an agreement for a plan of merger and made an announcement, as we'd done with American Savings and Loan Association, that we were going to acquire this bank. We then filed for regulatory approval, which was routine. The approval should have taken six months but was taking considerably longer than that. We heard that an objection had been filed to our acquisition which was delaying the whole process.

What I didn't know at the time was that the objection had been filed by David Paul, President of CenTrust Bank, someone who would later factor in to my acquiring Atlantic Federal (please see chapter 11) and who'd eventually become the poster child for the S&L crisis of the 1980s. Ultimately David Paul went to jail for eleven years. But all I knew at that point was that an objection to our application had been filed. I reluctantly made the decision to terminate with Sunset Commercial Bank, not wanting a long, drawn-out challenge to acquire it.

In time I'd learn for certain that CenTrust had filed the objection, likely because David Paul was a shareholder of Sunset Commercial Bank. They'd had their own eyes on acquiring it.

Again I was disappointed in not being able to get into the banking business. But that would not be the final chapter of my banking career, and again, not my only encounter with David Paul.

LIFE LESSONS LEARNED

- Try not to burn bridges; you never know when the relationship—no matter how bleak it seems at the time—will serve you.
- Not everything is as it appears. People and opportunities put in your path seemingly for one reason can open the door to something else—maybe even bigger and better—if you are patient, creative, and open to it.
- Deal-making is a fine art. It takes patience and flexibility.
- Luck comes to those who are prepared for it.

CHAPTER 10

HUNDRED DOLLAR SAVINGS ACCOUNTS 1982-84: KNOWLEDGE IS CUMULATIVE

"Seeing much, suffering much, and studying much,
are the three pillars of learning."
—Benjamin Disraeli

In the early 1980s, I registered on a lark to attend a seminar in New York conducted by the Practicing Law Institute. The PLI is a nonprofit continuing legal education organization chartered by regents from SUNY (State University of New York). The fee was $450, a relatively small investment that would eventually yield the kind of results one might read about in a work of fiction. But this was real life.

For a while I'd been intrigued from news reports about a group of investors who were buying up large blocks of public stock in companies, then selling their stock back to the same companies at enormous profits. The more recognizable names during this period were Sir James Goldsmith, T. Boone Pickens, and Carl Icahn, and there were dozens of others. Today these types of investors are called activist investors, or shareholder activists: individuals who purchase enough shares in a company to challenge its management or leadership. In the 1980s, they were pejoratively called greenmailers, a takeoff on the term blackmail. This tactic either forces the targeted firm to change its strategy so shares will go up in value, or leaves the company no choice but to buy back the stock at a premium to rid themselves of the intrusive activist investor.

The seminar handbook used case studies of Carl Icahn's activities. Icahn's strategy was simple:

1) Find a company not well managed and its price depressed;
2) Buy enough stock to appear you have a meaningful position;
3) Send a letter to management about the changes you recommend the company makes in running its business; implicit or explicit in the letter: If the company fails to comply, you may file a hostile proxy statement to oust their directors and replace them with yours;
4) Consider the company's offer to repurchase your stock in it, which usually comes, as they are afraid if you keep publicizing the company's value destructive way of doing business, other shareholders will jump on the bandwagon to replace them.

Goldsmith made $90 million from selling his stock back to Goodyear Tire Company; David Murdock made $194 million from Occidental Petroleum; Icahn's fortune came from Texaco, RJR Nabisco, and many others.

Transactions of this nature are SEC regulated. The way it works is if you are going to buy more than 4.9 percent worth of stock in a company (or divest yourself of it later on), a Schedule 13D must be filed, which is a beneficial ownership report. In that form, you must declare why you bought that stock—what your intentions are. From that point on, every time you buy more stock, even if it's just five shares, the Schedule 13D must be updated.

I thought the strategy was interesting and exciting but did not have the kind of money or access to debt to pull it off. I knew my financial limitations, though creatively I hoped I didn't have any.

I was sure I wanted to do something with all that information. Someone like Carl Icahn could go out and purchase $100 million worth of stock, shake up his target, and end up selling it back to that company for two or three times that. So what was I going to do? How could I adapt that magic formula to something within reach but that would still produce a significant profit?

I thought about all I'd learned in my career, arriving at the conclusion that I knew a great deal about limited partnerships from the creation and shapeshifting of I.R.E. In fact I was somewhat of an expert.

I knew that one of the required bylaws of limited partnerships was that if you own 5 percent of the limited partnership interests, and you wanted the general partner to solicit something from the investors in that limited partnership, the general partner was required to respond as well as provide you with the list of limited partners.

Soon I tested out what I'd learned in the seminar, applying it on a different level. I wouldn't have to go after a huge company. There were many hundreds of limited partnerships out there that other companies had formed during the time we were doing our own with Series I, Series II, and Series III. We'd just emerged from the recession and many of these limited partnerships were quite damaged, the real estate undervalued, and the investors unhappy. They were limping along. In chapter 8, I'd proposed converting our own limited partnerships to public corporations so those that wanted to could get out, but we could also take the individuals who remained all the way to the finish line as we rebuilt their investments in an improved economy.

Many other companies throughout the country had not thought this way, and their limited partnerships were on life support. The door was wide open.

With a little research, I discovered a limited partnership called Lexton Ancira in Kansas City was ripe for the picking. I was able to buy a little over 5 percent of it for about $250,000. I pulled out my Carl Icahn handbook and followed the steps to the letter.

Accordingly, I wrote to the general partner explaining that I.R.E had purchased 5 percent of the limited partnership interests and was demanding they call for a vote of the limited partners to replace the general partner with us. I said I thought we could do a better job. Period. The general partner called me immediately, negotiating to buy back my shares at $750,000 (a $500,000 profit), to which I readily agreed. The concept had worked like a charm.

My $450 seminar investment turned out to be highly profitable indeed. I now understood how the Icahns, Pickens, Murdocks, and Goldsmiths of the world were doing it, yet the concept of activist investing became distasteful to me. It felt as though I were fishing in someone else's pond—holding the targeted company hostage. Activist investors often have aggressive and abrasive personalities to the point they are feared. The companies they skew will do anything to shake them loose, and it was not a good fit for me. I could not go on in all good conscience, and discontinued the practice, though I probably could have gotten quite good at it. Today, activist investing is funded primarily by institutional investors such as pension funds (if they still exist), insurance companies, and some of the best-known hedge funds in the world. In fact Carl Icahn had tapped some of them when he started out, before he amassed billions. Activist investors are abundant today and operate as an accepted strategy.

But I was on the lookout for other investment opportunities, ones where I could be more creative than destructive.

Public Conversions

Though the opportunity with Shepard Broad and American Savings and Loan Association had not worked out, and Sunset Commercial had also fallen away, I had learned quite a bit about the savings and loan business. S&Ls throughout the country were languishing because of deregulation of deposits. Their deep losses were impacting their capital and if capital became too low, the government would take them over. To add to the problem, most S&Ls were mutuals, operating something like a nonprofit and nominally owned by depositors (just for the record, many insurance companies are also mutuals). They were not stock companies, with the benefit of shareholders who could inject capital if needed. In fact S&L depositors didn't care much about their ownership and likely didn't even know about it. Depositors were concerned primarily about their savings accounts and the FDIC insurance that protected them from loss. With few exceptions curiosity did not extend beyond that. Other than the ability to perhaps sign a proxy card that reelected the existing board of directors, depositors had no economic benefits or rights that a shareholder might have, as they were not shareholders.

At this point in time, the S&Ls had two problems: The first is that due to deregulation, customers were withdrawing their deposits as interest rates were higher in other financial institutions. S&Ls by design invest depositors' money in other assets, so cash was not sitting in a vault where it could be handed back to depositors. The mass exodus of customers and dearth of capital was leaving a decided hole for the government to come in and take them over.

The second problem was that in order to keep depositors' money at an S&L, the institution would increase interest rates it paid on savings accounts but that additional cost would create even more losses. Deregulation had lowered the boom and it was just a matter of time where, absent another strategy, they all would fail.

During the American Savings debacle, I'd really learned about how it all worked. Because S&Ls had no shareholders to access in order to raise capital in the times following deregulation, the government devised a system to allow these institutions (mutuals) to convert from depositor-owned institutions to public companies with shareholders. The guidelines were strict, but in the end the S&L would be public and capital would be accessible. A mutual would first have to offer its existing depositors the opportunity to buy stock, then offering what remained of the stock offering to the general public. This system, a kind of largesse when you think about it, was a great opportunity for an investor. Because these offerings became so popular with the general public, they were oversubscribed in the public offering and it was difficult to buy many shares in the offering. Their scarcity was discouraging, but I had an idea to work backwards to solve the scarcity issue and buy as much stock as I wanted.

The formula prescribed for conversion was complicated. If a savings and loan had a net worth of $25 million and it wanted to raise an additional $25 million from the public to increase its capital, it would sell the $25 million worth of shares to the public. The new shareholders would now own stock in a company with a $50 million net worth. Their purchase would be basically at half the subsequent capital—or half book value. To a shareholder, the capital would be described as book value per share. That's because the first 50 percent ($25 million) wasn't owned by the depositor and the new shareholders would get the free benefit of that first $25 million with the capital of the company now being $50 million—or full book.

If the offering had to be made to the savings and loan's depositors first, all I had to do was open an account and become a depositor at these savings and loans before they decided to do an offering. There were about fifty savings and loans in Florida at the time and I had no way of knowing which ones would want to convert to a stock corporation to raise money—or when they would. So I.R.E. opened $100 savings accounts at all fifty savings and loans. This cost us $5,000 and would entitle us to participate in the offerings as a depositor in any of these banks that decided to convert, before the stock was offered to the public. I was pleased with this approach in that it was more suited to my personality because the investment was passive. It would create the same financial returns as the greenmailing, without being hostile or activist.

A Closer Look

The government formula of stock allocation to the depositors was as follows: The bank would take the dollar amount of your savings account deposit(s) and divide it into the total amount of deposits the bank had. For example, if you had a deposit of $1 million and the bank had total savings account deposits of $100 million, you would be entitled to buy 1 percent of the $25 million offering of stock. Of course, most people didn't have a $1 million deposit because S&L depositors wanted the safety of knowing they had government insurance on their deposits, and government insurance was only up to $100,000.

As a result of the formula, I.R.E.'s $100 deposit would only entitle us to an infinitesimal amount of the stock offering. However I figured out two more elements: The subscription form for the offering, as required by the government, allowed depositors to subscribe for more than their pro rata amount if other depositors didn't exercise their right, and if there was availability left in the offering. Savings and loan depositors usually had no interest in buying stock because the stock market was riskier than having a government insured savings account. Particularly in Florida, many of these depositors were older—in their seventies and eighties, having lived through the Great Depression—which followed the stock market crash. They were cautious and stuck to what they knew to be secure. As a result, I.R.E. could basically increase the amount of our investment to any amount we wanted and we would likely get it.

Again, after the offering to the depositors and public shareholders, the stock which was basically being issued at half capital or half book value per share, would soon elevate to book value per share in the trading market after the offering to the public. That would be

149

a doubling of the investment, i.e. the stock one purchased for $10 a share would increase to $20 a share. In addition, by this time, the large northeastern banks had discovered Florida to be a great place to have branches and they wanted to acquire Florida savings and loans. Shortly after the offering, these northeastern banks would offer two times book value per share to acquire the entire savings and loan and change the bank and the branches to their bank name. If they now offered two times book value to the shareholders to buy the bank, the purchase price for the stock, in this example, would be $40 a share. That would quadruple the investment of $10 a share. Believe it or not, I discovered the formula worked that way every single time and if you could get the stock in the original depositor offering, it was like printing money! Now all I had to do was sit back and wait for these mutuals to convert to stock corporations. I was watching their capital being reduced by losses and I knew it was just a matter of time.

The first of the S&Ls to convert was First City Federal Savings and Loan Association in Bradenton, Florida. First City Federal had assets of $617 million and was looking to raise about $15 million in new capital or 1.5 million shares at $10 a share. We received the subscription form as a $100 depositor, which gave us the right to an allocation of 0.00000016 percent of the offering. That would calculate to $2.43 of the $15 million offering or basically rounded up to one share for $10. That was the infinitesimal part of the calculation. I carefully filled out the form subscribing for I.R.E.'s one share. But then I moved on to the next box that said, "Do you want to subscribe for more than your allocable share?" I checked yes and subscribed for 150,000 shares for an amount of $1.5 million dollars at approximately $10 a share. This represented approximately 9.9 percent of the offering, which was the maximum a shareholder could own of a bank or S&L, without prior regulatory approval. Under my theory, very few of the depositors would subscribe, so I.R.E. might be able to get its full 150,000 shares. As anticipated, the offering to depositors was not well subscribed, but in the public part of the offering, the shares were quickly gobbled up. Shortly after the completion of the offering, the stock traded up to $20 a share or book value, basically doubling our money. It worked exactly as I thought it would—with one wrinkle.

When the management of First City Federal completed the offering and realized we now owned 9.9 percent of their bank, they panicked. They couldn't understand how that could have happened. Their investment bankers had not advised them of the possibility of an interested party acquiring 9.9 percent of their stock. They immediately sued I.R.E. to slow us down. I'm not sure why they needed to slow us down because all we had done was buy stock in accordance with the terms they provided. Steve Arky, Gene Stearns, Alison Miller, and others from the law firm and I would be amused that they took that position because we had followed the letter of the law. We didn't even contact them to aggravate them and were totally passive in our investment. The only thing we did was file a required SEC report that indicated that we'd purchased 9.9 percent of the stock. So much for being passive!

In First City's defense mode, management's position was if their bank was going to be taken over by anyone, it was going to be an acquisition of the bank's choosing. First City Federal quickly announced it was seeking a strategic merger partner. In this way, their management could have some control over their salaries, benefits, even severance. A buyer, such as a northeastern bank, would agree to almost anything since it would be a small price to pay for an important strategic acquisition. Brooklyn-based, two hundred-year-old, multibillion-dollar Metropolitan Savings Bank became its hand-picked partner of choice, having trumpeted its intent to acquire a Florida institution. As mutuals in Florida were converting, they were being sold to well-capitalized northeastern banks that were seizing the opportunity to set up shop in the sunbelt with its exploding population.

Metropolitan Savings Bank was helmed by Luke Bayonne, from whom I received a call during First City Federal's litigation. Gene Stearns, Alison Miller, and I flew to New York to meet with him.

Gene and Alison were Steve Arky's law partners. Gene, a trial lawyer, and Alison, a securities lawyer, are senior partners in the firm of Stearns, Weaver, Miller. While I had previously worked with both of them at the law firm, this was really the beginning of an extraordinary friendship and professional association that has lasted four decades. Rarely a day goes by when I don't talk to one of them.

Both are amazing and fortunately they both have my back.

Eugene Stearns is an incredibly talented strategic thinker. He is the best trial lawyer I have ever known, and I am not alone in that testimonial. He can size up an issue quickly and tell you whether you will prevail or not. He is rarely wrong. His trial performance is straightforward without gimmicks or sleight of hand. He has an almost photographic memory and can recall facts at will. He remembers information about my life and business that I have long forgotten. Extraordinarily ethical and principled, he will litigate and appeal if necessary to win before he will give up on an issue he feels passionate about and when the law is on his side.

Alison Miller is my rock on securities law. She oversees all our securities filings including press releases, 10-Qs, 10-Ks, and registration statements. She reads our securities documents with an eye toward the past and present but more importantly how will today's disclosure look, with the benefit of hindsight, in the future. She is my "go to" person on all matters business and personal. She will be blunt and disagreeable if she thinks I am taking an important matter too lightly. I cannot fully express how important it has been to me to have someone like Alison who supports me but at the same time is brutally honest. She is practical and caring and will do anything for me, my family, or my business.

It was beyond freezing in Brooklyn that day. Three thin-blooded Floridians were no match for the weather as we hurried into bank headquarters in Brooklyn, taking the elevator to the top. Bayonne was a formidable figure with a thick Italian accent. He motioned for us to sit down.

"Number one," he began without pretense, "I want to buy First City. And number two, you're in my way. I want you to get out of my way, so I want to buy the stock you own."

I recall taking in an office that was as imposing as the man before me. Home court advantage, maybe, but not this time. "It's not for sale," I countered. He didn't like this at all, becoming somewhat agitated and aggressive.

"That's ridiculous," he said. "Everything's for sale."

So we had him, agreeing to sell our stock at two times book value. But there was more. I made the sale conditional on our obtaining a $5 million loan from his bank so we could continue to purchase bank stock in other S&Ls. He asked for collateral and we offered none, knowing an unsecured loan was in the bag. He was a hound dog, hot on the trail of a First City acquisition. He couldn't afford to look up. The lawsuit was withdrawn. My investment thesis continued to work exactly as I'd anticipated—even exceeding my expectations.

Gene, Alison, and I stood on the corner outside the Metropolitan Savings Bank building that day in the arctic weather, barely able to remove our hands from our pockets. Hailing a cab back to the airport could result in frostbite! Despite the conditions, we found a little warmth as we basked in the fervor of our deal.

All in all, I.R.E. made a $4.5 million profit on a $1.5 million investment in a short period of time (three times our investment, plus a seven-year $5 million unsecured loan with which to do this again).

Following Metropolitan's acquisition of First City, Metropolitan changed the name of the new enterprise to Crossland Savings Bank, reflecting it had branches from New York to Florida. In the recession of the late 1980s, Crossland went broke and was liquidated by the federal government.

One day the phone rang and the FDIC inquired about our $5 million loan. The Federal Deposit Insurance Corporation is the government agency whose job it is to deal with failed banks, so they would auction off portfolios of mortgages and assets owned by the failed banks. Investors would come in and buy them.

Our $5 million loan was a seven-year obligation on which we'd continued to pay, and on which we'd never missed a payment. No one at the FDIC auction really wanted it as it was unsecured, so we bid $800,000 for our own loan, and they accepted, saving $4.2 million in the end. It was never our intention to do something like that, or to pay it back early, just pay in accordance with our terms. But the government didn't want to wait and auctioned it off to our advantage.

Next up was Heritage Federal Savings in Daytona Beach, followed by First Federal Savings of Ft. Meyers. We bought 9.9 percent of each of these banks, with the same scenario unfolding. Both of them sued us. Gene Stearns was masterful in dealing with the litigation resulting from these frivolous acts. We never had any intention of taking over these institutions and were not aggressive in that regard, or in any regard, simply filing the proper SEC documents. Subsequently, the banks were sold at two times book value.

In December of 1984, Atlantic Federal Savings and Loan of Fort Lauderdale also did a conversion and offering. I.R.E. bought its customary 9.9 percent, but the dynamic was about to change. David Paul and CenTrust Bank appeared with an offer I couldn't refuse.

LIFE LESSONS LEARNED

- Continuing education and professional conferences should not be dismissed. More times than not, what I learned in a couple of days has allowed me to launch significant business ventures.
- Study people as much as information.
- Opportunities are everywhere. You just have to be open to them.

Eugene (Gene) Stearns

Alison Miller

Miami News
PM 75,000
Miami

JAN-9 -84

I.R.E. president Alan B. Levan shows new prospectus

The Miami News - A.G. MONTANARI

I.R.E. banks future on diversification

ROBERT ADAMS
Miami News Reporter

When Alan B. Levan began to set up limited partnerships for real-estate investors in 1971 at the age of 26, he had to overcome skepticism about what a person his age knew about buying and managing commercial property.

So he used a silhouette of himself instead of an age-revealing photograph when he issued a prospectus for his multimillion-dollar deals. Now he looks back wistfully at that period of his more youthful appearance. "Unfortunately, we don't have that problem any more," he said.

Now 39, Levan, chairman and president of I.R.E. Financial Corp. in Miami, said people with investment opportunities seek out his company. "You reach a turning point where a company can start to take off," he said. "That comes from seasoned management that has made some mistakes."

Last week, I.R.E, a company that specializes in real-estate syndications, announced that it had agreed to buy Sunset Commercial Bank in Miami for about $9 million. Levan (pronounced la-VAN) plans to convert the $75-million-asset bank into a stockholder-owned savings and loan association, subject to approval by state and federal regulators and Sunset's shareholders.

I.R.E.'s venture into the savings-and-loan field reflects Levan's desire to diversify the company's operations. "The larger you get, the less you want to put all of your eggs in one basket," he said.

Miami Herald
AM 450,000
S 580,000

DEC-26-83

I.R.E. buys stock of two thrifts

I.R.E. Financial Corp. of Miami enlarged its share in the state savings and loan industry by purchasing 249,700 shares of common stock of Fort Lauderdale-based Atlantic Federal Savings and Loan Association and 168,000 shares of common stock of Daytona Beach-based Heritage Federal Savings and Loan Association.

Miami Review
Legal Daily 8,000

DEC-30-83

I.R.E. purchases more thrift shares

I.R.E. Financial Corporation has acquired 40,000 additional shares of the outstanding common stock of Atlantic Federal Savings and Loan Association of Fort Lauderdale, thus increasing its holding to 9.9 percent of Atlantic Federal's outstanding common shares, according to I.R.E. president Alan B. Levan.

INVESTORS ARE HOT FOR FLORIDA THRIFTS

Thrifts such as the $1.7 billion Atlantic Federal Savings & Loan Association of Fort Lauderdale are expected to be the first to go. Atlantic Federal has a strong franchise north of Miami in Broward County, whose 1.4 million residents account for some $14 billion in deposits. "We have an almost inexhaustible supply of deposits here," says Atlantic Federal President Donald V. Streeter. Seven investor groups have already grabbed 5%-plus chunks of Atlantic.

Miami Review
Legal Daily 8,000

DEC-23-83

BRIEFS

I.R.E. Financial Corp., Miami, has purchased 249,700 shares of Atlantic Federal Savings and Loan's common stock, I.R.E. President Alan Levan has announced. This represents an 8.5 percent acquisition of Atlantic's outstanding common stock, which cost about $2.25 million. I.R.E. just completed its 9.9 percent acquisition of Heritage Federal's, Daytona Beach, common stock Monday for about $1.5 million.

READY TO RUN FOR THE FLORIDA GOLD

Alan B. Levan doesn't want to be confused with the gold-chain-and-leisure-suit crowd often associated with Florida finance. The prints and furniture in IRE Financial Corp.'s Coral Gables offices are English antiques. They convey President Levan's "very formal and conservative" approach to business.

Levan, 40, hopes a staid style will help IRE, a real-estate syndication and investment services company controlling $40.8 million in assets, become a force in Florida finance. It now owns part of three Florida thrifts and is expected to buy more, although Levan isn't tipping his hand.

Levan says a Florida vacation prompted him to leave Morgan Guar-

IRE FINANCIAL'S LEVAN: THE VALUE OF HIS THRIFT INVESTMENTS HAS ALREADY DOUBLED

anty Trust Co. and the New York fast track. Not that he's slowed down much. Partly as an antidote to his long hours, he has worked his three children, aged 11 to 15, into his business whenever possible. They might do mail room duty or sit in on deal closings.

Levan can be both pugnacious and gracious. After a former partner sued him, Levan's countersuit included charges of expense account cheating. Yet after Levan won a rough battle for a seat on the board of Atlantic Federal, its president, Donald V. Streeter, calls him a "remarkable asset."

Levan could say the same about Atlantic and his other thrift investments. They have already doubled in value, for a tidy net gain of $5.5 million.

AtlanticFederal

Savings and Loan

Savings Account

	DATE	WITHDRAWALS	SAVINGS	EARNINGS	BALANCE	
1	MAY2783		100.00		100.00	42
2						
3						
4						
5						
6						
7						
8						
9						
10						
11						
12						

SAVINGS ACCOUNT

*This $100 savings account was the catalyst
which resulted in a $6.5 billion banking enterprise.*

CHAPTER 11

ATLANTIC FEDERAL SAVINGS AND LOAN PROXY FIGHT: ABSENT THE WHITE KNIGHT

"Small opportunities are often the beginning of great enterprises."
—Demosthenes

In the late fall of 1983, I received a subscription document from Atlantic Federal Savings and Loan in Fort Lauderdale. Atlantic Federal was one of the S&Ls at which I.R.E. had opened a $100 savings account. It had suffered the slings and arrows of deregulation and was in the process of converting from a mutual to a public stock corporation to raise $25 million in capital. Founded in 1952, Atlantic Federal now had fifty branches and about $2.3 billion in deposits. It had operated on a traditional S&L business model by acquiring short term deposits, paying around 3 percent, and lending them out in fixed rate 30-year home mortgages at around 6 percent.

I filled out the subscription form as I'd done with the other S&Ls when they'd converted, subscribing for the requisite number of shares to which we were entitled. I then followed our pattern of subscribing for the additional shares up to 9.9 percent of the offering. When the offering was completed in December of that year, we received our 9.9 percent, filing the mandatory SEC Schedule 13D form advising the public of our ownership position. Shortly thereafter, Atlantic Federal sued I.R.E. for accumulating stock. We could almost set our watches by these frivolous lawsuits. It didn't take long for the court to dismiss it in our favor.

The following February I received a phone call from David Paul of the multibillion dollar CenTrust Bank, in Miami, who had previously filed the objection to I.R.E.'s acquisition of Sunset Commercial Bank. While we'd not yet met, I certainly knew who he was by virtue of the obstacle he'd thrown in our path. He and his bank were in the news from time to time, so his name had come to my attention more than once.

"You don't know me," Paul said at the outset of the call, "but we have a commonality of interests." I couldn't imagine what those interests might be.

"I'm the chairman and president of CenTrust," he continued, leaving nothing to chance. "You and I own shares in Atlantic Federal." He informed me that CenTrust owned 9.1 percent, and asked me if I'd gotten a copy of the new Atlantic Federal proxy, which I had not. I'd seen the previous proxy with the subscription documents, but that was back in December, and since then the offering had been completed. Another proxy had apparently been mailed, which I'd not yet received, so Paul proceeded to fill me in. Atlantic Federal was asking its shareholders to vote on a proposal to amend its bylaws to prevent a change of control of the S&L for at least five years. The primary issue with a proposed change like this is that the SEC mandates disclosure. There was no doubt the proposed bylaw amendment should have been disclosed with the original subscription documents in the fall.

It's quite possible Atlantic Federal knew that if it had disclosed its intent earlier, it would have had trouble raising the essential capital. Clearly, I.R.E. would not have invested. If the S&L had discussed it with its investment bankers, which it presumably had, it would likely have been advised to hold back so as not to dilute interest in the public offering. But whatever the sequence of events, major shareholders were now left in a conundrum.

"If this passes, it's going to negatively change the value of our investment," Paul said emphatically, "so we have to stop it. We have to make absolutely sure it never happens." If it passed, it would discourage a northeastern bank from acquiring Atlantic Federal, thereby preventing a 2x book offer. He further explained that while he was opposed to the change and wanted to take action, CenTrust and Atlantic Federal had the same bank regulator: the Office of Thrift Supervision. OTS regulators, according to Paul, do not like their banks fighting among themselves. I wasn't sure about that, but didn't really know him and at that point had no reason to doubt him. He asked I.R.E. to take up the fight.

I told him I would carry the flag. I wanted to protect I.R.E.'s investment. He sent me the proxy, which I brought to Gene Stearns, who confirmed that any intention to change the bylaws should have been previously disclosed.

While I had no interest in initiating a hostile proxy (we did not want to acquire Atlantic Federal), I surmised an opposition proxy would be popular among shareholders because they typically bought into the S&Ls for the same reason I did. This was to give the S&L money to build enough capital to keep itself solvent, but more importantly to hold the stock until a Northeastern bank bought it at two times book value.

Alison Miller prepared the opposing proxy. I had gained experience in reviewing proxies because of the conversions we'd done for Series I, Series II, and Series III. Additionally, my research of American Savings and also the proxies I studied at the PLI seminar added to my knowledge base.

I reviewed the proxy and actually slept on it for a night or two before giving final approval. It basically laid out the reasons why shareholders should vote no on the proposal. In the interest of showing Atlantic Federal's directors how serious I was about this objection, I.R.E. put up an opposing director. This seemed like a good strategy because Atlantic Federal had listed its directors up for reelection in the same proxy to amend its bylaws. It's one thing to issue an opposition proxy on a proposed bylaw change, but if Atlantic Federal were faced with losing a director seat, let's just say the heat would be on for a fast withdrawal of the proposed change. In fact, with Gene and Alison's concurrence, I put up a whole slate of highly qualified directors—five in all! We were investing all this time and expense, so why not aim for a stronger show of force? Surely now they would withdraw the amendment.

Atlantic Federal sued us for attempting to block the bylaw change and for nominating directors. There was again no basis for this second lawsuit: As shareholders we had the legal right to put up an opposing proxy and nominate directors.

When an opposing proxy is filed, the business is required to provide a list of all shareholders—or at the very least obligated to disseminate the information in the proxy to their shareholders. We were successful in obtaining the list from Atlantic Federal, immediately hiring Donna Ackerly of Georgeson, the same proxy solicitation firm we'd hired for our efforts to convert Series I, Series II, and Series III. Georgeson's job was to contact shareholders and encourage them to vote. Georgeson kept a tally and kept us apprised of which way the voting was going. I took the responsibility of contacting the larger shareholders, including Freedom Federal Savings & Loan in Tampa.

As had CenTrust, Freedom Federal had acquired a large amount—9.1 percent—of Atlantic Federal in the open market (they had not become depositors the way we had, but had still been able to acquire the larger block of stock). During my call they became quite sympathetic, aligning with us to vote to prevent the bylaw change.

At that point, we knew I.R.E. had 9.9 percent of Atlantic Federal's stock, CenTrust had 9.1 percent, and Freedom Federal also had 9.1 percent, which amounted to nearly 30 percent. Another shareholder who reached out held 4.9 percent and he indicated he would vote with us.

While it did appear we would win the proxy fight, we were still expending an inordinate amount of time, energy, and money on this campaign. We were defending ourselves against a lawsuit—again frivolous, but expensive and time consuming. I proposed to Gene that we drive up to Fort Lauderdale to meet with Atlantic Federal CEO and president Don Streeter, tell him we were going to win, and make the whole thing go away right then and there.

Fore!

Our meeting with Streeter caught us a little off guard. We arrived to find him dressed in loud golf pants and an equally loud shirt; the sartorial noise was deafening as we entered his office (unless you're fond of chartreuse), glancing around for the first tee.

One thing I'd learned about S&Ls was that as a rule, the people and operations were not as sophisticated as they were at other financial institutions where more was expected of them. The environment was more relaxed. Streeter was the son-in-law of the founder who had died a few years earlier.

Until that time, of course before deregulation, S&Ls had been tightly controlled, with strict terms prescribing how much interest they could pay for deposits. They generated long-term home loan mortgages, and that was about all they could do. There wasn't a lot of thought and creativity that needed to go into the day-to-day operations of an S&L—and nowhere near the stress and tension evident in other businesses—so the atmosphere tended to be noncompetitive and informal. In fact, it was more or less a punch-in and punch-out kind of mindset—an easy business. There was an unofficial principle ascribed to S&Ls called the "3-6-3 Rule": pay 3 percent for deposits; lend out the money at 6 percent; and tee off at the golf course by 3:00 p.m. Looking at Streeter in his Greg Norman sweater, there was no doubt in our minds he would not be late for the links so we got down to business. We asked him, point blank, to withdraw the bylaw amendment, providing him with proof of the majority of stock I.R.E., Freedom Federal, the anonymous shareholder, and CenTrust had. Additionally, Georgeson was sending us reports indicating large numbers of shareholders would be voting no.

"You need at least 50 percent to make this amendment pass," I said, "but we've got more than 50 percent opposed, which means it isn't happening for you."

Streeter jumped up. "That's ridiculous!" he shouted. "You don't have CenTrust. We have CenTrust!" He told us how CenTrust had been in the trenches with them all along, advising them on how to defeat our opposing proxy. Gene and I were flabbergasted. It just couldn't be. I told Streeter about the day David Paul called to enroll me in the cause, but Streeter just plain didn't buy it. He had a relationship with Paul, and no amount of explaining on my part could convince him that CenTrust was not squarely in his court. Gene and I scratched our heads, shook hands with him, and left.

On the hour-long drive back to Miami, we started to piece together what had just happened. We decided CenTrust likely had its sights on acquiring Atlantic Federal, a very large institution with fifty branches. If Paul was able to merge the two banks, the resulting entity would be one of the largest financial institutions in the region. If the bylaws changed, he'd never be able to acquire Atlantic Federal, so he targeted someone like me to take up the fight. He would appear as the good guy—the white knight, or something in Greek mythology called the *deus ex machina* or the god sent down from the heavens at the last minute to save the day. Except CenTrust wanted me to win so the bylaw change would fail. That way CenTrust would position itself as Atlantic Federal's protector, much in the same way First City Federal had gone running to Metropolitan Savings Bank to protect it and lock in all its management contracts, employee benefits, and severance packages.

After additional consideration of the circumstances, especially the fact that we were defendants in an Atlantic Federal lawsuit, we decided the only way to convince Streeter we were telling the truth was for me to file an affidavit as part of our litigation defense. Gene prepared it, explicitly stating that David Paul had contacted me to lead the charge to get the proposed bylaw amendment voted down.

Now it was part of the court record. To make sure Streeter—and not just his attorneys—actually saw it, we sent the court's stamped copy directly to him. The next day he called me, sheepishly admitting he'd been able to verify my side of the story and that he believed me. I asked him how he'd made that determination.

"I called David," he said, "and he told me it was true, but he said, 'that sonofabitch Levan should never have put it in writing because it was between the two of us.'" Realizing he'd been hoodwinked by Paul and would be defeated, he offered to withdraw the amendment, asking sarcastically if it made me happy.

"I'll get back to you on that," I said.

When I called him again, I addressed the five directors we'd nominated for his board, telling him we'd settle for just one. He initially said no. I became very firm, explaining he'd put us through a lot of trouble and expense with the lawsuits and proxy fight, and we meant business. He understood that if his shareholders were riled enough over all of this, they'd potentially elect all five of my nominees to their board, so he gave in, conceding one chair.

"Which of the five is it?" he wanted to know. He nearly exploded when I told him it was none of the above. I was the one.

"Anybody else—anybody on my board but you! It cannot be you!" he fulminated. I told him that was the deal. Without much choice, he ultimately relented, and I found myself on the board of directors of a $2.3 billion savings and loan.

When I thought about the events of the past few years, going back to the days with Shepard Broad and American Savings and Loan and even further, I flashed back to my time as a trainee at J.P. Morgan. Dinners alone every night in the company dining room so I could spend hours researching and studying well into the night in the company library. It was an effort I put forth to learn, but never in my wildest dreams did it occur to me I'd end up on the board of a $2 billion institution—certainly not at forty years old. Whether it was luck, hard work, kismet, being in the right place at the right time, or a combination of all four, I was grateful. I was fortunate to be where I was and I never lost sight of that.

As a sidebar to what happened, or perhaps as a strong measure of David Paul's personality, my son Jarett, then about age eleven, came home from school one day clearly distressed. He was president of his temple youth group and had an adult youth group advisor who worked closely with all the kids, year after year. Presidents are elected, and they come and go, but the adult advisor is the one constant who provides consistency and holds the group together. The adult advisor was someone Jarett looked up to.

When I asked about the source of his distress, Jarett said his advisor informed him that she could no longer interact with him—in fact, could no longer talk to him at all! I was concerned for him, and I didn't know where all this was coming from.

"What do you mean?" I asked. "Why on Earth would she say that?"

Jarett said the youth advisor was an executive with CenTrust and apparently just like former President Richard Nixon, David Paul had an enemies list. I'd ended up on it, and by association, my bright-eyed young son had become a casualty of the "cause." Dysfunctional didn't even begin to describe David Paul, issuing an edict like this that affected a child. At Jarett's age, children tend to become attached to their teachers, leaders, and advisors. They are role models and this should never have happened.

As I noted earlier, by 1989, David Paul became the poster child for the S&L crisis. CenTrust failed and was liquidated, and what's more, Paul had engaged in a host of unethical financial activities, pretty much thumbing his nose at the federal government all the way. He'd thought he was invincible and that laws surely didn't apply to him. It eventually came out that while his S&L ship was sinking, he'd used CenTrust money to refurbish his home and purchase artwork and gold plumbing fixtures that somehow ended up in his residence. He also kept a very large boat behind his house and had other assets that were paid for by CenTrust. The SEC and US Justice Department wanted to make an example of him, as they would one day do with me—only with me it was fiction, but with David Paul they were right on target.

On November 25, 1993, a federal court convicted Paul of forty-seven counts of bank fraud, in addition to numerous counts of mail fraud, filing false tax returns, and other offenses. Although he was looking at up to 350 years in prison, he was ultimately sentenced to eleven years and ordered to pay $60 million in restitution and a $5 million fine.*

In an interesting conclusion to the David Paul chronicles, at the government-sponsored CenTrust liquidation auction (just as Metropolitan Savings Bank's assets had been auctioned off when I.R.E. got to buy our loan back), all the assets were up for bidding. Paul had installed a dining room at his bank with fine china and crystal, silver, and linen. And of course there was expensive artwork (some at his home and some at the bank). Millions of dollars' worth

---

* "David L. Paul," Wikipedia, accessed September 24, 2017: https://en.wikipedia.org/wiki/David_L._Paul

of David Paul's misspent wealth was on display. I decided to attend the auction with my wife, Susie (more about her later in the book; Terri and I were no longer married). Paul had put us through a lot, both in business terms and through the vindictive personal actions he had taken that had affected my son. We were curious to see if there was anything on auction that might appeal to us as a kind of memento of his long overdue day in court. We didn't want to call a lot of attention to ourselves, so we entered quietly through a back door.

When the bidding started, a set of exquisite Limoges china with place settings for twenty came up. The china was emblazoned with the CenTrust logo, embossed in gold onto each item. We bid and got the whole set for a song, knowing that guests at our dinner parties would ask about the logo and we'd get to tell the story—a cautionary tale about the self-styled white knight who wasn't.

LIFE LESSONS LEARNED

- Knowledge is cumulative.
- Surround yourself with smart people—this, in my case, was Gene Stearns and Alison Miller.
- Mementos of history remind us of important lessons.
- Honesty and integrity always win out, even when surrounded by thieves and fools.

Miami News
PM 75,000
Miami

JAN-27-84

Atlantic Federal counters I.R.E. suit in proxy fight

MERWIN SIGALE
Miami News Business Editor

The proxy battle between I.R.E. Financial Corp. of Miami and Atlantic Federal Savings and Loan Association in Fort Lauderdale has ebbed and flowed anew.

It flowed late yesterday when Atlantic said it had filed a countersuit, alleging that I.R.E. and its president, Alan B. Levan, failed to disclose to Atlantic's stockholders and federal regulators that it eventually intends to seek control of the S&L.

But the battle ebbed on another front, as Atlantic said it was withdrawing the proposed anti-takeover amendments to its charter because the chance of winning stockholders' approval was "remote." Atlantic said, however, it still intends to "strongly oppose" I.R.E.'s slate of three nominees to the nine-member board and push for approval of a disputed stock-option plan.

The annual shareholders' meeting, where the issues will be voted on, has been rescheduled for Feb. 17.

Eugene E. Stearns, an attorney for I.R.E., said the allegations in Atlantic's countersuit "are totally, categorically untrue."

"I.R.E. Financial Corp. has no plans or interest whatsoever to acquire control of Atlantic Federal," Stearns said. "Its interest in Atlantic Federal is, and has been, only as a passive investor." He said I.R.E. "only got involved in this (proxy contest) by virtue of their surprise attack," referring to Atlantic's now-withdrawn proposals that would have made any takeover more difficult.

Stearns said the measures would "substantially reduce the value of the company's stock" but were not disclosed until after Atlantic converted from a mutual association to stock ownership last month.

I.R.E., which owns 9.9 percent of Atlantic's stock, sued last week to block the S&L's anti-takeover moves. Atlantic's other major shareholders are Dade Savings and Loan in Miami and Freedom Savings in Tampa, each with slightly more than 9 percent.

I.R.E. specializes in real-estate syndications. It has invested in several S&Ls and agreed to buy Sunset Commercial Bank in Miami and convert it into a shareholder-owned S&L.

Any takeover of Atlantic would not be permissible until December, one year after its conversion to a stock association.

Sun Sentinel
AM 82,000
Pompano Beach

JAN-27-84

Atlantic Federal sues I.R.E.

Atlantic Federal Savings & Loan Association announced Thursday it has filed a countersuit against its largest shareholder, Miami-based I.R.E. Financial Corp., over a bitter proxy battle.

At the same time, the Fort Lauderdale-based thrift said it was dropping proposed anti-takeover amendments that I.R.E. and other large stockholders had opposed. Atlantic Federal President Donald Streeter said the amendments had little chance of approval.

Atlantic Federal said its suit charged I.R.E. and its president, Alan B. Levan, with fraudulently failing to disclose in materials sent to Atlantic Federal stockholders and in filings with the Federal Home Loan Bank Board its intent to obtain control of the S&L once regulatory restrictions are removed.

I.R.E. on Jan. 19 sued Atlantic Federal in U.S. District Court in Miami to prevent the S&L from holding its annual stockholders meeting. The I.R.E. suit challenged Atlantic's proposed amendments and said the thrift's management deliberately concealed its intention to initiate anti-takeover measures that would alter the nature of shareholders' investment and reduce the value of Atlantic's stock.

Atlantic Federal later postponed its annual meeting to Feb. 17. The S&L's countersuit opposed I.R.E.'s motion to stop the annual meeting and included a motion to dismiss I.R.E.'s complaint.

— Karen Southwick

Miami News
PM 75,000
Miami

JAN-28-84

I.R.E., Atlantic settle proxy battle

MERWIN SIGALE
Miami News Business Editor

A proxy battle between I.R.E. Financial Corp. of Miami and a Broward savings and loan association has been settled.

I.R.E. and Atlantic Federal Savings and Loan Association said yesterday they had reached an agreement in principle to drop their respective lawsuits and "work together."

The two companies agreed that I.R.E. will obtain one seat on Atlantic's board — for I.R.E. president Alan B. Levan — instead of the three it was seeking. I.R.E. agreed to vote for a previously disputed stock-option plan.

I.R.E., which owns 9.9 percent of Atlantic's stock, sued last week to block anti-takeover measures that Atlantic wanted to submit to its stockholders. The Miami firm alleged that the proposals would reduce the value of Atlantic's stock and were introduced without notice shortly after the S&L went public last month with a stock offering.

Atlantic dropped the proposals Thursday, saying the chance of winning approval was "remote." But it countersued at the same time, claiming that I.R.E. and Levan secretly intended to seek control of the association. I.R.E. said it was only a "passive investor."

Levan and Donald V. Streeter, "negotiated our differences face-to-face," said Eugene E. Stearns, an attorney for I.R.E.

We Won!

IRE to acquire Atlantic shares

By L.A. HUGHES
Review Staff Writer

IRE Financial Corp. yesterday negotiated an option to acquire additional holdings in Atlantic Federal Savings and Loan Association from its old nemesis CenTrust Savings Bank, giving IRE controlling interest in the thrift.

"Fort Lauderdale-based Atlantic Federal, with its excellent Dade, Broward and Palm Beach franchise and its effective management organization has the means to create a profitable and stable statewide organization second to none," said IRE President Alan B. Levan in a written statement.

"Because Atlantic Federal and CenTrust have been adversaries in the past, we felt it important to attempt to purchase this block in order to eliminate a source of continuing conflict."

Levan has served on Atlantic's board of directors for about a year and is chairman of Atlantic's executive board.

Purchase of additional stock may be in the offing. "At this point there is no firm plan," said IRE corporate spokesman Marty Seigel.

"We hope we will, in the future obtain the right to acquire additional shares," Seigel said.

IRE paid CenTrust an option fee of $530,000. The exercise price for the 289,700 shares is $15.17 per share — 100 percent of the stocks' book value.

The transaction is pending approval of the Federal Home Loan Bank Board.

CHAPTER 12

CHANGE OF CONTROL: BEHOLD BANKATLANTIC!

"I am a great believer in luck. The harder I work,
the more of it I seem to have."
—Coleman Cox

Before David Paul's dishonorable discharge from the banking industry, he would make another appearance in my life. He had not yet attempted to rob his final bank, but was about to draw his gun on another one. Just like my old junior high and high school nemesis Nick, whose presence I'd ultimately taken great pains to avoid by enrolling in a university more than 850 miles away, for a long time Paul became the proverbial itch (or more accurately rash) I could not scratch.

But first…there are dreams we occasionally have when we seem to be someplace else, and we are there without a purpose. We wonder what we're doing, kind of going through the motions, with people who don't look at us or are unresponsive, or seem to be in another world altogether. That's pretty much what happened at my first Atlantic Federal board of directors meeting.

While I did know why I was there, and I certainly had a purpose, I was treated as though I weren't there at all. I was new on the board, sitting at a large, horseshoe-shaped conference table with Don Streeter and the rest of the directors. They were cordial and pleasant but in a detached, glad-handing kind of way. They were definitely guarded, maybe suspicious, often avoiding eye contact. I tried to engage them but to little avail. So I passed the first few minutes by noting the overhead projector, standard at pre-PowerPoint meetings like this, and fingering the notebook and brief agenda placed before me. I leafed through a copy of the financial reports at my place and picked up a pen, poised to take notes. Streeter and CFO Gerry Roberts proceeded to go through some numbers for the month, shown on the overhead projector, and adjourned the meeting. It was quick—just like that. There was no discussion about the future or even the near future—like next week. Atlantic Federal was bleeding with large losses and capital depleting, and there was no talk of planning. The proceedings lasted only an hour and the result, in simple terms, was a dry meeting. The agenda didn't provide a hint about what was really going on in the belly of Atlantic Federal. I asked if I could take the financial reports with me to study, as they'd not been provided well ahead of the meeting, which is how it's usually done, and was told they could not leave the boardroom. *What?* And instead of a routine monthly meeting, I was told the next board of directors meeting wouldn't be held for three more months. Again, *what?* What was going on here?

I later ascertained board meetings were indeed held monthly until I came on the scene. I was the only board member not on the executive committee, and Streeter had suggested to the rest of the board that it conduct all of its key business in executive committee meetings, which would now occur monthly, in lieu of having more frequent board meetings at which I'd be present.

I knew I'd come to the institution in an unorthodox way. It was certainly adversarial, but I'd made it clear my intentions were not hostile. In fact they were honorable. I felt privileged to be on the board and wanted to help. The fact is Atlantic Federal had been the aggressor, suing my company twice: once when we'd revealed through requisite SEC Schedule 13D that we'd acquired 9.9 percent of its stock, and once because we'd taken issue with its failure to disclose a bylaw change that would negatively impact I.R.E. and all shareholders. I was not an aggressor, only believing Atlantic Federal needed an adjustment to keep it viable, something I was confident I could provide assistance.

Sometimes it's hard to get people's attention, especially when they are working hard at avoiding you. At one point in my career I sent flowers to someone who was avoiding my calls. I filled out the card to say something to the effect of, "You must be really ill, because you've not returned half a dozen calls." It got his attention and a big laugh, but I wasn't about to send flowers to every member of the Atlantic Federal board of directors. They *definitely* weren't sick—just sick of me and they didn't even know me yet.

On the drive home to Miami, I decided the only way I'd be able to ferret out what was going on at Atlantic Federal and effect any change would be to make frequent appearances. So I made appointments to meet with the management team, and I walked around introducing myself to employees in order to gain their confidence. I wanted them to feel comfortable speaking from the heart about their observations. Without the benefit of people's experiences, what they believed were the institution's various strengths and weaknesses, fixing a downed S&L the way I really wanted to would not be possible. I didn't want to perform a patch job; I wanted to fill the plane with fuel and make it fly again.

On the other hand, it's important to note that my goal here (or anywhere at any time in my career) was not to surround myself with like-minded people. I believe the greatest disservice and impediment to growth—both personal and professional—is for people at the top to surround themselves with people that think the same way, or say they do, just to keep their jobs. Maybe the fact that I favored philosophy at Tulane means that the way I operate is rooted in logic. I put strong emphasis on making a logical choice or decision but in order to do that, one has to acquire a lot of information, perhaps some of it conflicting, from different sources with different experiences and points of view. I actually sought out people who did things differently—who challenged the way I thought or did things. So it wasn't necessarily that I was looking for sameness or symmetry of thought; I just wanted to know the management team and for them to know me.

Over the next month I went to Atlantic Federal several times. My first meeting was with CFO Gerry Roberts. While I'd not exactly been bowled over by him at the board meeting, his assistant, Jean Carvalho, impressed me to no end. Jean was as warm, welcoming, and engaging as she was professional—clearly the first person to be happy I was there. Her dedication and joy—about most everything—was infectious. In time she would become an executive vice president and valued member of my executive management committee, in charge of customer service and employee relations. When she passed away in July of 2017, it was as though my family had lost a member of its own.

During my meeting with Gerry, I asked how the bank determined the differing rates paid on one-, three-, six-, and twelve-month savings accounts, as well as two-, three-, four-, and five-year accounts. From the outside it seemed complicated and I figured there was some sort of alchemy to it.

"I know you post these on sign boards in the branches once a month," I said to him, admitting my ignorance of the process, "and I need some help understanding the formula." I was vitally interested because even during my time at Morgan Guaranty, I never knew how financial institutions came up with these rates.

In an instant, the guardedness I'd seen at the board meeting disappeared. Gerry flung the cuirass to the floor. He was a free man, chest broadening and eyes shining with pride. I guess he decided he could be of service to me. He knew his job and could demonstrate the knowledge intrinsic to it. He was about to let me in—to reveal the secret in the sauce. I was all eyes and ears.

"Come this way," he said, motioning me over to a table with a copy of the *Ft. Lauderdale Sun-Sentinel*. He opened to the financial page, pointing to all the banks listed and tracing the rate columns with his finger. Atlantic Federal was near the top and he was clearly pleased about that.

"It's simple," he said. "I just look at this page once a week and make sure our rates are a little higher than the highest rates at all the other banks. We want to keep the money we have and we want to attract more money, so we just pay a little more in all the different categories."

I couldn't believe what I was hearing. A $2 billion institution operating with a newspaper page as a blueprint? I didn't have a black belt in banking (not even close), but there had to be more science behind the way things worked than that.

In the next few weeks I met individually with each member of the management team. They were all extremely nice individuals but not sophisticated and business-savvy in the way they needed to be. The informal, maybe lackadaisical nature of those in the S&L industry would reveal itself to me over and over as time went by. I thought back to the Shepard Broad days. I knew what he'd faced in light of deregulation and his bank's potential demise, and I now had a deeper understanding of why he'd recruited someone like me with a reputation for innovating and getting things done.

At the next board meeting I was as delicate and diplomatic as I could be when suggesting the S&L might need some fresh ideas. Though it was early in the process, I'd developed a few, which I believed had the potential to begin to turn the institution around. But I had to find a way to make sure they were implemented despite a distrusting board.

Jack of His Trade

"You're not going to believe what I have to say, but just listen carefully." It was Gene Stearns on the phone, and I couldn't quite tell by his voice if this was going to be something for which I should break out the filet mignon. I don't drink, and I would become a vegetarian about ten years later, but back then I was a card-carrying carnivore so I'd sometimes celebrate good news with a hearty meal shared with colleagues or friends. Or, was the information Gene was about to share something for which I should brace myself? I wasn't sure so held my breath.

"I've got this really good friend named Jack Abdo who lives in Fort Lauderdale," he continued. Though they didn't know each other directly in college, I learned they'd known about each other that far back as they attended Florida State University at the same time. Gene eventually handled a securities case for Jack in the early 1970s. "He's a very successful homebuilder, absolutely brilliant, and interestingly he bought 4.9 percent shares of Atlantic Federal in the public offering," Gene said.

He went on to explain that Jack Abdo had been in Fort Lauderdale nearly all his life, and as it turned out knew almost every member of Atlantic Federal's board of directors personally and socially. "Coincidentally, Don Streeter just asked him if he'd be interested in joining the board," Gene informed me.

I exhaled, flashing on the possibilities this scenario presented, all of which Gene corroborated. He affirmed Jack would be a tremendous asset—a kind of mediator, if necessary, and certainly an ambassador of goodwill between the rest of board and me. He said when Streeter calls me to see if I would approve Jack, as he'd do with all board members, I should say yes without reservation. It all sounded good—actually maybe great. I couldn't believe my luck, though I have always believed luck is earned. It had been a long battle with Atlantic Federal and maybe luck's time had come.

Jack was approved, and at the next board meeting I met him for the first time. He immediately struck me as being quite sophisticated about business and other matters, and from that moment on we became the best of friends. The beginning of our friendship also marked the beginning of a lifelong partnership.

Jack, Gene, and I met to discuss Atlantic Federal soon after over lunch at the Banker's Club in Miami, and Jack and I got together a number of times after that first lunch, all independent of structured board meetings. At an S&L convention at the Breakers in Palm Beach, we really seemed to bond over dinner. Turns out we had a common upbringing by loving, caring parents closely tied to their immigrant roots—parents whose children meant more to them than anything. Well into the future, when his mother passed away in 1997, any opportunity he had to attend to my mother, Pearl, until her passing in 2015 was a chance for him to be with his mother again, or so he would tell me repeatedly.

Jack and I discovered we'd begun to orbit one another twenty-five years earlier as ushers at different movie theaters (*Where the Boys Are*—remember?) around the same time, though we didn't know one another. From an early age, both of us thrived on hard work and lots of it. We also lived for the real estate industry. The more we talked, the more we understood that our lives paralleled each other in so many ways. Over time we were destined to become as close as brothers could ever be. Symbiotic only scratches the surface of the kind of relationship we have to this day, both in business and as friends.

Jack was a kind of unofficial Fort Lauderdale and Broward County historian, having grown up in the area. He also had an exceptional memory. Because he was in real estate development, he could look at a site, perhaps with a restaurant that had been there for fifteen or twenty years, and recall what was there before...and even before that. Jack knew and retained detail upon detail upon detail, sharing a great deal with me about Atlantic Federal's history. I filed it all away and I owed him a tremendous debt of gratitude.

One day at the beginning of our association, we took a drive through a large residential development he'd built because I'd asked to see some of his work. When residents recognized the car, and who was driving, they lined up to wave and even blow Jack kisses. It was an incredible scene for buyers to appreciate their builder several years later. I'd never seen anything like it. Apparently he was more than respected—truly beloved for the quality of work he did and the way he treated people. A real estate rock star.

Jack never hesitated to tell me when he thought something was wrong, or he flat out didn't like something. He called the Tigertail Park Boulevard warehouses I'd built more than a decade earlier (please see chapter 5) "God awful" and worse. There is an expletive there, which is how much he hated them! Jack was all about quality and aesthetics. When he realized he'd hurt my feelings he backpedaled a bit, later telling me he felt terrible. But we had the kind of relationship where we could talk about anything with one another. Conversation, good or bad, only fueled the reasons for our association, of which there would be many over time.

As I tried to immerse myself with the other directors, I was trying to demonstrate I was just one of the guys. During the S&L conference I referred to earlier, I had a conflict with an I.R.E. real estate negotiation in Dallas going on at the same time. I wanted to attend the conference, but I also needed to be in Dallas. In order to do both, I attended the conference in the morning and when the S&L participants went off to play golf, I flew to Dallas to participate in the real estate negotiations. Then, I would fly back on the last flight in the evening so I could be at the S&L conference in the morning. I did that twice within the two-day conference. Often times, people are put off by how hard I work. Accordingly, I didn't tell anyone other than Jack that I took four airplanes to attend a conference twenty-five miles from the bank's main office.

As expected, Jack worked his diplomatic magic with the board, explaining that I wanted to learn as much as I could, which would only serve to empower the institution. One by one the directors came to me and expressed their concerns, chief among them that Atlantic Federal was vulnerable to a takeover by a Northeastern bank or David Paul and CenTrust. They asked me to work to keep them independent, giving me more and more responsibility, asking me to do committee work.

My Fault; My Fault; My Fault Again

One of the so-called chinks in the armor was my relationship with Don Streeter. He had never warmed up to me. There was a lot of animosity due to our adversarial history, and it was difficult for him to subordinate all that to the cause and trust me. I'm not sure I blamed him as we are all human—not machines—not devoid of feeling—but I needed to make sure we could at least live with one another. Thankfully, Jack and some of the board members suggested an idea to repair my relationship with him in a different kind of way.

In addition to his predilection for golf, Streeter was a competitive tennis player. Jack suggested we have a tennis tournament with him and Charlie Winningham, a tennis-playing board member. The idea was for Streeter and me to be doubles partners, and Jack and Charlie would throw the match, which would create a bond between the two members of Team Streeter-Levan.

Jack had a court behind his house and we all showed up ready to play, except for one small thing. I did not play regularly (in fact, I needed to go shopping for tennis clothes and sneakers and had required a lot of help from the salesperson). The match started with a lot of rah-rah, but unfortunately, I could not hit the ball over the net. In tennis, you switch sides in odd games, and as I was crossing the net after the third game, Jack and I crossed on the same side. He motioned to me, somewhat surreptitiously, telling me Streeter and I could not win the game, let alone the match, if I could not get the darned ball over the net! In fact Jack and Charlie were so bent on paving the way for us to win, they did their level best to hit many of their shots out of bounds, and/or directly into the net (as I did, only I didn't do it on purpose). Maybe it was adrenaline or a nod from the gods who showed a little sympathy to the suffering, but I was finally equal to the task. Streeter and I "won," which served to cement our relationship, somewhat, though I wasn't sure it could ever be strong. Unfortunately I was right.

I'd only been involved with Atlantic Federal a few months and another opportunity had presented itself. This was a big one. In time, the board asked if I would consider becoming chairman and CEO. Many times I silently thanked Shepard Broad for introducing me to the inner workings of the banking world. While I'd ultimately lost out in acquiring his institution, I had learned enough to sound reasonably intelligent to these board members, and enough to begin to formulate ideas about saving Atlantic Federal. This couldn't happen right away because it would take regulatory approval for I.R.E. to control Atlantic Federal, but they asked me to consider it so I went ahead and filed a regulatory application for change of control. After Shepard Broad and American Savings, I never figured on being asked again to control a huge financial institution. I was learning a lot about myself that I didn't know, which was both challenging and exhilarating.

The task now firmly at hand was for me to fix Atlantic Federal. I could not go out and raise capital until we got a change of control. No one would consider giving us money until they knew what the use of the money would be, and with an application for change of control out there, there were too many variables.

I was able to hire a recruiter and purge the management team. I was in a position to terminate CEO and president Don Streeter, which the board had wanted and with which I wholeheartedly agreed, and hire someone to serve as the face of the bank, in the role of president. If our application for change of control was approved,

I'd be able to step in as chairman and CEO. I also only hired people from commercial banks for management positions, people who had a different mindset—different conditioning, not individuals from sleepy S&Ls. Getting competent managers to leave thriving commercial banks for a drowning savings and loan was no easy feat. Granted, this was a $2 billion dollar financial institution with fifty branches, so there was some catnip there, but I needed to be absolutely sure I staffed it with commercial banking experts no matter what it took.

I did make an exception for my first hire. Though he came from a savings and loan, Lew Sarrica was just the expert I was looking for. An executive officer from Dollar Dry Dock Savings Bank in New York—a multibillion-dollar institution formed from a merger between Dollar Savings Bank and Dry Dock Savings—Lew was an extremely knowledgeable investment officer. I knew he'd be a strong asset despite his professional provenance. Ultimately, in addition to Lew, I was successful in completing my management team.

Along with improved staffing, among the early changes I made was to stop advertising savings rates in the branches. No more rate boards. We had fifty branches and I wanted customers to do business with us because of outstanding customer service—not strictly because of high deposit rates. Commercial banks thrived on customer service and low rates, and it was a model I wanted to emulate. They also offered checking accounts and all sorts of products, all again with that strong customer service, so their customers would opt for a variety of deposit products and personal investments. A couple of points on an interest rate were not as important as feeling good and secure about where one is banking.

The high rate–seeking depositors fled to the hills. This in turn reduced the amount of deposits from $2.3 billion to $1.3 billion. I also closed thirty branches. The hot, high-rate money was running off and we were now selling customer service instead of high rates. Even though we had $1 billion less in deposits, our costs went down so dramatically from interest and expense reductions that we were now making money. We never went back to posting rates and ultimately built the best branch and deposit system at the lowest rates in the entire state of Florida.

Though I could not yet raise capital in the traditional way through investment bankers, due to the pending application constraints, somehow we had to focus on capital. The bank had initially raised $25 million in its mutual conversion and public offering, but I didn't think it provided enough of a rainy day fund if the market collapsed again. Based on my history of raising investor money, we rolled out a $25 million subordinated debt offering. We sold it in the branches to our customers as an alternative, non-insured interest-bearing product and it was fully subscribed. I personally trained the branch personnel how to sell it. This was one of the few, perhaps if not the only, debenture offering in the country ever sold directly in the branches and without investment bankers. In those days, subordinated debt served as capital, so it gave us an extra cushion that was ultimately needed.

Next up was asset/liability management. Since we had solved the deposit problem by reducing the rates we were paying, which was the liability side of the balance sheet, we now had to fix the asset side. We were able to do this by inducing and incenting our borrowers to pay off their thirty-year fixed low-rate mortgages early and by making adjustable-rate mortgages king.

In summary, we had a new management team focused on customer service. We reduced savings rates, got rid of the majority of long term fixed-rate mortgages, built capital, and offered other loan products such as short-term mortgages to build profitability.

Meanwhile our change of control application was still pending with the regulators, and I couldn't officially become chairman and CEO until it was approved. The approval process dragged on because the regulators did not like having real estate people as head of their banks. Real estate people, although entrepreneurial, tended to operate by the seat of their pants instead of professional management. We kept telling the regulators that we were professional operators and had all this substantial public company experience with our partnerships, but the wheels turned slowly. It didn't help that there were multiple better capitalized parties over the next three years that tried to take the Atlantic Federal opportunity away from us by filing lawsuits, launching hostile proxies, and complaining to regulators.

Let the Games Begin

The most troubling of these challengers and agitators was CenTrust. At our first annual public shareholder meeting, CenTrust put up a new slate of directors. David Paul was fuming that he had introduced me to Atlantic Federal and it had backfired. Now I was the one filing the change of control application, not him. We were in a battle of proxies and certainly wits. Again I hired Georgeson, specifically Donna Ackerly, to assist us with proxy solicitation. It was coming down to the wire and voting was very close. We set up a war room at Atlantic Federal, staffed with employees who were calling other employees and even former employees, who owned just a few shares from the original offering. As the actual meeting day arrived it was going to be very close and every vote counted.

At the meeting, before the votes were counted, Paul criticized management for expenses being too high. Lib Ginestra, a typically quiet and demure board member, had had enough of Paul, stood up, and let him have it. "You come here and criticize our operations and you bring five expensive lawyers with you," she declared. "Talk about wasting money!" We were all very proud of her as we squeaked by with a narrow win.

Just so this proxy issue didn't happen again, I negotiated with Paul to take an option on his 9.1 percent stake. We would buy it upon our application receiving regulatory approval. I also took an option on Freedom Savings 9.1 percent. I anticipated now with about 25 percent either owned or under option, our approval would be smooth sailing. Of course, at some point, I was going to have to figure out how I was going to pay for the purchase of all these shares.

A few months later I got a call from the next challenger, so to speak, Dr. M. Lee Pearce. Pearce was a very wealthy and highly successful doctor-attorney in South Florida. Aside from his reputation in the medical and legal communities, he'd made a name for himself as an activist shareholder à la Carl Icahn. He told me he'd acquired 4.9 percent of Atlantic Federal and I should buy him out at a premium price. I knew exactly what he was doing, per my PLI seminar and the brief foray I'd taken into that world, but told him that since I.R.E. already controlled about 25 percent I didn't need his shares. While it was not a majority, I thought it was sufficient. Besides, I didn't have the money to buy him out. He said that was a mistake and I would regret that decision.

About a month later he called again, explaining he'd now acquired 9.9 percent of Atlantic Federal and I.R.E. should buy him out. He had become more of a nuisance and clearly a threat. I had a pleasant conversation with him but told him the same thing I'd said before. I didn't need his shares, they were too expensive, and I didn't have the money. He again said that I would regret that decision. At our next annual meeting, after we sent our proxy to the shareholders, Pearce launched a hostile proxy proposing one director. The unusual element about voting in the 1980s for the S&Ls is that voting was cumulative. A shareholder could spread his or her votes among all ten directors or cast all ten votes per share for one director. Since Pearce was only proposing one director, if he voted all his shares for the one director, he'd likely win that director seat. It was going to be a very close proxy fight—yet again.

As the meeting date approached, I heard a rumor that Pearce had purchased another 4.9 percent in someone else's name and that he could vote if he needed it. The reason he might not want to use it is because the regulators might determine that if his 9.9 percent and the 4.9 percent were voting as a block, it could be deemed to go over the 9.9 percent limit and become a regulatory issue for him. He'd be tangling with the SEC. But if he decided to take a chance and use the other 4.9 percent anyway, ignoring the possibility of a developing problem, there is no way we could have defeated him with his cumulative voting.

There was a lot of anticipation in the air on the day of the annual meeting. Gunter Ottenberg, from Southeast Bank, had been retained as custodian of the votes. In short his job was as official record keeper to tabulate the voting. The room was filled with lots of people in Pearce's camp, including lawyers, and lots of people in ours. I determined that if I could just get Pearce not to vote the 4.9 percent in his pocket, we had a good chance of winning.

I strategized not to vote I.R.E.'s 9.9 percent in advance and instead gave our proxy card to Jean Carvalho, who sat almost invisibly in the back of the room. After the meeting was called to order, Ottenberg rose and announced the total number of shares that had voted in advance, and that it constituted a quorum, with 70 percent of the outstanding shares represented, so the meeting could proceed. I could see Pearce's brain clicking that with the total number of shares at 70 percent of the outstanding shares voting, he was going to win his one seat—without pulling out his additional 4.9 percent, potentially putting him at risk later on.

In customary form, the chairman of the meeting asked if anyone present wanted to vote before the final votes were tabulated. I had asked one of the directors to chair the meeting. Jean Carvalho, in the back of the room, raised her hand, softly inquiring if this was the right time for her to vote her shares, just as we'd rehearsed it. Generally the only people who do that are the individual shareholders who have one hundred shares or fewer and want to vote them personally, as opposed to mailing them in advance. The chairman said yes, this was the time, and sent someone to the back of the room to pick up her ballot. Jean handed the person I.R.E.'s 9.9 percent proxy card in an envelope so no one could see the numbers or how she'd voted. She audibly thanked him for "being so kind as to come all the way to the back of the room" to collect her vote. It was a good performance in the event Pearce was listening. Ottenberg took the existing cards, plus Jean's card, to a private room to tally. I watched Pearce like a hawk and did not see him pull out the 4.9 percent proxy. We were squarely on track.

Ottenberg walked back into the room a few minutes later to announce the vote tallies. We had won.

Pearce jumped out of his seat, yelled foul, and said what happened was *impossible*. How could the total number votes have grown from 70 percent to 80 percent—more than 10 percent—from the quorum total to the actual total when only one additional person had submitted a proxy card? Ottenberg said it was correct and it was over, but Pearce demanded he go back and recount, a request Ottenberg obliged. Pearce sat there fuming the entire thirty minutes Ottenberg was gone, his round face purplish, cheeks puffing in and out. He was about to explode. His reaction was surely compounded by the fact that he had also filed a 40-page objection to our change of control application, likely as a kind of an activist shareholder vendetta because I would not acquiesce to any of his demands to buy back his stock at a premium.

When the tally came back the second time exactly the same, he complained to the SEC that we had rigged the vote. The SEC requested all voting cards be shipped to Washington, DC, where they were reviewed and sent back with the pronouncement there had been no impropriety. I subsequently called Pearce and negotiated an option to buy his shares. Surely, at 35 percent, I now had enough shares under control not to have to worry anymore. I just needed regulatory approval for the change of control and a plan to raise $15 million to buy all the shares I had under option. Time was running out, as the standard 18-month options I'd taken out were about to expire.

All in the Family

The change of control application had been gathering dust for more than two years. It had been delayed because of the proxy contests and the complaints by other bidders that I.R.E. was too small a company to acquire Atlantic Federal. Furthermore, regulators said, we were in the real estate business and they'd not had much success with real estate entrepreneurs acquiring their banks.

Under ordinary circumstances approval should not have taken more than nine months. If the options expired without our buying the shares, all would have been for naught. In time, the staff at the Office of Thrift Supervision in Atlanta, Atlantic Federal's regulators, told us we had ultimately convinced them of our worthiness and they had recommended approval several months ago, but the final stamp would need to come from OTS director Danny Wall in Washington, DC. The paperwork had been languishing on his desk.

As the director of the OTS is a presidential nominee, Gene suggested we visit Jeb Bush, then a Florida real estate developer. In fact Jeb lived in my neighborhood in South Miami with kids the same age as mine. Jeb's father, George Herbert Walker Bush, was at that time Vice President of the United States. We had a nice meeting with Jeb and I asked him if he could request that his father call over to Mr. Wall's office to inquire about the status of our application to change control. We made it clear his father didn't have to endorse or vouch for us in any way, just ask about the status. Jeb said he was reasonably sure his father would do that. The very next day Danny Wall signed the application for approval.

The only remaining issue was that we had to consummate the change of control within ninety days or the application would be nullified. This required the purchase of the optioned shares. I needed to find the $15 million and I needed it quickly. We were in a critical dash-for-cash mode.

I proceeded to knock on every Wall Street investment banking firm door to raise money for us but they didn't want to raise it for I.R.E., as a holding company, as opposed to directly for the savings and loan. That's just the way the thinking went. I finally secured a term sheet from E.F. Hutton—an eighty-year-old Wall Street Investment and Brokerage Company. The individual investment banker's name was Red Jahncke, and Alison and I headed to New York to negotiate the formal commitment letter. Red took us to lunch at the storied University Club, one of the last bastions of all male tradition, formed by a group of primarily Yale alumni in 1861. It was located on the second floor of a nine-story building. Red had made reservations for the three of us and we climbed a flight of burnished stairs to the second floor, approaching the maître d'.

"Mr. Jahncke," the maître d' began, eyeing our party. It was clear he had something on his mind. "I think you would be more comfortable in the first floor open restaurant." Red said no, that he wanted to sit up in the club. This pleasant but curious banter continued for a few minutes until the maître d' took Red aside, whispering something in his ear. I was oblivious as to what was going on, but Alison became more and more uneasy. The maître d' escorted us downstairs and we found a table in the first floor restaurant—open to the public.

Unable to control herself any longer, Alison blurted out, "This club is restricted as in 'No Women Allowed'! Isn't it?" Red sheepishly admitted it was true, though he'd never considered it when making the reservation. While his mistake was inadvertent, it was just one more jab with which we had to deal in our efforts to get our work done. To this day, Gene and I still talk about this indignity to Alison—a highly successful lawyer and respected leader in her profession—an affront we may not have considered as strongly at the time as we should have.

After E.F. Hutton signed the commitment letter, Red and I were scheduled to go city to city, branch to branch, to raise money from the E.F. Hutton retail offices, which was standard operating procedure. It was familiar territory for me because it was similar to the way we raised money for the limited partnerships, taking our dog and pony show on the road. The difference is this was a stock offering and E.F. Hutton was a big Wall Street wirehouse brokerage company in the same vein as Merrill Lynch.

Just before we left for our trip, however, another lawsuit showed up: Unicorp American, a large Canadian real estate conglomerate decided to crash our party. Red called me to say E.F. Hutton couldn't go forward because of Unicorp American, which owned shares in Atlantic Federal and was a very good client of E.F. Hutton. Red told me Unicorp had convinced E.F. Hutton to renege on its commitment to I.R.E. so the options would expire and Unicorp could buy Atlantic Federal itself.

Gene was crazed. He'd always said (and continues to say) I am more of a risk-taker than he is, but I'm not so sure. In his own profession he is no holds barred. At his home in his underwear, he tracked down E.F. Hutton's general counsel at 2:00 a.m., screaming into the phone that if they didn't go forward with our agreement, we would sue. "When this is over," he warned at 150 decibels, "I.R.E. will *own* E.F. Hutton for breach of commitment." By sunrise, E.F. Hutton had reconsidered its position. Gene had the Unicorp lawsuit dismissed with prejudice. I.R.E. took an option on the 9.7 percent Unicorp had accumulated. We now had almost 45 percent under option or owned. All we needed now was money to close the options and time was running out.

Red and I got on the road.

It was 1987, we were riding out another recession and unbelievably, E.F. Hutton was in trouble. At every E.F. Hutton branch we visited, we learned of another executive officer from the New York corporate office in the process of resigning or facing impending termination, including the president of E.F. Hutton. It was a highly chaotic and volatile environment, with E.F. Hutton imploding before our eyes, but we finally completed the task of raising $15,300 million out of the required $15,700 million. Al Nahmad, a friend, subscribed for the remainder. I.R.E. purchased all the options and completed the change of control prior to the deadline. I was now chairman and CEO of Atlantic Federal. Jack Abdo became our eminently qualified vice chairman. Mission accomplished.

Wrapping It Up

Gene gifted me with Perfection, a Hasbro board game with spring-loaded, odd-shaped pieces that had to be inserted and pushed down. Time was of the essence or they'd all pop out and you'd lose. Players had seconds to complete the task. Sound familiar? The "out of time" theme dominated my life! For a long time, hardly a year went by without a stay alive–type deadline staring me in the face, starting with the Hialeah land I sought to acquire and was unable to, the formation of I.R.E., right up to the ballad of Atlantic Federal. I never could have accomplished this without Jack, Gene, and Alison. Jack was a calming influence on the board. Gene was masterful in handling years of frivolous lawsuits. Alison did the securities work. I was proud to call them friends and colleagues then, as I am now. The four of us mastered the art of having a good time while getting the job done. Forty years later, we are still at it!

E.F. Hutton, caught up in a decades-long series of malfeasances and mergers, failed for all intents and purposes. Our offering was one of the last ones they completed. It eventually came back as EF Hutton America (sans the periods in the initials).

Unicorp American went broke as did Freedom Savings and Southeast Bank. CenTrust also went belly-up and David Paul went to prison. Overall about 1,400 of the S&Ls in the country were liquidated by the FDIC. Atlantic Federal survived and prospered.

Dr. M. Lee Pearce, despite his war cries and stunning defeat at the shareholder meeting that day, sent us a beautiful six-foot plant when we gained control of Atlantic Federal. Later on, he and I would find ourselves together again in another banking deal.

Sadly, Steve Arky, my close friend and attorney, and friend and law partner to Gene and Alison, committed suicide in 1984 at the age of forty-two. It would be impossible to describe the shock and grief we all experienced. One day we were all laughing and joking about conquests and then he was gone. It's a long story, but hard to understand the deep psychological pain some people go through. Unfortunately, none of us knew of Steve's personal demons until it was too late.

Following the change of control, we decided to change Atlantic Federal's name to BankAtlantic as we were emulating commercial banks. I wanted customers to think of us that way and not consider us the old S&L. I.R.E. became BankAtlantic Financial Corporation, or BFC—also an acronym for Building Foremost Companies.

Finally, just a few months after the upset at the University Club dining room, the old guard fell hard. In June of 1987, women were seated.

LIFE LESSONS LEARNED

- Surround yourself with good people.
- Good lawyers and relationships you can trust are crucial.
- Luck is earned.
- While timing may not be everything, it is extremely important.
- In business, if you have a good idea or opportunity, somebody always wants to imitate it or take it away. You have to think smarter and run faster.
- The ability to adjust to change in the economic environment is the key to survival—and prosperity.

CHANGE OF CONTROL: BEHOLD BANKATLANTIC!

Sun Sentinel
AM 82,000
Pompano Beach

AUG-12-85

Backer charts course for statewide S&L

Real estate magnate Alan B. Levan has big plans for Atlantic Federal of Fort Lauderdale, despite the loss of two key players on his IRE Financial Corp. management team.

By John G. Edwards
Business Writer

Can a real-estate magnate turn Fort Lauderdale-based Atlantic Federal Savings and Loan Association into the cornerstone of a thriving statewide network of S&Ls?

Alan B. Levan, whose IRE Financial Corp. controls a commanding share of Atlantic Federal stock, thinks he can. He believes the track record of IRE — despite the loss of two key players — speaks for itself.

A statewide network of S&L branches could ship funds from deposit-rich branches to regions where loan demand is brisk, according to Levan.

At the moment, however, Levan, 40, hasn't identified the expansion cities, hasn't applied for approval from government regulators, and is contending with Atlantic Federal's lackluster financial performance so far this year.

Eighteen months ago, IRE acquired stock in Heritage Federal of Daytona Beach, First Federal of Fort Myers and Atlantic Federal at a total cost of $6.65 million. The stocks' value has jumped to $12 million since then.

IRE, a Coral Gables-based company that sells and manages real-estate partnerships, has posted profit increases of 25 to 30 percent annually for each of the last six years. The $41 million-asset company earned $3 million, up from $2.7 million in the prior year.

Yet, the company has never paid a dividend to stockholders since going public in 1979.

"IRE is a growth company," Levan explained in an interview. "Rather than paying dividends, it reinvests its capital back in its business," said Levan, who took home $656,000 in cash compensation last year.

"IRE has been successful over the years, because it has extremely strong management," he said. "Its executives are well compensated and well motivated to produce profits for the shareholders."

A key IRE legal consultant, however, died this summer, and a major executive left the firm last year.

Stephen Arky, a merger and acquisition expert, committed suicide last month. Arky, 42, was reportedly despondent over his entanglements with failed ESM Government Securities Inc., a Fort Lauderdale-based company unrelated to IRE.

"Stephen Arky was an extremely close friend, a major adviser to our company and his death definitely leaves a void," Levan said. IRE today, however, relies on other attorneys "who know as much about the company as Stephen Arky did," Levan said.

Meanwhile, IRE was engaged on other fronts. The company disclosed plans in January 1984 to pay $9 million for Sunset Commercial Bank of Miami and to convert it into a savings and loan.

But the former Dade Savings and Loan Association of Miami, now known as CenTrust Savings Bank, filed objections with the Florida Department of Banking. Nine months later, IRE dropped plans to acquire Sunset.

Levan said he believes the best opportunities are in S&Ls, not commercial banks. And he wants to diversify so IRE's fortunes don't depend so much on the real-estate investment market.

When 13 Florida S&Ls made their first public stock offerings in late 1983, IRE got a chance to enter the thrift industry as an investor.

Within three months, IRE had invested a total of $6.65 million and held 9.9 percent of the outstanding stock of Atlantic Federal, Heritage Federal of Daytona Beach and First Federal of Fort Myers. Today, the stock has a market value of approximately $12 million.

Last week, American Pioneer Savings Bank of Orlando agreed to acquire Heritage Federal. Levan hasn't decided what to do with the First Federal stock. And IRE last week obtained an option to increase its ownership share in Atlantic Federal to 20 percent.

Levan hopes to acquire additional Atlantic Federal shares and launch an expansion program in Florida by acquiring existing thrifts and opening new branches.

By keeping the S&L headquartered in Fort Lauderdale, he thinks Atlantic Federal will enjoy an advantage over competitors that are moving their headquarters out-of-state.

"No matter how large we get, we will be able to make decisions at the customer level in Florida," Levan said. "We see that . . . as a remarkable opportunity for us, because our major competitors are almost all merging out of state, which gets the point of control far from the customer."

David L. Paul, board chairman of Miami-based CenTrust Savings Bank, which last week sold IRE the option on additional Atlantic Federal stock, questions Levan's expansion plan.

"You can't just rush off into the world without having the permission of the regulators," he said.

Others pointed to Atlantic Federal's anemic earnings as a hindrance. Atlantic Federal, a $1.7 billion-asset institution with 50 branches, reported last Friday that it had earned $60,000 in the first six months vs. $1.1 million a year ago.

"Atlantic Federal started doing things that will allow it to turn that around and turn it into a profitable institution," said Erwin I. Katz, president of Williams Securities Group Inc. in Tampa.

As for expansion, Katz said, "opportunities are going to present themselves." He called Levan "an astute business person" and IRE "a creative company."

Staff photo by JOHN CURRY
Alan B. Levan wants Atlantic Federal Savings & Loan to branch out statewide.

IRE FINANCIAL CORP.

IRE FINANCIAL CORP. is a publicly held, national financial services firm headquartered in Coral Gables that sponsors limited-partnership investment programs and acquires, manages and sells commercial properties on behalf of partnership portfolios.

The company reported revenues of $11.3 million in 1984 compared to $10.3 million in 1983 and $8.5 million in 1982. Net earnings were: $3 million in 1984, $2.7 million in 1983 and $1.5 million in 1982. Earnings per share were 44 cents, 41 cents, and 23 cents, respectively.

Total assets increased from $36.13 million in 1980 to $40.81 million in 1984.

SOURCE: IRE annual report

SEEING AROUND CORNERS

PAGE 35
WEDNESDAY, DECEMBER 11, 1985

THE WALL STREET JOURNAL.

© 1985 Dow Jones & Company, Inc. All Rights Reserved.

*IRE Plans to Make
Atlantic Federal S&L
Major Florida Player*

I.R.E. Planning Takeover of Atlantic Federal Thrift

Sun-Sentinel **Business** Tuesday, Nov. 19, 1985

Second bidder going after Atlantic Federal

First Centrust, now Dr. Pearce

34 THE WALL STREET JOURNAL WEDNESDAY, APRIL 9, 1986

IRE Financial Signs Option to Buy Stake In Atlantic Federal

By a WALL STREET JOURNAL Staff Reporter
CORAL GABLES, Fla.—I.R.E. Financial Corp. said it signed an option to buy Investor M. Lee Pearce's 9.8% stake in Atlantic Federal Savings & Loan Association of Fort Lauderdale for $16.67 a share.

*We Won again!
IRE takes option
of Pearce's shares.*

SEP-3 -86

Bidder for Atlantic Federal sues IRE's Levan

By JOHN G. EDWARDS

Another bidder. Unicorp now sues IRE.

Miami Herald
AM 450,000
Sun 540,000

AUG-21-86

Canadian investor bids for Atlantic

It's Broward S&L's 2nd offer in year

By DAVID SATTERFIELD
Herald Business Writer

A New York company controlled by a Canadian investor offered Wednesday to pay $21 a share, or $64.3 million, for Atlantic Federal Savings and Loan Association in Fort Lauderdale.

Ft. Lauderdale News
PM 129,000
Sun 238,000

AUG-21-86

Atlantic Federal has new bidder

By JOHN G. EDWARDS
Business Writer

Atlantic Federal Savings and Loan Association of Fort Lauderdale said Wednesday that a New York-based company has sent it the highest, written buyout offer yet.

Wall St. Journal
AM 2,100,000
New York

OCT-21-86

Unicorp Sues Board Of Atlantic Federal For 'Rejecting' Bid

By a WALL STREET JOURNAL *Staff Reporter*

NEW YORK—Unicorp American Corp., which has proposed to buy Atlantic Federal Savings & Loan Association of Fort Lauderdale, Fla., sued the thrift's board for failing to endorse its bid.

SEP-21-87

BANKING

Frustrated Unicorp loses fight to I.R.E.

Now for the conclusion of our continuing story, *Levan's Hope* . . . .

You may recall that when last we visited our little *menage a trois* about a year ago, Unicorp American Corp., a New York-based subsidiary of Unicorp Canada Corp. of Toronto, and Coral Gables-based I.R.E. Financial Corp. were locked in a heated battle for control of Atlantic Federal Savings & Loan Association of Fort Lauderdale.

You may also remember that both Unicorp American and I.R.E. Financial are real estate investment/financial services firms. And they both are controlled by strong chairmen — Unicorp by Canadian financier George S. Mann, and I.R.E. by Alan B. Levan.

*We Win Again! Centrust, Dr. Pearce
and Unicorp are history.*

Sun Sentinel
AM 151,000
Pompano Beach

FEB-10-87

Unicorp bows out of fight for Atlantic Federal

A federal magistrate in January recommended dismissing Unicorp's lawsuit against rival bidder IRE Financial Corp., which IRE's president said led Unicorp to consider a settlement.

Sun-Sentinel **Business** Wednesday, April 9, 1986 D

IRE wins bidding for Atlantic Federal

The Miami Herald

Business News

Friday, January 30, 1987　　　　The Miami Herald　　　　4C

I.R.E. can buy Atlantic Federal

By DAVID SATTERFIELD
Herald Business Writer

After a turbulent 16-month wait, Coral Gables-based I.R.E. Corp. received federal approval Thursday to acquire control of Atlantic Federal Savings and Loan Association, a Fort Lauderdale thrift with $1.9 billion in assets.

The Federal Home Loan Bank Board gave I.R.E. permission to exercise options it holds on 34.3 percent of Atlantic Federal stock. I.R.E. already owns 9.4 percent of the stock.

Exercising the options will cost I.R.E. about $15 million, a spokesman said. The company plans to raise that money through a common stock offering.

The deal will give I.R.E., formerly a real estate syndicator, control of Atlantic Federal and a 44 percent share in the S&L's annual earnings. It also will help the firm diversify beyond real estate, which has been hurt in recent years by oversupply and tax reform.

"I.R.E. is now a savings and loan holding company," said company chairman Alan Levan. "Atlantic Federal has made a dramatic turnaround. We are every bit as excited as we were when we made our initial investment."

I.R.E.'s federal approval came just days after Unicorp American Corp., the New York firm that tried to buy Atlantic Federal last year, revealed in filings with regulators that it may sell its Atlantic Federal stock to help finance its proposed acquisition of a New York savings bank. Unicorp

Please turn to **I.R.E./5C**

I.R.E. wins OK to buy Atlantic Federal

I.R.E./*from 4C*

owns 9.9 percent of Atlantic Federal stock.

Last October, Atlantic Federal's board of directors, which includes I.R.E.'s Levan, rejected Unicorp's $21 a share, or $65 million, buyout offer. Unicorp responded by suing Atlantic Federal, charging that Levan has been running the company without regulatory approval. But Unicorp appeared prepared to drop their bid.

"We are actively working with Lincoln Savings [a $2.3 billion-asset New York thrift] on a friendly basis," said Laurie Becker, lawyer for Unicorp. She said Unicorp would not pursue Atlantic Federal if it acquired Lincoln Savings.

Unicorp's offer to buy Atlantic Federal wasn't the first in recent years. In November 1985, the board also rejected an $15.50 per share offer by Miami physician and financier M. Lee Pearce, who subsequently agreed to sell his stock to I.R.E. The company also had an unfriendly fight over CenTrust Savings Bank and its chairman David Paul.

In the past year, lower interest rates and new management have revived Atlantic Federal, a traditionally conservative institution. For its fiscal year ended Sept. 30, Atlantic Federal earned $9.52 million, or $3.11 per share, compared with a loss of $1.6 million in the previous year.

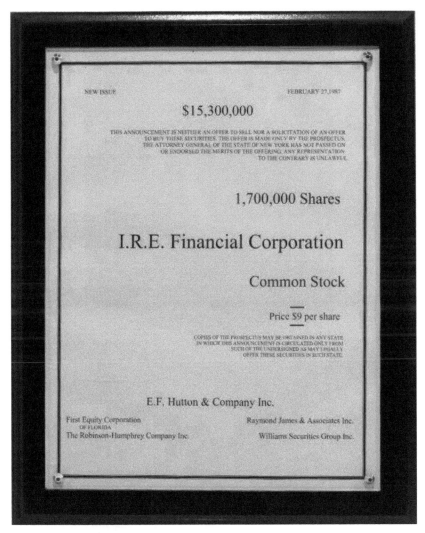

Stock offering to acquire Atlanta Federal, February 27, 1989.

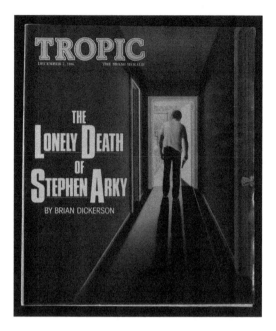

TROPIC

DECEMBER 7, 1986   THE MIAMI HERALD

THE
LONELY DEATH
OF
STEPHEN ARKY

BY BRIAN DICKERSON

DEC-29-87

Atlantic Federal hoists signs with new name, BankAtlantic

By LANE KELLEY
Business Writer

The name change for Atlantic Federal Savings and Loan Association in Fort Lauderdale became official on Monday, with new signs going up for BankAtlantic.

The new name for the state's 10th-largest thrift follows a previously announced name change for its majority owner, I.R.E. Financial Corp. in Coral Gables, which is changing its name to BankAtlantic Financial Corp.

The name change also represents an effort to identify with the banking industry and not the thrift industry. Alan B. Levan, BankAtlantic's chairman and chief executive officer, said the change more accurately depicts the services offered by the thrift, which have expanded beyond traditional home mortgages into home equity and consumer loans, full-service checking and commercial and corporate lending.

"The name change merely reflects an expansion of our business into a number of banking products," Levan said.

The name change should cause no inconvenience or interruption of service to the thrift's customers, said N. Mark Wright, BankAtlantic's president and chief operating officer.

"Checks, deposit slips, passbooks, certificates of deposit and other documents and printed materials remain valid and need not be returned or exchanged," Wright said. BankAtlantic accounts continue to be insured by the FSLIC for up to $100,000.

Last week, Levan announced that his firm would merge with the thrift in a deal giving the thrift's shareholders at least 2.5 shares of I.R.E. stock for every share of Atlantic Federal.

Levan will pay less for the thrift's stock than he had previously agreed to pay if that deal receives the necessary approvals

from shareholders and regulatory officials.

Earlier this year, Levan signed an agreement to pay at least $18 a share for the thrift's remaining stock within 12 months after acquiring control. But in mid-November, Levan said that agreement had been affected by October's stock market crash, or what he called "present market conditions."

Levan said the recent merger agreement between the two institutions should give the thrift's shareholders more than $13 a share for their stock, which is approximately what the stock has been trading for on the NASDAQ National Market System.

Levan said the merger agreement is fair to stockholders on both sides.

BankAtlantic has assets of $2.1 billion, two regional mortgage centers and 49 banking offices in Broward, Palm Beach and Dade counties.

CHAPTER 13

MARRIAGE: PARTY OF SEVEN

"I may not be your first date, your first kiss,
your first love or even your first marriage.
I just want to be your last everything."
—Anonymous

Divorce is never simple and a second marriage can be even more complicated when children are the primary concern. For them, issues of loyalty abound. Terri and I separated in 1986 and the next few years were a balancing act, both in terms of emotions and geography, until our divorce in late 1987. I was no longer living at home and though I.R.E. was in Miami, much of my business was now with BankAtlantic in Fort Lauderdale.

With all that my family had gone through, I did not want to upend things even more by moving out of Miami and nearly an hour away. Had I done so, I'd not have gotten to see my children every day when I drove them to school and attended school activities, sports, and other events. Terri and I believed our children needed both of their parents and I felt my several-hour roundtrip daily commute was a small price to pay. Though I was not down the hall in the master bedroom, or in the kitchen every morning, I stayed very close to my family's Coral Gables home—in fact in a neighborhood not far away.

Susie was never going to replace my children's biological mother and in the same realm I was never going to replace her children's father. That was not our goal. I was delighted to have two more children! Gina was eighteen, the older of Susie's two, and had moved out on her own. Lauren was seven and lived with us.

A second marriage can be fraught with challenges but we were determined to work through them. And we were completely in love. With Susie, I was swinging on the wrought iron gates again. We were also realistic and planned our September 2, 1988 wedding weekend with all five of our combined children in mind. The ceremony was a small gathering of family at our temple and then a reception at our house. Our honeymoon was close by at Marco Island, about two hours from Miami on Florida's west coast. We invited all five of our children and asked each to bring a friend. Our "Honeymoon for Twelve" was quite a spectacle and we had an outstanding time.

We had loaded ourselves up with lots of kid food (parlance for edible but sugary, gooey snacks) plus bagels and cream cheese for breakfast to last the weekend. We also snuck in an "illegal" toaster oven, which smoked continuously. It set off the alarm half a dozen times. Though we feared being asked to leave the Marriott resort, we could count on the burnt bagels and screeching smoke detector to elicit uncontrollable laughter from our kids—every time. Donny did an exemplary job of unwittingly locking people out of adjoining rooms, where the resort even had to call a locksmith to open doors, which made for more jokes and fun among the children.

The pool, the beach, and the game room opened other doors to lots of diverse activities and adventures—including the rented pontoon boat whose engine died in the Gulf of Mexico. Who says that if no one gets hurt, in the right frame of mind rescue can't be fun. It was! For me the adage about "happy wife; happy life," was only part of the picture. "Happy children; happy life" was just as important—to both Susie and me.

In fact, we never referred to Gina, Donny, Shelley, Jarett, and Lauren as stepchildren, as we believed that established some kind of label we never wanted for them. And they would call us whatever made them comfortable. The concept of a blended family, while not without its share of confusion, was somewhat easier because the children had known each other pretty much all their lives.

Susie, hired by Norman Silber to be my secretary in 1972, had progressed through the I.R.E. ranks for sixteen years and was now a senior executive at the company. While love and our personal relationship came slowly, our connection was undeniable. We were friends, business associates, and now we got to be together to live to our fullest potential in every respect.

There had been many occasions over the years when the families had been together. Donny and Gina were six months apart in age and had often played together on the office floor.

Gina had decided to live and work in Miami Beach for a while before enrolling in college. She attended University of Miami and graduated with concentrations in graphic design and marketing. She is now a marketing consultant for developers focusing on condominium development.

Lauren was seven at the time of our marriage. She was sweet and playful and had a large army of friends. She was the most challenging for me, as she was living with us and still very much in her formative years. I felt it was my responsibility to provide her a level of discipline as I had with the other children. Lauren was not prepared to accept a new male in the house and was somewhat rebellious. Often, when I would discipline her, she didn't want to listen because I was not her father and she would tell me she hated me. She constantly said she would never love me. I would calmly reply that I loved her and that my responsibility was not to be her father but to teach her good manners and behavior. I hoped she would come to love me but that was not a requirement.

One time when caught in a lie, I made her write "I will not lie, I will not lie," a thousand times. When she finished and obnoxiously said she didn't learn anything from that exercise, I made her write it another thousand times. My discipline was always sprinkled with love and sweet hugs. Much to my joy, she turned out to be a wonderful and loving young woman. And she had no scars from my discipline. In fact we laugh about it all the time. Lauren graduated from University of Florida with a degree in sociology, which she channeled into music, public relations, and event planning for music-related venues and festivals.

Lauren was not the only one who experienced my discipline. I always looked for opportunities to take my children's indiscretions and turn them into teaching moments. A few examples:

When Shelley was six, Jarett was taunting her one day and she grew frustrated with him. She called him an asshole right in front of me. When she saw the horror and surprise on my face, she tried to justify it by raising her voice and stammering, "But…but…but he *is* an asshole!" Shelley had her mouth washed out with soap.

When Donny was ten, he lied about taking his bath. I checked the soap and the tub. They were both dry. Donny was on time-out in his room for a week.

There are dozens of these examples. Of course, each punishment was followed by a warm hug and an "I love you." It was the act, not the person, that was getting the punishment. I learned well from my parents.

I'm happy to say none of the children went through the teenage years of rebellion. All five grew up to be independent, competent, genuinely nice people, not spoiled or feeling entitled.

As I write this book, four of our children are married with wonderful spouses. They've given us twelve phenomenal grandchildren.

Gina married Mario. They have three children: Mario's son Andy and Joaquin and Tomas. As an adult, Gina asked me to adopt her, which I excitedly did.

Donny married Judy. They have four children: Tyler, Jacob, Benjamin, and Julia.

Shelley married Jeff. They have three children: Tobi, Jordan, and Sydney.

Jarett married Dara. They have two children: Todd and Madeline.

Lauren met Travis and got engaged.

Our blended family has been a thing of beauty.

Susie and I celebrated our thirty-second wedding anniversary in September, 2020. She has not just been the love of my life, but my rock. We've worked together since 1972—forty-five years. She's been part of my every decision, my ups and downs, my successes and failures. She's Type A as I am and every bit as successful in her own right. We work well as a team—with each other, our children, each other's business, and our day-to-day life. It's a beautiful thing but we don't take it for granted. It requires constant nourishment, hard work and communication, and often times one-on-one Good and Welfare sessions, where in a safe, nonjudgmental environment, each is free to fully express a problem without interruption, always ending with a hug and kiss.

After an unforgettable honeymoon, Susie and I lived in Susie's house in Coral Gables with Lauren, and our housekeeper Petrona, and quickly set about figuring out, with the children, what would be the next family adventure. We decided on a winter vacation—which would be just three months away—in Vail, Colorado, scheduled around the holidays. This would allow all the children to ski if they wanted. Though it sounds like an oxymoron, there is, in fact, a one thousand-member strong (at least at the time) Miami Ski Club, of which my brother, the children's Uncle Jay, was president. He is an avid skier and had taken Donny, Jarett, and Shelley skiing out West a number of times, and they'd loved it. We were eager to introduce Lauren and Gina to the sport knowing another good time awaited all, setting December 23 as the day of departure. Until the unthinkable happened.

LIFE LESSONS LEARNED

- The heart has unlimited capacity for love. When it comes your way, and if it brings others along as well, willingly make room and genuinely embrace it.
- Experience is not lived in a vacuum. Be cognizant of others in the process that may be affected or simply want to be there with you.

MARRIAGE: PARTY OF SEVEN

Susie and Alan Wedding
9/2/1988

Our daughter, Lauren, as flower girl.

Zit (my father), Jarett, Susie, Alan,
Don, Pearl (my mother), Shelley, Jay
(my brother)

Honeymoon for seven in Marco Island, FL.

Susie and Alan

Susie!

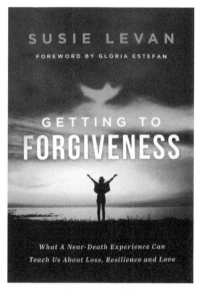

Susie owned and published Balance Magazine *for 10 years.*

Susie's memoir which became an Amazon #1 best seller.

After 120 editions and covers, I convinced Susie to be on the cover of her final edition.

MARRIAGE: PARTY OF SEVEN

Eight photos of our children

Jarett, Alan, Don

Jarett, Alan, Don, Shelley

Jarett, Shelley, Lauren,
Don, Gina

Shelley, Grandma Pearl,
Alan, Don, Grandpa
Zit, Jarett

Jarett, Alan, Don, Shelley
Susie, Lauren

Susie, Gina

Jarett, Shelley, Don

Don, Susie, Alan, Shelley,
Jarett, (in front) Lauren

SEEING AROUND CORNERS

First came the weddings…

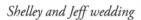

Jarett and Dara wedding

Shelley and Jeff wedding

Don and Judy wedding

Gina and Mario wedding

MARRIAGE: PARTY OF SEVEN

Then came the grandchildren …

*Alan, Jarett, Grandma
Pearl, Dara, Susie, (in front)
Madeline, Todd*

*Grandma Pearl, Alan, Shelley,
Jeff, Sydney, Susie, (in front)
Tobi, Jordan*

*Alan, Don, Grandma
Pearl, Judy, Susie, (in
front) Jacob, Benjamin,
Tyler, (coming soon
– Julia)*

*Grandma Pearl, Alan, Joaquin,
Mario, Gina, Susie, Tomas,
Andy (not pictured)*

All together

My parents, Zit and Pearl

My brother Jay and wife Lori   *My mother and my partner, Jack Abdo*

Having family fun

*Alan reading poetry to
grandchildren*

Quiet Sunday at home – working/papers everywhere

CHAPTER 14

THIRD HOUSE ON THE RIGHT: THE UNTHINKABLE

"Do not let the behavior of others destroy your inner peace."
—Dalai Lama

Kidnapping is something you see in the movies, or maybe read about in books. O. Henry's classic short story, "The Ransom of Red Chief," comes to mind. Maybe you glance at the headlines about a kidnapping in a foreign country, on a lazy Sunday morning, as you prepare a platter of cinnamon French toast (always my specialty) for your family. But a kidnapping doesn't happen to you—except that this time it did. It happened to my new wife, Susie, her seven-year-old daughter, Lauren (whom I always consider my daughter), and me, with our housekeeper and nanny, Petrona, also a victim.

By this time, I was heavily involved in managing BankAtlantic. We had been approved for the change of control the previous year and I was now chairman and CEO. With the new management team in place, there was an inordinate amount of work to do. I had established regular management meetings every Tuesday starting at 4:00 p.m. which would run late into the night. Now COO of I.R.E., BankAtlantic's holding company, Susie drove up to Fort Lauderdale with me and participated in the management meetings. Apparently, the fine details of our comings and goings were a pattern the criminals had observed and duly noted.

On Tuesday, December 20, Susie called Petrona around 6:00 p.m. from the bank as she normally did to check on the house and talk to Lauren before her dinner and bedtime. She always wanted to say goodnight. This time it was a very stilted conversation and Lauren was nowhere to be found. Petrona, a warm, highly competent, grandmotherly Salvadoran who had been with Susie and Lauren since Lauren was four months old, was strangely distant—wooden, almost. She continued to give Susie curt, often one-word answers to all of her questions, which went something like this:

Susie: Where is Lauren?

Petrona: Somewhere…somewhere in the house.

Susie: Well, okay, can I talk to her?

Petrona: No. Not now.

Susie: Is she sick?

Petrona: No.

Susie: Why not then?

Petrona: She's…sleeping.

Susie: *Sleeping?* Why would she be sleeping?

Petrona: She just is.

Susie knew Petrona's tone, mannerisms, moods, inflection, intonation, and as much as you can possibly know about someone who has lived with you and cared for your family since your daughter was four months old. Something was definitely wrong.

What we could not have known was that several hours earlier, someone had rung the bell to our home, claiming to be from a florist delivering a poinsettia plant. It was holiday time and there was nothing out of the ordinary about that, so the person was let in to the house. Two others followed, carrying guns, and the crime commenced.

Hanging up from Petrona, Susie just froze. She was pale and anxious and tried to tell me something was amiss. Being the practical, dogmatic, stoic that I was (and for better or worse still am), I did my best to rationalize her thoughts that something was wrong, subordinating them to the business we had at hand which was our marathon meeting moments away from starting. I just "knew" Susie was going into maternal overdrive. Period. As always, we had a lot on the table that night and I was eager to get going. But she was resolute. From that time on she was in the room but her mind was clearly someplace else. With no car in which to return home other than the one between us we'd used to drive up, I think she did her best to try and talk herself out of what she was feeling, for my benefit, enduring the light dinner we always provided and then the management meeting until 11:30 p.m. But by that time, try as she might, her fears had gotten the best of her. I tried again, albeit unsuccessfully, to talk her down off the ledge. A tense forty-five-minute to one-hour drive home awaited us.

Old Cutler Road in Coral Gables—the south end of Miami—is an exceedingly long, winding, tree-lined street where the trees actually form a canopy. As you drive along at certain times of the day, the dappled light makes it feel as though you are motoring through a fine painting. There are communities built off to the west and east sides of Old Cutler Road, with east being along Biscayne Bay. Our house was east but not on the water.

At 12:30 a.m., we approached the driveway to our home. The community, Hammock Oaks, was pleasant and tranquil and we were the third house on the right. Susie's house, into which I had moved, was relatively private—up on a ridge with a grove of forty-foot-high oak trees. It was only five minutes from my former house in Gables Estates where Terri and my children lived, and couldn't have been more perfect in that regard. But in others, like its isolation, it was not ideal, which we would quickly come to find out.

I felt Susie's hand on my arm as we entered the property.

"It's dark," she said, with a kind of slow grind in her voice. She pointed to the fact that the outside lights weren't on, something

Petrona had made sure to do for all the years they'd lived there. There were no lights on in the patio; no lights on in the garage; no lights on in the foyer that was partially visible from the outside through clerestory windows. Again I tried to talk Susie out of her concerns, suggesting Petrona had simply forgotten.

We exited the car and approached the front door, then noting that the alarm wasn't on, something indicated by a darkened red light. With Susie slightly behind me, I put the key in the lock and opened the door. Someone grabbed me by the arm and pulled me into the house. Susie took off running down the incline, screaming for help. In an instant one of the perpetrators was after her, tackling her at the bottom of the driveway, threatening that if anyone came as a result of hearing her screams we'd all be dead. He dragged her, largely by the hair, back in the house. Three men in wigs, sunglasses, trucker's hats, and gloves forced us to lie face down on the living room floor, hands behind our backs, with guns at our heads. In an instant they'd removed Susie's jewelry, our watches, and our three-month-old wedding rings. The only thing they didn't get was a necklace Susie was wearing—something of great beauty and sentiment—which was fortuitously hidden underneath her turtle-neck sweater. Later, she would remember she had it on and bury it beneath a pile of clothes in Lauren's upstairs bathroom hamper, hoping it would be missed by the perpetrators. They proceeded to rifle through Susie's purse, wherein she'd just cashed a $500 check for our family trip to Vail, for which we were supposed to leave in fewer than seventy-two hours.

"Where is Lauren?" Susie demanded, her voice wavering. "Where is my daughter and where is Petrona?"

The men told her they were upstairs and we would all get up there soon enough. Susie began to hyperventilate and one of them produced a brown paper bag from the kitchen, instructing her to breathe into it.

She was brought upstairs to see Lauren who was lying in her bed. Of course Lauren was still very young and it would turn out she was not unnerved by all this. She just didn't understand it and was filing it away where children of her age tend to file things away. Petrona was in the room as well and they appeared physically unharmed. Susie lay down with Lauren in the bed. Petrona, crouched beneath the window, was bug-eyed. In El Salvador, her native country, events like this always ended in murder so I could just imagine what was going through her head. The men pushed Susie back downstairs where she was told to join me, now in the dining room, whereby they explained that they were going to rob BankAtlantic tomorrow and that's why they were there. As frightened for all of our lives as we were, on some level Susie and I breathed a sigh of relief knowing then that this was not a home invasion. At least we'd be kept alive through the night and into the morning, long enough for them to carry out the next day's mission, perhaps with a flicker of an opportunity that we could figure out a way to survive.

The thing is, I really did understand and acknowledge to myself there was a high probability we would end up dead. I've said many times throughout this book that what has always allowed me to navigate in business, and in personal matters, is an ability not only to see around corners but to force myself to look at the downside. I exhaust any and all contingencies in my mind so that I have anticipated and am as prepared as possible for the worst. When you do that, as bad as it may be, some of the fear is gone.

Because of Susie's desperate screams for help, apparently one of the not-so-near neighbors had heard her and had alerted our community's Wackenhut guards. A patrol car had been dispatched and the guard rang the doorbell.

With one gunman watching out the window and the other two further back in the house, I was instructed to open the door and get rid of the guard. The message was it had better be an Academy Award performance or it would be my last. In a matter of seconds (which was all I had) I considered how I'd surreptitiously alert the guard that we were in trouble, but thought better of it. Instead, I told him I got home late and didn't see anything strange. It was a good decision, as it turned out, because one of the gunmen had moved close enough to me to close the door, which I'd not realized at first. If he'd shot me, it would have been at point-blank range.

The gunmen soon brought us upstairs to Lauren's room where we would all spend the night. In light of the circumstances I found the temerity to ask them how the bank was to be robbed, and they actually told me. The lead gunman and I would drive to BankAtlantic in Fort Lauderdale, where I would empty the safe, putting it all into a suitcase. That was all there was to it. Right: that was all there was to it. For now, they told us to get some sleep because we had a big day ahead of us.

I was consumed by thoughts about what I was going to do—not necessarily tomorrow, but right now. These were pre-cell phone days and even so, had this taken place a decade later clearly they would have confiscated those too. I wondered what opportunities were there to escape and even if I could manage to see a way, how I would take Susie, Lauren, and Petrona with me so they would not be killed. There was a bathroom in Lauren's room, and when we went in to use it we were not followed by any of the gunmen. But again, even if I'd jumped out the second floor window and didn't break any bones, limiting my mobility when I hit the ground, what would happen to my family if I couldn't get help to them in time?

It was now much past 1:00 a.m., when we'd planned on being in bed after our late management meeting. Susie and I were exhausted. Though she'd never be able to sleep she laid on the bed with Lauren, with Petrona still huddled under the window. I stretched out on the floor and surprisingly—at least surprising to Susie and Petrona—went right to sleep. I had disciplined myself enough to know I'd need all my wits about me in the morning, and a sleepless night would not have achieved that. I had to be able to function. To this day, Susie remembers that I was in such a deep sleep I was snoring, which I never do. Meanwhile she straddled the line between utter frustration with me and sheer incredulousness that I could sleep so deeply, or actually at all, at a time like that.

Reveille

At 5:00 a.m. a tennis shoe kicked me in the leg to awaken me. It wasn't a strong kick meant to inflict pain, just enough to rouse me, and maybe it began to tell me something about the gunmen—or at least one of them. This one appeared to be what one might call the mastermind—the one calling the shots. I didn't realize it at that moment but I was about to spend part of the morning assessing this man's personality—his character—his motives—his beliefs—really what made him tick. I would need to decide whether or not I could trust him not to kill Susie and Lauren, who were about to endure something most human beings will never experience in a lifetime.

Susie, though understandably fraught with fear about surviving our circumstances and especially getting Lauren out alive, had the presence of mind to be hard at work observing everything she could about this ungainly gang of three. She knew instinctively she had to key in on the details—perhaps things no one else would notice. She had become a human camera. She made indelible mental notes about their clothing: one was dressed from head to toe in red; another in blue; and the mastermind in white. She mentally logged their mannerisms, unusual identifying marks like birthmarks or tattoos on any exposed skin (so much was covered up), the cadence of their voices, accents, or regional distinctions, whether they were right- or left-handed, the size of their noses, their skin tone, and anything else about them.

When we were instructed to shower (walking to the bathroom of the master suite), and I to shave, as if getting ready for what would be considered a normal workday, Susie observed the mastermind speaking to a female on the phone in our bedroom. Because of the wig and hat he wore to conceal his hair, apparently he'd had to hold the phone a couple of inches from his ear, allowing Susie to pick up a higher voice as she passed through to our bathroom. Perhaps most outstanding about this one of the perpetrators was his skin tone, which Susie observed as albino, visible only when he momentarily removed his gloves. I did not notice that as my mind apparently worked differently. Granted I had taken a criminology class at Tulane—one of those fillers you take because you hear it's an easy A, but what was occurring to Susie never occurred to me. Instead I would try to get into his head, perhaps also a by-product of the class, but it would be the kinds of physical details Susie was identifying and memorizing that would be most important to law enforcement.

At about 6:30 a.m. we finished showering and dressing, whereupon they took us downstairs and outside. Susie was told to turn my car—a large navy blue Mercedes sedan—around in the driveway so that it was facing the street, with the trunk facing the front door. There was an early model Motorola Brick car phone and she recalls that fleeting moment when she had to make a decision whether or not to use it. But one of the gunmen had made her leave the passenger side door open so he could see everything she was doing. For Susie, lifting the phone would have been tantamount to pulling the trigger on herself and maybe the rest of us.

"Get in," the mastermind instructed when she'd re-parked the car. Susie hesitated but took Lauren's hand, believing they were going to be driven somewhere until the bank robbery was over with. She started toward the back door on the passenger side. He quickly opened the trunk. "Get in," he said again.

The three of us stood there. Susie and I were speechless—not breathing. Fortunately, again, Lauren was too young to comprehend what was about to happen, but Susie and I were beside ourselves.

"You'll get them back when we get the money from the bank," the mastermind told me, eyeing my wife and daughter. I vehemently objected. There had been no mention of this the night before. My family was either going to die of heat prostration or asphyxiation in the trunk, or come out with permanent mental and emotional issues even if they survived. I had to stop it. When I attempted to grab my family, the three gunmen became aggressive and I feared we'd all die on the steps of the house. I backed off. I was powerless. I asked at least for a pillow for Susie and Lauren's heads and they got Petrona to retrieve one. Susie and I hugged and kissed, teary-eyed, and she and Lauren climbed into the trunk together. The last thing I remember about the moment just before the car drove off was the abject terror and panic in Susie's eyes—which could destroy me if I let myself go there today. I'd had to stand by and watch the love of my life probably climbing into her tomb—with our seven-year-old.

The fact is with my claustrophobia, I'd not have survived fifteen minutes in that trunk. Susie did not have that affliction so at least she had that much going for her. I found out later she'd told Lauren they were going to play a game of hide-and-seek, and that Lauren would be with mommy so all would be fine. Though she believed they were going to die, her reason for living at that moment was to remove any sense of trauma for Lauren, something that prevented her from falling apart. Lauren had been born to Susie years after a time when she'd been told she could have no more children, years after Gina, and in the months and years after the kidnapping, Susie would come to believe there'd been a reason—aside from her intense love for this child—for Lauren's birth. She believed it was to keep her from giving up and succumbing to death as the hours ticked by in that trunk in the Florida heat.

* * *

As I stood on the steps, all I could do was return myself to the cause—the unimaginable mission—and do anything and everything to execute it as quickly as possible. But the gunmen decided it was too early to drive to the bank as it didn't open until 8:30 a.m. They took me back into the house for what seemed like an eternity. Eventually the mastermind took me outside again and got into the driver's seat of Susie's two-seater Mercedes SL, telling me to get in the other side. He told me he was driving us to the bank. An empty suitcase was lodged behind the two seats that abutted the trunk of the tiny car. He made it clear that if I followed directions and did not alert the bank guards or police, he'd phone me within forty-five minutes after I brought the cash out and he drove away. He said he would reveal where my sedan was located with my wife and daughter in the trunk. He asked me to write down my number, and I gave him the direct dial to my desk.

As we drove, he rested his gun between the throttle and dashboard, between the two bucket seats. When the car was in drive there was enough room for it. I could have grabbed it but what would that have accomplished? If I killed him and somehow survived the car crash, I'd never find Susie and Lauren alive—if at all. We were only an hour from the Everglades and in my mind—in Susie's as well, it would turn out—we feared that's where they would end up. If that were to happen, the car with their bodies would either never be found or if it were, it could take months or years.

I noticed a pock mark on his right cheek—the one I could see as I sat beside him—a detail observed much in the vein of what Susie had been doing. I couldn't help staring at him, figuring I had an hour to determine what to do. The plan was for him to wait in the car while I took the suitcase to the safe, removing the cash and bringing it back out to him. I realized at that point I would be in the bank totally without him: no gunman; no gun on me from anywhere. I would be among people and have access to a telephone. I could use it to call anyone and do what I wanted to do. But again I had to be monumentally careful, because as a result of my actions, I might never see my wife and child again.

I thought back to the criminology class at Tulane, a hundred years ago, the one I'd never have taken except for the easy A it promised. I focused hard, trying to dredge up what I'd learned that could be of use to me in this moment. I had found the course interesting from a psychological standpoint when we learned about why people choose a life of crime—what motivates them. As a businessman, I had a history of interviewing people for hiring and other purposes. I generally had a brief amount of time to essentially size them up, and now, in the car with this man, I had fewer than sixty minutes to do the same. I was about to become a civilian profiler. As counterintuitive as it sounds, I was bound and determined to find out if this criminal was someone I could *trust*—at least enough so that when he said he would call me in forty-five minutes, he would. As I started talking, trying to engage him, I was fortunate as he seemed to let me in.

"Why are you doing this?" I asked him, point blank, followed by a host of other questions. "Why do you not have a regular job?" "Is this the life you want?" "Have you ever killed someone?"

He answered all my questions, unruffled by them, basically saying life had not been good to him and he was getting back at society. He was sorry to involve my family and me, but there was no other way. He said he was a kind, truthful person and I should take him at his word. He didn't mean us any harm: It was just about the money. He was reflective, conversational, and pleasant, never appearing defensive or annoyed.

I asked him still more questions such as if his accomplices were part of a regular gang or if he'd just picked them up locally, and if he'd done this a number of times. He said he had done this a number of times—in exactly the same way. In retrospect I really don't know where all this came from, because in fact I was trying to profile a criminal and not hire a prospective branch manager, but the combination of my college class and professional experience served me well. I seemed to know what to do and was getting somewhere. My perception was crucial at this point. I had to feel, deep in my bones, that I could trust him enough to reunite me with my family.

I was also honest about myself with him, explaining I'd recently been made CEO and didn't even know the location of the safe. I thought it might be in the area with the safety deposit boxes with the large, ornate vault door but I was not entirely sure. And I really didn't know how much cash we kept on hand on a daily basis. That was all the truth. He told me I'd figure it out.

In the moments before we pulled into the parking lot and I entered the bank, I knew it was important for me to thank him for our conversation and tell him I thought he was a good person. I looked him in the eye through his sunglasses and said I believed him when he'd said he meant us no harm, and I was going to follow his instructions to the letter, trusting he'd give me the courtesy of calling me within forty-five minutes after I handed him the suitcase. I had to believe that unless provoked in some way, this really was just a job to him—his line of work. I took the suitcase from in back of the two seats and headed for the bank. Just as I left he reminded me that if I didn't deliver the money and let him drive out of there, I'd never see Susie and Lauren alive.

The executive offices were six floors up and there was so much adrenaline coursing through me, I hardly remember the elevator ride. Theoretically I had escaped, but I was really still shackled to the gunman. I walked directly into the office of the president, Mark Wright, shut the door, and told him the story as succinctly as I could. He gasped at the circumstances as we hurried back down the elevator to the location of the safe, which was in a small room behind the teller line. The safe was no different than one you'd see in a bedroom closet—just a bigger version, perhaps two-foot square, bolted to the concrete floor. It's unusual for the bank president, let alone the CEO, to go down to the safe and somehow we had to do this quickly and efficiently without arousing the curiosity of the tellers.

"We need to get into the safe," Mark told the head teller. She took a minute to try and make sense of things but opened it anyway because her boss had told her to. The bills were banded and there was $250,000 in there. I stuffed it into the suitcase.

The head teller, now clearly aghast, was told it was a matter of life and death and not to say anything to anyone. Mark then took her with him upstairs to make sure she kept quiet while I rushed out of the bank with the money.

The gunman rolled down the window and told me to put it in the same space it had been behind the passenger's seat. This was it—presumably the end of my participation in the crime—and I began to query him again.

"Are you going to call me *in forty-five minutes*?" I asked, grasping at an opportunity to reinforce what he had said. I could barely hear my own words, gripped by what was about to happen. He would be gone. That could be the end of everything. "I'm counting on you to do the right thing. I did as you asked. I'm holding you to your word. I'm trusting you," I told him, looking him in the eye again. I glanced at my watch. "I'm waiting for your call to come in exactly forty-five minutes." I was choking on my words.

"I will call you," he said, driving off. There is no way to describe how heavy my heart was at that point, knowing that no one else in the world except this man I'd never see again and his accomplices knew where my wife and daughter were. I had to suspend any doubt I may have had and hope I'd used the right psychology in impressing upon him that I was confident he'd do the right thing. I had to keep myself together.

Ticking Clock/Ticking Time Bomb

I rushed back into the bank, up the elevator, telling Mark the job was done. I sat down at my desk, immediately calling my attorneys, Alison and Gene. I got a hold of Alison who conferenced us with

Gene, who was in Colorado. The three of us had been through wars together for years, and all I could think to do was bring them into the situation. They wanted to call the local police but I cautioned them about doing so right away as it may sound the death knell for Susie and Lauren. Alison wanted to alert the FBI, and would, awaiting my signal, though, that I'd gotten the call or not gotten it.

In another instant it occurred to me that if the group of criminals consisted of more members, which I had no way of knowing, some of them may be holding others of my family hostage. I quickly thought to call my children—Donny who was in college now in Connecticut, and my ex-wife Terri to make sure the younger ones were at school. I was curt and didn't tell them the reason for my call. I just said I was checking in. I had little time and had to get to everyone. I called my parents and was satisfied they were all right. Mark sat in my office with me as the wall clock ticked away the minutes. With every tick it sounded like the mechanism on a bomb, minutes before it explodes, which was what the situation felt like to me.

Forty minutes had passed since the gunman had driven off and my heart sank. It was a feeling for which you can never find the words. Would he take this all the way to the end of the promised forty-five minutes, or was it just plain over? I was about to call the police, and call Gene and Alison (Alison, as it turned out, had jumped into her car with a colleague, Tony Menendez, and the two were speeding from Miami to the bank) when the phone on my desk rang. The mastermind told me where my car was. I repeated the location to Mark. Fortunately it wasn't in the Everglades, it was right there in Fort Lauderdale but I did not know the area very well. Mark indicated it was within blocks of the bank. For as long as I'd been connected with Atlantic Federal, now BankAtlantic, my pattern had been to drive directly up from Miami and right back down again, never going anywhere else. Alison and Tony had arrived in record time and had come up to my office and we flew back down to the lobby. Tony remained behind and Alison, Mark, and I jumped into Mark's car, driving off.

As it turned out my car was just minutes away and we fell upon it like blankets on a sudden fire. The doors were unlocked and I reached in to the driver's side to pop the trunk—with my life flashing before me. I was afraid of what we might find in there. Granted, it was December, but the sun had been up for hours. In South Florida, considered a tropical climate, December often only means 80 or 85 degrees, instead of 95, but there is generally high humidity that intensifies the heat. The temperature inside the trunk could have climbed to exceedingly high numbers, and with or without that factor they still may have suffocated. Susie heard us, and before the trunk was all the way open, she leapt out, sweat dripping off her face. Together we helped Lauren.

The miraculous details of their survival would only much later be revealed to me, long after that day, as the odds against anyone surviving hours in a trunk in Florida are incalculable. In time Susie recounted that while the car was moving they could feel the whoosh of air, perhaps coming from underneath, but when it stopped, they began to feel the effects of the heat and lack of air circulation. When Lauren had announced she was done with the hide-and-seek game, had to use the bathroom, and was hungry and wanted to get out, Susie had distracted her by saying I would be along very soon and she should close her eyes and try to nap, which she did. Susie could hear the change in her breathing and knew she was asleep. Whether or not she'd ever wake up, Susie had thought, was another story.

Though neither overtly religious nor spiritual, Susie said she began praying to God to take her, instead of her daughter—not to let a seven-year-old die that way. She recited the 23rd Psalm—which somehow came to her. At some point in the trunk after that she'd had a near-death experience, and when she'd felt herself come back into her body, both she and Lauren had seen a baseball-sized hole in the trunk through which fresh, cool air was rushing in. Susie said there was so much clarity, she and Lauren could see the telephone wires overhead and the kind of atmospheric dust particles sometimes visible when the sun shines through a window. By the time I got there, not knowing this story as of yet, both of them tried to show me the miracle of the hole (I didn't understand what they were talking about) but it had disappeared.

Air, Food, and Water

The next order of business was to get them into the air-conditioned car and get them something to drink as they were seriously dehydrated. Susie, Lauren, Alison and I piled into my car, with me at the wheel, stopping at a Burger King drive-through window for fluids, which was the closest thing. In a few more minutes we approached the bank parking lot, swarming with reporters—no police yet—just reporters. As Alison's office had called the FBI, who, as part of standard operating procedure had notified the Fort Lauderdale PD, the newspapers and TV stations had picked it up on their police scanners. Had I not waited out the forty-five minutes, with all this activity visibly mounting I might never have gotten the phone call.

My car was ambushed by photographers, snapping away through the front and back windshield. Alison jumped out, knowing I needed to steer my family out of there, just as one photographer planted himself in front of the vehicle deliberately preventing us from driving away. I was so intent upon getting Susie and Lauren to a safe, secure, private place, I screamed out the window that I would run him over if he didn't let us go. All manner of calm and repose had left me as I was no longer staring down the barrel of a gun, where I'd have to behave in order to survive. I had my life and family back so it was no holds barred. The photographer must have seen the look on my face and stepped aside.

I didn't know the area so didn't know where I was going. I simply started to head east over an intracoastal bridge, realizing I was on A1A—that coastal highway that, at 2,369 miles, runs all the way from Key West, Florida, to Fort Kent, Maine. In a more innocent time, A1A had been the route along which I'd hitchhiked back and forth to my summer jobs. Wherever it ran, it was peppered with a zillion motels and hotels for miles and miles. I pulled up to one and checked us in, where we spent the remainder of the day in an air-conditioned room, ordering room service and lots of fluids. I called the police to tell them where we were and they and the FBI promptly joined us. The police told us that the Coral Gables police had been dispatched to our house where they'd found Petrona tied to a downstairs shower door. She was shaken but okay.

Aside from the inconceivableness of the whole incident, what stood out most to Susie and me that day was the fact that the authorities were insinuating the kidnapping had been staged—by us! Perhaps it was the fact that we weren't acting the way they thought victims did, or should, proclaiming "woe is me." We certainly hadn't hung around the bank parking lot waiting for the police (in retrospect I had no idea what had been going through my head about police at that point, except to get Susie and Lauren away from the crazy mob scene). We also told the police we were leaving in forty-eight hours for our planned trip to Colorado, which did not sit well with them. They insisted we stay to get all the paperwork done, whereupon we explained that our family comes first and we didn't want to panic the other children.

To this day I don't know why my car, which I got back right away, was not impounded and held as evidence. But it wasn't, and at the end of the afternoon Susie, Lauren, and I got in and drove back to Coral Gables. Lauren ran to Petrona in front of the house and they embraced, but Susie stood there shaking. When we stepped inside the foyer, her knees buckled and she went down.

"I cannot stay here," was all she managed to say. With that, she slowly made her way up the stairs to Lauren's room, digging through the laundry hamper in her bathroom. The necklace that meant so much to her was still there, undiscovered by the kidnappers. Susie, Lauren, Petrona, and I packed a few articles of clothing, drove over to the Dadeland Marriott in South Miami, checked in, and stayed for three months until I could buy a more secure residence with tall iron gates. Except to empty the third house on the right when we sold it (which Petrona did almost entirely on her own, and I helped when I could), we never went home again.

About two years after the kidnapping, Susie and I were called to a Los Angeles courtroom to identify a defendant charged with committing bank robberies and kidnappings, similar to ours, throughout the country. Apparently someone had provoked the gunman as he was now also on trial for murder. Susie's meticulous observations of him were instrumental in the outcome of the case and he was sentenced to a long prison term.

Postscript:

Petrona was understandably ruffled, actually scared to death, but all right. She stayed and worked for us for another twenty-five years. When she retired, we continued to pay her full salary until her death. She was part of our family and a second grandmother to Lauren. Lauren cared for her until the day she passed away at ninety-four.

On Friday after the kidnapping, we left with the kids for Vail, Colorado. We didn't spend any time giving the children the gory details. We wanted to shield them and not make them nervous for their own safety. While the children were in ski school, Susie and I spent most of the trip in the sports clinic dealing with severe, paralyzing aches in her back, legs, and shoulders, cramped from the trunk and where she was apparently holding all her stress and trauma.

Lauren seemed unfazed and not traumatized in any way because Susie had sung to her and told her stories and said they were playing hide-and-seek. Susie clearly had a near-death experience in the trunk and had come back because it wasn't her time. She was not able to leave our new house for months. We had guards standing outside our front door, seven days a week, twenty-four hours a day, for more than a year.

Susie unfortunately suffered from post-traumatic stress disorder for two years, with recurring body aches and pains. She was eventually able to heal and come to understand the NDE with the assistance of a skilled and compassionate therapist. She became very spiritual and a voracious reader of everything metaphysical. Her newly found spirituality opened up a new perspective on life. It was difficult for me to grasp all the changes she was going through, but I was so in love and she was everything to me. After two long years, she was feeling more safe and secure again. Regretfully, because of our isolation, the security guard at our front door had become Lauren's best and only friend. Clearly, this was not a good situation for Lauren. We were finally able to eliminate the guards and went back to a more normalized life.

Susie also left her C-suite job, dedicating her new life to empowering and helping women overcome obstacles and succeed. Many years later, she became a circuit speaker to talk about her harrowing experience to hundreds of women. She created the nonprofit Work-Life Balance Institute and a magazine called *Balance.* I am very proud of her and what she has accomplished. She is constantly getting letters, cards, and emails from women who thank her for changing their lives. I am amazed at Susie's gift when I read these letters. We have been married thirty-two years. Susie has not only been the love of my life but my rock. We've worked together since 1972: nearly fifty years. She's been part of my every decision, my ups and downs, my successes and failures. As I said earlier, she's Type A as I am and every bit as successful in her own right. We work well as a team—with each other, our children, each other's businesses, and our day-to-day life. It's a beautiful thing but we don't take it for granted. It requires constant nourishment, hard work, and communication.

LIFE LESSONS LEARNED

- Be disciplined in your thinking and keep your wits about you no matter what. Not everything is life and death, as this was, but survival comes in different forms and composure leads to clearer thinking.
- Never take for granted that the people you love can be gone in an instant, and understand that family is everything. *Everything.*

$250,000 KIDNAPPING RANSOM PAID THRIFT CHIEF'S FAMILY FREED FROM CAR'S TRUNK

By **SALLIE JAMES**, Staff Writer
SUN-SENTINEL

DECEMBER 22, 1988

The three men had held the family hostage all night in their Coral Gables home. In the morning, family members were separated into two late-model Mercedes-Benz autos and the chairman was dispatched to his institution, officials said, while the man's wife and daughter were reportedly being held in the trunk of the second Mercedes.

Robbers flee with money; hostages OK

THE ASSOCIATED PRESS
FORT LAUDERDALE, Fla. — Three robbers held a bank executive and his family hostage overnight, then stole nearly $250,000 from the bank's vaults before fleeing, authorities said.

$250,000 paid to free two kidnap victims

Pertrona / Lauren's Nanny

CHAPTER 15

THE ABCs (ALWAYS BE CONNIVING) OF ABC

"Nothing more completely baffles one who is full of tricks and duplicity than straightforward and simple integrity in another."
—Charles Caleb Colton

It was now 1990 and once again the economy was on life support, fighting for its life. Deregulation of the nation's many thousands of savings and loans institutions by the federal government in the 1980s, and their consequent demise, had resulted in a kind of financial turmoil that infected everything from mortgages to employment to consumer confidence. Between 1985 and 1996, 1,043 (one-third) of the nation's savings and loans had failed. The S&L crisis was getting worse and the government had created the Resolution Trust Company (RTC), which was auctioning off hundreds of billions of dollars' worth of S&L assets because the government had no ability to generate cash or liquidity from the assets it was taking back. Discounts on these assets were ranging from 75 to 90 percent.

Fortunately, BankAtlantic was operating more like a bank since our change of control while most S&Ls were failing in this financial firestorm.

The market was crazy and the price of real estate had dropped by about 40 to 50 percent. BankAtlantic's holding company had changed its name from I.R.E. to BankAtlantic Financial Corporation, or BFC. As mentioned, I.R.E. had formed all these limited partnerships, having raised millions of dollars. Nationally, real estate entrepreneurs and the general partners of limited partnerships were trying to figure out just how long the recession would last and then figure out when it ended, just how long it would take to recover. Questions about having enough cash to get to the other side loomed large, all day, every day, infusing crucial decisions that had to be made about survival and sustainability.

Accordingly, a great number of the general partners and limited partnerships around the country, separate from BFC, proposed *rollups* by merging all their partnerships together. Most of these transactions were poorly structured with a bias in favor of the general partner. As a result, the SEC and various congressional committees were holding hearings to better understand them and determine whether new rules were required.

BFC was faced with a huge dilemma: How do we protect our limited partnerships—our investors—and secure the value of the real estate we owned? We had a fiduciary responsibility to these investors and had to take some kind of action because the market was getting worse and worse with no end in sight. We knew rollups were not the best solution and believed there had to be something else we could do.

I came up with a strategic concept that protected the investors, different from what everybody else was doing. It protected the limited partners' downside risk while improving the likelihood of their return of capital. We had their best interests in mind. Instead of a *rollup*, or merger, in 1989 we proposed an *exchange* into I.R.E. We would not lose sight of our responsibility to these financial partners, leaving them twisting in the wind the way other companies had. We decided instead to protect them. We fixed a price based on current appraisals that we thought was appropriate for the real estate value, telling the investors, "I.R.E. will guarantee you $30 million in the aggregate." So instead of having real estate that could go up or down in value (at the moment it was plummeting), we offered to assume responsibility and risk, guaranteeing the limited partnerships a $30 million pie. When the time would come for us to sell the real estate, if it ended up having to be sold for less than $30 million, the limited partnerships would have a guarantee of that fixed $30 million from the full faith and credit of I.R.E. Instead of the investor taking the loss, I.R.E. would take the loss. However if we were able to sell the real estate for more than $30 million in the aggregate, we would give the investors 100 percent of the excess—anything over $30 million. The guarantee would be in the form of debentures, or debt of $30 million, guaranteed by I.R.E. These debentures would be payable in full in twenty years, which fell within the thirty-year legal partnership life timeframe.

The interest payable by BFC on the debentures would be 8 percent the first year, 9 percent the second year, and 10 percent the third year and thereafter. If we deferred the interest payments, and if for whatever reason we could not make them, the interest rate would jump to 12 percent. So for us, if it was accruing at 12 percent, this would give us even more incentive to pay it off early—not wanting to wait the twenty years. Even if we didn't defer, as the economy recovered and interest rates came down BFC could pay off the debentures earlier if it desired. It was a very good arrangement for the limited partners.

At that point the only thing on which the limited partners were relying was the strength of BFC as opposed to the real estate as an entity. When somebody issues debt—a debenture—you're relying on the issuing party to have the wherewithal to pay off the debt. In short there was no edge for us—totally different from the way other companies were structuring their survival deals. Again if BFC survived the recession, the investors were going to get 100 percent of the real estate liquidation number—with a fixed $30 million dollar minimum—no matter what BFC's losses. It was our way of saying we got you into this. It's our responsibility and also our duty to protect you and get you out.

The *exchange* had to be approved by two-thirds of investors. The voting was made by proxy in the format prescribed by the SEC. Investors had thirty days to decide how they would vote.

When the votes were tallied, two-thirds voted in favor of having a guaranteed debenture as opposed to the volatility of the economy and falling real estate values. As the partnership units were never designed with a liquidity feature, the debentures were similarly structured. Since the economy was depressed, no dividends were being paid on the partnership units so the prospect of receiving interest payments was seen as an enhancement.

The Truth by Any Other Name

In the summer of 1990 I received a call from Bill Willson, a producer with ABC's primetime news program *20/20*. Willson was looking into the limited partnership industry per the current rash of rollups that were going on—specifically because the general partners were coming out way ahead of the limited partnerships. Apparently he'd attended a recent SEC seminar to familiarize himself with the subject when some of the unhappy one-third of our limited partnerships (who'd lost out to the two-thirds of voters in favor of our proposal in the proxy) had reached out to the media. He was poised to fly in from New York to Miami to hear my thoughts about the industry and "our" rollups.

I told him our transaction had been unique in the industry. We didn't have anything to do with *rollups* so I didn't believe he could put us in the same crowded category at all. I emphasized our fiduciary responsibility to our investors, which is why our programs were structured as *exchanges*—not *rollups*.

The fact is Willson had called several times before I'd taken his call. He was extremely persistent. I'd avoided any interaction with him because I knew the agenda put forth by a purported news program like *20/20* or other programs of that ilk was totally biased. They were marketed as news programs but had none of the general news guidelines. Instead, it was always a hatchet job on a particular individual or company. It was pure titillation. The worse they made the subject look, the more entertaining.

Ultimately, I reached out to Gene Stearns who suggested I take the call, however, with a plan that Willson could come down to meet with us with our objective being to point him in another direction.

Gene and I spent several hours with Willson to no avail. He wasn't listening. He didn't care about how our limited partnerships functioned. We explained that our *exchange* followed strict SEC guidelines and the documentation was legal, and ethical, overwhelmingly approved by our investors. He just wasn't buying anything we had to say. The fact that it was done differently from others in the industry, and that we could provide industry experts to corroborate what we were telling him was of no interest to him. We emphasized BFC was assuming the risk for our investors. But what we were doing simply didn't fit his pictures, and when we said (again and again) that his "factual premise was all wrong," his response pretty much summarized *20/20*'s modus operandi: These kinds of "news" programs are predicated on a bias.

"I don't care about the truth," he said unapologetically, in fact flagrantly, wearing it like a badge. "The truth is irrelevant to me." He told us we can go on camera and defend ourselves.

Though we knew it going in, we were still aghast that he'd confirmed ABC takes the position of persuading viewers of the program over to their unsubstantiated point of view by the way they structure the story. ABC wanted to feature BFC and me in one of its segments.

Willson wanted me to appear in front of the camera, something often known as "attack photojournalism."

The features of the show always included an on-air correspondent asking slanted and shocking questions to an individual that would be impossible to answer. No matter how he answered the question it was designed to make him look like he was hiding something even if he wasn't. Every individual subject of the show came out looking bad with questions like "how often do you beat your wife?" Or "How did you hide the money you stole?" It was advertised as television news but it was designed as entertainment. The worse they made the subject look, the more entertaining. Almost always they would interview a purported victim who would have a sad sack story to tell ending in "woe is me."

Because they're putting the subject on camera, a smile or frown as a response can be edited and distorted—attached to another question. If they're chasing the subject down a street—in TV news vernacular known as the "perp walk," done in such a way that the subject has to defend him or herself by swiftly ducking into a car or closing a door or putting a hand up in front of the camera, it's distorted to mean the subject is uncooperative because of something to hide. A microphone and a large, heavy camera thrown up two inches away from a face, especially after a chase, can feel threatening, and one's natural instincts are to block it to prevent a collision. Again the hand up can be distorted. They can use it any way they want. We didn't know for sure that they'd do this in a story like ours but we had to be prepared.

Willson was beyond tenacious in our offices that day, trying with everything he had to persuade me to appear on camera. He said I should just tell my story. He said John Stossel would be the correspondent and Hugh Downs the anchor. Gene and I agreed unconditionally at that point that this was not a good idea. There was no way I'd get a fair and balanced representation of the facts. We knew interviews were edited—twisted in a way to fit the show's agenda, which was already a losing proposition for me. We told Willson he should just run the story without comment or video from me, but he said this was television and they needed the visuals. He left disappointed and came back at us by phone, resulting in at least six more hours of discussion on the subject. He was clearly fixated on BFC. Unfortunately all conversations ended the same way: We could not convince him that what we did was nothing in the realm of rollups.

Frustrated, *20/20* set out to entrap me into a confrontation with a rolling video camera. They sent a crew to my office and staked out my house with broadcast vehicles, even flying overhead with helicopters for B-roll so that my wife and daughter and I—even our housekeeper, Petrona—were made to feel like criminals. The stress was indescribable. Anyone entering or exiting our home was targeted. This went on for weeks. By that point, I knew they had invested so much time, effort, and money in the story there was no way this program was going away.

Gene called Willson and offered a compromise. We wanted to negotiate, agreeing to the interview if we were allowed to review and approve it before it went on the air or at least have a third party independent review of the material. That was a no-go as far as they were concerned. Alternatively we offered for them to submit their questions, whereupon we'd go into a TV studio and respond to them on tape as long as they would run it all unedited, in its entirety, which they also vetoed. We further offered to provide them with experts in limited partnerships, and some of our investors who were in favor of the exchange. *20/20* said no, that they wanted me. It had to be me.

Ultimately they agreed to send us four or five questions, per our protocol. I went into a studio and Gene asked me the questions off-camera with the idea that when we sent it to *20/20*, they would use John Stossel so that it looked as though he were the one asking

225

the questions. We completed the task and then they decided it just wasn't enough for them.

Mr. Levan Goes to Washington

More time passed and one day a process server came to my office delivering an official-looking document. It was a subpoena from the all-important Subcommittee on Oversight and Investigations of the House Committee on Energy and Commerce. Gene and I were mystified. It turned out that this subcommittee was chaired by Rep. John Dingell (D-MI). The title of the hearing was "The Rollup of Real Estate Limited Partnerships by the BankAtlantic Financial Corporation."

Was this for real?

Bill Willson got a United States congressman to call a special one-day hearing in Washington specifically on our limited partnership exchange just so *20/20* could get its Alan Levan video? Talk about the power of the press.

As Gene and I knew, the only way to physically attend a congressional hearing is to drive up and then walk up to the building. You have to get out of the car by opening the door, closing it, walking down a sidewalk, up the steps, down a long hallway, and into the chamber. So another reason for the hearing is Bill Willson gets exactly what he wants: the perp walk.

Cameras are rolling, getting you squarely between the eyes with microphones in your face. Questions are pointed, such as "Why did you orchestrate this rollup?" You can choose not to answer, which makes it appear as though you are guilty and want to avoid the question. If you say, "They are not rollups, they're *exchanges*," they persist by saying, "Yes, but why did you do these rollups?" Then they'll ask it a third and fourth time. The goal is for you to lose your composure and either throw your hand up in front of the camera or take a swing at the cameraman, or the reporter holding the microphone, to get the camera and microphone out of your eyeballs and away from your teeth.

It was an all-day hearing. Theoretically, Congress uses hearings in the way of fact-finding to make laws. In reality, Congress uses hearings so its members' (perceived) skills and prowess can be trumpeted to anyone who will watch on TV or read about it. It is picked up by an array of media outlets as representatives work hard to make a point or argument, or berate someone. And the only item on the agenda was I.R.E.

That day there was testimony from a wide variety of characters including the SEC, BankAtlantic's regulators because BFC was the holding company for BankAtlantic, various congressmen, and me.

What is a regulator who is now in front of a camera going to say? He's not going to offer anything supportive. He's going to say, "Well, hmmm, based on what you've said, Congressman, we really do need to investigate this matter." All of which makes for great TV ratings.

Now it was my turn. You are under oath, so anything you say falsely is considered perjury. I was fully prepared for my testimony. I made an opening statement and then Congressman Dingell, Chairman of the Subcommittee on Oversight and Investigations, grilled me for about forty-five minutes. I could tell his questions were designed by Bill Willson to trip me up but I handled myself well. I also knew that Dingell was a proponent of the Glass-Steagall Act.* In short he was not in favor of banks gaining more and more power. He was a natural and willing shill for Bill Willson, because what Dingell got out of the hearing was a forum from which to ask the regulators how they could possibly approve BFC as a holding company for BankAtlantic. In fact it was the new banking powers that had created the thousands of S&L failures. He was actually correct in his view of runaway power, but it was the axe he had to grind on our backs that

---

* https://www.investopedia.com/terms/g/glass_steagall_act.asp

was incorrect. Dingell was suggesting the idea that we had designed and executed these rollups to be able to infuse the resulting capital into BankAtlantic. He was implying we were not proper stewards and had been unfair to our investors.

I did the best I could to parry his accusations and by the end of my testimony I was confident and angry. I was the last one up. I had listened to other witness' testimonies all day, which was all nonsense. Just plain nonsense.

I took a deep breath. I told Dingell that I did not appreciate being summoned there. I took offense at his insinuations about my company and me. In other hearings, Congress had paraded S&L executives that had blatantly plundered their institutions before committees and they deserved to be filleted. We had done everything right by our investors with transparency and following SEC rules. I believed we'd had an elegant solution to a challenging problem. All of the testimony was designed to make it look as though we did something wrong. Hard as they tried, the participants could not identify anything we had done that was not ethical and completely by the book. By the end of the hearing, and as a matter of public record, Representative Dingell actually told me he liked me. As I exited the chambers, the ABC cameras were still rolling. They were able to capture me while chasing me down the hall, sitting down and standing up. They stuck a microphone and camera within two inches of my face and asked the exact same question twenty times so that I would have to answer it twenty times. All the while they were just hoping to get me on camera frowning or being frustrated or just waiting for the one time I would tell them to go fly a kite. The cameraman even followed me into the bathroom.

Smoke

Though we'd come out reasonably well under the circumstances, when we got back to Florida Gene and I were now on edge, trying to anticipate *20/20's* next move. We contemplated a number of possible scenarios but to our surprise, they issued a press release which was distributed to the local press, something we had not considered. It said they were going to air a segment on Alan Levan and BFC in the next few weeks, providing some details as to the nature of the segment.

The result was a media feeding frenzy. Miami and Fort Lauderdale are large cities, but how often did they get a local executive on a national "news" program? *20/20* had essentially positioned the segment as an exposé: catching somebody in the act. This was very big news, and the press got to work in anticipation of the broadcast with stories largely speculating on what the segment would really be about. With all this, *20/20's* South Florida viewership numbers would go through the roof, just as they'd planned. It was scheduled to air during sweeps week in November of that year when broadcasters use viewership numbers to determine advertising rates. (Sweeps occurs in February, May, July, and November.)

By law, for the press, libel doesn't enter the picture if they can quote another source. The inaccurate articles were unrelenting and media outlet upon outlet upon outlet in turn quoted another outlet, and another, so the non-story, as it was, exploded. Though the show hadn't even aired, it seemed everyone knew about it, with customers of BankAtlantic appearing at our branches, articles in hand, concerned about the viability of the bank and their deposits.

When the segment finally ran it was outrageous. It was no different than the hundreds, if not thousands, of other *20/20* stories distorting the facts in the name of entertainment and to skew ratings. They falsely implied I had refused any contact with ABC and had something to hide. Parts of the videotape Gene and I had gone into a local studio to meticulously record had been altered in the realm that they'd changed the lead-in questions reportedly asked, my answers presented out of context. ABC portrayed statements made by a member of Congress at the hearing in such a way as to create the false impression he was yelling at me when I wasn't even in the room at the time. Other statements and footage were also manipulated. We had offered to provide our expert and investors who had voted yes to the exchange to appear on camera, but instead they'd found their own negatively biased "expert" and had ferreted out investors who'd voted no to it. In addition to errors and misleading references, there was absolutely no balance to the reporting at all. Bill Willson later said it was all my fault since I'd refused to appear on camera to defend myself.

The story was inaccurate and misleading. Gene was so outraged he sent another one of his written missiles which got the attention of the ABC corporate executives. While they rarely do this, in January of 1992, ABC aired three unprecedented retractions and corrections to the segment, read by anchor Hugh Downs.

First, ABC admitted it had overstated the value of one of the real estate properties in the exchange because ABC had not taken into account a substantial mortgage on the property.

Next, ABC clarified its statement that "Levan wouldn't talk to us." They admitted that although the two sides could not agree on the ground rules for an on-camera interview, Levan had indeed communicated with the network in various ways, including sending a videotape of pre-approved questions—questions conceived by ABC. *20/20* had falsely reported this point too, where they'd said we'd sent a videotape with answers to questions we'd anticipated ABC might ask—not that we'd answered the actual questions they'd sent us.

Finally, ABC admitted editing portions of that submitted videotape to the point that it may have mislead viewers. They also acknowledged that the exchanges were legal and the devaluation of real estate was caused by a volatile economy, not BFC.

But the damage was done. The big story was damning and the press had a field day. Try as we might, we could not get any of them to stop, take a step back, and consider the truth—the vindictiveness—of what had been done to us, all in the name of ratings. Each of them took the position that if *20/20* saw a story there, they should see nothing less. The stories that begot more stories and still more stories generally had lead-ins that went something like, "As reported on the ABC news program *20/20*...." It's the proverbial "where there's smoke, there's fire" aphorism—despite the fact that the origins of that smoke clearly came from the end of a *20/20* producer's cigarette—or something like that.

We were in a terrible dilemma. BankAtlantic was in a vise. People were starting to lose confidence in an institution that served as the custodian of billions of dollars' worth of depositor's monies. One of the issues in the *20/20* story was that investors could not liquidate these debentures (of course, that's how we'd set them up, as the original limited partnerships could not be liquidated either). And *20/20* jumped on this, saying they couldn't be sold at face value, soliciting interviews from brokers who'd said even if they could buy them, they wouldn't do so at face value, only perhaps five or ten cents on the dollar...if they would buy them at all.

If people are not comfortable with their bank, they're going to take their deposits out. If too many customers cash in at the same time to take their deposits out it becomes a bank run. No bank maintains a safe with enough cash to refund everybody's deposits. Reference that scene with James Stewart in *It's a Wonderful Life*.

We became increasingly concerned about this scenario because of all the stories about how we were losing money and taking advantage of our investors. We had to find a way to stem the tide and though litigation was never something we had seen as an offense/preemptive strike either at I.R.E., Atlantic Federal, or now BankAtlantic, and we'd rarely been a plaintiff in a lawsuit, we believed it was the only way to stop the noise. If we filed suit against one of these media outlets, perhaps the others would decide they don't want to have to defend themselves as well. Then again, it was only a possibility each local outlet would fall in line. So we decided we needed to aim high, directly at *20/20,* declaring false light, invasion of privacy, and defamation. If we went to the top of the pecking order, perhaps the local press would stand down because they'd not want to have to defend their behavior. If you shoot the leader, the underlings scurry away. And it worked. The moment we filed the lawsuit against *20/20* and ABC, you could hear a pin drop from the rest of the media. I like to say the silence was deafening.

We really had no interest in pursuing ABC, or anyone else, but had no choice. We knew the case would be difficult to win and even if we did, the verdict would likely be overturned by an appellate court because of First Amendment rights and freedom of the press. What's more, ABC is a huge entity with deep pockets and other resources. ABC took the case very seriously and hired legendary First Amendment lawyer Floyd Abrams to defend it. Gene could not argue the case for us because he was considered a witness to all the events—intimately involved in every step along the way from Bill Willson's first couple of phone calls when I'd brought him in. He just could not be a significant witness, which we needed, and argue the case. Alan Fein, a talented litigator at his firm, volunteered for the job.

The discovery process took about four years. Among the smoking guns we found was a memo from an ABC staffer that said, "Since Levan won't cooperate by standing before the camera, let's make him look really bad." It was just a little incriminating! In fact the individual who wrote the memo was called to testify, at which time he admitted that *20/20* just makes up a story and if people don't want to defend themselves, that's up to them.

"Does that give you the right to undermine the truth with bias… to tell a story that's simply not true?" Alan Fein had asked.

"We just tell it like we see it," was the response.

Also integral to the outcome of the case would be producer Bill Willson's declaration to Gene and me the very first day in my office.

"I don't care about the truth. The truth is irrelevant to me," he'd said.

The case went to trial over seven weeks in 1996. Both Bill Willson and John Stossel were called to the stand. Bill Willson had, for all intents and purposes, cloaked himself in the First Amendment. John Stossel was another story.

From my attorney Alan Fein:

Prior to the trial, at the deposition, John Stossel, clearly slouching in his chair, couldn't have been less interested in being there. We posited he had been counseled by Floyd Abrams to evoke the refrain "I don't know" or "I don't remember" to just about every question. He gave us dirty looks. He put on quite a show in his own right. At the trial, impeccably dressed and well-coiffed, he talked about his litany of Emmys for consumer reporting, what a great guy he was, and how much he knows.

In the first hour of my cross (examination) at the trial, I basically took his deposition transcript, making a list of all the questions to which he had answered "I don't know."

"So you claim to know a lot about this transaction, this exchange," I said to him. "But isn't it true that you don't seem to know about X, and don't know about Y, and you don't know about Z?" This went on for an hour and occasionally he'd speak up.

"Well, I did know about this," he'd say. "And I did know about that."

So I'd suggest we take a better look at the part of the deposition where he'd said he didn't know, and we'd play that part for the court. It was excruciating for him. The jury, which seemed to like him on direct examination, started to hate his guts, so to speak. It was pretty obvious he was a fraud, and he slinked off the stand as the jury stared with steely eyes. Their arms were crossed and they were shaking their heads. It was a highlight of the trial.

The whole thing is stunning, though, the fact that a national news organization could work hand-in-glove with a congressional committee to create the faux drama that they'd been trying to create, which—much to their chagrin—resulted in this trial. (The 20/20 broadcast) is something that went to the essence of who Alan Levan was, and is, and if it were left to stand unchallenged that would be the way he'd have been branded forever. Members of my firm had known him for decades, and this just wasn't who he was.

* * *

On December 18th the jury found in our favor, awarding us $10 million in compensatory damages: $8.5 million to me and $1.5 million to BFC. The jury concluded that the gist of the broadcast was false and that ABC knew it was untrue or had serious doubts about its accuracy.

The money was the least of our concerns and objectives. Restoring our honor and integrity were high on our agenda.

Alan Fein had taken an interesting tack. In a defamation suit like this, he had to show the court that I was more than a suit and tie. I was a living, breathing human being who was quite susceptible to attack and that I felt pain. I was not cuirassed in a corporation. There was no wall up around me. He knew that like most CEOs I was reserved and conservative in nature. Corporate America doesn't usually attract people that like to let it all hang out. But this time it would be necessary—a central component to the outcome of the trial. The jury needed to see the real person, what was inside, so that when damage was done to me I felt it not just from a business perspective but deep in my heart and soul.

Alan Fein likes to say I was disrobed. He encouraged me to open up about my life—to talk about things I wasn't necessarily comfortable opening up about, exposing myself for all the world to see. He asked me to talk about my wife; my children; my parents; the kidnapping. He knew it was crucial for the jury to see me as vulnerable—just like everyone else. I had to be genuine, not stoic or practiced and contrived, and they had to be able to relate to me. I must say when talking about the kidnapping, which I'd tried to compartmentalize for years since it had happened, I absolutely broke down. It was probably as surprising to me as it was to the court, but it all came gushing out…maybe for the first time. It turned out to be a painful experience for me on the witness stand, like running down Main Street completely naked, but I understood that what Alan Fein was doing was the result of his mastery as an attorney and I was incredibly fortunate to work with him.

The $10 million was among the highest damage awards (maybe the highest) in history ever returned against a news organization. Part of the reason is that our suit was one of the few times that anyone dared take on a major news organization. A bona fide example of David and Goliath. In my case it was a function of integrity. We took them and their "gotcha' journalism" with all its ramifications to task and we won.

The Flip Side

It was a foregone conclusion that Floyd Abrams would appeal. Under the First Amendment there is freedom of the press—a broad topic. For the press to violate its responsibility under that heading is extremely technical. It has wide and varied discretion as to how to execute the concept. The actual malice standard was hard to prove, though we'd done it, but it would be hard to sustain. We'd had something almost no plaintiff would have had, and that was the statement by Willson that the truth was irrelevant to him, but as it turned out the appellate court judge, the Honorable Bard Tjoflat, was an extremely conservative jurist infamous for having no patience for large verdicts against corporate entities. Probably that had something to do with it; the appellate court overturned the verdict. Still, we'd made our point, reclaimed our honor, and it was back to business as usual.

For the record, I wholeheartedly support freedom of the press as an important element of democracy. But with that, I do believe the press has a responsibility to stick to the facts, tell the truth, and not fabricate information and report inaccuracies as the truth under the banner of a news organization. While we didn't collect the $10 million, it was never our intent. We'd sued because we had to stop the buzzards from flying over my soon-to-be dead carcass had events gone the way ABC wanted them to go. Throughout my career, and something I hope has come across in this book, *persistence and determination for doing the right thing have always prevailed*. What's more, this concept was about to take its place in a series of events that were to befall me in a way I couldn't possibly have imagined—even through the inconceivability of the ABC trial. It goes all the way back to what my father explained to me the summer I worked my first job as a cabana boy in Miami Beach, toiling all day and not getting paid.

"You have to stand up for yourself," he'd said. "You have rights." And I understood from him that if you always do the right thing, the truth will prevail.

(The ABCs of) LIFE LESSONS LEARNED

- Always stand up for yourself.
- Be sure to do the right thing.
- The truth will prevail if you persevere.

Alan Fein   *May 1997*–Florida Trend

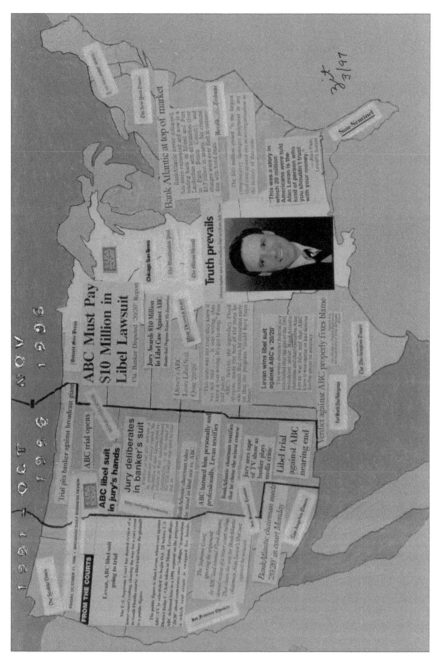

Collage of newspaper articles created by my proud father after our 20/20 win.

CHAPTER 16

HOPE IS NOT A BUSINESS PLAN: THE GROWTH OF BANKATLANTIC

"The man who will use his skill and constructive imagination to see how much he can give, dollar for dollar, instead of how little he can give, dollar for dollar, is bound to succeed."
–Henry Ford

When I arrived at Atlantic Federal in 1984, it was singularly focused on attracting high rate savings accounts and making thirty-year low fixed rate single family mortgages. It had $2 billion worth of assets and fifty branches. Its capital was weak and it was losing money. Its management team was not equipped to deal with the changing regulatory environment and banking's new competitors. The mismatch, between the high savings rates it was paying plus overhead expenses, and the low rate fixed long-term mortgage income it was receiving, was creating losses and bleeding its bottom line.

I had been fortunate to attract the chief financial officer of BankOne, the sixth largest bank in the country at the time, to join BankAtlantic as CFO. I was really excited he accepted the position because he bought into my vision and soon the opportunity to create something special. After accepting the position, he changed his mind and instead wanted to be president. I told him I didn't understand the banking business well enough to allow him to completely take over management. I believed that risk was just too great. Just as I had done with building my first apartment building, I jumped personally into running BankAtlantic. He felt bad about disappointing me and agreed to spend an entire week of his vacation tutoring me on running the bank.

As I explained in previous chapters, the US government had basically decided S&Ls had been created in the last century for the purpose of providing mortgages for home loans. They were consequently out of step in the last decade and a half or so of the twentieth century. These were long-term fixed rate mortgages, and many, for example, were 5 percent and 6 percent for thirty years. That was fine in the heyday of S&Ls because the savings rates were pretty much regulated at 3 percent. Deposits would be brought in at those numbers—with the one or two percent overhead. Then if mortgages were lent out at 6 percent, it was easy to make money on assets, which was a very attractive living for a no-brainer type business. Also as noted earlier, most S&Ls were mutuals so they weren't even public companies with accruing access to capital. They were simply there as a community service, like old insurance companies where nobody really owned them.

In 1977 the government had allowed Merrill Lynch to create its cash management account—CMA—on which you could write checks, whereupon they were paying a high rate of interest which was not government insured and also not government regulated. Other money market funds of this ilk had existed including Fidelity, Vanguard, Wellington, and Dreyfus. In time, they would all implement check writing. They could pay customers higher rates than the S&Ls and as a result the money was flowing out of the S&Ls into these other institutions. This was known as disintermediation. The S&Ls panicked, trying to find a way to keep their depositors' money. While Merrill Lynch and the money market funds invested in higher yielding liquid assets, the S&Ls had been mandated to invest in long term, fixed rate single family home mortgages. As a result, the S&Ls did not have access to the higher yields in which these new competitors could invest in.

In order to solve this problem, the government deregulated savings accounts so the S&Ls could now raise the rates they were paying to be competitive and retain the deposits. Unfortunately, this created another problem. The S&Ls were now paying more interest on savings deposits than the interest they were earning in mortgages—and they couldn't get rid of the mortgages because why would anybody pay off a low interest thirty-year mortgage, particularly now that the mortgage rates were up? The S&Ls were upside down and bleeding. Merril Lynch and the money funds were not burdened with the decades-old requirement that the S&Ls provide long term fixed rate mortgages to customers.

Interestingly, we decided the key to sustainability was to *shrink* out of the problem. Our banking regulators had advised us against, it, but I believed they were wrong. There was no way we were going to hold on to the direction in which we were going and grow out of it. Hope is not a business plan.

We aggressively reduced the rates we were paying on savings accounts. The institution shrank from $2.3 billion in assets down to $1.3 billion and we closed thirty out of fifty branches. We slashed expenses and brought in a new management team. I personally signed every check (over time amounting to thousands of checks) so that we didn't spend a penny we didn't need to. I had used this archaic but effective technique with I.R.E. in the recession of the 1970s. While 1,400 S&Ls were closed by the government under these conditions, BankAtlantic survived. We had made it to the other side, limping but alive.

By 1991 the recession was over for BankAtlantic. We were now ready to focus on rebuilding the franchise and growing it in a completely different way. While we were essentially an S&L and not a commercial bank, I wanted our customers to perceive us as providing commercial banking services. The government had destroyed the S&L model by allowing non-regulated, non-bank entities to begin providing checking accounts at high interest rates, but fortunately they also allowed the S&Ls to start providing commercial banking services. We were going to jump on that opportunity. We didn't start with much. We did not have a single desktop computer anywhere at the bank and while we had two ATM machines, neither one was functioning. Checking accounts and commercial loans at BankAtlantic were nonexistent.

We viewed the opportunity as a blank canvas where we could do anything we put our mind to—anything at all. I felt the same as when I'd joined JP Morgan as a trainee in the 1960s: optimistic, enthusiastic, and excited.

We had changed our name from Atlantic Federal Savings & Loan to BankAtlantic, jettisoning anything that smacked of an S&L so our customers would identify us as providing commercial banking services. We knew we had to reduce and consequently stopped advertising our rates, which had been a big draw, focusing on unparalleled customer service to attract people instead.

We redesigned our logo with three horizontal lines before the "B" in BankAtlantic to demonstrate fast motion and high energy.

Our new signage was red on the top and blue on the bottom, merging in the middle, where it met a bold white BankAtlantic. We created a distinctive branch design for both our new and renovated branches. We were reinventing ourselves, charging into the next age of banking. Growth was imminent.

We acquired the $180 million MegaBank in Dade County; $450 million Bank of North America in Fort Lauderdale from Dr. M. Lee Pearce; and $950 million Community Savings in North Palm Beach. While Pearce had lost the fight for BankAtlantic during the ugly proxy battle, he'd ended up being a real gentleman about it. When an opportunity came up for us to purchase Bank of North America, my negotiations with him went smoothly. We were raising capital from Wall Street to help us continue to grow BankAtlantic. We'd risen from the ashes and just couldn't be contained! I was swinging on the wrought iron gates again.

A Chink in the Armor

Shortly after the purchase of MegaBank, the US Department of Justice advised us that it had been doing surveillance on MegaBank's Brickell Avenue branch in Miami for money laundering connected with Colombian drug cartels. The manager was in question. They asked if we would cooperate in allowing them to wiretap the branch phones and fax machine without a warrant. They had their reasons for doing it that way, which were undisclosed to us. Of course I said yes. They also insisted we not change any procedures at the branch and certainly not terminate the manager—nothing that would alert her that anything was going on.

After a year of surveillance, they believed the branch manager to be guilty of a money laundering crime. Around that time she resigned. I wasn't sure if it was to take a better offer, or because she suspected the federal government was closing in on her somehow, but she was gone. We asked the authorities if we could inform the CEO of the new bank we'd learned she was going to about the investigation, and they said absolutely not. I feared she would just do it again.

Unbelievably, despite our unending cooperation and offer to do the right thing when the branch manager left, the Justice Department accused BankAtlantic of money laundering and wanted us to pay a $90 million fine. They said we were criminals. I was angry and flat-out refused.

In time I was summoned to Washington to a meeting in the Sam Rayburn building with about ten Justice Department officials. Gene and Alison went with me. They accused BankAtlantic and certainly me of single handedly threatening the integrity of the entire US banking system by allowing money laundering to be conducted in our branch. Astonishing! I did not want to have to litigate with the Justice Department so BankAtlantic did reluctantly pay a $10 million fine—just to get rid of them. I almost never paid someone to go away, clinging to my rights and the knowledge that I had not broken the law, but in this case I decided the repercussions from my not doing it may have outweighed my acquiescence.

Ultimately, the other bank where the branch manager went was accused by the Justice Department of money laundering as well. I figured they'd be paying a fine to get rid of the Feds, just as we did. It seemed to me the government just kept assessing fines, rather than arresting anyone. Sounded to me like a scam to build the Justice Department's Christmas fund.

Cruise Ships, and Stratospheric Concepts

We also installed ATMs in all of our branches. But we didn't stop there. BankAtlantic was the first to develop satellite-based technology for ATMs on cruise ships. We installed BankAtlantic ATMs on all the Carnival, Royal Caribbean, and Celebrity cruise ships. We established an exclusive relationship with Walmart for BankAtlantic ATMs in all their superstores in Florida, Alabama, and Georgia. This was tremendous fee income for us, helping to increase our capital, taking advantage of every technological opportunity we could to keep BankAtlantic innovatively in step with modern banking moving into the twenty-first century.

We excelled in asset liability management—the rates paid for checking and savings accounts and what's charged for commercial loans. It was a simple matter of proverbially cracking the code or figuring out the formula, something not that difficult as commercial banks had been doing it for a hundred years. It was just that S&Ls

didn't do it or didn't know how to do it. The management team I'd hired came primarily from commercial banking, replete with intimate knowledge of sophisticated systems focusing on price sensitivity in the areas of thirty-day, sixty-day, and one-year rates.

It may be an understatement to say we focused on diversifying and increasing our assets with a variety of products. With Jack Abdo's and my expertise in investing in and developing commercial real estate, we developed a very strong niche for commercial lending. We became known in the market as the "go to" bank for commercial real estate construction loans. We were financing single family housing developments, apartment buildings, shopping centers, warehouses, retail net leases for construction of the likes of Walgreens or Publix, and high-rise condominium construction. We grew our commercial portfolio to $2 billion of high quality commercial real estate loans. We also created portfolios of $2 billion in residential mortgage loans, $750 million in home equity loans, $300 million in small business loans, and $1 billion in investments. BankAtlantic had grown to $6.5 billion.

Another innovative capital-builder we undertook in this twelve-year period was in the realm of investing in tax certificates. Everybody who owns a home or building pays real estate taxes. In Florida, these taxes are assessed in November and you have the option to pay them early but if not, they are due by the end of May.

If these taxes are not paid, municipalities still need the tax money to cover the budgets that fund their various operating costs. A decade or two ago, they started auctioning off tax bills that are in arrears in the form of what are called tax certificates. For example, there would be an outstanding tax bill (certificate) in the amount of one thousand dollars for a certain address, and the price that bidders would bid began at an interest rate of 18 percent. Whoever bid the lowest interest rate won the certificate. The bidder would still have to pay the one thousand dollars, to the municipalities, but it became a question of how much interest the homeowner was going to have to pay the winning bidder as the owner of his or her tax certificate. If almost nobody wanted the tax certificate, a bidder could scoop it up at 18 percent, but if everybody wanted it, it may sell for as low as 10 or even 5 percent.

When the homeowner or commercial building owner ultimately paid, it would be the one thousand dollars plus the accrued interest. If they didn't pay, every year the rate of interest would accrue to the certificate owner. In time the latter could foreclose, just like with a delinquent mortgage, ending up owning the property. Even if the property owner had a first or second mortgage, or a mechanic's lien, these tax certificates took precedence over it. A tax certificate, considered a municipal lien, was the absolute first lien on the property.

Hundreds of millions of dollars of these tax certificates were routinely sold through the state of Florida in each of its counties. We figured out how the business worked, realizing it was a tremendous opportunity for BankAtlantic in that the return on investment was even better than our mortgage loans.

Assembling a team, we attended these auctions religiously and in fact were the only institution or large buyer in the state that was doing so. Most of the attendees were clubby, wealthy individuals, some of whom were doing it illegally, deciding how to divvy it all up so as not outbid one or the other, allowing the certificates to be acquired at the full 18 percent interest rate.

At an Orlando auction one year, a wealthy individual investor actually showed up with a gun, threatening our employees, saying we didn't belong there. He claimed the opportunity to buy tax certificates was only available to individual investors—of course that is illegal. We got chased out of Dodge that time, but other than that it worked out very well as a profitable source for BankAtlantic. We became the largest buyer in the state. Ultimately, after a decade of dominating the market, all of the private equity firms and other financial institutions jumped on the bandwagon, so it was no longer cost-effective for us because the yields went way down, but for a long-time tax certificates were a solid revenue builder.

The real success of the bank was our deposit base. With most S&Ls, checking deposits were mostly an afterthought. Their core product was savings accounts. People would have their checking accounts at commercial banks from which to pay their household budgets and businesses would have checking accounts so they could take care of payroll and run their operations. We wanted to turn checking accounts into a core revenue product for the bank, competing as we were against Bank of America, Wachovia, Southeast Bank, and Barnett Bank—all big banks of the period—multi-, multi-, multi-billion dollar banks with branches in Florida. So what could we do?

My son Jarett headed up this area of retail banking. Jarett had already been on the teller line during summers at Atlantic Federal around age fourteen or fifteen. He took his job very seriously and it showed.

One time an older teen teller said to him, "I don't understand why you work so hard. You're going to be chairman of this bank someday." Jarett replied, "You don't understand. I need to work a whole lot harder than you do just to keep my job." That kind of story sends two messages. One, it tells you about Jarett and his work ethic. If you are going to do something, do it right. But it also goes back to my mother's teachings, including the lessons she taught my brother, Jay, and drove home to me at age nine, when we assisted her with those PTA mailings. Jarett would go on to business school and get his BBA and also a law degree, so he'd be a real asset to us.

* * *

With Jarett's key involvement and creativity, we came up with a unique and important concept to separate us from the other banks. When you are competing against huge national banks that have large marketing budgets, you can't outspend them, so you need something that makes you stand out. I went back in time to my days running for office at Tulane, and there was no shortage of ideas—particularly the collateral I'd prevailed upon Avis to send, in chapter 3, which, though staunchly inside the rules and ethics playbook, had started a small earthquake. We needed that kind of a shaker-upper at BankAtlantic. So we came up with seven-day banking. From what we knew, there was only one other bank in the entire country at that time, New York's Commerce Bank, that was doing it.

Our branches were open every day of the week, including Saturday and Sunday. We rebranded ourselves "Florida's Most Convenient Bank." The other banks thought we were crazy but it worked to our advantage. BankAtlantic became regionally famous as the seven-day bank. Jarett even created a mascot and called him "7." A BankAtlantic associate would wear the "7" costume and would be seen all over town at ice hockey games, festivals, flea markets, on street corners, and at large venue events. The mascot was so popular we even had several of them so they could spread out to cover multiple events at the same time. We created "7" cloth dolls and "7" piggy-type banks for kids to land us squarely in everyone's home, every day of the week.

What the other banks never understood was that this was a marketing concept, not a customer usage strategy. We understood this from the apartment business. One of the most important features in an apartment complex is the gym. We would build beautiful, state-of-the-art gyms. When tenants would talk to their friends, they would always talk about the magnificent gym in their building. When asked if they used the gym, they would generally respond, "Not yet, but it's available when I want it." Seven-day banking was the same. Not that many people took advantage of banking on Saturday or Sunday then, but it was available and had everyone talking about us. We were novel, modern, and even revolutionary—all in the name of marketing and customer service.

Commerce Bank sued us for usurping their idea. Of course, they lost and when they did, threatened to open Commerce Bank branches all over Florida—especially right across from our branches. We didn't mind. There was enough business to go around.

Then we took things further. We declared every Friday to be Red Friday Day. All the associates, even the executives, would wear a red BankAtlantic shirt on Fridays. After a while, many of our customers coming into our branches would wear red on Fridays. Our drive-thrus would carry doggy treats. The dogs would go crazy with anticipation, as their owners, our customers, came to BankAtlantic. On Thanksgiving, we would deliver thousands of pumpkins to the branches for our customers' children to paint in a designated area in the parking lot. The energy from the top down at BankAtlantic, and the electricity and passion among the associates, was delivered to the customers in the form of great customer service. Our signs were cocky and boldly trumpeted "Yeah, We're open. We're open when you need us—seven days a week."

Jarett started a program of free checking/free gift. We would give away George Forman grills to new customers who opened checking accounts. We opened hundreds of thousands of low cost checking accounts at that time, ultimately resulting in over a million checking accounts. We placed free coin counters in all of our branches. That created a buzz as well. It worked like a charm. We had created one of the most valuable deposit franchises in the state. These low cost deposits funded the lending portfolios at attractive margins. (We didn't know it at the time, but these deposits would become the most valuable driver in our eventual sale of the bank.)

Based on a contact Jarett had, we were able to secure the naming rights to the 17,000-seat ice hockey arena in Broward County. We now had our name on a major arena. The BankAtlantic Center hosted the Florida Panthers and hundreds of other events every year in the arena. This included hundreds of major celebrity concerts (think Barbra Streisand and Lionel Richie), religious events, local graduations, Monster Trucks, and more. BankAtlantic became a brand name in South Florida.

On the capital front we were constantly accessing capital on Wall Street. We were no longer doing it ourselves nor through financial planners. BankAtlantic had major investment banks such as Bear Stearns, Ryan Beck, Lehman Brothers, Friedman Billings Ramsey & Co., and Keefe, Bruyette & Woods raising money for us. We did equity raises, subordinated debt offerings, and convertible subordinated debt offerings. Compared to the fits and starts the bank had in the early years, we easily raised hundreds of millions of dollars during this period to keep our capital strong and fuel our growth.

Funding People's Futures

During these growth years, we created the BankAtlantic Foundation to assist in community needs. We started providing money and services to other nonprofits in the region, channeling more than $15 million into South Florida charities including Habitat for Humanity, the arts, museums, education, and organizations for the homeless. We didn't want to be known strictly for our innovations, but as a bank that gave back to the community that supported us. Robin Reiter had joined us earlier from Southeast Bank to help create and set up the BankAtlantic Foundation. After Robin retired in 1999, our daughter, Shelley, who'd worked under Robin, became executive director.

In 1997 BankAtlantic listed its stock on the prestigious New York Stock Exchange, and by 2003, BankAtlantic's market capitalization reached over $1 billion.

Culture and Communication

We were innovative and had fun doing it. We attracted hundreds of people to our annual shareholder meetings. In addition to the financial material, Jack and I would appear on video clowning around. We had annual employee events called Red Carpet Night with several thousand associates, providing awards, motivation, and education about the successes of the prior year and the goals for the coming year. Each would be fun-filled with antics, costumes, videos, and general rah-rah. On one occasion we had our meeting in the BankAtlantic Center with three thousand associates in attendance. Billy Joel was scheduled to be in concert at the BankAtlantic Center the following week so I was on stage dressed like Billy Joel doing a lip sync of *Piano Man*. All three thousand associates were up on their feet in their red BankAtlantic shirts with cell phones lit, like candles, singing and rocking back and forth with me. It was a sea of red. It was an awesome experience that marked the crest of the wave we were gloriously and gratefully riding.

* * *

One of our most important policies was to regularly hold town meetings at the individual branches and conduct regional meetings as well. When you think about it, good communication is a key component of success on any level. We understood the importance of providing a forum for associates to be able to voice any questions or concerns that may come up for them, and also to make sure we properly disseminated anything by way of continuing education. If we had good or bad news to share, we wanted our staff to hear it directly, honestly, candidly, straight from the top, rather than in the form of rumors, conjecture, and the kind of office gossip that is known to take on a life of its own at the water cooler.

The BankAtlantic culture was infectious. It was the key to our success. We treated our associates like family and they in turn treated our customers the same way. We had 3,000 associates working every day to engage and delight our customers.

Years after the sale of the bank, and even today, when I run into a former BankAtlantic associate, they say it was the best time of their lives. Their employment experience before and after BankAtlantic was just not the same.

These comments are so heartwarming to me and I take them with sincere gratitude and appreciation. I look upon the BankAtlantic days as very special. It truly was a family. Because of the vast experience, innovative ideas, and practices of Executive Vice President Susan McGregor, who started in a lesser position and over time was promoted to EVP and chief talent officer, we instituted the BankAtlantic University. In this arena we used specially designed curriculums and built bridges to educate and promote our associates, which we called them instead of just employees, supporting their career trajectories and efforts to rise as high as they could in the organization, resulting in leadership and succession plan opportunities for many.

* * *

When It Rains…

In 2004-2005, a series of hurricanes including Charley, Frances, Ivan, and Jeanne struck the state of Florida, particularly central Florida and the Palm Beach area. We had branches in their paths throughout the state. We wanted to help the community and paramount to that, we needed to help our associates. Maybe too few businesses understand that and even if they do, they don't act on it.

The damage to many of our associates' homes was incalculable. We put affected associates in hotels. We got generators for associates who had family medical needs requiring electricity. We had vans come from the other side of the state full of supplies. We would have trucks with hot meals go out at certain times to designated locations, telling our associates to be there. The gas stations were closed so we had gas trucks come behind our building in the dead of night, and we would quietly communicate to our associates so we didn't create a riot for gasoline: "You can bring two cars per family, but you have to be there between 1:00 and 3:00 in the morning and just quietly drive in," and we would fill their cars up with gas. We did everything we possibly could to make their lives better and keep the wheels of business turning as they continued to get their paychecks.

We had hundreds of great associate stories going above and beyond. Perhaps this summarizes them all:

We had a part-time associate in West Palm Beach. The area was completely under water. The cars were flooded; she couldn't get out of her neighborhood. She borrowed a canoe, placing her two-year-old son inside. She paddled to a neighbor's house somewhere down the road to drop off her son, borrowed their car, which was not submerged, then drove to work. Part-time or otherwise, associate loyalty was rampant.

Once we had generators, we opened all the branches and encouraged associates and customers to come in and charge their cell phones. Our associates responded overwhelmingly to help their communities, maybe in direct proportion to our support of them.

For many years, we received phenomenal local and national press. BankAtlantic and I were featured in *Business Week*, the *Wall Street Journal,* and hundreds of articles in *American Banker, Miami Herald, Ft. Lauderdale Sun Sentinel, South Florida Business Journal,* and other local and regional publications. We were the darling of the banks and every year we came up with new and innovative ideas. While nothing is perfect and as with any business there was still the occasional bump in the road, we won award after award for our growth, innovation, earnings, stock price increases, and community service. We even won the J.D. Power award for customer service in banking in the state of Florida, during the Great Recession in 2008.

Over a period of twelve years, 1991–2003, we had grown BankAtlantic to $6.5 billion dollars in assets, one hundred branches, three thousand dedicated associates, and one million customers—all checking account holders and we'd started with none. We had totally converted BankAtlantic from a single service, high savings rate payer to a low-cost institution with checking accounts and commercial banking services. Along the way, we had become the largest Florida-based financial institution. At that time there were some Florida banks that did become larger than we were, but they collapsed because of the unsustainable ways in which they grew.

Our management team had a lot to be proud of. In addition to me, it consisted of Jack Abdo, vice chairman; Jarett Levan, president; and our executive vice presidents: Jean Carvalho, head of customer service; chief operating officer Lloyd DeVaux; chief credit officer Jay McClung; chief investment officer Lew Sarrica; chief commercial lending officer Marcia Snyder; chief talent officer Susan McGregor; and Jim White and his successor, Valerie Toalson, chief financial officers.

With the help of stellar management and our equally stellar associates, without whom none of this could have happened, we'd defied the odds. This included turning around a cascade of doubts from our bank regulators that we couldn't make it work and admonitions about even trying. From a sleepy S&L we had created a vibrant, profitable, potent financial institution in Florida. It was an exhilarating journey.

LIFE LESSONS LEARNED

- Create a culture where people are valued and appreciated. Pursue your passion in an environment that is fun, fulfilling, and energizing.
- People are the heart and soul of your business: not only customers, or management, but your employees (associates) as well.
- Real success involves transparency and communication.
- The BankAtlantic culture was the key to our success. We had 3,000 ambassadors working every day to engage and delight our customers.
- Hire up. People that work for you should be brighter and more talented than you. "Subject matter" experts can be rock stars.

From these humble headquarters...

to this new logo...

to these new headquarters.

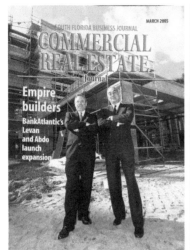

Alan and John E. Abdo (Jack) – From the moment we met, we became lifelong friends and partners. With the exception of my family, no one individual has had a greater impact on my life and career.

STRATEGY

Business Strategy
   Build Low Cost Deposits

Marketing Strategy
   Differentiation
   Florida's Most Convenient Bank
   7 Day Branch Banking
   Midnight Hours
   24 Hour Call Center

Execution Strategy
   Sales Training
   High Energy
   "WOW!" Customer Experience

Expansion Strategy
   Retailer Mentality

TEN KEYS TO VICTORY

– Leadership
– Assertive Selling
–Embrace Change
– Exceed Expectations
– High Integrity
– Low Interest Rate Risk
– Operational Excellence
– Operations Risk Management
– Superior Credit
– "WOW!" Customer Experience

Bank Atlantic
Florida's Most Convenient Bank

- Founded in 1952
- *"Florida's Most Convenient Bank"*
- 100 branches*
- Headquartered in Fort Lauderdale, FL
- Operated in top 6 counties in Florida*
- Total Assets of $6.5 billion*
- Sold to BB&T in July, 2012

L to R
Back: Jack Adbo, Jim White, Lew Sarrica, Lloyd DeVaux,
Mark Begelman, Jay Fuchs, Jay McClung
Front: Alan, Marcia Snyder, Susan McGregor, Jarett Levan

Dr. WOW!

Alan and Jarett
at Associate Paint Party

Alan at Red Carpet Night

Alan at Associate Gala

BankAtlantic "7"

Jack and Alan sitting on a park bench discussing strategy.

Alan and Jack filming video for annual shareholder meeting.

Filming another video

Red Carpet Night, thousands of associates wearing red

Britto – BankAtlantic

Even red at community walks

Alan, Jarett, and Jack

Susan McGregor, Alan, Jarett –
Branch ribbon cutting

BankAtlantic / Family
oriented bank

Alan – town hall meeting

Business Briefing

It's official: BankAtlantic Center

The Sunrise arena formerly known as Office Depot Center had a new name as of Tuesday — the BankAtlantic Center.

The Center of it all

MARKETING

Panthers' arena gets BankAtlantic name

■ It's out with Office Depot at the Sunrise home of the Florida Panthers, now known as the BankAtlantic Center.

BY CHRISTINA HOAG
choag@herald.com

The Florida Panthers have a new name at their Sunrise arena as of Tuesday: the BankAtlantic Center.

The Fort Lauderdale-based bank took over the stadium's naming rights from Office Depot in a deal that marks an unusual third marquee change in the arena's seven-year history.

The 10-year agreement, with an option to extend for another 10 years, also represents a major foray into sports marketing for BankAtlantic, which holds smaller sponsorships with the Florida Marlins and the Tampa Bay Lightning.

Just a month ago, the bank announced a minor sponsorship as the Florida Panthers' official bank.

•TURN TO ARENA, 2C

J. ALBERT DIAZ/HERALD STAFF
TEAMING UP: BankAtlantic's mascot '7' will appear with the Panther's mascot.

Panther's arena gets BankAtlantic name.

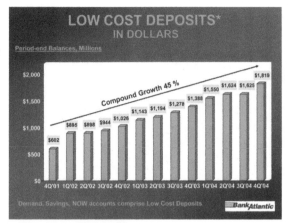

Low Cost Deposit

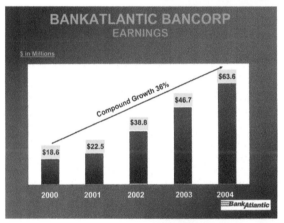

Earnings

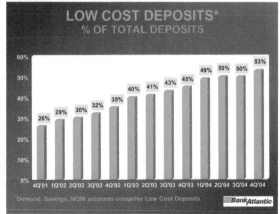

BankAtlantic grows...

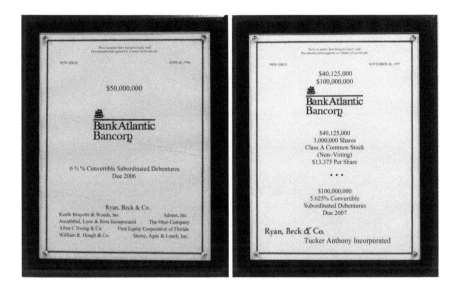

BankAtlantic Capital Raises – still growing.

BankAtlantic Capital Raises – still growing.

HOPE IS NOT A BUSINESS PLAN

Business Week

Sun Sentinel

Miami News

South Florida Business Journal

South Florida Magazine

Jarett, Estate Lifestyle Magazine

Forbes Magazine: Alan – Bank Atlantic with Beetle (VW)

South Florida CEO Magazine

Alan and Lloyd DeVaux, Florida Banking Magazine

CHAPTER 17

LIFELONG LESSONS
AND GIVING BACK:

MY DINNERS WITH BEVERLY, LUCIANO, JIMMY AND ROSALYNN, THE DALAI LAMA, ET AL.

"As you grow older, you will discover that you have two hands,
one for helping yourself, the other for helping others."
—Audrey Hepburn

I'm not sure what was more inspiring: Being front row, center, in a tiny Plains, Georgia, church where former United States President Jimmy Carter was delivering one of his famous Sunday sermons, or watching him tirelessly wield a hammer on a sweltering Georgia day at a Habitat for Humanity site. In both cases, in so many ways, meeting him made me realize that for some people giving back was at the heart of their lives.

My parents had always done more than talk about the value of giving. They volunteered their time in our New York and Florida communities, including at our schools, synagogues, with Boy Scouts, and in hospitals. Sometimes their giving was in the form of a check, but more often it took the form of hands-on participation in whatever was asked of them and even what wasn't. When my mother went into an assisted living facility in her last years, she served on the board to help make things better for all of her fellow residents. Of all the life lessons I learned from my parents, helping others was probably the most powerful.

Die Fledermaus in the House

In the late 1970s, when I was still running I.R.E., Greater Miami Opera CEO Bob Herman invited me to join his board. I was not passionate about opera and didn't even know much about it. In truth I'd never attended an opera, but Bob and I had come into each other's orbits and so he posed the question. I said yes, recognizing that this would be my first opportunity as a young professional to give back. I also figured I'd be able to learn something.

By reputation, Bob Herman was an excellent business manager. He'd worked at the New York Metropolitan Opera under director Rudolph Bing and had taken the Greater Miami Opera (now Florida Grand Opera) to world class status. It was considered a highly prestigious nonprofit, with its board comprised of a cadre of well-respected leaders in their professions. Bob Herman was also extremely skilled, talented, and an expert in running the organization more like a business than a typical nonprofit.

While on the board, I volunteered to create a corporate giving society. Traditionally, and especially back then, an arts organization like this had no corporate support. Its programming was supported by wealthy dowagers. So I took on the task of creating such by raising corporate money. Over time I was able to raise about $150,000—more than half a million dollars by today's standards. But no matter how much I enjoyed opera or not, my mission was really not about myself. It was to support an arts nonprofit that many thousands in the region loved, and to make it accessible to people who could not afford to go. As a bonus, my family and I also got to participate in pre- and après-performance cocktail parties and dinners, including dining with Beverly Sills and Luciano Pavarotti.

A Matter of Habitat

During my time at BankAtlantic, we started supporting the Broward County region's Habitat for Humanity. Habitat's mission is to eradicate poverty housing and provide housing for deserving low income recipients in need. The houses are built by volunteers. The Broward County chapter is just one of hundreds of chapters throughout the world. Because Susie and I demonstrated a strong interest in Habitat, working hard for the organization, we were invited to go to Habitat's corporate office in Americus, Georgia, to meet with its charismatic founder and president Millard Fuller. His passion about eliminating poverty housing in this country was infectious.

During our trip, Habitat for Humanity was conducting a *blitz build* where twenty houses would be built in a single area within one week. There were six hundred volunteers. Of course Millard Fuller had recruited a very hands-on former president Jimmy Carter to be the face and spokesperson for Habitat, and he and Rosalynn were there. Millard and his wife, Linda, invited us to dinner with the Carters. And what an incredible dinner it was. Just the six of us talking about the issues of the day, politics, and giving back to society. This was followed by the opportunity to attend one of the former president's Sunday church sermons the next morning in Plains, Georgia. BankAtlantic was Habitat for Humanity's first corporate supporter in Broward County, with our example serving to enroll other businesses in the cause. Over the years we provided the funds for sixty homes and our associates volunteered to help build them. I had the pleasure of dedicating each of the homes and emotionally handing the keys to the deserving homeowners and their children. We also provided Habitat with their offices free of charge and serviced their mortgages. In 1992, during the time of Hurricane Andrew, we worked with the national office to provide Habitat with 200,000 square feet of free warehouse space to store building supplies to help alleviate the devastation in South Florida.

For two decades, Nancy Daly had taken the helm of Habitat in Broward County, and she is both extraordinarily passionate and dedicated. One Sunday night a number of years ago, Nancy called me with an urgent request.

Habitat for Humanity ReStores are a highly successful concept where donated new or gently used appliances, building materials, furniture, plumbing, lighting fixtures, home accessories, and more are sold to the public at a fraction of retail prices. All proceeds go to the organization. Nancy needed a million dollar loan by the next day to purchase a property that had suddenly become available. It was the ideal place for a ReStore and she'd been looking for a long time. While I'd never made a unilateral lending approval before and all loan applications had to go through the standard loan committee lending approval process, I knew what this meant to Nancy and Habitat, committing right there on the phone to her. She was immediately able to tell the property's seller Habitat for Humanity had the loan to purchase the building.

This particular ReStore makes enough money from sales to build five to eight houses a year.

Education Beyond Tulane—YPO

YPO is a nonprofit which stands for Young President's Organization and is a global platform for chief executives to engage, learn, and grow. As we learn, we give back to the next generation of CEOs. YPO empowers more than 26,000 members in more than 130 countries.

One of my great fortunes was the opportunity to join this organization. It has shaped our lives, given us lifelong friends, provided continuous education from business to health, and provided many wonderful experiences. My closest friends and confidants are members of my YPO Forum, a group of eight local CEOs: Leonard Abess, Joel Altman, Mark Begelman, Phil Bakes (deceased), John Guarino, Phil McKnight (deceased) and Stephen Riemer. I've been the moderator of our forum for twenty-seven years.

In addition to the local and national meetings, we've traveled internationally with YPO, all extraordinary experiences. These YPO conferences, called universities, are hosted by local chapters in their respective countries with a full week of education during the day and social events in the evening. Because of their CEO status, the hosts are able to provide access to world class educational resources, speakers, and opportunities. The education and enlightenment from each of these universities was incredible.

At a YPO university in London, we met four of the royals: Prince Edward, Prince Philip, Princess Margaret, and Princess Anne. In Florence, we had a private party on the Ponte Vecchio and dined at the home of a Medici family member. Susie had a private tea with Salvatore Ferragamo's wife Wanda. In South Africa, we met Desmond Tutu and Nelson Mandela. In Paris, we toured the Louvre on a day the museum was closed to the public. Our tour guide said in the eleven years he had been a guide he had never been that close to the Mona Lisa because of the crowds. Susie and I took all five of our children to a week-long university in St. Moritz, Switzerland, hosted by YPO.

In Cuba, a top Cuban official recalled that he and Fidel Castro, Fidel's brother Raul, and Che Guevara were assembled in the very same conference room in which we were sitting when they had the "holy shit" moment that they had taken over a country in 1959. He reflected that they were twenty-nine to thirty-one years old the time. All of us YPOers could relate to our very own "holy shit" moment when we realized our businesses had been successful.

One of the annual YPO programs is a week at the Harvard Business School, with YPO attendees from around the world. The course uses the traditional Harvard case method and is taught by HBS professors. I've attended this program for twenty-three years and have been a moderator twenty-two years.

United Way

Susie and I have been member of the United Way Alexis de Tocqueville Society for more than thirty years. This is a wonderful organization that supports the community in so many ways.

Broward Workshop

I've been a member of the Broward Workshop, also for more than thirty years. This organization is comprised of Broward County's largest CEOs and chief decision makers, representing one hundred of Broward County's major businesses and professions. Through the Workshop, business leaders seek to facilitate positive solutions to Broward County's critical community issues.

Broward Center for the Performing Arts

BankAtlantic was a charter donor in the development of this Broward County gem, serving as a large multi-venue performing arts center theatre and entertainment complex.

Funding Exponentially

I recall taking frequent mental notes about all the good that the Southeast Foundation, under the auspices of Southeast Bank, was doing in the community. The premise was for a percentage of the bank profits to be channeled into the foundation, which would in turn donate them to nonprofits serving various important community causes. I admired the model and thought BankAtlantic should do something similar. I was able to recruit Robin Reiter (please see chapter 16), who had set up the Southeast Foundation, to create ours. Over time, the BankAtlantic Foundation contributed in excess of $15 million toward bettering the community, for scholarships, libraries, education, arts, and poverty. The work continues today through the BBX Capital Foundation.

Kid-Sized Achievement

In the ninth grade I made ashtrays in Junior Achievement, creating a tiny company to produce them and make a profit as the organization's objective. It was an experience I never forgot. In Broward County, JA again came into my purview through Scott Rassler, who was on the Junior Achievement board of directors. But this time I had an opportunity to contribute in a big way—and for thousands of young people to learn how to succeed in business as I had.

JA Executive Director Melissa Aiello had an idea. She'd secured a site at Broward Community College North, now Broward College, for the purposes of building JA World. She wanted to build a large building where the space would be filled with kid-sized mock storefronts that included a bank, restaurant, car dealership, utility company, various retail establishments, and much more. The banking mock storefront would be built out to resemble an actual branch with a teller line and customer service desk, and more, or a clothing store, restaurant, and anything else. All fifth and eighth grade Broward County students, following completion of their JA course in financial management (owning a business; designing a household budget; saving to put a child through college), would get to come spend a day at JA World, working for one of the establishments to learn what it was like to have a job. My son, Jarett, who was working with me by then, and I thought it was one of the most inventive ideas we'd heard, so much so that we immediately agreed our bank would be JA World's first tenant. Brochures advertised the fact that we'd gotten on board with the program so that others would follow suit. Other businesses quickly followed. BankAtlantic and the other storefronts would pay rent to subsidize the cost of the program.

A Community Calling

The government requires all banks to provide a certain amount of minority lending…a very important part of banking. Many banks do it begrudgingly, because they are required to, but we always felt it was the right thing to do.

Marcia Barry-Smith headed up our BankAtlantic lending program to low income but hard-working, deserving borrowers. Marcia was with us for decades doing God's work. Marcia left when we sold the bank, but recently Jarett and I received this letter from her:

> *"I don't know if there's such a thing as an unrecognized mitzvah but you both have so many of these to your credit and you should know.*
>
> *In a meeting yesterday, a woman couldn't stop talking about how we changed her life—17 years ago! We approved a very difficult loan, got her a subsidy, and our own $5,000 FHLB grant. She could then bring her daughter from their country as she now had a safe place to stay.*
>
> *Fast forward, that daughter has graduated from law school last year and the mom still lives in her condo—now free and clear. The sense of pride, the affordability and stability that this achievement gave Christina allowed her to create the same in her next generation.*
>
> *For all the times both of you defended me and supported what we did for the less fortunate, against many dissenters, for paying it forward, I thank you. And it is written."*

Captains of Industry

Susie is typically starstruck over Hollywood celebrities—I am the same but over successful CEOs. One of the most unique experiences I ever had was with JP Morgan in the mid-2000s.

I was invited to a JP Morgan conference in Deer Valley, Utah. I believed it to be a typical four-day banking conference. We had attended similar conferences by other banks numerous times. When Susie and I arrived, we were greeted with a big surprise. The first person I met and introduced myself to was Craig McCaw. I asked what bank he was with. He said rather routinely that he created McCaw Communications and Cellular One and had recently sold it to AT&T, becoming the largest individual shareholder of AT&T. My head was spinning. It turned out this was not a banking conference at all, but instead a CEO conference comprised of about one hundred CEOs of the largest corporations and private equity companies in the world. In attendance were individuals like Henry Kravis (co-founder of KKR), Barry Diller (chairman of IAC), Stephen Schwarzman (CEO of Blackstone), Jamie Dimon (CEO of JP Morgan). Apparently, I had not read the invitation carefully. I realized I was going to spend four days with the titans and captains of industry.

We attended the JP Morgan Conferences for six or seven years. It was fascinating. One year I walked into lunch and Jack Welch (the CEO of GE for twenty years) asked me to sit with him and his wife Suzy. It was a reserved table and I had the most enjoyable lunch dining with Jamie Dimon, Tony Blair (former Prime Minister of the United Kingdom), Cardinal Dolan (the Archbishop of New York), Jimmy Lee (Vice Chairman of JP Morgan Bank), along with Jack and Suzy. The learnings and inspiration I garnered from these conferences is incalculable.

I often recall my days at JP Morgan as a trainee—what a ride it has been.

Finding Your Passion at NSU

Created in the 1950s in a storefront, Nova Southeastern University today is a national gem with 23,000 students, 150,000 alumni, and an operating budget of more than $600 million. It is the eighth largest nonprofit university in the country.

I was asked by then-president Ray Ferraro to join its board of trustees in 2000 and I became chair of the finance committee. George Hanbury, who had been chief operating officer of the university for thirteen years took over as president and CEO in 2012. Dr. Hanbury is someone highly accomplished from a strategic and business prospective and passionate about the mission of education. I am now chairman of the board of trustees.

Susie and I co-founded two NSU auxiliary organizations: the NSU Fellows Society and the NSU Ambassadors Board. The Ambassadors Board was designed so that membership would be comprised of C-suite executives in the community. The goal of its members is to introduce people to the university and become knowledgeable about its eighteen Schools and Colleges.

There are currently two hundred C-suite NSU Ambassadors Board members. A former Tulane friend, Stan Linnick, someone I'd tried to persuade to come to work with me at I.R.E. in the 1970s, finally retired from Exxon after thirty-five years. He is executive director. The name was recently changed to the Susie and Alan B. Levan NSU Ambassadors Board.

Susie and I also co-founded the NSU Fellows Society. I'd determined that five hundred donors had each contributed more than $50,000 over the last fifty years. This was a fragmented group without a lot of contact with the university after making their gift. As I learned in business, your best customer is your existing customer. I organized this group of five hundred donors by creating the prestigious NSU Fellows Society and breaking them into donor levels. The university now has a group dedicated to actively communicating with these existing and new donors. It is currently in the midst of a $250 million capital campaign, the largest nonprofit undertaking in Broward County. It appears that NSU will easily reach and exceed this target because of the community recognition of its progress and accomplishments. *US News and World Report* has ranked it as one of the top two hundred colleges in the country.

The fourteenth Dalai Lama visited NSU in 2010 and Susie and I sat at his table. He wrapped his blessed white scarf around each individual that had lunch with him as though he were embracing everyone. Clearly he's a man who exudes calm, kindness, and light. But long before his visit, I felt blessed to serve at NSU. The fact is I feel blessed by the opportunity to give back.

LIFE LESSONS LEARNED

- Quite simply, my parents got it right. Giving back is a blessing.
- Lifelong learning will keep you young, sharp, and promote personal development.

Alan, Rosalynn and President Jimmy Carter, Susie

Habitat for Humanity event in Plains, Georgia with the Carters

Celebrating forty years of BankAtlantic service to the community.

Delivering the keys to a new Habitat for Humanity home owner.

Susie and Lionel Richie – United Way event

BankAtlantic
FOUNDATION

2 0 0 2   C o m m u n i t y   R e p o r t

Shelley Margolis
Executive Director
BankAtlantic Foundation

FROM THE EXECUTIVE DIRECTOR

It is a pleasure to share with you BankAtlantic's 2003 Community Report.

2003 was a great year for BankAtlantic and the BankAtlantic Foundation. We were busy putting smiles on children's faces, handing over keys to new homes, teaching financial literacy, and much more. We were doing good deeds for the community, all while having fun in the process. Since 1952 BankAtlantic has seen communities grow and prosper. It is an important investment for us to give of our time and money back to the community.

Shelley (Levan) Margolis, Executive
Director, BankAtlantic Foundation

Giving money away

BankAtlantic
executive
Shelley
Levan
Margolis
helps choose
community
groups to
fund.

DOUBLE ROLE: Shelley Levan Margolis is vice president of community relations at BankAtlantic.

Community recognition

NSU Board of Trustees – 2002

Alan, NSU Presentation

Alan and Dr. George L. Hanbury II, President of Nova Southeastern University

Stan Linnick, Rhoda Linnick, Susie, Alan. Stan is Executive Director of the Susie and Alan B. Levan NSU Ambassadors Board.

A visit to NSU from the Dali Llama Dali Llama, Susie, Alan

George Hanbury, Jana Hanbury, Susie, Alan

HARVARD | BUSINESS | SCHOOL

Harvard Business School CEO/WPO Presidents' Seminar 2010
January 31 - February 5, 2010

Alan B. Levan, Harvard,
Leader of Leaders recognition,
2000-2016

Harvard Business School CEO / WPO Presidents' Seminar 2011
January 30 - February 4, 2011

Harvard Business School CEO / WPO Presidents' Seminar 2013
January 27 - February 1, 2013

Harvard Business School CEO/WPO Presidents' Seminar
January 31 - February 5, 2016

Harvard Business School CEO Presidents' Seminar
February 4 - 9, 2018

Each year, about 160 CEOs attended from around the world.
I moderated for twenty-two years.

Young Presidents Organization

Vermont, L to R, back – Phil McKnight, Phil Bakes, John Guarino, Mark Begelman, Stephen Riemer. Front – Leonard Abess, Alan, Joel Altman

Nashville

Leonard's plane

Aspen

Alan – Yikes!   *With Joel*

Thirty years of friendship and education – Forum trips to Las Vegas, Deer Valley, Georgia, Orlando, Panama, Mexico, Columbia, Nashville, Florida Keys, NYC…Family trips to Orlando, Aspen, Cuba, Brazil, London, Paris, Florence, Switzerland, South Africa, Manaus…

CHAPTER 18

TALES FROM A DIVERSIFIED HOLDING COMPANY

"A journey of a thousand miles starts with a single step."
—Chinese Proverb

Most bankers train to be bankers and spend their entire lives as bankers. Jack Abdo and I got to BankAtlantic, Atlantic Federal when we met, through a totally different route. We were entrepreneurs first; real estate developers and investors second; bankers third. It was this difference in training and experience that allowed us to be innovative in the management and growth of BankAtlantic. Just because we were now bankers didn't stop our creative juices from flowing well outside the teller windows. We invested in and/or owned, and continue to own, many businesses along the way. In fact sometimes the pursuit of other businesses was a kind of wild ride we couldn't have anticipated.

Jack and I have a very interesting yin-yang relationship. Not only is he a savvy stock market investor, but he's known to come up with outside-the-box opportunities leading to unconventional relationships and ultimate successes. I have to make the decision to fund his finds, so to speak, and if I say we have no funding available he continues to negotiate (with the seller and *me*!), keeping the former on hold until I figure out how to do it. Jack is undeterred by any hesitancy on my part. He knows if I think something through long enough I'll figure it out. Over more than thirty-five years, many dozens of opportunities have come up for us, including perhaps the wildest ride of all: Benihana.

It was the mid-1990s. Benihana, the well-known Japanese style steakhouse, was now headquartered in South Florida and Jack was approached to join the board of this publicly traded company. Alan Fein, the partner at Stearns Weaver Miller was representing the company and needed someone in Broward County to serve on the board.

Rocky Aoki, who'd founded Benihana, was a dyed-in-the-wool maverick and Renaissance man. A Japanese-born wrestler, he'd qualified for a spot on the Japanese 1960 Olympic wrestling team, later ending up in the United States on a college wrestling scholarship. His future would include avid car and power boat racing (the latter of which nearly killed him during a 70 mph test run in 1979), using vehicles and boats that brandished the Benihana name. He broke a record for the longest hot air balloon flight, piloting a Benihana-branded balloon, traveling 5,208 miles across the Pacific from Japan to California. He was a backgammon world title holder.

It all started when Rocky was studying restaurant management in New York. The story goes he leased a Mr. Softee ice cream truck in Harlem in which he worked seven days a week, and on which he posted a sign alleging his wrestling prowess in the event someone was thinking of mugging him. By 1964, at age twenty-five, he'd saved $10,000 from his ice cream initiative with which to convince his father to co-invest in the first Benihana. It was a four-table teppanyaki (iron griddle, though the literal translation is iron plate) restaurant on West 56th Street that featured Japanese chefs in acts of culinary showmanship. In the years that followed the Benihana chain flourished, opening restaurants throughout the United States.

In 1999 Rocky was forced by his board to resign as CEO after pleading guilty the previous year to insider trading. He was still the major shareholder through the Aoki Trust with a dual class super voting stock structure. On his way out he convinced his board to appoint his accountant as his successor. The management style from that point shifted to more of a caretaker scenario compared to the panache Rocky had exhibited, and on which he'd built an empire. Over the years the company name had continued to have brand significance, however the quality of food and ambience had begun to diminish. One might say there was a dulling of the brand.

Jack had an idea somewhere around 2005 that BankAtlantic Financial Corporation (BFC) should consider owning Benihana. While the food quality and entertainment value were way down, and certainly management was in disarray, he was convinced the Benihana brand could not be killed off. People were still lining up to celebrate birthdays and anniversaries as they'd been for forty years. He just needed me to figure out how to acquire Benihana.

The opportunity presented itself in 2010 when Benihana needed money. Jack recommended to me that we should make a large investment: $20 million in convertible preferred stock on which we could get an interest rate, something we'd convert to common stock when the time was right. Additionally, after years of trying, Jack was able to convince the board to retire the existing CEO and have him leave the board. There had been no strong leadership or governance for a long time. I was appointed to fill the vacant board seat.

Following a detailed report on the company's state of affairs, the board engaged Richard Stockinger as the new CEO. He unofficially reported to me (we didn't own Benihana; just controlled a large part of it), and though he was extremely good in his role, his early days were off to rough start. The vestiges of Rocky, now deceased, were everywhere. Old habits, like mavericks and visionaries, die hard.

The Asian chefs were not fluent in English. Nevertheless Rich was determined to build morale and called a town hall meeting in Dallas. Every Benihana chef in the United States attended. Also attending the meeting was Taka Yoshimoto, the chief operating officer, who'd been with Rocky and Benihana from the very beginning. Rich's presentation was extremely motivating as he sought to inspire, promoting a Benihana renewal program he'd designed to refresh the brand in every way—certainly at the restaurant level. Taka was there in part to translate Rich's message to the group in Japanese.

A few weeks later one of the chefs reached out to me in broken English, requesting a meeting. He'd been with Benihana a long time and had known Rocky personally. I was pleased to accommodate him, immediately flying him to Florida, whereupon he told me that Taka's translation had included admonitions not to believe a word Rich Stockinger was saying as the CEO would soon be fired and consequently would not be there very long. I thanked him for his great honesty, reaffirming that I'd protect his anonymity.

Afterward, given the fact that I was not quartered at Benihana's corporate headquarters, I reserved a conference room at their offices and asked Taka to join me. I confronted him with what I'd been told. He spent the next half hour defending his actions, complaining about all the things that were wrong with the company and why he was integral to its future. He made a strong pitch about why Rich Stockinger should not be CEO and all the reasons he (Taka) should. I listened politely, my arms gently folded, never once interrupting him, letting him go on as long as he wanted. When he stopped, I said succinctly in response, "Thank you for that explanation. Today will be your last day." I was not CEO and didn't really have full authority to do that, especially since Taka was also on the board, but I did it knowing both Rich and the rest of the board would support me under the circumstances.

As a business owner I've had the unfortunate though necessary experience of terminating many people over the years, including people in very high positions. It's never pleasant or easy, and I always tried to temper a termination by saying it was my fault—perhaps I'd not properly explained the parameters of the job, or maybe it's a different company now than it was when the person first came to work. But this was different. Frankly this termination was a breeze. Subterfuge, betrayal, and company disloyalty do not begin to align with any company policy. With Taka gone, it cleared the way for Rich to redefine the company, implementing his Renewal Program that included new menus, a wider selection of better quality food, more thoughtful and efficient ordering of food supplies, and a new management team. He did an outstanding job in rebuilding a world class brand that had been tarnished. Sales and earnings improved dramatically.

Crowns and Thorns

Among the reasons the Benihana brand had fallen apart was that some years back Rocky had become ill and his third wife, former Tokyo beauty queen Keiko Ono, had taken over the reins of the Benihana Trust. The trust was the largest shareholder. Keiko was difficult to deal with—a real challenge—as she wanted to run the company. She was a very unpredictable, unreliable, self-absorbed individual who seemed to try and use her looks to get her way. Along the way we'd learn that she'd hire lawyers and not follow their advice so they'd quit. She was always changing lawyers and business consultants. She'd make deals with us and never honor them. One time she wanted me to meet with her in New York about an issue we'd been discussing. I kept trying to find out where in the city we were meeting. Finally my executive assistant, Carolyn, was able to ascertain she'd planned for us to meet privately at her residence. I balked, explaining I'd arrange to see her in a restaurant, conference room, someone's office, but there was no way I was going to meet her in the privacy of her home where she might train her "looks" on me. When I said no, she abruptly canceled the meeting.

She'd visit the Benihana restaurants, telling the staff she'd soon be running things. She was a real sword rattler. Keiko was also constantly battling Rocky's children—both during his lifetime and after his death—for control of the trust and Rocky's money.

We had multiple proxy contests with Keiko. She'd propose board members and in the dual class stock structure, she had a large percentage of the vote. We had a very narrow margin by which to defeat her.

In each case I hired Donna Ackerly from the proxy solicitation company Georgeson. She and others worked the phones in order to get the votes. We were able to easily defeat her each time, but on one occasion, though Donna and her team worked themselves to the bone, they had not received enough votes for us to win. Donna was still at it on the day of the shareholders meeting and in fact at 10:00 a.m., when the meeting started, we were still behind. Rich was running the meeting, adhering to the standard agenda of a five-minute presentation of the state of the company followed by a reading of the proxy vote.

We'd arranged things so that Donna had a phone at the back of the meeting room, so she could continue to work the shareholder list until the last second. The room was filled with about fifty people including Keiko and her current crop of advisors. Just as the meeting began, Donna signaled to me that she had a lead on someone who might change his vote. It was somebody in St. Louis with multiple shares, which could help us turn the corner. The problem was the vote had to go through the shareholder's brokerage company that holds the shares. When business is done with brokerage houses the stock is in "street name," meaning shares have the brokerage house's name on them though they belong to the shareholder. This was the case with the St. Louis-based shareholder whose vote we desperately needed. It was incumbent upon him to communicate his plans to his broker, who then had to communicate to his brokerage company. The brokerage company had to communicate to Broadridge Financial Solutions, essentially a clearing house that managed the shareholder process, and in turn Broadridge had to communicate with Georgeson, which would relay the information to Donna at her post so the vote could be counted in the tally. Unfortunately the whole process would take a minimum of an hour, so I had to let Rich know he had to stall.

We were going for a Benihana filibuster. The longest filibuster is history was one presented in relation to the Civil Rights Act in 1957 by Senator Strom Thurmond: twenty-four hours and eighteen minutes. While we weren't going for a record, I told Rich he had to come up with a song and dance, whereupon he looked at me as though I'd just asked him to slowly take his clothes off (not such a bad idea under the circumstances—it would stall things). More realistically, I thought perhaps laying out his extensive business plan in painstaking—or more likely painful—detail would be just what the doctor ordered. Fortunately, Rich was passionate about all the changes he had made at the company.

"Rich," I said resolutely, jumping up amidst a slightly puzzled crowd, initiating the act, "I think maybe the shareholders would be interested to know *all* about your Renewal Program. Tell them how you buy the food, where it comes from, how you measure its quality, how you are organizing things, *all* about that," I said, averting my eyes from anyone and everyone who might be looking at me in disbelief. In fact I thought I could feel nearly fifty pairs of eyes boring a hole right through my head.

But as restless as people became, and as unpopular as Rich and I were becoming that morning, it worked. Rich droned on and on, and Donna finally motioned to me that the vote was in place. I motioned to Rich that he could stop, making a slice across my neck as they do in live TV. Rich took a deep breath and much to the crowd's relief, said in midsentence, "So that's it!" Donna read the vote and we won our position by a hair, bringing a foaming Keiko to her feet as she'd thought she had things in the bag.

The following year, we had another proxy contest at Benihana. I was looking to jettison the Aoki Trust super voting class, under the dual class stock structure, so we wouldn't have to expend the time, money, and energy every year fighting against a super majority. I was able to get most of the large shareholder institutions to agree to this, with one exception.

The fact is there'd been a large shareholder who was suspicious to me, someone who I thought was definitely in Keiko's court and that there must be a story behind this. I called him, wanting to secure a vote from him, stating that all the other big shareholders were voting to eliminate the super voting class, which would mean Keiko would lose her stronghold. I told him I wondered why he wasn't voting that way. During our conversation there was something he said, involving the word "incentive," that really suggested to me he was operating as a group with Keiko, receiving incentive compensation for his vote. If an individual is in concert with someone else this way, it needs to be disclosed in an SEC schedule 13D, or a beneficial ownership report. If you're an independent shareholder, certainly you can do what you want. But I got the feeling there was more to this person than that. I confronted him directly.

"You know," I said, pausing a bit, "I've kind of gotten the impression you're working with Keiko." He denied it. I persisted. "I've got a lot of experience in SEC governance and I think, based on what you said in our conversation, you should have filed a 13D describing your relationship with Keiko. There's a violation here."

Again he denied being connected with Keiko, at which point I told him whether he was or wasn't clearly was not for me to decide, and that I'd simply turn the matter over to the SEC to investigate the nature of the relationship. There was silence at the other end of the phone. "I suspect you have some kind of financial arrangement with Keiko where she's paying you for these shares, or she's doing something with you, or you with her, where you are no longer an independent shareholder," I continued, refusing to let go. "You can vote any way you want, but I'm going to bring in the SEC."

He asked me to hold off, saying he needed time to think about things. He called me back fifteen minutes later. "I've done nothing wrong," he began. "There's nothing here, but I'm going to change my vote. Will you agree not to turn this over to the SEC?" I responded that the extent of my interest was in an honest election. Period.

When he changed his vote, along with most of the others, we were in a much better position, neutering Keiko's voting rights to far less than the 50 percent she had, in fact down to 12 percent, matching her economic ownership. She no longer had a hammerlock on the company. That put us in a position to offer to buy Benihana or sell it to a third party. We couldn't sell it previously because Keiko would have rejected every prospective sale. We'd proposed selling it before but she'd not been interested; she was after only absolute control. We were subsequently able to sell the entire company to a private equity firm for more than BFC was willing to pay had we gone ahead and bought it ourselves. As directors of Benihana, which was a public company, we had a fiduciary responsibility to represent all the shareholders and obtain the best price, even if it meant BFC didn't get to own it. So for us the sale was bittersweet, though we got the same high price for all the shares BFC owned as the other shareholders. We became a seller instead of a buyer but it worked out well all around. In fact we sold Benihana to the private equity firm at $16 a share. When we'd come on board just a few years earlier it had been trading at $6. We'd successfully raised one of the world's most identifiable brands up from the ashes.

BankAtlantic Development Corporation

While the 1933 Glass-Steagall Act provided that commercial banks should focus strictly on banking, and not real estate ownership, the

S&L charters did allow for real estate development and ownership. So while my goal had been to change everything about the fact that BankAtlantic had been created as an S&L and had been stuck in that mold, when it came to eyeing real estate potential I was glad it was an S&L.

Among the first opportunities for us to delve into real estate was in the early 1990s when we formed BankAtlantic Development Corporation. Jack had a relationship with three individuals who were apartment developers and we entered into a joint venture with them to build apartments. Our half of the partnership became a wholly owned subsidiary of the bank. Even though BankAtlantic was an active commercial lender, I required the development management team to secure construction financing elsewhere. I didn't want to convolute things by having BankAtlantic lending to its own ventures. Many of the S&Ls had gotten into trouble by lending to their own subsidiaries without controls in place, making for a conflict of interest, and though it often took discipline not to take the easy road, I was steadfast.

We started with three institutional-grade apartment complexes, meaning that when they're completed, they're the kind of buildings institutional investors and major insurance companies such as Prudential, Aetna, or Equitable would be proud to have in their portfolios. Institutional grade means they're built to last forever. Quality is king. Jack Abdo has always been obsessed with quality and location. Actually, what Jack is obsessed with in real estate begins with an *e*: everything. We built and rented the buildings out, eventually selling them to insurance companies. The profitability boosted BankAtlantic's bottom line so we decided to build three more apartment developments. We also sold these to insurance companies.

On the heels of BankAtlantic's highly profitable foray into real estate, we began looking for other opportunities.

Treasure on Treasure Coast

In 1995 Jack sourced our ability to buy the St. Lucie West Corporation. He'd had a long-time relationship with president Pete Hegener. Pete had been hired by a private equity firm to develop a large plot of land, roughly a 4,500-acre tract toward the southwestern end of the city of Port St. Lucie on Florida's Treasure Coast. The proposed community was named St. Lucie West. At Jack's encouragement, we were able to have BankAtlantic purchase the St. Lucie West Corporation from the private equity firm for $20 million. The tract consisted of seven square miles bordered by I-95 on the east and by the Florida turnpike on the west.

Jack took responsibility along with Pete for designing the master plan for nine thousand homesites and the infrastructure: water; sewers; roadways; utilities. The homesites were then sold to local and national builders to build and sell the homes themselves. Ultimately the entire city of St. Lucie West was built out with nine thousand homes, houses of worship, schools, parks and recreational facilities, and millions of square feet of commercial, industrial, and retail facilities. St. Lucie West even had an arena, site of the New York Mets spring training camp.

Here again is where my focus on the downside (what's the worst that can happen, and can I/we live with it?) and avoiding conflicts of interest come to the forefront. BankAtlantic provided the equity but refused to commit to the construction financing. Again that's where many of the S&Ls had gotten into trouble by lending to their own subsidiaries without controls in place. Not only did avoiding conflicts of interest serve us well over the years, but even the avoidance of the appearance of a conflict of interest was important. It's the discipline I've had from my first years in business when I.R.E. had the multitude of partnerships, some with strong cash resources and some with none. When we and others were in stressful financial environments, it would have been so easy to take from Peter and give to Paul, as the saying goes. But as easy and tempting as it is to comingle money, I would never allow it. We prevailed upon Pete to get independent financing for whatever was needed and each time, a prospective lender would ask why his owner, BankAtlantic, wasn't providing the construction lending. But high compliance was always at the top of my agenda. In about three years, our profits soared, tripling our initial $20 million investment in St. Lucie West.

Masters of Tradition

Embracing our relationship with Pete, we decided to have him source another site. We were gung ho to go again. Round two. This time Pete found a 9,000-acre tract, double the size of St. Lucie West, just south of it and directly on the west side of the Florida turnpike. It was actually a former cattle ranch. We decided on the name Core Communities for our real estate enterprise now, for the reason that we were branching out and making a bona fide business out of the kind of master planning we'd done for St. Lucie West. We were going to develop this tract, which we named Tradition, Florida, even more comprehensively than we had St. Lucie West. It was going to be more upscale and offer more.

We wanted Tradition to reflect a 1950s-era warm, open, friendly town but with a modern sensibility. It would have a very large town center, 18,000 homes, and 13 million square feet of commercial space including warehouses and shopping centers. Work opportunities would be there. The community would be self-contained. In 2008, the Torrey Pines Institute for Molecular Studies, Florida Center for Innovation, as well as the Gene Therapy Institute and Mann Research Center were located in Tradition Research Park (though some have since moved). We master-planned Tradition as a fifteen-year build-out.

Soon Tradition became a model discussed around the country—recognized as one of America's best places to live. It was the 2009 site of HGTV's Green Home. We are reasonably confident that when Disney built Celebration, Florida, they first took a good, hard look at the way we'd built Tradition. Our master-planning concept was pivotal in redefining communities.

Alan Sherman Said It Best

As I wrote in chapter 1, when I was eight years old my family and I moved from Brooklyn to Freeport, Long Island. The fabulous '50's suburban shuffle was in full swing. People couldn't wait to get out of their tiny, cramped, third-, fourth-, or fifth-floor walk-ups in concrete enclaves to somewhere the grass was greener (or actually where there was some grass to begin with). While Freeport was not a planned community, many on the island were, including the most famous: Levittown in Nassau County, New York.

Levittown was built between 1947 and 1951 by the firm of Levitt & Sons, founded in 1929 by Abraham Levitt. Sons William and Alfred served as the company's president and chief architect and planner, respectively. Levittown was the first truly mass-produced suburb and was widely regarded as the archetype for postwar suburbs throughout the country. William Levitt, who assumed control of Levitt & Sons in 1954, is considered the father of modern suburbia in the United States.* Since its inception, the company had built more than 200,000 homes.

At one point in the mid-1990s Levitt & Sons had come to BankAtlantic for financing. We served as lender for their three Florida division active lifestyle retirement construction communities. The company had reduced its size and scope from its New York heyday, now operating strictly in Florida and Puerto Rico.

Earlier than that, we'd signed a contract to purchase Oriole Homes, a large, local, family-owned and run developer of housing

---

* https://en.wikipedia.org/wiki/Levittown, New_York. Accessed August 15, 2019.

communities. We'd ultimately rejected this opportunity because we were not pleased with the results of our due diligence. Consequently Jack had been on the hunt for another home builder to acquire. Elliott Weiner helmed Levitt & Sons, which was owned by Starrett Corporation, controlled by New York real estate titan Paul Milstein. Elliot didn't feel he got a lot of support or even attention from Starrett, restricted to building a few projects at a time, so at his urging Jack approached Starrett about BankAtlantic purchasing the Florida division of Levitt & Sons to add to our real estate stable. Jack was successful in negotiating our purchase in 1999.

Though we'd once been Levitt's lender, now that we owned the company we passed the lending torch to other banks just as we had with our other ventures. In time Levitt & Sons would actively build eighteen retirement communities in Florida, Georgia, South Carolina, and Tennessee, all designed with 350 to 500 homes and a large clubhouse with organized recreation for active adults.

A Favor by Any Other Name

As a matter of form, I would take a trip to Atlanta once or twice a year to meet with Jack Ryan, our banking regulator at the Office of Thrift Supervision. We'd talk about how and what the bank was doing and any plans. Of course the OTS was frequently in our bank, performing routine examinations, but I thought it was a good practice to proactively fly up and tell Jack Ryan what we were up to.

The OTS knew we were making a lot of money in our real estate enterprises, and of course as an S&L we were fully chartered to be in that business. On one trip, however, Jack Ryan said, "Alan, it's obvious you guys are experts in real estate. You're really good at real estate lending, but I see you're also really good as real estate developers." I nodded, wondering just why he had raised the point. "The problem I'm having," he continued, "is that there are hundreds of S&L CEOs and presidents up here all the time who say to us that

282

they want to do what BankAtlantic is doing. They want to be in the real estate business—specifically real estate development because it is so profitable for your S&L."

He went on to say that clearly the other S&L heads and their management teams did not have Jack Abdo and my expertise in the area, so while they were sanctioned to do it, the OTS discouraged them because they simply were not qualified. "They're going to get into a lot of trouble," he concluded.

I understood his problem but I was a little surprised at the request that followed. "I would like you to consider getting the real estate operation out of the bank," he said.

I paused, studying him for a moment before I responded. "If I understand what you're asking me to do, you're asking me to spin the real estate operations, of Levitt & Sons, and Core Communities, out of the banking structure." He nodded and I continued, trying to conceal as best I could my incredulousness, not so much at the idea but at the luck that had just befallen us.

"Jack, you do know we've invested $50 million in these companies between the money we put into St. Lucie West, which then stayed in Core Communities to build Tradition, and the money to purchase Levitt & Sons," I said. "We're making a lot of money, but that's quite an investment. And you want me to spin it out of the bank into a separate, independent company?" We looked at each other for a few seconds, whereupon I knew what I had to do. He'd just given me the green light. "To my knowledge," I continued, "regulators do not ask their banks to reduce their capital. They ask them to increase it. You are asking me to reduce the bank's capital by $50 million by creating a new, separate company with which the bank has nothing to do."

He nodded emphatically. "Alan, I would consider it a favor if you would do that for me."

There it was. A favor. The upshot is it was a fantastic opportunity he didn't comprehend. We'd created these companies by infusing money from the bank into these subsidiaries. Now we were going to be allowed—actually urged—to take the money out of the bank-owned subsidiaries for whatever we wanted to do with it. I tried to keep as straight a face as I possibly could. I told him that as a *favor*, I'd accommodate him.

It was a once-in-a-lifetime opportunity. In 2003 we spun Levitt & Sons and Core Communities out of BankAtlantic into a separate NYSE-listed company we'd called Levitt Corporation. We also listed BankAtlantic Bancorp on the NYSE at that time. BFC now owned 55 percent of a public real estate development and master planning company as a totally separate entity in addition to BFC's 55 percent ownership interest in BankAtlantic.

Levitt Corporation, as an independent company, could now raise its own capital. We went to market and did so, just like BankAtlantic Bancorp was raising capital. It enabled us to accelerate the growth of Tradition—before the recession—and release the brakes so Levitt & Sons could be fruitful and multiply resulting in the aforementioned eighteen active retirement communities in four states.

Ryan Beck

There is no underestimating the power and possibilities that come from continuous education. I call it cumulative knowledge. I.R.E. had come from my curiosity about what turned out to be a pivotal seminar (please see chapter 6), and overall I get lots of ideas from attending seminars and conferences.

At a banking conference in Scottsdale, Arizona, titled "Are You Looking to Buy or Sell Your Bank?", upwards of four hundred bankers, investment bankers, and others attended, eager to learn. Keynote speakers addressed topics such as how to grow your bank, buy a bank, how to handle governance issues around banking, exactly how to sell a bank, and so much more. It was all intriguing to me because we'd purchased three banks: Megabank; Bank of North

America; and Community Savings Bank. We had the capital and were looking to buy other banks to grow our franchise.

One of the speakers was Ben Plotkin, president and CEO of Ryan Beck, an investment bank that bought and sold banks. They operated as the middle man with about four hundred brokers in total. I wasn't at all familiar with Ryan Beck and listened carefully to what Ben had to say. Most of the speakers at these conferences and seminars represent companies looking to pick up clients and generate business from attendees. At a coffee break following Ben's presentation, I took the opportunity to approach him about finding other banks to buy, wondering if he'd be interested in working out an arrangement where he'd send us opportunities that may cross his desk.

"By the way," he said in response, "did you know we're a full-service investment bank? We also raise equity and debt for growth. We're a banking boutique (smaller than a wire house, which is a Wall Street bank with many hundreds of offices and thousands of brokers), so if you have any need for what we do...."

We certainly did! Over time Ryan Beck became our primary investment banker—our lead underwriter—raising hundreds of millions of dollars of debt and equity for BankAtlantic.

When I really understood how things worked in the investment banking business and knew we could make money from it, I thought we should pursue owning a company like Ryan Beck. In fact we got to buy Ryan Beck, though it was a public company. Ben Plotkin went to his board on our behalf, having brought the idea to me in the first place. They approved the sale to BankAtlantic for $40 million, with Ryan Beck becoming a wholly owned subsidiary of BankAtlantic Bancorp. He was an excellent investment banker and wanted to focus on his strengths. After the purchase we left Ryan Beck alone to do what it did best, though Ben now reported to me as CEO of the ownership group.

One day Ben called to tell me about a business called Southeast Research that did research and analytics on banks, selling their reports to interested parties. I was familiar with them, having done business with them in the past. I gave Ben my imprimatur and he negotiated to buy Southeast Research. For Ryan Beck this wasn't because the company was ultra-profitable. Rather it was because it had a large cadre of research experts in the banking field, so Ben wanted to take this company and roll it right into Ryan Beck's research group to beef it up...to produce a peerless, robust research and analytics department providing additional services to its clients.

Next on Ben's agenda was the acquisition of Gruntal & Co., one of the oldest brokerage companies in the vein of Merrill Lynch. In fact Gruntal & Co. was more than one hundred years old with a name known to everyone in the financial world. As prolific as the company had been for generations, it had changed hands and fallen on hard times, making some bad investments—perhaps bad acquisitions outside of the brokerage space that had depleted its capital.

Gruntal was in the crosshairs with its regulators forcing a sale or they'd shut it down. For all of its problems, the company still had $20 billion in customer funds in its escrow accounts, trading every day through seven hundred brokers (hankering for a solvent parent). Another company, Ladenburg Thalmann, had wanted to buy it but the deal had fallen through so Gruntal was ripe for the picking. Actually the regulators were conducting a shotgun wedding so we didn't have to pay a penny for Gruntal & Co. as it was near bankruptcy. We elected to take the assets. We wouldn't have wanted to buy it outright anyway because it had all sorts of liabilities that we couldn't get our arms around. We acquired the branch offices, brokers' contracts, and customer accounts, including the $20 billion in escrow accounts owned by the customers. Former Gruntal brokers were ecstatic because with an investment banker providing them product, they had expanded earnings potential. They could now sell IPOs and other financial products, not just trade stocks.

The Gruntal deal was a real game-changer, with Ryan Beck exploding from four hundred brokers to more than one thousand. Ryan Beck went from about $4 or $5 billion in customer accounts to something in the vicinity of $25 billion, with tens of thousands more customers.

The end of the Ryan Beck story is that in 2006, using my knack for seeing around corners as I'd done with I.R.E. and at other times, I was concerned we were diving into another recession. I told Ben we needed to think about selling Ryan Beck. Ben introduced me to Stifel Financial Corporation chairman and CEO Ronald Kruszewski. Stifel is an investment bank that was larger and more generic than Ryan Beck. In short Stifel had a more diverse menu of companies for which it could raise funds, whereas Ryan Beck was an investment banking boutique. We sold Ryan Beck to Stifel Financial Corporation for $125 million in the first quarter of 2007 at the door to the recession. Our investment in Ryan Beck had been $40 million. What we took was all stock, so we essentially sold it for 100 percent stock in Stifel. When the announcement was made that Stifel was buying Ryan Beck, over the next six months Stifel's stock shot up with us being a major beneficiary. I started a plan of liquidating the Stifel stock and by the time I was done, we'd sold Ryan Beck for a $100 million profit. Stifel integrated Ryan Beck into its business and has been very successful with it.

Share and Shares

Once again Jack Abdo's prolific work life, which is often indistinguishable from his social life with his business dinners at least five nights a week, led us to the front door of Bluegreen Corporation.

"We should *really* get involved with them," he said repeatedly about the NYSE-listed company. Bluegreen had originally been a land sales company under the Patton Corporation name, but when George Donovan, at that point CEO, had joined the company in 1991, he brought with him years of experience in the vacation ownership industry, converting it to a timeshare company and changing their name to Bluegreen.

"I know we're not in a position to buy it, but I'd like to stick my toe in the water," Jack said. "Maybe we can make an investment in Bluegreen that will lead to great things." As usual his instincts were keen; his enthusiasm infectious.

He asked me to accompany him to Bluegreen headquarters, the former 170,000-square foot IBM headquarters in a Boca Raton warehouse. We were to attend a meeting he'd set up with George Donovan. Bluegreen or otherwise, history had been made in that particular building as the PC was invented there, and I was eager to go.

George Donovan was quite pleasant when we asked about Levitt Corporation investing. He indicated that Bluegreen was a public company and not looking to raise any capital. He said if that ever changed and he didn't want to go through investment bankers, he'd call us.

"Do you have any issue with Levitt Corporation buying stock in your company on the open market," I asked him as a professional courtesy as we left. He hadn't told us anything confidential, so Jack and I felt comfortable in becoming regular shareholders just like everyone else. George told us he'd be pleased if we did.

Many years back, when I'd first formed I.R.E., and certainly when I became involved with Atlantic Federal/BankAtlantic, I'd made it my business to buy five shares of stock in every bank I could find that was a similar business to mine. This way I would be mailed the quarterly and annual reports. I'd done the same with a few shares' worth of stock for every real estate development company, syndication company, home building company, and more—also so I could get their reports. In this way I kept myself abreast of every idea and disclosure I possibly could. I wanted to do this with Bluegreen. It was clearly an innovative company under George Donovan who had the vision and creativity to convert the conventional timeshare model to a points system. This would enable the timeshare owner to use the points any week at any resort in the Bluegreen system in the United States and Caribbean.

During this time, Bluegreen was going through a transition. Unfortunately in converting to a points system, aka a club system, the company experienced a substantial reduction in income because it was a difficult conversion. Bluegreen was a trailblazer in the concept, something that often comes with a marketing challenge until people fully understand the new advantages. The concept actually became an industry game-changer and standard, with major players like Wyndham, Marriott, and Hilton ultimately adopting it. But for about the first eighteen months, it was extremely disruptive for Bluegreen. Earnings went down. Stock went down dramatically. That's when we bought ours for about seventy-five cents a share when it had previously been trading at five dollars. We bought 5 percent of Bluegreen stock and were now getting their reports.

One day, a year or two later, the phone rang with George Donovan professing to Jack he was embarrassed.

"I did need some capital," he began. He explained he'd been approached by Morgan Stanley and some other investors. He'd subsequently raised $50 million through them, giving them a few board seats, thinking Bluegreen was all set. "They're killing me," he said, explaining that instead of putting senior executives on the Bluegreen board, they'd put newly minted MBA twenty-five-year-olds.

"They don't know anything about the timeshare industry; they hardly know about business," George said, swallowing hard. "They're unhappy about what we're doing and are disruptive in my board meetings because they object to everything I'm proposing. I can't get anything done. I can't get allocations to buy new inventory to build new buildings and as a result, the business is suffering and not only that, they want to fire me because they don't think I'm doing a good job as CEO." He asked if there was any way Levitt Corporation could buy them out, saying he'd put us on the board so we could effectively control Bluegreen.

Jack went to work with Morgan Stanley and other investors that were in this for the $50 million. They were suffering huge losses in their investment. They'd put their money in, not realizing the transition Bluegreen was going through. They proceeded to tie George Donovan's hands at the board meetings so he couldn't make appropriate decisions. It was a huge mess so Jack was able to step in, negotiating for us—actually Levitt Corporation—to buy them all out, paying less than what they had in it. They were willing to take the hit. With the 5 percent we already owned in the market, and the purchase, we now owned 23 percent of Bluegreen. I became chairman and Jack became vice chairman, of course sweeping the twenty-somethings off the board and back to the video arcade at the mall. The company flourished under our control. George now had Jack's and my support, as well as that of the entire board, and he could confidently execute his business plans. The company grew to more than fifty resorts owned and managed by 8,000 employees. In 2005, George Donovan retired. We appointed George's second-in-command, John Maloney, as CEO.

LIFE LESSONS LEARNED

- When the road gets rocky (or in my case Rocky), see where it takes you and adjust your course accordingly. You'll get to your destination—even a new and better one.
- Sometimes it's better to go to great lengths not to take the easy way. Though it may prove difficult in the short term, it will pay off later on.
- Opportunities are everywhere. You just have to be open to them.
- Luck or expertise? I don't know if there is a difference if you are constantly looking and learning.

Summary

This overview tells you what we do rather than <u>who we are and how we approach our business</u>:

<u>First</u>, our culture is entrepreneurial. Our objective is to make portfolio investments based on the fundamentals: quality real estate, the right operating companies and partnering with good people.

<u>Second</u>, our goal is to increase value over time as opposed to focusing on quarterly or yearly earnings. We expect our investments to be long term, and we anticipate and are willing to accept that our earnings are likely to be uneven. While capital markets generally encourage short term goals, our objective is long term growth as measured by increases in book value per share over time.

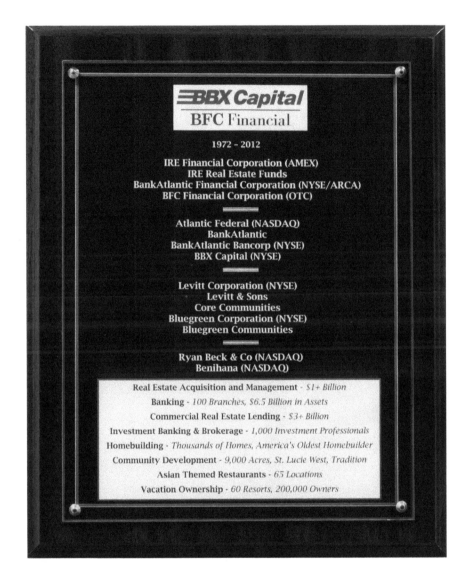

≡BBX Capital
BFC Financial

1972 – 2012

IRE Financial Corporation (AMEX)
IRE Real Estate Funds
BankAtlantic Financial Corporation (NYSE/ARCA)
BFC Financial Corporation (OTC)

Atlantic Federal (NASDAQ)
BankAtlantic
BankAtlantic Bancorp (NYSE)
BBX Capital (NYSE)

Levitt Corporation (NYSE)
Levitt & Sons
Core Communities
Bluegreen Corporation (NYSE)
Bluegreen Communities

Ryan Beck & Co (NASDAQ)
Benihana (NASDAQ)

Real Estate Acquisition and Management - *$1+ Billion*

Banking - *100 Branches, $6.5 Billion in Assets*

Commercial Real Estate Lending - *$3+ Billion*

Investment Banking & Brokerage - *1,000 Investment Professionals*

Homebuilding - *Thousands of Homes, America's Oldest Homebuilder*

Community Development - *9,000 Acres, St. Lucie West, Tradition*

Asian Themed Restaurants - *65 Locations*

Vacation Ownership - *60 Resorts, 200,000 Owners*

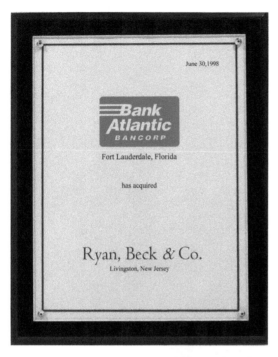

TALES FROM A DIVERSIFIED HOLDING COMPANY

Sun Sentinel

THE HEAT IS ON *Miami Herald*
AT BENIHANA

Bluegreen Vacations Overview

68 Resorts
214,000 Vacation Club Owners

Bluegreen's Fountains Resort, Orlando, Florida

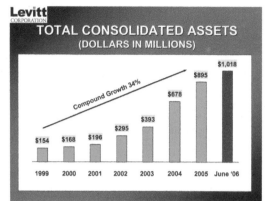

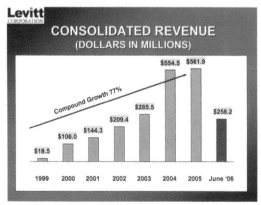

Seth Wise, Levitt and Son's Developments

Levitt & Son's
Alan – Bellagio Community

Jarett and Seth

CHAPTER 19

STORM CLOUDS—AND THE STATE BIRD OF FLORIDA

"Those that cannot remember the past are condemned to repeat it."
—George Santayana

It was 2004 and the economy was booming. Except for a few months of slowdown here and there, it'd been a long time since the country had been hit with a recession. The 1990s had been the longest period of consistent growth in American history and the subprime mortgage crisis was a few years away—not yet on the radar. Most Americans were employed and life was good. Business was also good…maybe too good. Jack Abdo and I started to become uneasy, particularly about the way things were going in the real estate industry.

At BankAtlantic, we'd built a first-rate real estate lending team. Our real estate Major Loan Committee was working in overdrive, processing all the commercial real estate loans coming in for approval. Our real estate portfolio had swelled to $2 billion. We were financing residential housing developments, shopping centers, owner-occupied office buildings, apartment building development, and high-rise condominium development. Construction was everywhere and the developers were making money, as were the banks lending to the developers. There were so many cranes in the sky hoisting building materials the joke was the crane had become the state bird of Florida. But at the same time, there was a strange undercurrent brewing.

First, it's one thing for developers to take risks in order to build their buildings, as they generally understand the risk. When you think about it, there are a lot of moving parts in real estate, especially when you're a developer. You have to find the land; you have to design the project; you have to secure the financing; you have to build; and you need to find the buyers who want to occupy what you're building. In getting from A to Z, a zillion things can change: the market changes; interest rates change; the economy changes. It could be as simple as someone builds a comparable project next door and becomes a competitor, pulling your usual customers away and attracting other prospective buyers or renters. They sell it for less or more expensively, depending on the project's criteria. They put in a fabulous fitness center and other amenities. So when a project takes three or four years to build, and sell out, and mortgages amounting to $10, $20, or $50 million have to be personally guaranteed, there's a tremendous amount of risk the developer takes and naturally the bank does as well. And for all of that expertise and risk, developers get paid an exorbitant amount of money when they are successful.

In order for a developer to finance the construction of a new high-rise condominium building, it needs to demonstrate consumer acceptance to the bank. Historically, the best way to demonstrate consumer acceptance is with preconstruction presales. If the developer wants to build a high-rise condominium that will cost $50 to $100 million, the lender will lend 75 percent of the amount of construction, after the developer has buyers' contracts of at least 50 percent of the units. Presales assure the lender that the building has met consumer acceptance as the individual buyers have to put down 20 percent deposits. This concept has always worked well for the developers, the buyers, and the bank. The developer would generally offer a preconstruction price discount to encourage early decisions from prospective buyers. Upon meeting that presale requirement, the bank will start to fund construction and the developer starts to build. It generally takes three years from the first presale contract to the completion of the building and the buyers moving in. During the course of the three years, prices would increase from the early presales because as the building was going up, and finished, buyers could see how beautiful it was.

Non-real estate, speculative investors figured out they could sign a presale agreement putting down 20 percent of the purchase price to buy a condominium unit, and then later put the unit on the market, all before closing and occupancy, reselling it at a significant profit. If a unit went up $100,000 in price, they could now sell it to make a real windfall without doing anything else. And the developers were all too willing to accommodate. They began to solicit presale buyers (investors) so they could reach their presale requisite in days instead of the usual months it took to get there. This allowed construction to accelerate.

Jack and I had started to observe this phenomenon everywhere: cab drivers, waiters, estheticians, everyday folks were becoming investors—racing to participate in the presale market as it was. Why not? Vegas had nothing on odds like these. When you could earn enough in a very small timeframe to send your child to college, provide some security for yourself and your family, maybe finance a dream of yours, I repeat, why not? The caveat is that it's one thing if developers or sophisticated investors are making a profit because they are investing substantial amounts of money and understand the risk. It's another issue entirely if average people who know nothing about the business are making $50,000 and $100,000 basically without doing a thing. We intuitively knew this kind of flipping was creating a market that could not sustain itself.

Tantamount to that, if someone is going to occupy a unit, if it's really where they want to live, they're going to make sure it meets their high standards and specifications. Is the price right? Are the amenities ample? What about the square footage and finishes? If you're going to spend your hard-earned money and bring your spouse and children to live there for the next five, ten, fifteen or more years, it had better be exactly what you want.

Flippers, on the other hand, couldn't care less about any of that. Flippers see only dollar signs, knowing in six months they could double their money. Flippers do not go to any lengths to make sure the quality of the building is what it should be, so there is no dialogue along these lines with the developer. Compound that fact with the reason the lender, who lends 75 percent of the construction costs, wants 50 percent in presales for the assurance that the project is viable—that the building has authentic buyers who actually intend to purchase the unit and move in when it's finished. In that way, even if no more sales beyond the 50 percent are ever made, when the construction is complete, the lender then recoups 70 to 80 percent of the construction loan as the individual units close. But if flippers who are part of that initial 50 percent presale get involved, there is neither assurance it will meet with critical consumer acceptance nor that they will actually follow through and buy the unit.

You may recall that my father, courtesy of a friend he had in real estate, participated in this kind of activity in a small way in the early 1970s when condos were valued at $50,000 to $75,000, making a tidy sum of $5,000 to $10,000 a pop. He had no understanding of the risks. Fortunately he got out before the market collapsed during the 1973-75 recession, where people ran away in droves so as not to have to close on devalued condo units on which they'd paid a deposit. I'd seen it firsthand and was grateful my father was not affected. Jack and I were concerned that if prices started to fall as a result of a glutted, oversold market, presale flippers would forfeit their deposits and walk away, rather than put up more money to actually purchase the unit.

I met with our BankAtlantic lending group multiple times to tell them what Jack and I were feeling. Our lending group assured us that our developers were on the up and up—definitely not involved with flippers to satisfy the presale requirements. Nevertheless we were uneasy because we had a portfolio of $600 million in high-rise condo construction loans. If we made a mistake on the market it would be catastrophic. We asked our lenders to slow down approval of the new loans, whereupon they promised they'd only present new loan requests that reflected the highest quality all around, likely indicating prospective buyers were authentic.

No developer ever intends to build an ugly or substandard project anyway. Developers consistently believe their project is always the best, state of the art, most beautiful, ultra-high end, and at the best pricing. Developers are eternal optimists—sometimes blindly optimistic. Pessimists need not apply.

Jack and I began asking the loan officers for the developers' presale list of buyers' names. If we'd see separate names of an entire family who'd purchased multiple units in one building we'd know something was up. Many of the buildings were also geared toward older residents, so if we found presales to buyers in their thirties and forties, another red flag went up. We couldn't prove much but suspicion mounted.

To digress, and as established in previous chapters, the economy in Florida turns on real estate. In many states it's all about agriculture or manufacturing, but in Florida, real estate and construction are pivotal. If you have fifty buildings going up from South Miami Beach to North Miami Beach, think about how many construction workers are employed on those projects. Consider how much HVAC is being purchased, how many installers are employed, and the vast number of materials suppliers in the loop. What about the concrete business? Truck drivers? Painters? Drywallers? Roofers? Flooring people? Carpenters? The list is infinite, and it's not only condominiums. Houses are going up everywhere in massive developments. So when the music stops, everything does. Unemployment reigns and hundreds of thousands of people need to cut their spending habits. Forget about not buying real estate, they're also not buying new TVs. They're not going to movies or restaurants. They're not buying clothing or cars. They're not doing home improvements. They're spending far less at Christmas. They're not able to pay their credit card balances. The fact is Florida has always been known as a boom or bust state in real estate because when it slows, and prices start to stabilize or go down, people get quite nervous. It's been said Florida is a bellwether—the first into a recession but also the first out. At the first signs of recovery, people are out there buying again, but when it's bad, it's really bad.

When all this started, we recognized many of our loan officers were not that old, consequently had not lived through what happened in the '70s. They just hadn't seen it. All many of them had was a reference point of years of unprecedented economic growth in America, never experiencing a real downturn. And other banks and lenders were much the same way, employing a relatively new crop of people as an older regime had retired.

I took all this into account and finally drew a line in the sand.

"We're done," I told my ashen staff in 2004. "We're not doing anymore condominium construction lending."

I knew that with $600 million in construction loans in the portfolio, it would still take three years for that size portfolio to run off; for us to get our principal back on our loans as each unit closed. And just because we stopped new lending didn't mean we'd get that $600 million back right away. That money still has to go through the cycle of building the buildings, selling them, closing them, and BankAtlantic getting paid back for these construction loans. I simply decided to micromanage the $600 million and make sure we got it all back. Once again I was seeing around corners and took an unpopular stance, exactly as I'd done in the 1970s with I.R.E.

Our lending staff was up in arms as their stock in trade was developers. They spend their careers cultivating relationships with these developers, who could go to any bank, but they come to us because of solid relationships they have and because BankAtlantic is a good lender. We understand the business possibly better than anyone given Jack's and my extensive backgrounds in real estate, long before we were bankers. We were now cutting off our loan officers' opportunities for bonuses but more important than that, we were destroying everything they had worked for with their developers. It was one of the hardest decisions I've ever had to make. It was going to cost BankAtlantic $30, $40, $50 million in lost income from new loans, but I had this bad feeling about what was coming.

I've always taken the position that you watch the downside and the upside takes care of itself. My objective has always been to make sure we are sustainable in business—that we can survive to be in business when the worst, which can come again and again, is over. While the loan officers were focused on the impact of their bonuses, my primary focus was to be prudent and protect the bank's capital. Though Jack and I could not guarantee where all this was going, we had a pretty good idea. We knew for sure that an ugly recession would be catastrophic. But what made the decision even more difficult was that our competitors—the other banks—continued to do business the way they always had. I didn't feel much better four years later when we were proven right, because everyone else lost their shirts. But in 2008 when the bottom fell out of the housing market and the other banks took a bloodbath, all $600 million of our condominium portfolio had been paid in full.

Builder Bank Loans: A Loan by Any Other Name

Our real estate lending department had been dealt a huge blow to its budget by my mandate to stop new condo construction lending. Being as resourceful and resilient as the department was, it identified a new kind of loan to generate income.

Residential single family housing was still booming. National public homebuilders such as Lennar Corporation, KB Home, Toll Brothers, and others were building like crazy in Florida and around the country. These developers would identify a large tract of land on which they wanted to build hundreds of homes, but sometimes for optics and accounting reasons they did not want to acquire the land themselves. For example too much money invested in land wasn't earning any money until they created the subdivisions, so their balance sheets might reflect inventory they weren't going to be able to use for several years.

Accordingly, homebuilders would work with an intermediary to buy the land and sell them the lots as they needed them. These intermediaries, known as land bankers, would approach lenders, including BankAtlantic, to borrow the money to buy the land so they could deliver the individual lots to the national homebuilders when they were ready to build on them. The banks were interested because the national homebuilder had already been identified as the buyer and had put up substantial money in deposits for improving the entire property with streets, water, sewer, power, and more. The intermediaries, or straw men as I came to refer to them, would make their profit by buying a large land parcel for one price and selling smaller lots to the national homebuilders at a marked-up price.

Jack was generally against these builder land bank loans because we were not dealing directly with the homebuilder. We were lending to intermediaries who were signing the loans, guaranteeing the debt, but who did not have the financial strength that the direct borrowers would have. These borrowers really had no control over what was ultimately going to happen once the land was acquired. It was totally dependent on the national homebuilders. If the homebuilders stopped "taking down lots," in vernacular, how were the intermediaries going to be able to pay us? Again, they were completely at the mercy of the homebuilders.

In many cases, when an application of this kind came to our Major Loan Committee, which was comprised of about six people including Marcia Snyder, head of our lending group, and Chief Credit Officer Jay McClung, with Jack as vice chair, Jack voted against it. Back in the mid-1980s, I'd established a precedent that all major lending would be done by consensus, meaning all of us had to agree. The voting mechanism for disagreement was determined by a soft no or a hard no vote. A soft no could be overruled if everyone else wanted to go ahead with the loan, at the discretion of the committee chairman, which I was. If someone gave a hard no, even if it was the only no, it could not be overruled. Jack was not in favor of builder land bank loans. He was uneasy with the concept and would generally vote a soft no. Much to my eventual regret I overruled him, many times, for the following reasons.

BankAtlantic's loan officers had convinced me that since we were only lending at 65 percent of the land purchase price and the homebuilder had put so much money into the project, we were secure. After all, the market value of the land could decrease 35 percent and BankAtlantic could still be protected to recoup its 65 percent loan to value loan. Besides, at that point, in this country we had never seen a housing market decline of the magnitude as was to befall us. Even during the recession of the 1970s, housing was relatively strong. We ultimately lent about $200 million on these builder land bank loans.

As we entered 2006, the slowdown in sales and subsequently construction was palpable. Bear in mind we actually owned a homebuilder, Levitt & Sons, so we didn't have to rely on a host of outside builders and developers telling us what's going on in the market.

We knew it firsthand. Our source of marketing trends was our own subsidiary. Some of the buyers on these individual houses were beginning to default on their contracts. Levitt & Sons assured us they were not encountering flippers, though it would later be apparent their assessment was incorrect. We were observing other signs of a slowdown in that new condo sales were nonexistent and prices were no longer rising. The information from the Federal Reserve and Treasury was confusing to us, as they continued to say the market, at worst, was in for a soft landing.

At that point, we felt an obligation to disclose in our 2006 SEC annual 10-K and 2007 quarterly 10-Q filings that we were concerned about the market. While we'd not had any loan delinquencies or defaults, as a public company it was incumbent upon us to disclose *what we knew, when we knew it*. All we had at that point in time was a hunch that the economy was headed for trouble, so we disclosed what our feelings about it were. As we compared our filings with those of other local and national banks, however, we saw no such disclosure, which was quite strange because all banks competed for the same customers and same type of projects. Quarter after quarter in 2006, 2007, and 2008, we continued to disclose our concerns, which was our responsibility to do. We said we were subject to the economy and if the market were to devalue, then BankAtlantic would potentially experience devaluation in its loans. If it were a mild devaluation we'd be okay. But if it were substantial, we would see deterioration and loss in our portfolios. Again, we were the only bank making this disclosure. Our stock started to decline because we were making these doom and gloom observations about the economy. Since we were the only bank making the disclosure, investors assumed our portfolio was worse than those of other banks.

The Federal Reserve held to its declaration about a soft landing and rebound. Nevertheless I was meeting with our loan officers, and a lot of the land bank loan intermediaries were coming in seeking modifications and extensions because their take downs were slowing from the national homebuilders, impacting the rate of required pay downs on the loans. If the intermediary was supposed to have been paying us at five lots a month, which has now slowed to two lots a month, I considered that a major problem.

Meanwhile, we'd had an opportunity to divest ourselves of Ryan Beck, which we sold to Stifel Financial, the large regional brokerage house. This generated $140 million, a substantial profit and cash, which I used to shore up our balance sheet.

I was bracing for the worst. Treasury Secretary Hank Paulson and Ben Bernanke, president of the Federal Reserve, kept saying despite the slowdown of the economy, things were okay and going to continue to be okay. I certainly didn't have the overview they did, but what I did know was that in the state of Florida conditions were getting worse.

Our second quarter report to investors, filed in early August 2007, reported continued deterioration in the real estate market and greater risk to the land loan portfolio. We told investors that devaluation of real estate is "likely to result" in higher credit losses for all housing loans. As before, our bad news caused our stock price to fall below that of our competitors who continued to publish rosy and optimistic projections.

During this time my son Jarett became president of BankAtlantic. He'd done an outstanding job for many years in building out a branching system and creating low-cost deposits. If anything, the appointment was long overdue and the board readily approved it.

The October Surprise

Through August 9, 2007, we had been the lonely—*only*—voice of doom. Our competitors said everything was fine when it was not. Our stock prices relative to our competitors continued to decline because we consistently told the truth when they did not.

By the end of the third quarter of 2007, I was very concerned about potential cracks in our portfolio. None of the loans were delinquent on September 30, 2007, but I had this pit in my stomach that we were headed for a meltdown. I could just feel the delinquencies coming. I wanted to be sure our disclosure was accurate. I asked the loan officers and credit professionals at the bank to scour these land bank loans to identify potential problems so we could disclose all of them at one time, as opposed to the drip, drip, drip of bad news over several quarters.

The teams worked around the clock to determine the extent of any potential problems. Again the bedrock of securities law is to report *what you know, when you know it*. After thirty-five years of being a public company CEO, having filed many hundreds of 10-Q and 10-K reports, I certainly knew it was against the law to conceal a known fact or trend if it would impact shareholders. To me, the known trend was a declining economy. If the trend continued, the impact on our portfolio and others would be dire. There was constructive debate internally because some of the loans were less than thirty days late. But many of the land bankers had told us their homebuilders had stopped purchasing lots and as a result, the land bankers would not be able to make loan payments in the future. Banking guidelines said we could wait ninety days to see if they would pay. My position was why wait if we already knew they'd be in default.

We downgraded virtually all our builder land bank loans. On October 25, 2007, BankAtlantic Bancorp reported a loss of $12 million as a result of these builder bank loans. It was precisely what I had been issuing warnings about in previous 10-Q disclosures.

Wall Street's reaction was brutal. Our stock dropped and New York analysts that followed our stock were quoted in the media, calling us "lending cowboys," as though we were reckless lenders. Shareholders were angry that we took these losses and called us incompetent.

The odd thing was we were the only bank in the country that reported lending losses and expressed any concern about our portfolio in our disclosures for September 30. There was barely a whisper of delinquencies or problems in other banks' portfolios. Jack and I were incredulous. *How could we be the only dumb ones on the block?* How is it *none* of the other banks had the same problems with their loan portfolios? Though we had the same kind of borrowers as other banks and similar loans, was it that somehow they had underwritten them better than we had and weren't having the same problems? Had we made serious underwriting mistakes when no one else did? We felt like absolute idiots!

Based on the relative disclosure, no one would know we owned one of the healthiest banks in the market. No one would know that the principal difference between our stock price and theirs was honesty and full disclosure.

But in fact, time would reveal we were not the only ones. We just recognized and acknowledged the problems, disclosing them prudently and early. Other banks faced the same dilemma, just waited as long as they could—actually nine months, into the second quarter of 2008, when the market went into freefall and they could no longer ignore nor conceal anything—to disclose them.

We took very few losses in the non-builder land bank loans. They performed just as we thought they would. Despite the fact that their value may have gone down, these developer borrowers had secondary sources of income for collateral that they had been willing to put up. Where the intermediary land bank loans were concerned, we took a $15 million hit. Twelve months later, the financial market went crazy and the world as we knew it came to an end, so to speak, with multi-billion-dollar entities like Lehman Brothers, Bear Stearns, and Washington Mutual going under.

While we had no idea we were headed into the Great Recession, based on our experience and intuition we were sure we needed to protect our downside and disclose *what we knew, when we knew it.* This served us well because BankAtlantic survived while thousands of other banks did not. Unfortunately, that's not how the SEC would see it.

LIFE LESSONS LEARNED

- Use logic and caution in assessing a situation. Be prudent. If it seems too good to be true, it probably is…or will be in time.
- Transparency means you can live and work with a clear conscience—with far less wasted energy. There's nothing worse than trying to operate atop of a mountain of concealment and lies. Even Sir Walter Scott knew it in his 1808 poem "Marmion," when he wrote:

  Oh what a tangled web we weave
  When first we practice to deceive.

- Conventional wisdom of others is not always correct.
- Always protect the downside. The upside will take care of itself.

ER CONVENTION FACILITIES SOUGHT   SUNDAY   SPECIAL SECTION: TIPS FOR SMALL BUSINESS

SINESS   C

SATURDAY, OCTOBER 27, 2007 | EDITOR: LISA GIBBS lgibbs@MiamiHerald.com | 305-376-3578 or 954-764-7026 ext. 3578   A

EARNINGS

Loan woes slam BankAtlantic

■ Problem real estate loans sent BankAtlantic into the red in the third quarter, sparking a share price tumble. The loss surprised analysts who had predicted earnings of 10 cents a share.

BY JANE BUSSEY
jbussey@MiamiHerald.com

The deteriorating housing market took its toll on BankAtlantic Bancorp in the third quarter. The Fort Lauderdale-based banking company said Friday it lost nearly $30 million while experiencing a seven-fold increase in its problem loans in three months.

The bank fell into the red for the quarter that ended Sept. 30, with $29.6 million in losses, compared to earnings of $2.5 million for the third quarter of 2006.

BankAtlantic's 52-cents-per-share loss compares to a profit of 4 cents a share in the same period a year ago.

The loss surprised analysts who had predicted earnings of 10 cents a share.

BankAtlantic shares led the New York Stock Exchange in percentage declines Friday. Shares tumbled nearly 40 percent, dropping by $2.93 to close at $4.72. Friedman Billings Ramsey also downgraded the stock to "underperform."

BankAtlantic Bancorp. is the

parent of BankAtlantic, which has 100 branches in Florida. Bank deposits are federally insured up to $100,000.

The bank traced the bulk of its loan problems to 11 commercial real estate loans totaling $148.7 million that were placed on nonaccrual status in the quarter. This pushed nonperforming loans from $21.8 million in the second quarter

•TURN TO BANKATLANTIC, 3C

BankAtlantic was the first bank in the country to report loan problems. In a true "punish the messenger" scenario, ten years of litigation followed this appropriate and forthright disclosure. As the global economy entered into a major recession, every bank in the country subsequently made the same disclosure, but ten months too late.

CHAPTER 20

CLASS ACTION: TRUTH BY HINDSIGHT

"Keep true, never be ashamed of doing right;
decide on what you think is right and stick to it."
—George Eliot

Ialways figured the odds of my being accused of securities fraud were about as good as four feet of snow falling on Christmas Eve in my South Florida neighborhood. But it happened. Not the snow. In 2007, I was accused of securities fraud—tried once by ambulance-chasing class-action lawyers in 2012 and the SEC in 2014 and 2017.

For the record, I'd been CEO and chairman of three public companies on the New York Stock Exchange and chairman of a fourth, all simultaneously. Most CEOs have a tenure of eight to ten years at one company and seem to move on to another, but I'd been with BankAtlantic, BankAtlantic Bancorp, and its predecessors I.R.E. and BankAtlantic Financial Corporation (BFC) for thirty-five years.

I had a solid track record. While I did not I have a black belt in securities law, I was knowledgeable and highly experienced. I'd filed hundreds of 10-Q and 10-K reports with the SEC. In fact, I believe I have filed more 10-Qs and 10-Ks than any CEO in the United States, including the limited partnership filings I did in the 1970s and '80s.

I was meticulous in my filing and disclosure process, overseen by a sophisticated group of professionals that included lawyers, accountants, and other experts in their fields. The process was designed so that there were multiple checks and balances to ensure accuracy.

The financials were compiled by the internal accounting staff. They were then reviewed by the controller and chief financial officer. Next they were reviewed by the outside auditors, Price Waterhouse Coopers (PWC) and then by the Audit Committee of the board of directors.

Disclosure followed a similar track: Controller to CFO to PWC to external lawyers, Alison Miller of Stearns Weaver Miller, and finally to the company's disclosure committee.

In short, I ran a very tight, very public ship. The financials and disclosure filings required my signature and that of the CFO, but the drafting, editing, and reviewing all took place outside of my influence. If worse news was required based on my viewpoint, I would send it back for additional negative disclosure.

After we announced quarterly earnings, BankAtlantic's protocol was for interested shareholders and some outside stock analysts to join us in an earnings conference call. In addition to my presence as CEO, BankAtlantic's chief financial officer, chief credit officer, chief operating officer, president (my son Jarett), and vice chairman (Jack) would routinely be on the call. If anything was said by management or by me that was an inadvertent mistake or misstatement of the facts, it could be corrected immediately by filing form 8-K.

During these calls, regardless of the fact that no delinquencies had yet surfaced in our portfolio, I believed the responsible thing for me to do was to express my concern about the builder land bank loans discussed in chapter 19. So I did. I'd also said I was less concerned about the rest of the commercial loan portfolio, because the non-builder bank loans were made to borrowers doing the actual development and with considerable resources as opposed to being intermediaries.

By the end of the third quarter of 2007, I had become increasingly concerned about the softening economy. I encouraged our credit and accounting people to report losses for many of these builder land bank (BLB) loans even though they had not yet become delinquent. I could just feel the market deterioration and felt an obligation to write them down. I believed my actions were prudent and good disclosure. Almost immediately, ambulance-chasing class-action lawyers filed a lawsuit charging that BankAtlantic and I had knowingly made false statements about the health of certain loans and had failed to disclose concerns about the portfolio. The suit was partially based on three sentences I uttered in a July 2007 investor conference call:

"There are no asset classes that we are concerned about in the portfolio as an asset class."

"That portfolio [residential development other than builder land bank] has always performed extremely well, continues to perform extremely well."

"The one category that we just are focused on is this land loan builder portfolio because just from one day to the next the entire homebuilding industry went into a state of flux and turmoil and is impacting that particular class .... There are no particular asset classes that we're concerned about other than that one class."

These cogent, concise, and accurate statements described the current state of affairs at BankAtlantic. No attempt at subterfuge. No smoke and mirrors. And no one took issue with these statements... until they did.

I felt sick to my stomach. Here I was, brutally honest about the state of the economy and our portfolio and for that I am being accused of securities fraud.

How was it that BankAtlantic was the only bank in the country that reported concern for the economy and was willing to announce losses? Every other bank in the country hid its problems in July of 2007 and instead reported them in the third quarter of 2008 (nine to twelve months later) as the economy worsened from smoke to a five-alarm blaze.

Whenever a loss is disclosed, as it was, and despite my nearly four decades of flawless filings and conscientious business practices, lawyers from class-action firms come running, assuming there might be a shareholder feeding frenzy. They show up sans any research or information. If you report a loss on Monday, they'll file a lawsuit on Wednesday. The reason they file so quickly is that because there are different law firms involved, each wants to be the first to the courthouse as so many of them drink from the same (contaminated) well. Despite a lack of due diligence to determine if there's really any liability, they just file a boilerplate suit, left to be figured out as they go along. It's kind of like sticking your plastic lounge chair in line in front of Best Buy in the wee small hours before Black Friday even begins, so you can get the Sony 55-inch XBR Ultra HD TV you want—though you are not sure it's even in stock. But you're going to call it that way, and you're going to act on it.

The legal fees of 20 percent obtained in an out-of-court settlement, can line the firm's bonus box for years.

Each law firm wants to be the one the judge selects to try the case and in this instance, a firm by the name of Labaton Sucharow LLP won the coveted prize—with six other firms consolidating their cases into what was now the lead law firm's case.

My experience is that class-action lawyers like these are gunning for a quick settlement. Period. They hate to go to court because it's expensive and most often they lose, so they just stir the pot looking for a settlement. Large companies tend to settle because litigation is a thorn in their side and they want to be done with it. They basically pay the lawyers to disappear. Certainly over all the years they represented me, and through a galaxy of frivolous and other throwaway lawsuits, Gene, Alison, Alan Fein, Grace Mead, and dozens of other lawyers at Stearns Weaver Miller would each attest to the fact that I could never be railroaded into caving. I will not settle. I did whatever it took to prove I was on the right side of the law and always will. It was a matter of integrity, reputation, and principle to me.

The first hurdle that the Labaton Sucharow lawyers had to overcome is whether they had any basis for the fraud claim. This should have been a no-brainer for the judge. There was no evidence to support this claim and the judge should have summarily eliminated the case on a motion to dismiss.

In order to solve that problem, the Labaton Sucharow lawyers filed a document that claimed they had confidential witnesses who knew we had done terrible things. The lawyers would say, "We have information from 'somebody' in the lending department who personally observed the company hiding information, or these 'witnesses' knew the information BankAtlantic was disclosing was simply not true." They claimed they had five or six of these confidential witnesses and did not have to disclose their names—only describe how they would have been privy to this kind of activity and information and what their positions were in the company. That was how they got past Gene Stearns' motion to dismiss. The judge should never have allowed the case to go forward.

As we knew, it would turn out that these confidential witness statements were bogus. The Labaton Sucharow lawyers had invented them, along with distorting who the witnesses themselves were. Their methodology had been to interview former employees who had worked in other areas of the bank and who were likely ferreted out by the plaintiffs' firm in fabricating the case. It would soon be apparent that these witnesses had no knowledge of the basis of the suit. What's notable about this law firm is that they'd been cited and fined a number of times in previous cases for producing bogus confidential witnesses. But at that point Judge Ursula Mancusi Ungaro had already allowed them to get past the motion to dismiss and start discovery. It had begun to feel like echoes of the ABC *20/20* affair, where the producer and other staff members stooped to subterfuge to achieve their objective.

For class-action law firms like this, these lawsuits are a numbers game…a very lucrative one. If they muscle their way into ten boiler-plate suits of this ilk, even knowing nothing about the circumstances to begin with, and can get themselves past the pivotal motion to dismiss, even illegally, they can often weasel defendants into a settle-ment of millions of dollars. This is big business to these firms, much like standard ambulance-chasing lawyers handing their card to a bleeding victim on the side of the road, hoping to pick up a case.

Over the course of two years, in gearing up for the trial, Gene filed a number of petitions with the court to require the plaintiff to reveal the identities of these confidential witnesses. On November 30, 2009, the judge ruled that the former BankAtlantic employees who had allegedly accused our executives of making improper, risky loans as part of a securities fraud class-action lawsuit could no longer conceal their identities. The main reason we wanted to know was so we could depose them to learn what they knew, how much they knew, when they knew it, how it came about, and anything else. Now we'd get to the truth.

Mark Arison, lead attorney for the plaintiff, said the witness statements had been based on transcripts of interviews with them. As this is crucial information, the attorneys would have interviewed them directly and personally. But when we began to dismantle these people, Arison soon backpedaled, saying he didn't conduct the actual interviews, saying the people who did the interviews must have gotten it all wrong and he'd just used their information.

In one instance that came to light, a conversation with a witness had been recorded where she'd said she worked at the bank but not in the department in question. She serviced residential home mortgages and really didn't know what was going on in commercial real estate, which was the basis of the suit. The report called her a confidential witness in the commercial real estate division anyway. The reality is she knew nothing about anything. The affidavit filed by the law firm said exactly the opposite.

Still, despite the fact that we'd deposed all the so-called confidential witnesses and had gotten to the truth, Judge Ungaro ruled the case could not be dismissed at that point because we were way past the motion to dismiss phase and well into discovery.

Also, at one point Judge Ungaro said that as an attorney she used to handle securities fraud cases. She admitted that was twenty-four years ago before she became a judge. She said in essence that life had changed so much and she was having a little trouble catching up, basically having trouble getting her head around it. So securities law, as it was, was no longer consistent with her experience. By her own admission she was out of her element. Judges operate on their own experience to a large degree, and federal judges like Ungaro deal with a lot of criminal cases, but clearly this one was not a criminal case. It was something entirely different.

A Witness by Any Other Name

Aside from the so-called confidential witnesses that we'd discredited, the Labaton Sucharow team proceeded to call several other witnesses from BankAtlantic. Among them were Perry Alexander, a senior lender in his fifties who'd been passed over for promotions a few times because he was never able to grow the department, and Amy Engleberg, a loan workout officer probably in her late thirties or early forties. They were still both employed by the bank. Unbeknownst to me and others in management until the trial, these employees had been sending catty emails back and forth to one another during work time like two high school teenagers.

When we started to execute the builder land bank loan strategy, apparently Perry had sent Amy an email saying, "I hate these deals.

The Major Loan Committee is blinded by greed and focused only on interest rates." In another email, he called the Major Loan Committee a "sneaky pack of liars." Amy's response was to disparage the quality of the loans, identifying seven of them, referring to them as "stinker loans in the portfolio." She also called them "ticking time bombs" and "explosive piles of crap."

It seemed hundreds of these inappropriate emails had flown back and forth between them over a period of several years. They were critical of many people and many undertakings at the bank. It is unnerving to have bank officers who don't approve of what's going on, maybe don't appreciate their jobs as a result, possibly hate working for you and all you stand for, and you don't know it. You think they're team players and/or if there are any problems, they would come to me, but I couldn't have been more wrong. I was blindsided.

Perry and Amy's position in court was that we'd failed to disclose the condition of these builder land bank loans to the marketplace. But on the stand, when Gene asked if they'd ever read any of our 10-Q or 10-K reports where we disclosed my concern for the BLB loans, they both said no. Had they ever listened to the conference calls when all of this was disclosed? Again they both said no.

What was also apparent was that because I had eliminated condominium lending in an effort to keep us afloat in a sagging economy, Perry was bitter because these condominium loans were how he achieved his production goals. I had taken away his ability to produce what he was comfortable producing. He never spent time developing other kinds of loans because unlike many of his loan officer colleagues, he didn't look for new business. He felt cheated. He also admitted, upon cross examination, that he had never expressed his concern to me, had an Irish temper and anger management problems, had a female boss, Marcia Snyder, he resented, and that his email communications were immature and not fact based. He'd never taken it upon himself to look into the loans themselves—just didn't like the concept.

Actually, Perry's distaste for the builder land bank loans was well founded. Jack Abdo, as mentioned previously, didn't like the idea either. As time went by I became concerned about these BLB loans and had regretted not acting in concert with Jack. So Perry's thinking about the loans wasn't wrong, but the way he went about conducting himself unprofessionally for years clearly was. It would cost both him and Amy their jobs. The press, of course, loved the descriptive adjectives Perry and Amy used in their emails and used them on dozens of headlines about the case and the trial.

We were now getting close to the end of the six-week class-action trial. Judge Ungaro had ruled early on, even before testimony and evidence, the three sentences in question were misleading, constituting securities fraud. During the trial it became obvious the disclosure was not misleading. Gene then asked the judge what she was going to do about that ruling, based on all she'd learned during the rest of the trial. She replied she'd really not made a decision about that yet.

On multiple occasions during the six-week trial, Gene and Judge Ungaro vehemently argued with one other over what the law was regarding a particular issue. Gene knew the law backward and forward but Judge Ungaro could not bring herself to agree with him. Numerous times the judge ordered Gene to sit down and be quiet, but he continued to argue the point. "Sit down Mr. Stearns, or I will hold you in contempt of court," the judge would command. If she had only listened to Gene, she would have saved everyone six weeks of a frivolous trial and not created the mess she did.

She even had the gall to accuse me of "truth by hindsight," that I didn't think the statements were correct at the time they were uttered, but proved correct over time. If she was paying attention during the trial, she surely knew the three sentences and all the disclosure was correct and appropriate from the beginning.

Before her jury instruction, Gene had argued and argued and argued yet again with Judge Ungaro that if she said what we thought she would end up saying, it would prejudice the jury—that the jury should be given the opportunity to make up its own mind about those three sentences. How can you have a jury trial and basically take that decision away from them, with the judge saying, "I've already found..."? How can you have a securities fraud trial when the judge says she has already decided the defendant is liable? What kind of trial is that?

But shortly thereafter, in her charge, or instruction, to the jury she said specifically, "In a prior ruling, I determined that the three sentences in a July 2007 conference call were misleading and were securities fraud." So there it was—communicated to the jury that the judge, who is the highest ranking individual in the courtroom, has already decided I was liable. She essentially poisoned the well before the jury had a chance to deliberate because it was now out there in neon lights.

So we lost, with the jury finding us liable. Strange as it was, I felt the judge was shocked by the jury's decision—that she hoped we would win. An appeal on the ruling, regarding the three sentences, which was imminent, would reveal her erroneous prejudicial ruling to the jury. Gene was emphatic that this loss resulting from the prejudicial ruling would never stand in an appellate court. Jurisprudence warranted that if we disagreed with the verdict, we first had to ask for a rehearing with the same judge to reconsider the jury's decision before it can be appealed. Gene filed the brief, saying, "Even though the jury came to this conclusion, the jury's decision was wrong because of *your* ruling, and it's judicial error, so you, as judge, should throw out the jury's decision and award the case to us as defendants."

Fortunately, the judge reconsidered, realizing Gene had been right all along and she had prejudiced the jury. She overruled the jury's verdict. However in order to save face, the ultimate reason she gave for her decision was not the three-sentence ruling, rather some technicality. In any event we were exonerated. On April 26, 2011, she ruled in our favor.

Naturally the plaintiff appealed this action to the Eleventh Circuit Court of Appeals. On July 23, 2012, the appellate court agreed with Judge Ungaro's decision to throw out the verdict and find in our favor. Interestingly, the appellate court didn't agree with how she came to that decision—the technicality—but it stood that the lower court should have found in our favor. Judge Ungaro then nominally sanctioned the Labaton Sucharow lawyers and fined them for the confidential witness scheme.

But it wasn't over yet.

About Alison: It is such a blessing to have Alison Miller always watching my back with her eagle eye and knowledge of the SEC rules of disclosure. We don't do a filing or issue a press release without her review.

About Gene: Gene Stearns had proven to me many times over that he is a master in the courtroom and he is an expert on the law, which is often frustrating to the judges. Not only is he the best strategist I've ever worked with, he works to the bone to understand every piece of evidence and nuance in a trial. He has a photographic memory that allows him to go into a courtroom and argue a case without notes—just facts and intuition.

About Jack: Jack Abdo was by my side the entire time. He sat at the defendant's bench with me, with his unwavering support.

I'm proud to call Alison and Gene my lawyers and friends. I'm proud to call Jack my friend and partner.

The trio was also with me during the two SEC trials to follow in chapter 22.

Susie also attended court every day. She understood all the issues and players in the trial—backward and forward. Every night during the drive home and dinner, she would strategize and coach me on perceived weaknesses in the class action's case and what our response should be. As always, she was insightful and a calming influence on me, as she would be during the two grueling SEC trials to follow.

LIFE LESSONS LEARNED

- Never take for granted that events in your life will automatically follow a logical, equitable course. Chances are they won't, so you have to be prepared to challenge what's wrong and defend what's right.
- Never take for granted the people who support you.
- Justice is random.

BROWARD WEDNESDAY, OCTOBER 13, 2010

DAILY BUSINESS REVIEW

CLASS ACTION

BankAtlantic Bancorp accused of hiding woes

BROWARD MONDAY, OCTOBER 4, 2010

DAILY BUSINESS REVIEW

JUSTICE WATCH John Pacenti

BankAtlantic parent's class action set for trial

BROWARD MONDAY, OCTOBER 11, 2010

DAILY BUSINESS REVIEW

CLASS ACTION Shareholders have sued executives over risky real-estate loans

BankAtlantic trial ready to begin on Tuesday

South Florida
OCTOBER 22-28, 2010
$4.50

BANKATLANTIC lending exec blasted loans

South Florida
OCTOBER 15-21, 2010
$4.50

Does BankAtlantic trial show how S&L regulators failed?

South Florida
NOVEMBER 5-11, 2010
$4.50

Plaintiffs make damages case in trial against BankAtlantic

FEDERAL COURT Judge says issues should go to jury

ATTORNEY: BANKATLANTIC PUNISHED FOR **ITS HONESTY**

by John Pacenti
jpacenti@alm.com

An attorney representing BankAtlantic Bancorp told a federal judge Friday that the holding company is being punished for being the only one that was honest with its shareholders about loans going bad before bad mortgages triggered the financial meltdown.

But U.S. District Judge Ursula Ungaro remained steadfast that many of attorney Eugene Stearns' objections to a shareholder class action against the Fort Lauderdale-based company were matters for cross-examination and for a jury to decide.

Ungaro

Levan

Attorney Eugene Stearns said BankAtlantic Bancorp CEO Alan Levan "spoke what he thought was true" during an investor conference call.

DAILY BUSINESS REVIEW
BROWARD   THURSDAY, NOVEMBER 11, 2010

SHAREHOLDER SUIT Jury to get BankAtlantic case Friday

PLAINTIFF ATTORNEY SAYS LOANS WERE LIKE 'TIME BOMB'

South Florida BUSINESS JOURNAL
Wednesday, October 13. 2010, 2:24pm EDT

BankAtlantic exec grilled about land loans

South Florida Business Journal

Miami Herald

MiamiHerald.com | **THE MIAMI HERALD**

BANKING

BankAtlantic lied about risks, jurors told

DAILY BUSINESS REVIEW

SHAREHOLDER SUIT Real estate loans challenged
CEO calls banking "risky business"

Daily Business Review

Daily Business Review

DAILY BUSINESS REVIEW

SHAREHOLDER SUIT Former employee testifies

Officers warned that market was softening, attorney says

DAILY BUSINESS REVIEW

SHAREHOLDER SUIT Statements scrutinized
Plaintiff attorney, executive spar in cross-examination

Daily Business Review

South Florida Business Journal

BankAtlantic case nears climax

South Florida Business Journal - by Brian Bandell

Sun-Sentinel

Jury finds BankAtlantic misled shareholders

Sun Sentinel

AMERICAN BANKER

BankAtlantic Loses Class Action

American Banker

Sun Sentinel

BBX loses fraud case, will appeal

Case dealt with loans that turned bad during real estate downturn

Sun Sentinel

The Miami Herald

BANKING

BankAtlantic liable for stock fraud

Miami Herald

THE WALL STREET JOURNAL.

Jury Finds Bankers Misled on Risk

Miami Panel Says Top Executives Are Liable for
Damages After Misrepresenting Values of Loans

Wall Street Journal

BROWARD   TUESDAY, DECEMBER 28, 2010

DAILY BUSINESS REVIEW

SECURITIES Attorney claims prejudicial errors

BankAtlantic retrial sought

by Wayne Tompkins, DBR. Claiming 'overwhelming' and prejudicial errors, the attorney for BankAtlantic Bancorp is seeking a
new trial in a securities fraud class action case conducted in U.S.
District Court in Miami.

Daily Business Review

LEGAL WIN: A judge's ruling boosts the outlook for BankAtlantic **P2**

A Message from Jarett

I am pleased to announce that this morning we declared victory in the shareholder class action lawsuit brought against BankAtlantic Bancorp, as the Judge has entered judgment in BankAtlantic Bancorp's favor. We have stated all along that we believed the verdict was contrary to law and would eventually be set aside. We are thrilled with this decision. Please click here to read the press release.

DAILY BUSINESS REVIEW

BBX Defeats Shareholder Lawsuit in Case That Could Trim Merger Litigation

Sun-Sentinel

BANKATLANTIC BANCORP.

Judge reverses jurors' verdict

The ruling vacates shareholders' lawsuit

JOSH RITCHIE/STAFF PHOTOGRAPHER
BankAtlantic Bancorp. Chairman Alan Levan said he was "very pleased" with the judge's decision overturning the Nov. 18 verdict of the jury in Miami.

South Florida BUSINESS JOURNAL

BankAtlantic fires back at class action attorneys

SOUTH FLORIDA BUSINESS JOURNAL | APRIL 29–MAY 5, 2011

Legal victory could be turning point for BankAtlantic Bancorp

BankAtlantic seeks to punish class action attorneys

Bloomberg Businessweek
Get our new FREE iPad app now

THE ASSOCIATED PRESS   April 26, 2011, 1:36PM ET

Judge voids BankAtlantic investor lawsuit verdict

As anticipated, these ambulance chasing lawyers only wanted a cash settlement. When I refused, they were forced to defend their position in court which didn't stand the light of day. Ultimately, they had to pay our legal fees for defending their baseless claims.

CHAPTER 21

RECESSION (AGAIN): 2008

"The Man in the Arena"

"It is not the critic who counts; not the man who points out how the strong man stumbles, or where the doer of deeds could have done them better. The credit belongs to the man who is actually in the arena, whose face is marred by dust and sweat and blood; who strives valiantly; who errs, who comes short again and again, because there is no effort without error and shortcoming; but who does actually strive to do the deeds; who knows great enthusiasms, the great devotions; who spends himself in a worthy cause; who at the best knows in the end the triumph of high achievement, and who at the worst, if he fails, at least fails while daring greatly, so that his place shall never be with those cold and timid souls who neither know victory nor defeat."

—Theodore Roosevelt

Once the $8 trillion housing bubble burst in mid-2008, the country entered a severe recession. The Great Recession officially lasted from December 2007 to June 2009, though it began to rear its ugly head much earlier. Like a skipping stone its effects continued, mounting and multiplying for months and years after that. In 2008 and 2009, the labor market lost 8.4 million jobs. It was the most dramatic employment contraction of any recession since the Great Depression, and the longest recession since World War II.[*]

---

[*] Robert Rich, Federal Reserve Bank of New York. "The Great Recession." www.federalreservehistory.org/essays/great_recession_of_200709

The recession hit Florida harder than many other states mostly due to the collapse of housing prices. Between December 2007, and March 2010, Florida saw an average of a thousand jobs a day disappear, largely in the housing industry. Unemployment in the state went from 3 percent in 2006 to 12 percent in December 2010.

We'd been sued by our investors and investigated by the SEC during the recession, as a result of it. My ability to see around corners and the strong sense of responsibility I'd felt to disclose what I did, when I did, calling it early the way I did, had totally backfired. My premonition on the economy was correct—what I missed was the SEC's desire to find a scapegoat for their own failures.

During this period, October 2007 to March 2009, the S&P 500 Index decline was 57 percent. IndyMac Bank failed and was seized and closed by federal regulators on July 11, 2008 with $32 billion in assets. On September 7 of the same year, Fannie Mae and Freddie Mac were taken over by the government. On September 15 of 2008, the financial services firm Lehman Brothers filed for bankruptcy. It was the largest bankruptcy in US history, with Lehman Brothers holding more than $600 billion in assets. Merrill Lynch, AIG, Countrywide Financial, and many others required forced marriages or government support to ward off failure.

A US federal bailout was announced on September 8, 2008 with $85 billion to AIG alone. The receivership of Washington Mutual Bank by federal regulators on September 26, 2008, was the largest bank failure in US history with $307 billion in assets. JP Morgan bought the assets with federal assistance and wrote down the value of Washington Mutual's loans by at least $30 billion. In September of 2008, Congress approved a $700 billion bank bailout known as TARP, an acronym for the Troubled Asset Relief Program. During the recession, more than nine million US homes entered foreclosure, representing more than $450 billion in losses. The Florida banking industry incurred the largest percentage decline of banks during the recession of any state. More than half of Florida's 308 financial institutions during the recession either failed or were sold to other banks.

Included in the run-up to 2007 was a very strong market—really the longest post-war economic boom on record. The tenet in this country, echoed by many leaders, is that home ownership is everyone's right. This kind of thinking influenced the reckless behavior of Congress, Fannie Mae, Freddie Mac, credit agencies, investment banks, and mortgage originators. Suddenly everybody was qualified to purchase a home, resulting in a wellspring of negative amortization or subprime mortgages (affectionately called "no documentation loans" or "liar loans"), in which your credit history didn't matter as much as it once did.

Fanny Mae and Freddy Mac would buy these loans from originators, aggregating them into pools of hundreds of millions—ultimately billions—of dollars. They'd be securitized with a triple-A rating, pools of them packaged and sold to domestic and international investors. This created an inflationary cycle related to real estate values. So between 2001 and 2007, the market kept climbing up and up with mortgages on these properties. The entire banking industry in 2004 to 2008 was drinking from a fire hose of subprime mortgages—the negative amortization referred to earlier. It was high volume and highly profitable. But BankAtlantic had none of that. We'd resisted the temptation to load up our balance sheet with these exotic mortgage products. It takes a lot of discipline to stick to your principles. In 2006 and 2007, we saw the market getting somewhat murky despite Fed Chairman Ben Bernanke's and Treasury Secretary Hank Paulson's assurances that whatever was going on may persist for a quarter or two, followed by a soft landing and rebound. But the subprime housing issue did not appear to be contained and we were concerned, particularly about how it all related to BankAtlantic's portfolio.

In August of 2007, French bank BNP Paribas froze three investment funds because of losses stemming from US mortgages. This was the touchpoint of a global credit freeze where lending just stopped. Lines of credit were frozen, particularly impacting national homebuilders in this country who in turn faced a liquidity squeeze. That was the time the intermediaries had come to us, unable to make their payments, asking for more time, and why we wrote down the loans we did in that October period.

I recall not understanding what was happening, preferring to imagine a homebuilder conference attended by all the national homebuilder executives, with too much coffee and donuts. Some over-caffeinated developer had grabbed the microphone to say the end of the world was coming, causing a reaction on the part of all of the homebuilders to stop taking down their lots at the same time. But that fantasy scenario wasn't the case. We didn't know why, but the neon signs were flashing, the economy was tanking, and we had to face it—immediately.

To preserve cash and ensure liquidity, homebuilders such as Miami-based Lennar Corporation with its many dozens of subdivisions throughout the state decided to conduct a fire sale of homes that were completed, but not yet sold. If they were building a four hundred-home community, with fifty on spec, they decided they didn't want to risk waiting around to see if buyers would come, choosing to put them on the auction block instead to raise cash. Traditional buyers could not get financing because the mortgage market was drying up, so the only ones in a position to acquire these homes were cash buyers—sometimes for two-thirds or even half of what the homes were worth. The national homebuilders took a bath with write-downs of more than $100 billion, but they were more interested in the immediate cash to remain solvent.

People were enraged that they'd paid full price for a home, only to see the one next door in the same development offered at half of what they'd paid. It was a miserable, frightening time with no end in sight.

Because of massive unemployment, homeowners put their homes up for sale, only to find out that their neighbor's foreclosures and property devaluations left their own homes worth substantially less. In vernacular, you were upside down on your mortgage. This, in turn, reduced the value of the loans in our portfolio. It was getting ugly.

Falling Knives

Through years 2007 to 2012, not a day passed when there wasn't more bad news about the economy...often colossally bad news. It was unrelenting stress and chaos and impossible to avoid. Everything was drip, drip, drip—like Chinese water torture. You had to rush to get the news each morning so you could figure out how to deal with it that day and the next and the next.

Every single day the national and local news screamed about some new bankruptcy, bank failure, or national or global crisis. At BankAtlantic, Bluegreen, and Levitt & Sons, the crises were daily as well; the class actions, the SEC investigation, borrowers requesting modifications and extensions, loan defaults, loan devaluations and write downs, liquidity, capital requirements, bank examiners, home prices plummeting, staff reductions, stock price freefall, etc.

I've said before that in a crisis I am at my most steady, organized, and certainly disciplined. I work at compartmentalizing so I can keep working. It's important to evaluate the downside—the worst that can happen—and the consequences. As I visualize all that, I ask myself if I can live with it, which determines the course of action I will take. I put each issue into a bucket and work very hard to solve each problem. My staff and I had to anticipate what was coming and know exactly what we'd do about it. The timeworn excuse, "How could we have known?" was always unacceptable to me. In business, I never allowed things to get to that point. All too often, though, painful, unpopular decisions are required, such as the significant downsizing I'd had to do with I.R.E. and BankAtlantic, but that is why so many held onto their jobs and the businesses went on, maybe in a different form, but if it had all disappeared everyone would have lost. I was never afraid to be proactive, think way outside a more conventional box, make difficult, unpopular decisions, and be fully accountable for them.

In December 2008, I attended a private equity seminar in New York. The keynote speaker was Stephen Schwarzman, CEO of Blackstone, the giant private equity firm. I had met Schwarzman several times at JP Morgan conferences in Deer Valley and had arranged a private meeting with him, at his office, before his speech. He was quite pessimistic about the market. In his speech, he said that he was concerned about the debt markets and the economy and was advising all of Blackstone's controlled companies to cut back expenses, prepare for a difficult market, and reduce their reliance on the credit markets.

Bluegreen's model was wholly dependent on the credit markets. During the recess, I went into the hallway and called John Maloney, CEO, and Tony Puleo, CFO of Bluegreen, to tell them what I had just heard. I was quite confident and firm when I charged them with putting a business plan on my desk within sixty days to significantly cut Bluegreen's staffing and overhead and reducing our reliance on credit. Within sixty days, they gave me a plan on reducing our staffing and closing about a third of our sales offices. Bluegreen relies on the debt markets as it generates timeshare sales and without an efficient debt market, there would be a cash crisis at the company. By March 31, staffing had been reduced from 8,000 to 4,000, and all non-required overhead had been eliminated. As Schwarzman had predicted, the debt markets totally froze and credit for even the strongest Fortune 500 companies was not available. These changes allowed Bluegreen to survive the recession and prosper after it was over.

We desperately needed to raise capital for Levitt & Sons and BankAtlantic. But the credit markets were closed and dead. Not a penny was being raised by Wall Street for banks or homebuilders.

Levitt had eighteen communities in Florida, Georgia, and Tennessee. By 2007 home sales, which had slowed to a trickle over the previous few years, were nonexistent. This was a situation that required me to defy convention. It was life or death, financially. When we needed to raise capital for Levitt & Sons, the homebuilding subsidiary of Levitt Corporation, which was bleeding profusely the same way all homebuilders were, I created a unique instrument called a rights offering.

A rights offering, or stock offering to existing shareholders (no outsiders) comes with a very large price discount incentive. We offered a capital raise to Levitt Corporation shareholders, encouraging them to double down—to invest more money. If they were in the stock at five dollars, we'd take the stock down to two dollars and fifty cents, saying we'd offer them more stock in the same pro rata we had to the total number of shareholders and outstanding shares, but at a discount to the current market. So, if you owned 5 percent of the company before, participating in the same pro rata you'd still own 5 percent after the offering. If you didn't choose to participate, you may be diluted down to 4 or 2 percent, so most people who had the money would participate.

To my knowledge, other than Levitt Corporation, no other public company had ever used this technique to raise capital. It probably never occurred to them. They just didn't figure it out. There was historical evidence of it in the 1920s and '30s, but it had been decades since anyone had thought of it. The concept had come to me because I'm a voracious reader and had read about this years earlier where companies in Europe had utilized it. Somehow I'd retained it, able to pull it out as a creative solution at the right time.

We raised $185 million for Levitt Corporation through the rights offering. Now the question was if I would put that money into Levitt & Sons, its homebuilding subsidiary, to allow it to survive. Ultimately I made a decision not to, unsure of how long the recession would last. At that point Levitt & Sons was losing about $30 or $40 million a year, and I just couldn't see the end of it. If things continued for another three or four years, we'd have blown through all of it and Levitt would still be in trouble.

I went to the banks that had lent construction funds to Levitt & Sons and asked them to work with us. We weren't asking them to forgive the debt, just requesting a longer period of time to pay it back or as another option reduce the interest rate during these impossible times. We offered significant debt repayment concessions for our own BankAtlantic customers during the recession, so we didn't think it unreasonable that other banks would work the same way with us. Unfortunately, they all turned a blind eye. It was still early in the economic collapse. None of the other homebuilders had yet disclosed to the banks their deteriorating condition. Once again we were the first. "You raised the capital. You have the money now," was the typical response. "Just put it in. We're not going to work with you."

The hard decision I made was to put Levitt & Sons into bankruptcy. I'd never done that with any company under our umbrella, and the decision was nothing less than daunting. The stigma of bankruptcy was unfathomable. But ultimately I came to the conclusion that Levitt Corporation, the parent company, could use that $185 million more constructively rather than try and save Levitt & Sons. In late 2007 we put Levitt & Sons into bankruptcy, preserving the $185 million at the parent, Levitt Corporation.

On February 24, 2011, our regulators, the OTS, hit BankAtlantic with a cease-and-desist order (your basic CYA methodology) so the bank could not make any more commercial loans. Actually, they were late to the party because we'd prudently made that decision a year or two earlier. The regulators just needed to have it on record as their decision instead of ours. And though we were in full compliance with capital standards, they required us to increase our capital. Demands like these become a noose around a bank's operation, as mentioned earlier, and are the reason most banks never come out of it as they end up in a death spiral.

The concept of the rights offering worked so well at Levitt Corporation, I decided to use it at BankAtlantic to raise capital. In fact, we did five rights offerings over a two-year period at BankAtlantic, each time chasing the downward spiral of the stock. BFC participated in the rights offerings along with the other BankAtlantic shareholders, but, in reality, other than us, very few other shareholders really believed the bank would survive. Over the period, we invested the $185 million from Levitt Corporation in BankAtlantic, allowing the bank to survive, and increasing our ownership from 25 percent to 53 percent.

Media Massacre Redux

Following IndyMac's failure in 2008, bank analyst Richard X. Bove penned an article titled "Who Is Next?" It listed of the all the banks likely to fail, and BankAtlantic was on the list.

Bove knew nothing about us and had not studied our balance sheet—only looked at losses. We had learned from the *20/20* experience that once this kind of defamation is out in one media outlet, all the others pick it up. If it is slander or libel, they are not accountable for it as long as they can quote their source, in this case the errant Bove. This is just the kind of "news" that starts a run on the bank. Even the *New York Times* ran a multi-page story about Bove and BankAtlantic with the headline "The Loneliest Analyst." It was not flattering to BankAtlantic or me. In fact there'd been many dozens of stories and photos of the lines around the IndyMac branches… people attempting to withdraw their money.

On December 28, 2009, BankUnited, a Miami S&L, had a massive collapse, dealing a $4 billion blow to the FDIC. Its depositors were panicked, and that concern rubbed off on us.

Hundreds of banks did fail but ours was not one of them. We had to sue Bove to get him to retract his statement. We weren't interested in the money, just in sending a message to other news outlets not to echo his unfounded prediction because we'd go after them. In

July 2010, Bove printed a retraction and we dropped the suit. His employer at the time, Ladenburg Thalmann, paid us $350,000 for his reckless reporting though without admitting any wrongdoing.*

One of the more disappointing characteristics of human nature was that so many of our commercial loan customers decided to strategically default on their payments. They had the ability to pay but elected not to. We were among the most revered real estate lenders in the market. Jack and I and our loan officers knew our customers personally and had worked very hard to design lending solutions for their particular needs. As the economy continued to fail, we offered to give them more time to pay if they worked with us by providing stronger guarantees or additional collateral. Many of our borrowers accepted our offer of help, but, as the press kept forecasting our demise, many commercial loan customers strategically jumped ship because they viewed us in a weakened condition. Their thinking was that if BankAtlantic failed, we'd be taken over by the FDIC and they'd be in a position to negotiate significant discounts—to buy back their loans from the government. By 2012 we'd written down more than $500 million in loans and filed hundreds of foreclosure actions against these customers. When we filed, some countersued us claiming it was our fault for lending them the money so we were just as responsible as they were! It was truly the age of insanity.

The market was deteriorating fast. Loans that were okay in one quarter would need to be written down in the next quarter because the market and valuations were dropping so quickly. And then written down again in the next quarter.

Among our more colorful borrowers was developer Dan Catalfumo. Catalfumo had been described in the press as a titan of

---

* Andrew Martin and Louise Story. "The Loneliest Analyst." *The New York Times.* September 11, 2010. http://www.nytimes.com/2010/09/12/business/12suit.html?pagewanted=all

the South Florida building industry. He'd been a BankAtlantic borrower for years as we financed a number of his projects, along with financing he'd obtained from half a dozen other banks that included Bank of America and Seacoast National Bank. In 2006 to 2007 he told us things were slowing down and he needed some help. We modified some loans and gave him extensions. Then at one point he stopped making payments to all of his lenders, including BankAtlantic. One by one each bank settled, discounting their loans and just getting whatever money they could recover. Catalfumo had a lot of judgments against him. He told the banks to stand in line because he didn't have any money, so they wouldn't be able to collect on any foreclosure actions. He had filed for bankruptcy.

Jack Abdo took over responsibility for all our commercial foreclosures during that period, and in fact still does. Through forensic accounting and investigation, Jack found Dan had stashed $75 million in a Cayman Islands bank. We determined that when Catalfumo had seen the market turning in 2006 to 2007, he'd begun skimming money from his own projects knowing that at the time of total market collapse he'd simply file bankruptcy and walk away from it all, while knowing he had stashed millions in the islands.

Theoretically this cache of money was untouchable in the states. Catalfumo owed us $48.5 million and Jack went doggedly after it. Perhaps "pitbullishly" is more like it. Just after 2012 we were able to get a judgment and attachment on those funds. We got from him every penny he owed, plus default interest and legal fees. I believe we were the only bank to be paid in full.

More of Less

During what seemed like an unrelenting recession, on a regular basis we'd had to identify the extent of the continuing losses, make sure our capital was strong, ensure we properly disclosed the situation to our shareholders and regulators, keep our employees motivated, prevent our deposit customers from withdrawing their funds, keep our loan customers from taking advantage of us because they thought we were going under, and also manage the other companies in our portfolio including Bluegreen Corporation and Levitt Corporation.

The freeze in the credit markets gave the timeshare industry a terrible blow and we had to reduce Bluegreen's workforce from eight thousand to four thousand employees.

The recession roared. It was interminable. Like a bad candidate elected to office, wreaking a path of destruction, it seemed it would never stop or leave.

On October 15, 2010, the NYSE threatened BankAtlantic with delisting because our stock had fallen from over a billion dollar market cap to less than $35 million, below the NYSE minimum requirement. Fortunately the NYSE never forced us to delist, because so many of its listed companies were in the same situation. We were also battling the shareholder lawsuit and trial and the two SEC lawsuits (see next chapter) and trials during this time.

Jarett had the responsibility of shrinking the bank. In 2007, we had $6.5 billion in assets and three thousand associates. Surgically, over the next few years, Jarett reduced our asset size down to $4.5 billion and reduced our employee count from three thousand to twelve hundred. It was very painful. It was a double-edged sword: We provided severance to our departing associates, but it created a charge against our income that reduced our capital further. We knew it would negatively affect our capital, but we always tried to take care of our associates the best we could so we made the decision to offer a generous severance.

Since the branch associates are the first line of communication with the deposit customers, we needed to have frequent town hall meetings with the remaining associates. These meetings allowed them to grieve about their departing friends and other employees, under-stand the economy, the losses, the class action and SEC litigation, and what our short- and long-term goals were. Our culture was always about strong communication and transparency, and this was not a time to go into hiding.

We survived through our creativity, resourcefulness, discipline, initiative, luck, and sometimes by the skin of our teeth.

Even as all this turmoil was going on, in 2010 BankAtlantic won the J.D. Power Award for customer service in banking for the State of Florida. It was a proud moment indeed.

In 2011, we quietly put the bank up for sale. More about that in Chapter 23.

LIFE LESSONS LEARNED

- Read everything you can, even if it may currently seem unrelated to your business or interests. File things away. You never know when you will be able to apply something (in this case the rights offerings) to a pivotal situation.
- Always take the time to evaluate the downside of a pending situation or action to see if you can live with it. It will give you the confidence you need to make the right decision.
- "How could I have known? Everyone else made the same mistake," is not an acceptable excuse.

With the recession mired in its seventh quarter, making it one of the longest on record, BankAtlantic chief executive Alan Levan said he is focusing his Fort Lauderdale-based bank on credit, core earnings and capital.

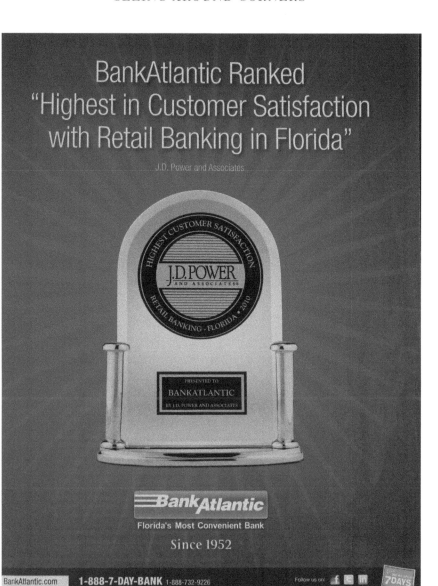

CHAPTER 22

SEC VS. ALAN B. LEVAN AND BANKATLANTIC: GUILTY UNTIL PROVEN INNOCENT

*"Press on. Nothing in the world will take the place of persistence.
Talent will not; nothing is more common than unsuccessful
men with talent. Genius will not; unrewarded genius is almost
a proverb. Education will not; the world is full of educated
derelicts. Persistence and determination alone are omnipotent."*
—Calvin Coolidge

During the class-action lawsuit, Labaton Sucharow had been feeding information to the SEC, which was thrilled to receive it. This way the SEC didn't have to spend time and money acquiring information on its own. The objective of the class-action lawyers, however, was to apply more pressure: Sharing information with a government agency would force our hand and lead us to settle. Obviously, that didn't happen. In time, the SEC came after us. And, on a couple of occasions, though he subsequently denied it, Labaton Sucharow lawyer Mark Arison told Gene that if we settled the class-action suit, he could make the SEC case go away.

The SEC's Miami office had sent us a subpoena and notice of investigation in 2007, right after the class-action lawsuit was filed, saying it saw our stock had dropped. The notice said it didn't understand the reason for this, suspecting there had been a disclosure violation, and wanted us to cooperate with some information requests and under-oath interviews. But they don't ever tell you whether they consider you a witness, or whether you are a target of the case. They just ask you to cooperate. Of course we cooperated: we sent them millions of pages of documents and presented about ten individuals for interviews, including me.

When It Rains

As a public company, we were now obligated to disclose that we received information requests from the SEC. We did that in our November 8, 10-Q filing. The class-action news was bad enough but now this disclosure made headlines in the local press that of course impacted not only our customers but also the bank examiners.

Bank examiners are government bureaucrats. They come into the bank on a regular basis and write quarterly reports to their supervisors and for the file. For years and years, we'd gotten a clean bill of health with summaries such as, "…this is a well-run institution; management is astute. They have a very large real estate lending portfolio but seem to manage it well. There are no delinquencies." While they'd typically never come out and say a company was excellent or even very good, "we think the institution is stable" is the best you can hope for, which we received.

Banks are rated by the bank examiners on a scale of one to five. Management is rated. Credit is rated. Internal governance is rated. Willingness to cooperate with the examiners is rated. We had always gotten the highest marks. Suddenly they see losses, the class-action lawsuit, and the SEC bearing down on us. It was CYA time. They become very exposed with decades of their reports that say we've been doing everything right and now they are on the line. A bank that fails while receiving good reviews is career-ending for an examiner. So they issue a report saying they are downgrading everything. Management is not as good as they thought it was. They downgrade our loans and now give us negative reports. But the fact is nothing had really changed other than the economy and the SEC investigation. We did nothing wrong except prudently sound a warning bell. We hadn't made a single change in the way BankAtlantic did business...in the way we operated.

In a paralyzing catch-22, a negative report from your regulator restricts your ability to operate. The bank examiners decide that you cannot make any more commercial loans. (They knew we had already decided on our own to halt commercial lending.) You cannot hire staff or initiate any new business ventures. You cannot do this or that anymore. Basically, your hands are tied behind your back, so you cannot run your business. For many banks, these restrictions force them into failure because they can't generate new income. By the time the bank fails a year or two later, the examiners have been reporting problems for two years, though they may have been the direct or indirect cause of the problems. When a bank fails, it is catastrophic for the FDIC insurance fund, the depositors, the tax payers and the shareholders, but now the examiners can point to the file and say they recognized the problems and their careers are safe.

The SEC investigation dragged on for several years, as did the class-action litigation. While we were confident our disclosure was appropriate and forthright it was an eerie feeling having the SEC digging around. Fortunately, Alison had reviewed the disclosure before it was filed in 2007 and both Alison and Gene, in 2007, felt absolutely sure the filed 10-Qs and 10-Ks and my conference calls met all the requirements of the law. With the benefit of five years of hindsight they felt 200 percent confident. During the five years of investigation, the SEC also came up with a bogus accounting issue that they said was fraudulent. We couldn't find anyone who agreed with them—not our accountants, PWC, not our audit committee, not third-party accounting experts we engaged. Were these SEC lawyers stupid or just out of control?

After we won the class-action litigation in 2012, I thought surely the SEC case would die a sudden death and the SEC would fold its tent and go away, realizing we were one of the good guys. After all, the SEC's issues were exactly the same as the class action we just won. Unfortunately, that was not to be.

Instead, the SEC sent us a Wells notice in late 2011. It is required by law for a government agency to send a Wells notice when it is planning to bring an enforcement action. Congress's original purpose of the Wells notice is so the government informs you they have made a decision and it gives you a last chance to defend yourself so they can make a final determination about whether to bring litigation and insure the government doesn't go after innocent people. The SEC uses it for a different reason. After expending lots of resources investigating someone for five years, there is no way it would admit it has wasted taxpayer money in pursuing a nonsense case. Instead the SEC wants you to tell it upfront what your defenses are and what your trial strategy will be. Of course, we responded with all the legal arguments we had in a last-ditch effort to convince them they were barking up the wrong tree. So, there you have it: the SEC knew every legal strategy, every defense, and that my statements were true at the time and were particularly true with the benefit of hindsight.

And if that wasn't enough, the events in question happened in 2007. It was now 2012. The SEC and the world now knew about the Great Recession, the worst economic debacle since the Great Depression in 1929. The SEC also knew we won the class action on the same claims, that BankAtlantic never failed capital and survived while thousands of banks did not. Not only did we do nothing wrong, I should have been the poster boy for good disclosure. I thought I should have received a medal.

Astonishingly, with all this information, they still sued us in January 2012. I was devastated. As dismayed as I was with the ridiculousness of the class-action litigation, I was shocked and angry with the Enforcement Division of the SEC.

The SEC simultaneously put out a press release saying BankAtlantic and Levan used accounting gimmicks to conceal from investors the losses in a critical loan portfolio. Robert Khuzami, director of the SEC's Division of Enforcement, said at the time of the suit, "This is exactly the type of information that is important to investors, and corporate executives who fail to make that required disclosure will face severe consequences."*

When the SEC is involved, no matter what the outcome, just the publicity can cripple your business. People assume where there's smoke, there's fire; if the SEC is suing you, there's got to be something to it. When BankAtlantic's name came up in conversation, people would shake their heads and roll their eyes.

On more than one occasion I called Gene to say I didn't get it. I just didn't get it at all. Why was the SEC doing this? What did it see that we didn't? Prior to all this I was held in high regard. BankAtlantic and I had received many honors and awards. We were synonymous with strong ethics. But now, in light of the class action and the SEC taint, everything was called into question by third parties. I was constantly put in a position of having to justify my actions on so many fronts, particularly because the *South Florida Business Journal, Ft. Lauderdale Sun Sentinel,* and *Miami Herald* began to run with every crumb. In fact, despite the fact that all of the trials were civil in nature, the *SFBJ*, on one occasion, referred to what was happening to us as a criminal bust. In the *SFBJ* alone, there were 1,092 articles or mentions between 2007 and 2017, all

---

* U.S. Securities and Exchange Commission press release. January 18, 2012. https://www.sec.gov/news/press-release/2012-2012-13htm

341

of them negative, related to the SEC case. Many of them were front page headlines and stories.

I was offended and humiliated. I didn't know what hit me. What had I done? Why was this happening? What country were we in that I was guilty (and of what?) until proven innocent?

This not only went to the core of all I'd worked to achieve professionally, and my efforts to take care of people along the way just as much as I did my business, but it cut to the quick in a personal sense. I never let on because I always had a confident smile, but it felt like...I don't know...a betrayal. I was not a machine. I felt it in my gut. My heart ached.

The SEC case, like the class-action suit, was largely based on the same three sentences with which Judge Ungaro had prejudiced the jury, where I'd expressed my concerns regarding performance of the builder land bank loans, uttered during an earnings conference call in 2007. Regardless of the fact that no delinquencies had yet surfaced in our portfolio, the responsible thing for me to do had been to express my concern about the builder land bank loans. To reiterate, in those calls, I also said I was less concerned about the rest of the commercial loan portfolio because the non-builder land bank loans were made to borrowers with considerable resources and collateral. These three sentences were clear and accurate statements—nothing more; nothing less.

The SEC appeared to have been investigating exactly the same claims presented in the class-action lawsuit, saying the disclosure we'd made was securities fraud, along with an accounting issue we were alleged to have had.

Where the latter was concerned, the SEC claimed that our accounting for the year ending December 31, 2007, was fraudulent. We had loans on our books that were held for investment, meaning they were going to be on our books for the long term. It decided we should have put these loans in a category of "held for sale," meaning we wanted to sell them. If in fact they were supposed to have been put in a bucket of "held for sale," we were told we should have written the loans down by several millions of dollars. Because we didn't do that, now we were alleged to have committed accounting fraud. The BankAtlantic Audit Committee, with a rigorous internal process, said our accounting procedures were appropriate. Our national accounting firm, PriceWaterhouseCoopers, with its own rigorous accounting procedures said our accounting protocols were appropriate, along with our methods of disclosure.

Life in a Vise

An SEC investigation is extremely serious for a number of reasons, and for me, personally, even more so because I'm CEO of a public company. What would our board of directors say? What would these people do? What consequences would it all have on me? I'd seen it happen time and time again where a CEO was forced to settle with the SEC, essentially admitting wrongdoing, whether it be true or not, or be thrown out of the company. The question I kept asking myself was, "Is my job and entire career in jeopardy?" The SEC works on the same strategy and principle as the class-action lawyers: look for a settlement in which a business or individual "admits" to wrongdoing, then pays a fine to avoid the lengthy and expensive process of going to trial.

The litigation had an ominous beginning. At our very first pretrial conference before Judge Scola, the SEC lawyers told the judge that the evidence was so incriminating, he didn't have to read the 10-Qs and 10-Ks. I could not believe what I was hearing. I could not believe the SEC would be so unethical. The SEC said the three sentences in the conference call were obviously false because why, otherwise, would BankAtlantic have reported a loss? *What?* Do these people know securities law? And unbelievably the judge must have agreed with them because shortly thereafter he rendered a summary judgment order that the three sentences were false. I was sinking into my chair wondering what the hell was going on. Again! The bedrock of securities law is that you consider the total mix of information. Am I the only one who knows that? Clearly if the SEC had bothered to look, the three sentences were correct and the 10-Qs and 10-Ks were correct. Gene did an incredible job explaining this to Judge Scola, as he had in the class-action trial with Judge Ungaro. He told Judge Scola it was reversible error, but to no avail. The SEC also convinced Judge Scola that PWC shouldn't be allowed to testify on the grounds that I had lied to the accountants. Not only had I not lied to the accountants, I had never even discussed the accounting treatment with them. The judge bought the SEC's argument hook, line, and sinker. How can you defend yourself against accounting fraud without your accountants? He actually ruled PWC could not testify at trial. Gene was crazed. And I thought federal judges were supposed to be smart.

When the SEC brought its suit for accounting fraud, PWC conducted what it called a "look back" analysis to determine if the accounting treatment for 2007 was correct. It concluded that it was. Since this was fatal to the SEC's accounting claims, the SEC moved Judge Scola to prevent a jury from hearing that testimony. Judge Scola granted that motion as well.

On the long road ahead, there were ten counts of fraud in the SEC lawsuit. One of the settlement demands from the SEC during this time was a monetary fine, an admittance of securities fraud, and a lifetime officer bar, meaning I could never again be an officer or director of a public company. Fundamentally, only criminals get that kind of treatment. I would never agree to that. I couldn't live with myself if I had to admit I committed securities fraud. An officer director bar would be career-ending for me. I had spent my entire life running public companies and this would put an end to that.

The judge kept delaying the trial date and at some point, Gene told me that Judge Scola was never going to try the case. I wasn't sure I understood.

"He's gotten himself into the same box as Judge Ungaro when she made the ruling about the three sentences," he said. "The ruling is incorrect and he'll soon realize that it's going to be deemed judicial error. The judge is never going to want to hold a trial and defend his ruling."

Gene explained that Scola would wait until a new federal judge was appointed, with an empty docket, whereupon Scola would kick this case in his or her direction. President Obama ultimately appointed three new federal judges for Florida's Seventh Judicial Circuit Court, and one of those judges, Judge Darren Gayles, received the case from Judge Scola on June 20, 2014, the day after his appointment.

As fate would have it, Judge Gayles decided not to override Judge Scola's ruling on not allowing our accountants to testify and on upholding the three sentences summary judgment that both Ungaro and Scola said constituted securities fraud. When challenged by Gene, Judge Gayles, a brand-new federal judge, added that personally he'd not have made those rulings, but he would uphold them out of respect to Judge Scola. Gene argued with him numerous times about it, but the judge's reasoning was that he didn't want to show any disrespect by substituting his own opinion.

"When we appeal this," Gene told him in sharp retort about the three sentences, "it'll go to the appellate court as *your* ruling." Gene knew he had the law on his side. He was trying to convince yet another judge that his decision would be considered judicial error and it would be embarrassing to him to be seen in that way, right out of the starting gate. But Judge Gayles was not accustomed to being called on the carpet by lawyers and chose to proceed the way he was on course to.

In his roughly hour-long opening statement at the beginning of the trial, SEC staff attorney James Carlson said over and over that I was a liar. I don't tell the truth. He told the jury that the judge is going to tell them Mr. Levan is a liar. You can't believe anything Mr. Levan says. Mr. Levan is surely a liar, and this is all about lies. In fact, in his closing argument he called me a liar seventeen times.

An excerpt from court transcripts of the opening statement from Mr. Carlson:

> *"The defendant Levan kept investors in the dark. You cannot count on Mr. Levan to tell any investors the truth, but you can count on us to go through these lies and pick them apart and present them to you. We ask you to hold him and his company guilty for violating federal securities laws."*

What horse shit! Carlson lied through this entire opening statement and for that matter the entire trial. During the opening statement, Eric Bustillo, the Miami regional office director and Carlson's boss, was in the courtroom, proud as he could be.

While we'd been denied permission to have our accounting firm, PriceWaterhouseCoopers, testify at trial, the SEC's former chief accountant, Lynn Turner, who now spends his time providing expert testimony for SEC enforcement actions, was allowed to testify in support of the SEC's case. Typically, experts are supposed to be independent fact finders, poring through reams of material, issuing independent opinions. This often takes months of intensive research and analysis. Upon Gene's cross examination of this expert, we learned from Lynn Turner that he spent a mere three billable hours on the phone, all with the SEC, before rendering his opinion that our accounting was fraudulent. Continuing, on cross examination Gene asked him if he felt any other accountant would come to the same conclusion he did. His response was a show stopper.

"No one in my profession would come to the same conclusion I did without doing more," he responded under oath. He admitted he did not do more. When asked if the three sentences were false, he said he wouldn't go that far. How sad and unfathomable that the enforcement division of the SEC would stoop to using such unethical tactics in the enforcement of the SEC's high standards and idealism. Its trial strategy was unscrupulous, with the objective to distort the facts and confuse the jury, or basically win at any cost. It was outrageous. What country were we in?

Other SEC tactics included putting Jarett on the stand, trying to trip him up because he was the bank president. The SEC knew Jarett's job function at that time was managing the branches and did not include disclosure, real estate lending, or accounting treatment. But they spent countless hours on those subjects in an attempt to prejudice the jury that we did something wrong solely because he was my son. For the record, Jarett was approved as president by the BankAtlantic board of directors because he earned the position and deserved to be president. And, as relates to Jarett's time on the witness stand, he told the truth, held his own, and did a great job. I was very proud of him.

The SEC also tried to befuddle the jury by spending days going into lengthy and confusing diatribes about builder land bank loans, dissecting loan after loan after loan. This was a total waste of time because we had already reported these loans were a problem. It's not securities fraud for a bank to have loans go bad; only if you fail to disclose the problem. Then what was the SEC's purpose? Only to confuse the jury.

The SEC used an internal memo addressed to the lenders and major loan committee that I'd written in February of 2007 disclosing my concern about the economy, the market, and the builder land bank loans. I said in the memo, "The early bird gets the worm," so we needed to make sure these loans were properly and meticulously documented. I also indicated if the borrowers were going to ask for loan modifications or extensions, we should use it as an opportunity to request more collateral to shore up the loans. In the event the market ultimately collapses, the other banks will want to do the same and borrowers won't be able to satisfy everybody, so we'd better get more collateral from them first.

The SEC had a field day with these communications, distorting and misinterpreting them, accusing me of "knowing" and not disclosing that "non"-land bank loans were a problem (they were never a problem) when in fact the memos were referring to builder land bank loans: the intermediary loans. It was chaos—a maelstrom of immaterial material. The SEC threw so much at a bewildered jury, sometimes even we were confused. After a while it became patently clear that once the SEC announces a case it can never back off. Seems they would lose rather than admit the evidence doesn't support their claims.

Unbelievably, the trial dragged on for six weeks. Finally the trial was over, and Judge Gayles gave final instructions to the jury. And again this judge informed the jury that our disclosure on the three sentences constituted securities fraud. James Carlson had a field day with the closing argument calling me liar, liar, liar. The jury reached its decision on December 15, 2014. In spite of all the SEC misinformation and name calling, it found in our favor on all counts except the three sentences. After all, how could a jury ignore a judge? It also found against us on the accounting. We cried judicial error on the three-sentence ruling and decreed we'd lost the accounting issue because the court had refused to allow PriceWaterhouseCoopers to testify. We were disappointed but pleased that we had won everything the court had not prejudiced the jury against.

The SEC immediately issued a press release that it won. We issued one the same day that said it was a split decision...that we won everything we could win, but we certainly could not win the securities fraud claim on the three sentences when the judge had already ruled they were misleading. And we could not win the accounting issue when we were prevented from bringing in PricewaterhouseCoopers, our own accounting firm, to testify.

The next day we issued another press release stating, "A decent and hardworking group of jurors was misled by a jury instruction that is just wrong." The judge did not take kindly to this press release.

Virtually every day during the trial there was an article in the *South Florida Business Journal*. Brian Bandell was an *SFBJ* reporter who was fixated on covering the class-action litigation and now the SEC trial. Brian was typically quite diligent, but in covering the SEC trial he got very busy multitasking on a number of stories. He'd show up for the morning testimony, which generally was the SEC presenting a witness. He'd need to leave by lunchtime to return to the newspaper to write his article, along with whatever other stories he was covering. Most often he was not in the courtroom in the afternoon for Gene's cross examination of the SEC's witness. Gene's cross examination destroyed each witness and revealed the stupidity of the SEC's argument. So, Brian's stories included the SEC case but not our defense. Bandell actually ended up winning an award for his coverage of the trial. On December 15, the front page of the *SFBJ* had my picture from top to bottom on the front cover with the following headline: "SEC wins fraud verdict against BBX (BankAtlantic Bancorp had become BBX Capital Corporation) CEO Alan Levan." The next week another full front cover spread, "Levan. He fought the law and the law won."

No Remorse

At the penalty hearing. the judge, apparently peeved that we'd been claiming judicial error and that we'd taken the position that for all intents and purposes we'd actually won, said my press releases demonstrated that I showed "no remorse." I'm thinking, *that's the kind of language one hears at a criminal trial.* But this had not been a criminal trial—or had it? Sometimes I wondered. The judge hit us hard. The sanctions against me included a two-year officer and director bar. The judge fined BBX Capital Corporation $4,555,000 and fined me $1,302,902. The *SFBJ* wrote that regulators forced me out as chairman and CEO. The board of BankAtlantic, incidentally, about which I'd been deeply concerned, had stood behind me 100 percent every day for the duration of the trials. When I had to resign as chairman and CEO, there was never a thought of them asking me to leave the company. Jarett became acting chairman and CEO. I assumed the role of founder and manager of strategic planning and non-executive advisor to management and the board of directors.

Cake, Ice Cream, and the Sweet Taste of Victory

Once again we had to appeal to the Eleventh Circuit Court of Appeals, involving the jury decision, the officer and director bar, Judge Gayles' ruling on the three sentences, and the prohibition of our accountants testifying.

Perhaps my favorite moment in the course of this long running nightmare was an oral argument when one of the three judges on the panel asked the SEC appellate lawyer if there was *any* evidence in the record—and she emphasized the word *any*—warranting a summary judgment finding three sentences in the hour-long conference call false. The best the SEC's lawyer was able to say was that two district court judges had made that finding. For the first time it appeared that sanity would emerge in this long running nightmare. Someone with authority had asked the obvious question.

On September 28, 2016, the appellate court overturned everything the SEC had won, and determined that Judge Gayles had committed judicial error. It was a tremendous birthday present. The case was remanded back to Judge Gayles for a retrial strictly on the three sentences and accounting issue, stipulating this time that PricewaterhouseCoopers be allowed to testify.

After years of the SEC's unrelenting efforts in court and in the media to destroy my company and me, it fell silent. The chest-pounding in the name of justice, which had been a popular SEC battle cry, stopped. SEC lawyer Jim Carlson had no comment for the press. It would be inconceivable to me that the SEC would want to try the case again. It surely would take a beating without the erroneous order from the judge bolstering its case. Gene told the SEC he was 100 percent sure we would win, as was I. Not a scintilla of doubt.

Unbelievably, the SEC decided to try the case again! It had no case in the first instance. But now, the Eleventh Circuit Court of Appeals eliminated whatever hope it was holding on to. Gene said, "The fact that the SEC would pursue a case against a company that set the highest standards for disclosure reflects badly on its enforcement decisions. There was pressure on the agency to sue somebody; it sued the wrong people." Still, the SEC persisted.

When I would tell people and the press that I was 100 percent confident we would win, they looked at me as if I were delusional. Why would the SEC bring a case against someone who is innocent? That was the constant refrain.

Because the jury decision was reversed, I was allowed to assume my former positions as chairman and CEO. I also received a refund of my $1,302,902 as did BankAtlantic its $4,555,000.

On February 26, 2017, I emailed Michael Piwowar, Acting SEC Chairman, with a copy to Eric Bustillo, Miami Branch Chief,

> "This retrial is scheduled to commence in twenty-five days, on March 20, 2017.
>
> It will be the first SEC trial under the Trump administration. This case, which the SEC has pursued for nine years under the Obama administration is going to result in an SEC loss and an embarrassment to the new administration and the incoming SEC Chairman.
>
> Don't take my word for it. I only suggest that you ask Director of the Miami Regional Office Eric Bustillo whether he believes this is a case which will result in a win for the SEC.

If you cannot get a resounding, career strong 'YES,' I suggest you put a spotlight on this four-week trial commencing in twenty-five days. (The Appellate Court reversed the judicial errors from the first trial which originally gave energy to this case.)

Thank you for your attention. A response would be appreciated."

On March 23, 2017, I sent another email,

"THIS SIX WEEK TRIAL WILL BEGIN IN TWO DAYS!

This trial will not end well for the SEC. I suggest you get the Director of the Miami Regional Office Eric Bustillo to commit in writing that this is a case which he believes he can win. He has wasted nine years and millions of taxpayer dollars on a frivolous case which will be an embarrassment to You, as acting Chairman, the SEC and the new administration.

I will be forwarding this email addressed to you to all members of the House and Senate. Also, as you know, these emails to you are available under the Freedom of Information Act.

Thank you for putting a spotlight on this case."

The second SEC trial began on March 27, 2017. If you're tallying, it was the third trial including the class-action lawsuit. I put out a press release saying the SEC claims were all baseless, I wasn't going to settle for anything other than a complete vindication, and I was looking forward to ending this abusive ten-year SEC campaign.

The SEC tried the exact same case. The same witnesses were brought back. These included accounting "expert" Lynn Turner; Perry and Amy who, in addition to appearing at the class-action trial had reappeared as witnesses in the first SEC trial (and about whom the press had picked up all their negative, gossipy comments and whose testimony we'd later learn that the jury tended to discount), and other alleged witnesses.

The SEC's opening statements were again bombastic, but Jim Carlson had to refrain from calling me a liar because the judge's disclosure ruling had been overturned. We went through another six-week trial that really should have lasted three days. The SEC went through the same unethical, stupid, disgraceful tricks it did in the first trial. The whole thing reminded me of a toddler telling you a joke and when you laugh, telling the same joke again and again, anticipating the same response. After the first time, it doesn't happen. Every single live witness testified that the words I spoke were true and explained why.

The SEC's closing arguments to the jury were pathetic. I watched ten years of my life being played out to a jury of my peers, for the first time without a judge's foot on the scales of justice. The SEC's lawyer, Jim Carlson, took an hour telling lie after lie. You may think that is an exaggeration, but it is not. By that point the SEC's claims were in shreds and lying was all they had left. The arguments they had used to persuade two judges to grant summary judgments without a trial were revealed as having not a tiny bit of factual support.

The trial finally concluded on Friday, May 5, 2017, and went to the jury at 3:00 p.m., this time without the silly instructions from the judge. Court adjourned two hours later, set to reconvene on Monday morning. We assumed the jury would be out deliberating for several days.

On Monday morning, May 8, Susie, all our children, and I gathered at the cemetery to lay the one-year stone, called an unveiling in Jewish tradition, at my mother's grave. We had arranged this date months earlier. Sadly, my mother, who had attended every day of the class-action trial and the first SEC trial, died shortly after that trial at the age of ninety-eight. I will always regret that she did not get to see the culmination of our long, painstaking battle. All of my values—surely my work ethic and tenacity—had come from my father and her. The service was very emotional with our rabbi leading us in prayer and memory. Just as it concluded I received a call that the jury had already made a decision, after only a three-hour deliberation.

We were all together, so my entire family and I raced to the courthouse. If you subscribe to this sort of thing, which my wife, Susie, definitely does, I'm sure my mother had something to do with the logistics because I'd scheduled the unveiling for a date when I could not imagine the third trial would still be on. Perhaps my mother knew and wanted us all to be together on my final day in court, and so we were.

The courtroom was silent as the jury came back in. The foreman spoke.

"The jury finds in favor of the defendants on all counts."

Ten years and $20 million in litigation costs later, we were free. I was completely exonerated. It was a clean sweep victory on all counts of the SEC's frivolous lawsuit. I was so emotional and angry, I went over to the SEC bench and said they should all be embarrassed. I walked away realizing I got no reaction from them. I pivoted around and yelled at them, "You are the scum of the earth!" looking for a more satisfying reaction. Success! This time they were shocked. The security guard led me out of the courtroom.

The SEC still had the right to appeal by July 8, which was a Saturday. On Tuesday, July 11, Gene sent me a short email saying the "SEC's failure to file a notice of appeal made the Final Judgment, well, final. The nightmare is over!"

Gene Stearns and his legal team had been brilliant. With the exception of the erroneous orders from Judges Ungaro, Scola, and Gayles, the cases would have been dismissed at an early stage. It was an uphill battle all the way.

Upon Reflection

Abusive federal regulation and enforcement is a major issue that must be addressed. This was the subject of press releases and talking points in speeches I had opportunities to deliver following the last trial. My observations appeared in numerous publications, including the *Miami Herald, Ft. Lauderdale Sun Sentinel, South Florida Business and Wealth*, and *Florida Trend*. It is regulatory enforcement run amok. It took a jury only a few hours to completely dismiss a meritless case the SEC spent nearly a decade and many millions of taxpayer dollars pursuing. It tried to shoot the messenger and doing so is not an acceptable enforcement strategy. Full and fair disclosure is the bedrock of securities law, and I passed with flying colors. The SEC did not.

Though I'd not thought about them in years and years, I was swinging on the wrought iron gates again.

LIFE LESSONS LEARNED

- Though your insight and opinion may be unpopular, don't be afraid to express them and take action, especially if others may be negatively affected if you don't.
- Stand your ground against all odds and at all costs. There is no substitute or plea deal for a clear conscience and the truth.
- Wealth and success go up and down. Sometimes multiple round trips. The only constant is reputation and integrity. That's the only important thing.

SEC office wants BankAtlantic action

BY BRIAN BANDELL

BankAtlantic Bancorp has defeated a shareholder class action lawsuit, but soon may have another legal opponent: the SEC.

In the first quarter report, the Fort Lauderdale-based bank holding company (NYSE: BBX) revealed it received a letter from the SEC's Miami office, stating its intention to recommend that the SEC file civil action against BankAtlantic Bancorp for violations of federal securities laws. BankAtlantic Bancorp Chairman and CEO Alan Levan received a similar letter that indicates the SEC's intention to target him, as well.

South Florida Business Journal

Tuesday, May 17, 2011 3:01 PM ET ∴ Extra

BankAtlantic Bancorp discloses SEC subpoenas

SNL Financial

Press Release

SEC Charges Florida Bank Holding Company and CEO with Misleading Investors about Loan Risks During Financial Crisis

FOR IMMEDIATE RELEASE
2012-13

Washington, D.C., Jan. 18, 2012 — The Securities and Exchange Commission today charged the holding company for one of Florida's largest banks and its top executive with misleading investors about growing problems in one of its significant loan portfolios early in the financial crisis.

SEC probes BankAtlantic Bancorp

South Florida Business Journal

With great fanfare the SEC issued this press release. NOTE: see if you can find a press release at the final conclusion of this matter. HINT: there is none!

HE FOUGHT THE LAW AND THE LAW WON

Former BankAtlantic CEO Alan Levan lost his civil fraud case and could be banned from publicly traded companies. but he's not giving up yet. **Pages 16-17**

South Florida Business Journal. Front page news again.

BBX, CEO lied about bad loans, jury finds

Miami Herald

Ex-BankAtlantic CEO Levan gets bar order, fine in SEC lawsuit

Alan Levan barred from serving on any public company board for two years

Levan and firm must also pay fines totaling $5.85 million

Judge rules Levan purposely misled investors

Miami Herald

BBX and CEO fined $5.85M

Company misled investors on loans losses, jury decides

Sun Sentinel

Retreat is not an option for CEO

Facing trial, BBX Capital exec wants name cleared

Sun Sentinel

$5.8 Million in Fraud Penalties Ordered Against BBX, Levan

Daily Business Review
Sun Sentinel

For his part in SEC violations at BankAtlantic, Alan Levan faces $1.3 million in civil penalties and a two-year ban on serving as an officer or director.

Levan has lost

SUBSCRIBER CONTENT: Dec 19, 2014, 6:00am EST

Al Lewis
Editor-in-Chief- *South Florida Business Journal*
Email | Twitter

The inescapable fact of the week is that a federal jury found Alan B. Levan and BBX Capital Corp. liable on civil accounting and securities fraud charges.

BBX, Levan and his losing legal team have done a fine job trying to spin this fact with a press release.

They've called the verdict mixed since they won on some charges. They've split hairs over the charges they lost. They've promised to file a motion to set aside the verdict. They swear they can win on appeal. They've even declared that the jury was misled.

A smarter response would have been to quietly promise an appeal and decline further comment until that appeal was decided.

Levan's bluster hasn't levitated stocks of his companies. They're hovering near their 52-week lows as of this writing.

He has risked inflaming a judge, who will likely decide whether to ban him from ever running a publicly traded company again, as well as the Securities and Exchange Commission, which already has his number.

The world is filled with executives who've been sacked with civil fraud charges and swear that they're innocent. That it was all a bum rap from those pesky regulators.

Levan is currently standing in a long line of them.

South Florida Business Journal

SEEING AROUND CORNERS

Daily Business Review

Sun Sentinel

SEC refunded my $1.3 million payment – how sweet it is

THE REAL DEAL
SOUTH FLORIDA REAL ESTATE NEWS

The Real Deal

Alan Levan, BBX win appeal of 2014 court judgment

The appellate court reversed penalties of $1.3M against Levan and $4.55M against BBX

October 01, 2016 10:15AM

Alan Levan

Fort Lauderdale-based BBX Capital Corp. said it won its appeal of a 2014 court judgment against the company and its former chairman and CEO Alan Levan in a case brought by the Securities and Exchange Commission.

LAW360

11th Circ. Axes SEC Win in BankAtlantic

Law 360

REUTERS

BBX, ex-CEO win new U.S. trial in SEC financial crisis case

Reuters

SünSentinel
May 17, 2017

Shareholders welcome back CEO

BBX Capital's Alan Levan was cleared of SEC charges

By Marcia Heroux Pounds

Sun Sentinel

Sun Sentinel

Alan Levan renamed chair, CEO of BBX Capital

FEBRUARY 7, 2017, 4:35 PM

A lan Levan is back as chairman and CEO of Fort Lauderdale-based BBX Capital.

Levan restored as CEO of BBX Capital, awaits trial with SEC

Alan B. Levan of BBX Capital Corp.

South Florida Business Journal

South Florida Business Journal

Levan and BBX overturn SEC's victory on appeal

Brian Bandell

Alan B. Levan could soon resume his position as chairman and CEO of BBX Capital Corp. after a federal appeals court overturned a Securities and Exchange Commission judgment against them.

It's unclear whether the SEC will pursue further action.

DAILY BUSINESS REVIEW

Banker Facing Retrial Accuses SEC of 'Intellectual Dishonesty'

Daily Business Review

Former BankAtlantic CEO Alan Levan says he's ready to confront a Securities and Exchange Commission lawsuit that's headed to a retrial after appeal.

Re: SEC v BankAtlantic Bancorp and Alan B. Levan
Alan Levan

To:	chairmanoffice@sec.gov
CC:	oig@sec.gov ; miami@sec.gov ; Alan Levan
Sent On:	Sunday, February 26, 2017 4:09:33 PM
Archived On:	Sunday, February 26, 2017 4:09:56 PM
Identification Code:	eml:d58f10b8-5f91-4312-9365-6ec21baac74e-2147329055

> Att: Michael Piwowar, Acting U.S. SEC Chairman ,
>
> This retrial is scheduled to commence in 25 days, on March 20, 2017.
>
> It will be the first SEC trial under the Trump administration. This case, which the SEC has pursued for nine years under the Obama administration is going to result in an SEC loss and an embarrassment to the new administration and the incoming SEC Chairman.
>
> Don't take my word for it. I only suggest that you ask the Miami Branch Chief, Eric Bustillo, whether he believes this is a case which will result in a win for the SEC.
>
> If you cannot get a a resounding, career strong 'YES' , I suggest you put a spotlight on this four week trial commencing in 25 days. (The Appellate Court reversed the judicial errors from the first trial which originally gave energy to this case).
>
> Thank you for your attention. A response would be appreciated.
>
> Alan B. Levan
> Chairman
> BBX Capital Corporation
>
> Sent from my iPad

My last ditch effort to request integrity from the SEC.
They ignored my email.

HE FOUGHT THE SEC AND WON

May 8, 2017

Banker Alan Levan's determination to fight the Securities and Exchange Commission paid off on Monday when a federal jury rejected all of the remaining civil fraud claims against him.

The case against the former leader of BankAtlantic ends one of the longest running legal sagas regarding the Great Recession in South Florida, which saw numerous banks fail and get taken over by regulators.

Alan B. Levan and
Eugene Stearns—victorious!

The Miami Herald

May 9, 2017

Federal jury clears BankAtlantic, former CEO Alan Levan of all charges

Miami Herald

DAILY BUSINESS REVIEW

May 9, 2017

Federal Jury Clears Levan and BBX on All SEC Claims

"I am pleased this negotiable nine-year ordeal is finally over and I has vested in complete exoneration," Fort Lauderdale banker Alan Levan said in a statement.

Daily Business Review

THE WALL STREET JOURNAL

Jury Clears Former BankAtlantic CEO in SEC Case Over Soured Real Estate Loans

Wall Street Journal

THE REAL DEAL
SOUTH FLORIDA REAL ESTATE NEWS

Jury verdict exonerates Alan Levan and BBX Capital

Levan: "This is really regulation run amok. The SEC Enforcement Division is just out of control"

May 08, 2017 06:00PM
By *Mike Seemuth*

Alan Levan

Alan B. Levan, chairman and CEO of Fort Lauderdale-based BBX Capital Corp., won a five-year court fight with the U.S. Securities and Exchange Commission over public disclosures of loan quality by BBX's corporate predecessor BankAtlantic Bancorp.

The Real Deal

SOUTH FLORIDA SunSentinel

May 9, 2017

Alan Levan acquitted of all charges

Jury clears former
BankAtlantic CEO

Sun Sentinel

Florida Trend

Breathing Easier

After nine years, Alan Levan, chairman and CEO of **BBX Capital**, is out from under a U.S. Securities and Exchange Commission cloud.

BBX associates wrote on the glass of my office in celebration.

SEEING AROUND CORNERS

From:	Eugene Stearns <EStearns@stearnsweaver.com>
Sent:	Tuesday, July 11, 2017 9:20 AM
To:	Alan Levan; Jack Abdo - Abdo Companies; Jarett Levan
Cc:	Alison Miller; Grace Mead
Subject:	SEC

On Friday, the SEC's failure to file a notice of appeal made the Final Judgment final. The nightmare is over.

Eugene E. Stearns, Esq.
Stearns Weaver Miller Weissler Alhadeff & Sitterson, P.A.
150 West Flagler Street, Suite 2200
Miami, FL 33130
Direct: 305.789.3400
Main: 305.789.3200
estearns@stearnsweaver.com

STEARNS WEAVER MILLER
WEISSLER ALHADEFF & SITTERSON PA

The nightmare is over
NOTE: NO PRESS RELEASE FROM THE SEC THAT THEY LOST! And
that they wasted millions of taxpayer dollars on a frivolous lawsuit.

Miami Herald

CHAPTER 23

SALE OF BANKATLANTIC: CHARTER MEMBERS OF THE UNDERDOG CLUB

"Business is like a man rowing a boat upstream.
He has no choice; he must go ahead, or he will go back."
—Lewis E. Pierson

I loved banking. For me it had a sense of philanthropy. Sure, the bank was a for-profit institution, but you'd lend money so people could fulfill their dreams. Some days I felt like the Good Humor man, back in my old Brooklyn neighborhood on steamy summer nights. People were glad to see me, and it felt good to provide something that gave them so much pleasure. I couldn't believe how lucky I was to have my job.

We worked with small businesspeople, real estate developers, and corporate borrowers. We did business with consumers, either buying a home or seeking improvements for which they needed financing. Our loans helped people build their wealth, put their children through college, buy a car, take a vacation, and prepare for retirement. We did it in a professional, sophisticated, and highly efficient manner, and I made it our business to treat people with courtesy and respect, just as I wished to be treated.

Then there was my competitive side, pitting BankAtlantic against the big banks. It was us as the underdog against Bank of America, Southeast Bank, First Union, Wachovia, Barnett, Colonial, BankUnited, Barnett Bank, AmeriFirst (originally First Federal… the nation's first S&L), and dozens of others in our marketplace. We were a $6.5 billion institution—by most standards a large bank, but small in comparison to the behemoths with assets in the $200 and $500 billion and trillion range. But I loved matching wits with them in the areas of creative, innovative, customer-friendly, and efficient ways of building a bank and corporate culture. Frankly we took great pride in being the scrappy thorn in their sides as we built our business from one billion dollars in assets to $6.5 billion. We achieved this by doing things they were too busy or too big to do, or maybe things they didn't deem profitable enough, were beneath them, or they just didn't care about. We were a great innovator in putting the first ATMs on cruise ships and building our commercial real estate lending department, along with seven-day banking and free checking.

Though I had a competitive streak, it wasn't easy to watch the demise of these Goliaths of the Florida banking industry. They were stalwart, traditional, and iconic in their own right. They were all mostly liquidated or acquired, falling one by one into the claws of the Great Recession. In fact the only large bank survivor of the economic war in Florida of that time other than BankAtlantic was Bank of America, albeit with government assistance. Of course, BankAtlantic received no government assistance.

My staff and I loved the family feeling of BankAtlantic, basking in the comments and letters received from our customers as they compared us to other banks. Even our employees—called associates because we felt it elevated them to where they should be—told us BankAtlantic was like no other bank for which they'd ever worked. Workplace culture is one of those things you can't spend a lot of time talking about: either you have it or you don't. It's nothing you can dictate over and over. Like the trickle-down theory in economics, a good feeling about your workplace and your role in it starts at the top, reflected by each and every manager, down through every single level. We were proud to have a culture that did exactly that.

Communication was always paramount so we held our frequent town hall meetings throughout the company at the corporate level and at our one hundred branches to keep everyone informed. We wanted associates to hear any news, including updates about the trials and any negative press, directly from the top rather than hearing things around the water cooler. We wanted management to know what associates had to say, whether they expressed outright or did it anonymously if that was easier for them. We held our annual red carpet events at the BankAtlantic Center with thousands of associates in attendance. Most often I would make an entrance in costume in a big reveal. We celebrated our associates and our success. Of course every Friday was Red Friday where associates wore red, as did many of our customers. Fridays were an exciting, even boisterous time at the bank because everyone got into the spirit. Though to some it may sound saccharine, management, associates, and customers were one big extended family and life couldn't have been any better. While the titans of the banking industry thrashed and fell around us, BankAtlantic thrived.

Lowering the Boom

By 2011 I'd now been CEO of a public company, I.R.E., which became BankAtlantic Financial Corporation (BFC), for forty years (1971–2011), and CEO of BankAtlantic for twenty-seven years (1984–2011). Tough times or otherwise, I considered every day a privilege. There was something very special to me about being CEO of a bank. I'd never intended to be in this industry but sometimes your life chooses you instead of the other way around, and for a good reason.

Frankly there are also not many individuals who can say they were consistently CEO of one public company for nearly four decades. That kind of longevity at that level exists in rare cases but not as the norm. The average tenure for a public company CEO is five to seven years, with many of them hired guns by a private equity firm that acquires a bank to build short-term profits and sell it. But I was still running my marathon—in one place—and exactly where I wanted to be. Jack Abdo and I had decided some years back that one day Jarett would take over, eventually carrying the flag to the next generation. By 2011 we'd been in the business so long the Levan name was virtually synonymous with BankAtlantic. Maybe the best way I can describe what I felt every day about my business was a quiet pride…something that simmered in the deepest moments of reflection. I'm not sure a lot of people have that in their lives and I never took it for granted.

But things were about to change. We were now in the fourth year of the Great Recession. Though the economists purport it ended in 2009, that's simply a metric: two quarters of reducing GDP and so on. People did not get their jobs back and real estate certainly had not rebounded in 2009. In 2011 it wasn't the losses that kept me up at night. I knew the market would improve as it always does. And it wasn't the search for capital. We'd been resourceful and I had confidence I could stay ahead of capital requirements. It wasn't even the class-action lawsuit and SEC investigation going on at that time (the trials were yet to come) that made me lose sleep. I knew we were right and daunting as it all was, I held it in my heart that ultimately we'd be vindicated. The one variable that was so uncontrollable was the regulatory environment and the bank examiners. They were constantly changing the rules.

A strong example of this is that the economy was having a difficult time rebounding as credit was still very tight. As a result, the Treasury Department and Federal Reserve would make an announcement saying banks should be understanding of their borrowers' issues and cut them some slack. If people had a loan coming due, it should be all right to extend it if the bank determined they were on the right track.

Those times were like a hurricane. Everything was topsy-turvy. People were generally well-intentioned and they just needed more time to right their ships. According to the Fed and Treasury, banks were being too restrictive, given the harsh economic climate and the clamping down of bank examiners. Banks should now loosen the reins, they said emphatically, allowing customers to extend or modify their loans or even consider providing credit to people whose credit had been "dinged" in the storm.

But the bank examiners paid no attention to that. They were still in CYA mode, constantly tightening the screws, inundating the files with negative information and dire warnings and restrictions *just in case*. If one of the banks on a bank examiner's watch was identified for questionable practices—even for extending credit, as the government was suggesting, to someone with a less-than-stellar record, the examiners considered it the bank's offense. If a bank went under and there weren't a lot of red marks on its record to begin with, it was career-ending for that particular bank examiner. They all feared for their jobs. Examiners treated every bank and every prospective borrower as a bad guy with ulterior motives: guilty until proven innocent.

We and our customers were never again given the benefit of the doubt. Many of these examiners were the same ones who'd been around in 1984 when the approval process for our change of control application (please see chapter 12) had met with innumerable obstacles because they were fearful about having real estate people heading up banks. The wheels had turned very, very slowly at the time, though once we won them over and continued to prove ourselves, they'd spent twenty years staunchly in our corner.

Now the pendulum was swinging the other way again. They were fearful of making the wrong decision—any wrong decision—as their jobs hung in the balance. It seemed every time we turned around we were walking into an examiner's fist. We could not make commercial loans; we could not raise salaries; we could not hire anyone. Could not this. Could not that. Could not this again. We were in a stranglehold. The regulatory environment was such that examiners were afraid of being criticized and again, they feared for their jobs. Banks were failing all around us and often it was the examiner pushing them over the cliff.

In some ways it also felt as though we were moving toward the Canadian banking system where the only banks were five large national ones; government aid and new regulations coming out in this country seemed to favor large national and regional banks—not us. TARP (Troubled Asset Relief Program) funds were made available by the government and using many billions of dollars, it was bailing out behemoth entities such as Bank of America, AIG, and GE Credit. But these funds were not available to institutions on a smaller scale if we ever needed them.

The joy of banking began to sour. I no longer awoke with enthusiasm; no longer embraced my work. Sure, it's business, and I'm a CEO who prides myself in compartmentalizing to get the job done, but there was a hole inside of me that had never been there before. My dream of BankAtlantic remaining in my family dwindled from a crackling bonfire to a smoldering ember.

The big question: What do we do now?

The thought of selling BankAtlantic was traumatic and fraught with emotion. But when I got myself on top of it, as with most things, I approached it as a brand-new challenge. I just accepted it, jumping into creative challenge mode and no longer grappling with it. I didn't allow myself to dwell on what I was about to give up. My dad had always told me not to stew...to move on...and here was another opportunity. The question shifted: How do we orchestrate a sale?

Florida: In the Prime

We knew we had to proceed with caution. Acknowledging BankAtlantic was for sale would send signals to the press, which would assume we were being forced to sell because we couldn't meet capital. None of that was true and the speculation and rumor mills would take on a life of their own. It would impact our associates and our customers, which would set in motion a whole new set of negative dynamics. In short there would be chaos and at the very least make for a dark environment. So it would all have to be done quietly, skillfully, strategically, and impeccably.

I advised our executive management team and board of directors. Next I engaged an investment banker who met with Jarett and me, suggesting BankAtlantic's value might be $600 million minus the $285 million in trust-preferred debt (preferred stock) on BankAtlantic Bancorp's balance sheet. That was a far cry from the $1 billion market capital in 2006. The Great Recession had clearly taken its toll; we had reported losses for about fifteen quarters. But I believed we could rebuild the BFC Financial platform, not necessarily in banking, but some kind of diversified platform with the proceeds. As BFC owned half of BankAtlantic Bancorp, BFC would get approximately $150 million from the sale.

Next we prepared a list of prospective buyers and sent them all non-disclosure agreements. An offering circular was prepared and I was very pleased with the large response we received from the marketplace. After all, we had one hundred branches throughout the state. We had highly valued low-cost deposits—perhaps the best in the state—a magnet to any prospective buyer. We'd had outstanding customer rapport and feedback for years. I was truly optimistic.

The prime contenders were some of the largest banks in the United States and Canada: TD Bank; PNC; Capital One; BB&T; among others. To a large extent they expressed interest because unlike most states where the population doesn't change much and growth in deposits can become stagnant, if not decline altogether, Florida is different. People continuously move to Florida with the principal industries being real estate and tourism. Their money comes with them. National banks know they can go to Florida, raise deposits, and use the funds in other states. Florida may not provide enough places to lend money in terms of manufacturing or plants that need to be built, but the Northeast and Midwest do and money can be channeled there. So what we were offering was an opportunity to gain a foothold in the present and certainly the foreseeable future. Florida was the envy of every major bank in the country, and I knew they'd be salivating about ours.

Choreography 101

At the same time we had a big task ahead of us. We had to balance various banks' requests for information and onsite inspections in the realm of their due diligence without setting off too many alarms. We didn't want a lot of internal or external questions about what we were doing. "Who are these people and why are they here?" could never come up—from anyone. We had to juggle our responses and keep our identity secret from the marketplace and also from one bank to another so they could each accomplish their due diligence. They all needed access to loan files, the ability to conduct branch inspections, and anything else that might be warranted under the heading of due diligence.

In the process, BB&T was interested but dropped out early. We learned they'd been working on another acquisition and all of their time and resources were going into that. Banks have advance acquisition teams and generally focus on one thing at a time in this respect.

TD Bank had been soliciting to buy us for years and I'd always maintained I wasn't interested. At times they'd even come in with maps and other materials to demonstrate how it would all pan out if we'd only work with them. Headquartered in Toronto, they had hundreds of billions in assets and a large US presence, but not in Florida. They were elated that we were now for sale. CEO Ed Clarke invited Jarett and me to visit him in Toronto.

I've never been particularly impressed by movie stars or Hollywood people in general in terms of being in their company, but being in the company of CEOs of major companies? That was always intriguing to me! My curiosity cup runneth over. I always wanted to learn about their background and understand what they did to get to where they were. I wanted to know how they managed the titanic world they ruled. I wanted to know the key to their success. I had read hundreds of biographies, starting in high school, hungry for information on how very successful businesspeople achieved their success. Meeting Ed Clarke was going to be an experience.

Toe in the Water

Clarke's office was capacious with a top-of-the-world view of downtown Toronto. He was most welcoming and met with us for an hour, pitching us on why BankAtlantic's culture would fit so well with that of his bank. We wanted to make sure our associates and customers would land well. But we also spoke the language, knowing the word "merger," which came up often, was a euphemism; it was bank speak for, "We buy you and sayonara. We'll take it from here. Throw the rule book in the trash and don't let the door hit you on the way out." We had to be very, very careful in structuring a deal.

Clarke said he'd arrange for his advance team to fly down and review our commercial real estate files. They already knew a lot about our branching system, which appealed to them, having approached us over the years. Jeff Mindling, our chief credit officer, would coordinate their due diligence visit.

When Jarett and I returned to Florida we felt optimistic. It appeared as though when all was said and done, they'd make us an offer that would knock our socks off. They just wanted to get through our commercial loan files to make sure we'd written down the loans appropriately, and that the ones that were performing were really performing. All would be good. A large conference room—more like a ballroom—was secured at the local Marriott with a couple of days scheduled for the TD Bank people to spread out and do their thing. It began on a Saturday and Jarett and I drove over to see how it was going. The sight that befell us was dazzling.

Forty people lined the tables. TD Bank had assembled a team from all over the place—not only a Toronto crew, but bank personnel representing all of their Canadian and US regions. They pored over hundreds and hundreds of files Jeff had produced reflecting our commercial real estate borrowers and the loans themselves. Some of these files were two and three inches thick, and the TD Bank people meticulously went through them, scribbling notes, firing questions at Jeff about a particular borrower or credit. It was clear TD was rigorous when it came to acquisitions, which is probably the reason it'd grown to be the size it was. The bank had it down to a science and it was dizzying to watch.

The evening was to consist of TD Bank-hosted cocktails and dinner with our executive management group. TD attendees were not necessarily from the due diligence team, but an executive team representing the states and Toronto. The conversation was naturally all about the acquisition and how they were chomping at the bit. We understood we'd receive an offer very shortly and would be exceedingly happy. They had matched up their human resources executive officer with ours; the head of their commercial lending department with ours; and the same with their investment and chief financial officers. All of our management people did an air-tight job in keeping anything and everything about a potential sale close to the vest. It seemed like a fait accompli and yet it left a strange taste in our mouths. Unless there was a flood and ark being built about which we'd not gotten the memo, why would they need two of everyone as they professed? Still we moved forward. We were savvy enough to know there'd be issues there that needed to be worked out but beyond that were open to going ahead with a sale if the numbers added up.

Two days later another bank group came in. We accommodated them because until we had a deal with TD Bank, we were still for sale. Jeff put them in another hotel so the teams would not run into each other and moved all the files over. Another interested party also came shortly thereafter, and they were accommodated. We went through the same song and dance with several others and everything needed to be done neatly, efficiently, and as quickly as possible to get the commercial loan files back to where they lived so as not to raise suspicion among bank associates or anyone else about transporting the files off premises.

In 2011 we were still pre-digitized in terms of commercial files. Though our deposit information had been digitized and was backed up and transmitted elsewhere every night in the event of a disaster, commercial files were still paper, maintained in fire-retardant vaults at corporate headquarters. Jeff was running between hotel ballrooms with the files, getting more than his share of exercise. It was hectic but exciting to see how much interest our bank was generating.

Wrong Number

In the weeks that followed the silence was deafening. The investment banker we'd hired called TD Bank multiple times. They became hard to reach, and when they could be reached, said they were working on some other matters and it would be a while before they could really talk to us. That was their response, or lack of response. Ultimately they just died on the vine. There was no offer letter; no negotiation; no further discussion.

In time Coral Gables-based Bank United also stepped aboard. The bank itself had failed and we were dealing with a new group that had purchased the assets with government assistance. We'd been skeptical of Bank United because we just didn't trust them. We didn't know if the new regime was really interested or just poking around to see what BankAtlantic was up to…maybe taking notes about our customer base. Our investment banker encouraged us to let them in though. Following their review, just like TD Bank, we never heard from them again.

One day I got a call from Richard Fairbanks, CEO of Capital One Bank—a veritable kingdom. Fairbanks said he was interested in expanding into Florida and BankAtlantic would be an ideal merger partner. Capital One had built its business on credit cards and had been a public company, not a bank, and then at the time federal bailouts were made available it worked to their advantage to convert to being a bank. Capital One had become a bank because they figured out that getting access to branch deposits would be a low-cost way to fuel its credit card business. Florida branches would be a great resource.

I knew a lot about Richard Fairbanks because for decades I'd been a member of the Young Presidents Organization, first mentioned in chapter 17. YPO is a global network of young chief executives in more than one hundred thirty countries. In additional to the local, national, and global meetings, as mentioned we met for one week each year taking classes at Harvard Business School. One year we studied Capital One's growth and saw just how brilliant Fairbanks had been in founding and building it. When Capital One became a bank, Fairbanks became known as the only founder of such with all other large bank CEOs in the country essentially professional managers brought in to helm existing banks. This gave Fairbanks a certain mystique.

Capital One was interested in BankAtlantic, sending in a team to review our loan files just as the others had done. He invited Jarett and me to visit him at his headquarters in Virginia, followed by at least five separate conversations I had with him lasting two or three hours apiece. In those discussions we primarily talked about how we would come to a valuation. We never talked about an exact price, but his point of contention was about our commercial loan portfolio, which had a lot of non-performing loans. We'd written them down and continued to write them down. "This is high risk for us," he said on more than one occasion. "Our price is not going to be in the range you were hoping for."

I would counter that we were at the end of the cycle. "We've written them down and I'm thinking close to $600 million less the $285 million in trust-preferred stock." In turn he'd say that was not what he was thinking because while our deposits might be worth that number, the commercial loan portfolio is a huge "deduct" from that.

We never agreed on a number, and this was my first (eye-opening) conversation that the commercial lending portfolio was the problem. TD Bank had never expressed it; they'd just looked at the portfolio and disappeared. Richard Fairbanks really wanted to buy BankAtlantic and at least gave me the professional courtesy of talking to me candidly.

Next up was PNC Bank. They sent a coterie of thirty to forty credit analysts to review the commercial loan files. PNC loved our deposit system and had already announced their plans to build twenty or thirty branches in Broward County. We already had twenty or thirty branches in Broward County that they could have instead of building them. It was an ideal fit—the stuff of financial fantasies. After several weeks of anticipation, their offer of $125 million dollars arrived. It was woefully short of the $600 million our investment banker had initially said we could get. It was a real lowball number and I needed to know how PNC had arrived at it.

Surprisingly, PNC sent us the data I asked for—the spreadsheet showing their calculations. While they were valuing our deposits at 10 percent, there were multiple deducts including for the troubled commercial loan portfolio, the trust-preferred, and so on. I was immensely disappointed but agreed to continue the dialogue. PNC CEO Jim Rohr sent his spacious private jet to pick up Jarett and me to whisk us to Pittsburgh, corporate headquarters of PNC Bank. Call it kismet but our headquarters at the time was in an area of Fort Lauderdale called Cypress Creek. Our building was literally on the runway of an executive airport. It was always fun to look out and watch private planes coming in and taking off, and now we'd be on one of them. It was echoes of traveling to TD Bank, this time in style, only I hoped we could turn this one into a win.

Jim's car and driver met us on the tarmac of a private airport in Pittsburgh, whisking us to PNC headquarters. We met up with our investment banker, who had come in from New York, convening for a few minutes before entering an executive conference room where Jim Rohr, his investment banker, and a PNC acquisitions person greeted us. We spent an hour talking about the national economy, the Florida economy, the recession, and why a combination of PNC and BankAtlantic was a formula for success. Rohr used the word "merger" and Jarett's eyes locked onto mine because we knew what that meant. It wasn't good. We kept getting the message that PNC was a whale and we were essentially a speck—a grain of sand on a hot Florida beach. PNC could do so much more if it acquired BankAtlantic because it was Big Daddy and we were a tiny bank with an interesting deposit franchise they wanted. I was getting irritated and his continuing diminution of our importance was wearing thin on me. But I'd done enough negotiations in my life to know to keep calm, remain in my seat, and see what the next few minutes held. I was still hopeful and optimistic that I could get PNC to raise its offering price of $125 million.

Then Jim Rohr dropped a bomb. "Actually," he said, "the BankAtlantic franchise is only worth $50 million!"

The offer letter we'd received the previous week had said $125 million; now we were down to relatively nothing. I was livid. I lost my cool, blurting out a resounding "*What?*" that was probably heard more than three hundred miles east in Philadelphia.

At that point, their investment banker took over to explain that our commercial loan portfolio was a disaster. Apparently when they'd issued the letter last week, they hadn't thoroughly assessed the damages and were going to have to deduct more from their intended purchase price. He was adamant—in fact fist pounding adamant—that it was a take it or leave it offer. There was not a penny more. Without hesitation, I left it. Accepting it was tantamount to letting someone steal BankAtlantic while I sat by and watched—even waved them through. Perhaps their intel-gathering had turned up the other banks that had tossed their hats in the ring and then pulled them out, and they'd decided they were our last hope, but the exploitation factor and lack of decency was more than I could take. Transacting at a less-than-fair price was never all right. They'd dragged us all the way to Pittsburgh just to drop us on our behinds.

The meeting ended abruptly and we were now standing in the hallway. Our investment banker expressed concern that we were not taking this offer seriously enough. I was pissed off. With the hasty goodbyes, Jarett and I weren't sure we'd be availing ourselves of the same mode of transportation back to Fort Lauderdale, but the driver soon appeared in the hallway and drove us back to the plane. I was steaming the entire flight, deciding to take one of the plastic drink cups with the PNC logo on it as a souvenir and reminder of the day, just as my wife Susie and I had purchased rogue David Paul's Limoges china for pennies on the dollar at the government-sponsored CenTrust liquidation auction. It's interesting because as a rule I don't remember the bad times in my life. It takes an enormous effort to do that. But for some reason on a couple of occasions, including this one, it gets seared in my brain as unforgettable.

Brushing Off the Dust

At the next BankAtlantic board meeting, our New York investment banker was invited to attend as he had over the past few months. He was expected to provide reports as to how the sale process was going. When it came to the PNC issue, he swallowed deeply a few times and his tone changed as he suggested that was really the best offer we'd gotten and we should take it. In fact it had been the only offer. "The market is the market," he said, justifying his position. "We've reached every possible bank that could be interested and had the ability to pay and the market has spoken," he said. "Those that weren't interested just weren't. Those that were afraid of the commercial loan portfolio disappeared. Only PNC is left. If you believe in supply and demand, and if you believe in the market, then the only choice you have is to accept it."

He proceeded to bring up the shareholder class-action litigation and the SEC investigation. We were still taking losses and had trust-preferred securities we needed to take care of, and his argument for accepting the paltry PNC offer became stronger. I perceived the directors were buying his argument.

I sat there, telling myself I'd be damned if I was going to let go of BankAtlantic after thirty-five years for $50 million dollars. The public shareholders would receive $25 million of that and BFC would walk away with the other $25 million and its tale between its legs. I firmly believed we would survive the recession. We just had to keep focused and our heads above water. I told the directors it would be a huge mistake to succumb to those numbers and we should go it alone. I've always had a highly supportive board and they agreed with me.

I terminated the investment banker for even suggesting we sell the bank for $50 million. This was the same individual who'd valued us at $600 million dollars less than six months earlier. I was angry and at the same time I just didn't know: I thought we were the prettiest girl at the party but we couldn't get a dance. We had come up dry.

What had come battling out of all of this, however, was our commercial loan portfolio was scaring people to death. Banks knew it would be a drag on their earnings. It didn't scare *us* as we'd seen some percolation—money coming into the market—and we'd done another quarter or two of appraisals and appraisals had stopped dropping. They had stabilized. But as far as selling the bank I didn't have a lot of time to figure out what my next step would be. The end of the second quarter was around the corner and we needed capital before June 30. I'd pulled many rabbits out of many hats in the form of downsizing and rights offerings, but this time I needed more.

I went back to the PNC analysis of how they justified their price of $125 million. One of the line items was a 10 percent deposit premium and then deductions for the risk of the commercial loan portfolio. This meant that if deposits were $150 million, they would pay $15 million to acquire them. Our Tampa region had $150 million in 10 branches. With that intel, I had a short-term action plan.

Calling PNC's acquisitions officer, I said I would sell them our Tampa franchise for a 10 percent deposit premium. Only performing loans would go with the sale, so no discounts there. We would retain everything else. I was very aggressive on the phone but there was a method to my madness. I told the acquisitions officer I'd felt manhandled at our unfortunate meeting in Pittsburgh. He had seventy-two hours to make a decision and not a minute more. I warned him not to come back to us and try and negotiate because if he did, I'd pull my offer off the table. PNC came back within the seventy-two-hour window and we sold BankAtlantic's Tampa branches at precisely the number I'd asked for. The profit on that transaction solved our capital issues for that quarter. Another rabbit pulled out of the hat.

While we celebrated the success of the Tampa sale, we were still bemoaning the fact that it didn't solve our long-term issues. I spent time turning over everything that had happened in the past six months. Banks had expressed a lot of interest but then I couldn't get them to the table. They appeared to relish our low-cost deposit franchise and our one hundred branches in Florida—prime banking territory—but similarly were repelled by our real estate lending portfolio. It had been easy to sell the Tampa branches as the deposits were quite valuable. So it was incumbent upon me to structure things differently in order to sell the entire organization.

I recalled an obscure deal I'd read about years earlier—in fact, twenty-three years earlier in 1988, to be precise. At that time Philadelphia's Mellon Bank had been drowning in problem loans that scared away investors. The bank was failing, unable to raise capital. Mellon was one of the oldest, most venerated banks in the country. In order to obtain what it needed, the bank created a transaction where good assets were separated from bad. In other words Mellon extricated all of its problem loans simultaneously, creating a new entity for these loans called Grant Street, leaving the bank a pristine organism with deposits and performing loans, capable of raising capital.

Mellon then raised sufficient money to make sure capital was strong enough to support itself, having shed itself of the bad loans. Grant Street became a real estate company, raising money from investors favoring distressed properties at a discount. The goal was to eventually liquidate Grant Street, with investors turning a profit on the money they'd put in. It was a unique, elegant solution to a problem referred to at the time as good bank/bad bank. I had been intrigued at the time I first read about it and was again now, as I recalled it. Whoever had designed it was brilliant. Could it be dusted off and work here? I decided to use the same structure for BankAtlantic.

Frankly I wasn't afraid of our commercial loan portfolio. I thought we'd seen the worst of it and the market was stabilizing. Jack Abdo and I had weathered several recessions and knew that whenever Florida emerges from one, real estate comes charging back. In fact real estate values always got better than they were before the prior recessions. I figured that was the way it was going to work again. We knew the borrowers intimately and were familiar with the locations of these properties. TD Bank and PNC—and other banks that had considered purchasing BankAtlantic from us—did not have that advantage, so they were wary. But I knew that if we set up our own Grant Street in order to sell what was currently in bad shape, we'd do well in the end. We just had to present a different kind of package.

A new offering circular was produced that featured our performing loans plus a 10 percent premium for the deposits, minus the branches PNC had bought. At first I decided not to engage another investment banker to assist in structuring the transaction largely based on my disappointment with the first one. I also recalled the time I started out in my real estate career. I'd had ideas for a building and had gone to every bank in Miami for financing and every one told me to do this, do that, change the windows and the front door, consider more landscaping, change the apartment size and on and on. At the end of the day it was all conflicting information and nobody wanted to finance the project anyway. Never again! When I formed I.R.E. I didn't make the same mistake. I structured the product, held firm to my convictions, and took it to market. I wasn't about to invest a lot of time and energy giving people input. They could take it or leave it. I wasn't going to budge.

Steve Jobs employed the same modus operandi, though it would come years later. In creating Apple he reportedly didn't believe in market research. His position was that consumers don't know what they want. If you ask them, they're going to tell you a bunch of different things they think they want based on their current perspective. But Jobs believed if Apple really wanted to change the paradigm, it was going to have to give them something no one had ever *thought* to want. Then when they saw and understood it, they'd not be able to live without it. That's the way he created the iPhone.

In addition to retaining what I called the scratch-and-dent loans, amounting to $600 million, I decided we would also keep the $285 million in trust-preferred bonds (a liability) at the holding company. This time we were selling only BankAtlantic, not BankAtlantic

Bancorp, which we would keep as a public company on the NYSE. Because the $600 million in real estate assets would be spun out into BankAtlantic Bancorp that was no longer a bank with accruing banking constraints, I knew we'd be able to get creative and do other things with the portfolio. Also, that $600 million dollar figure was the written down number on the loans, which had been worth much more in their original form. I figured these loans would turn to gold for us when the market came back, presumably just around the corner. The fact is I estimated the "bad" portfolio was really worth more than the bank.

After I structured the concept, I did end up going to two other investment bankers. I wasn't going to work with anyone who didn't fully endorse it. The two I approached believed it to be viable and thought they could find a buyer.

The next part was the most fun yet.

Seven or eight months had passed since BB&T had told us they'd been interested, but the timing had not been good. This time, things were different. There were issues to be worked out with the trust-preferred stock but overall they liked what they saw and agreed to buy BankAtlantic. We had a buyer. The contract was signed on November 1, 2011, to close no later than August 1, 2012, pending regulatory approval. Though BB&T said that if they'd terminate any of our associates, they'd take care of them, we didn't leave it at that. We made sure contractually that severance was provided for every single employee, saying that if BB&T's severance package was better than ours, they had to pay them, but if not they were to pay them the kind of severance we'd identified. We also negotiated severance for our executive team—the individuals that had gotten us through the past five grueling years and had helped build the bank overall.

Trust *Un*preferred

BB&T had stipulated it would never take over the $285 million in trust-preferred securities. Those would remain with BankAtlantic

Bancorp as our responsibility. As soon as we announced the sale, however, the holders of the trust-preferred bonds—individuals and hedge funds that had purchased the bonds opportunistically at the height of the last recession for pennies on the dollar—immediately sued BankAtlantic Bancorp. The reason for the suit was to force BankAtlantic Bancorp to pay off the bonds now. These bonds still had another twenty-five more years before they were due. They wanted to force us to pay them off now because BankAtlantic Bancorp was no longer going to be a bank, and an early payoff would significantly increase their yield.

BankAtlantic Bancorp ended up in a Delaware court, the venue of jurisdiction for these trust-preferreds. We had an expedited trial and the court came back highly critical of BankAtlantic Bancorp and me. The judge decided BankAtlantic Bancorp had no ability to pay off the trust-preferreds, so if BB&T wasn't going to assume responsibility, the sale to BB&T could not happen. A great deal of negative press ensued and BB&T was not happy about any of it, including the fact that we'd told them the trust-preferreds would not be a problem (which we'd truly believed). BB&T canceled the agreement to purchase the bank.

I revived my initial concept and went straight back to them.

"You've been through due diligence. You know what you've got here," I said. "This is the best banking franchise in the state. Our low-cost deposits are flawless. If you will agree to pay $600 million and assume the $285 million dollars' worth of trust-preferred bonds, we will owe you $285 million, collateralized by the $600 million in real estate loans and assets. Think of it as a bank loan—look at it as though you are loaning BankAtlantic Bancorp $285 million. We're going to keep the $600 million in real estate loans but we'll pay you back the $285 million dollars for the trust-preferred bond obligation you are assuming."

They accepted the terms, saying they'd pay off the $285 million trust-preferreds at closing or within thirty days, which they did. We had the $600 million in scratch-and-dent real estate assets and loans and BankAtlantic Bancorp was obligated to pay back $285 million. Our contract provided we pay it off in seven years by liquidating parts of the $600 million in real estate we'd retained.

BB&T accepted it! The purchase was now back on, pending regulatory approval. As usual, the wheels turned slowly and we were being asked by bank examiners to increase our capital and respond to hundreds of questions. They actually waffled on it until July 31 when they finally approved it—the day before the scheduled August 1 closing, which had not changed.

Essentially we got the $600 million purchase price for the sale of BankAtlantic, which was the number with which we'd started, though it was in real estate instead of cash. I believed the real estate was far more valuable than the cash, something none of the other banks had had enough vision to see.

As will be discussed in the next chapter, it didn't take us seven years to pay off the $285 million. It took us only three years because we sold off a portion of the real estate and channeled some of it into joint ventures to build apartments, housing communities, and shopping centers. It turned out the real estate loans, called junk by everyone, were really gold. It was no surprise to me or Jack. Obviously, the Delaware judge got it dead wrong!

The underdogs had their day.

LIFE LESSONS LEARNED

- Cliché or otherwise, never say never.
- Be far more creative than the other guy. Learn to spin what others think is useless into gold. It's not always possible, but trying is.

The Miami Herald

50 CENTS
109TH YEAR, NO. 49 ⓒ2011
MiamiHerald.com
WEDNESDAY, NOVEMBER 2, 2011
BROWARD & KEYS EDITION

BANKING

BB&T in deal to buy BankAtlantic

AMERICAN BANKER.

BB&T to Bulk Up in Florida with Deal to Buy
BankAtlantic

BB&T to buy local bank

Deal with BankAtlantic
excludes some assets

BY DOREEN HEMLOCK
Staff writer

Sun Sentinel

'Bittersweet' end for local banking giant

by Gregg Fields, DBR. There's
going to be bare-knuckled competition in South Florida banking
now that BankAtlantic has been
sold to BB&T.

Though it has a low pro-
file locally, BB&T is a North
Carolina powerhouse with 1,800
branches across 12 states and
the District of Columbia. It has
remained steadily profitable even
as its Tar Hell brethren Bank of
America and Wachovia (which
was taken over by Wells Fargo)
got pummeled by the financial
crisis.

The BB&T franchise will be a
true contender, the sixth-largest
in South Florida. And analysts
say the relatively rich price
it paid for BankAtlantic's 78
branches shows South Florida

JILL KAHN

Chairman Alan Levan said the final
agreements to sell BankAtlantic were
hammered out in negotiations until
5:30 a.m.

has enduring appeal to financial
institutions, despite the sluggish
economy. But it also means the
end of yet another high-profile
South Florida bank.

"It's bittersweet," said Alan
Levan, the longtime chairman.
SEE STORY, PAGE A7

Daily Business Review

CHAPTER 24

'TWAS THE NIGHT BEFORE EXPIRATION: GROWTH OF THE COMPANY 2012–2017

"Never let a good crisis go to waste."
—Winston Churchill

The approval for the sale of BankAtlantic to BB&T moved slowly at first, and then it literally happened overnight. It took nine months, and then the night before the contract expired, we finally got regulatory approval. Until that moment we just didn't know anything. It's difficult to plan for the sale of your business while you are still running it and don't know if the sale will actually happen, and at the same time make pivotal plans for what lies ahead.

But on July 31, 2012, the sale was consummated. The following day we assessed what we had. We'd given up the BankAtlantic name, and while we didn't sell BankAtlantic Bancorp, the holding company, it nevertheless contained the BankAtlantic name so we were required to come up with something else. We soon changed it to BBX Capital. BBX was BankAtlantic Bancorp's NYSE trading symbol, which was well identified in the marketplace, so it was a logical step.

The organizational structure was the same. BankAtlantic Financial Corporation (BFC) still owned 53 percent of BBX Capital and BBX

Capital continued its listing on the NYSE. Because BankAtlantic was a 100 percent subsidiary of BankAtlantic Bancorp, BBX Capital was the recipient of the "proceeds" from the sale to BB&T. The proceeds consisted of $600 million of scratch-and-dent (my description)—most often referred to as junk or toxic assets by others—residential and commercial real estate loans. In the renegotiated deal with BB&T, we now owed BB&T the $265 million with a maturity date of seven years. We weren't producing any income at that moment because most of the $600 million was not income-producing. It was mostly raw land. We immediately focused on the task at hand.

With the sale of BankAtlantic, BFC still controlled 53 percent of BBX Capital. BBX Capital's assets consisted of $600 million of real estate and loans and $285 million worth of debt to BB&T.

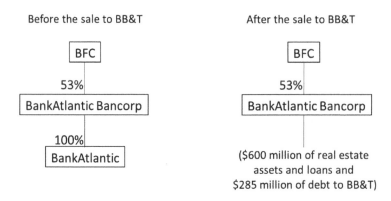

I was chairman of the BBX Capital executive management team. Jack Abdo was vice chairman, Jarett Levan was president, and Seth Wise was president of BBX Capital Real Estate. With BB&T's permission, we asked approximately forty BankAtlantic associates to stay with us and work for BBX Capital—we needed them for accounting, finance, and servicing of the real estate portfolio. Since we remained a public company, we were still obligated to audit our financials and continued to file SEC 10-Qs and 10-Ks. At the moment, we had no business other than real estate, and no strategic plan.

Previously, BankAtlantic Bancorp had no employees since it was just a holding company for BankAtlantic. It totally depended on the bank for all operational services and infrastructure. The bank had hosted human resources and IT, and was responsible for maintaining office space, telephones, payroll, accounts receivable, and accounts payable. In short, the bank handled all the systems and protocol. BankAtlantic Bancorp never had anything to do with these operations. It was just the holding company that owned the behemoth BankAtlantic. Now BBX Capital was left with nothing in the way of infrastructure in which to operate.

Part of our agreement with BB&T was for BBX Capital to stay on the premises until year-end. When we were working out this agreement long before the sale ultimately happened, it had never dawned on me that by the time we'd transacted the sale there'd be only five months left in the year—and sometime in December, BB&T was planning to shutter the single-purpose building that housed our offices. BB&T had other offices in South Florida, with corporate offices in Winston-Salem, North Carolina, and they had no need for that building, so we had to be out. We'd have no street address, telephone number, furniture, human resources, computer system, or payroll systems—absolutely nothing. We were suddenly under a lot of pressure, not only to pay our overhead and pay down the debt, but also to find a suitable place from which to operate.

We were probably the only NYSE-listed company in history with $600 million in assets and absolutely no infrastructure and no business plan.

Our immediate plan was to find office space, continue to manage our assets, and generate enough cash to pay overhead and pay down the debt to BB&T. Beyond that we had no strategy for BBX Capital. The only thing that was certain, maybe even cause for brief celebration, was that because we were no longer a bank, the bank examiners and regulators were gone. Granted, we were functioning in crisis mode, but at least the shackles were off, and it felt good to breathe the air outside the prison walls.

With the clock ticking loudly, finding space was not as easy as it might have been in earlier years. Once a prospective landlord did his or her due diligence, the SEC lawsuit came up and we were refused occupancy. There was still an eight hundred-pound gorilla on our back. We lost a lot of time in our five-month scramble to relocate because of our reputation problem. In one case we offered to pay the entire first year rent in cash, but we were still turned away. No landlord wanted to associate with us. Finally, at the eleventh hour, we landed in a good space, thanks to Terry Stiles, a BankAtlantic borrower and good friend to all of us. Terry was the developer of the Bank of America building in downtown Fort Lauderdale. He was not deterred by the SEC litigation and leased us eighteen thousand square feet of prime office space.

Prose and Plans

There were very few positive articles in the press about us even after the sale of BankAtlantic. Among the good ones, however, were *Opportunist* magazine, which heralded me on its January 2013 cover. *Florida Trend* wrote in its September 30, 2013, issue that I was "un-distressed," meaning I was operating in distressed properties and had assembled a basket of so-called toxic assets from the sale of BankAtlantic that I considered anything but toxic.

But overall the press was negative; most articles were still about the SEC situation, or at least mentioned it. It was a tough time in that respect, but we needed to turn our attention to working on a strategic plan for BBX Capital.

What we did know was that we were entrepreneurial and good at creating value. We decided we would operate differently from other public companies and focus on value creation instead of quarterly earnings. All of our public communications began to carry the following two paragraphs:

"Our goal is to build long-term shareholder value as opposed to focusing on quarterly or annual earnings."

"Since many of BBX Capital's assets do not generate income on a regular or predictable basis, our objective is to achieve long-term growth as measured by increases in book value and intrinsic value over time."

First on our agenda was to continue to collect funds from defaulted commercial loan borrowers. Jack Abdo took on this responsibility, and there couldn't have been anyone more suited to it. Jack is someone who, once he gets his teeth into something, performs like a terrier. He was as aggressive as he could be within the parameters of good business practices, and he got us to where we needed to be. If customers were willing to work with us in a reorganization plan for their loans, we worked with them. But for those who strategically defaulted, or simply walked away from their obligations, Jack vigorously pursued collection. Among the great stories of this era was the pursuit of Dan Catalfumo, the wily, colorful borrower with the Cayman Islands cache mentioned earlier.

Next we needed to liquidate the real estate portfolio to give us funds to pay the overhead and pay back BB&T within the seven-year contractual term. Seth Wise, our partner and president of BBX Capital Real Estate, and his team took on that task. The fact is keeping the real estate was far more valuable than receiving cash from the sale to BB&T, something that none of the other banks had the vision to see or care about. There were hundreds of pieces of real estate in the $600 million in assets we'd retained, so we broke them into three categories: (1) "sell immediately" for properties we doubted would go up in value, (2) "hold for development," or (3) "hold for increase in value" for sale later, for properties we were more optimistic about. In short, we segregated the portfolio. The real estate we decided to develop was further broken down into "joint venture" or "build it ourselves," using our own land. Seth did a masterful job in analyzing this portfolio and setting it up for sale and value creation.

* * *

The true test of character is how people handle themselves in challenging times. Because of our long history at BankAtlantic in dealing with developers, we knew who had handled themselves appropriately during the recession, and these were the real estate people we were eager to partner with in this phase of our business. Among our strong associations during this time were Armando Codina and Jim Carr of CC Homes for residential housing; Joel Altman/Altman Development Corporation for multi-family units; ContraVest, also for apartment communities; and Phil Procacci of Procacci Development Corporation for hotels. We also partnered with Terry Stiles/Stiles Corporation for office buildings and retail, and a number of others we considered experts in the industry. With these partnerships we built apartments, residential housing communities, student housing, shopping centers, and office parks. We entered into nineteen joint ventures and independent development deals. The real estate loan portfolio, called junk and toxic by everyone, turned out to be golden, which was no surprise to me.

Between 2012 and 2017, we sold 481 separate real estate assets. Thank you, Seth! Most were land parcels obtained through foreclosure. We commenced 92 commercial foreclosures and lawsuits. We collected $100 million in judgments. Thank you, Jack! By August 2013, within twelve months of the sale to BB&T, we'd gotten the $285 million dollar BB&T debt down to $150 million. By the following August we'd paid it down to $15 million. We'd soon pay off the entire debt—four years early. And we still had retained hundreds of millions of dollars in cash and real estate to boot. Clearly Judge Lassiter in the Delaware court had gotten it wrong.

Tying the Knot—Once and For All

BFC had been a misunderstood entity since 1987. The fact is, we'd never set out to create the complicated web of businesses we did. At that time, after we'd acquired control of BankAtlantic (then Atlantic Federal), we wound down its I.R.E. real estate operations to focus on the bank. It was always confusing to investors because over time BFC had become just a 53 percent–owned holding company (without any operations) for BankAtlantic.

I had tried to simplify the story by merging BFC and BankAtlantic in 1987, but because of investor issues that merger was never accomplished. It continued to be a dream of mine over the next twenty-nine years to merge the two, but the story became more complicated instead of less. Over time BFC had become a holding company with controlling interests in Levitt Corporation, now Woodbridge, Bluegreen Corporation, as well as BankAtlantic Bancorp.

All of these companies had listed on the NYSE, albeit controlled by BFC. I was simultaneously chairman and CEO of three NYSE companies: BFC, Woodbridge, and BankAtlantic Bancorp, and chairman of Bluegreen, also on the NYSE.

Since BFC continued to have no operations other than its controlling interest in these companies, it had become apparent that BFC's long-term dream to put all these companies together was never going to become a reality. This was especially true with the onslaught of the Great Recession and shareholder and SEC lawsuits, all of which muddied the waters. But I've always known that opportunities come to those who are prepared for them.

While BFC's stock had begun to rally after the sale of BankAtlantic, the stocks of BBX Capital, Woodbridge, and Bluegreen had been slower to recover. During the recession, the Dow Jones Industrial Average had lost over 54 percent of its value and our affiliated companies had been not immune to this debacle.

Woodbridge, formerly Levitt Corporation, and BFC were delisted from the NYSE because of their low stock prices and BankAtlantic Bancorp, now BBX Capital, had been put on probation from the NYSE for the same reason.

I wondered if this was the opportunity I had been thinking about for decades to clean up BFC's complicated corporate structure. During the recession, BFC had increased its ownership in each of the companies to over 50 percent from all the rights offerings and strategic purchases in support of shoring up their capital.

But the obstacles were still immense. All mergers are complicated. And for BFC the task at hand was monumental. Nationally, in my experience, a majority of mergers end up with ambulance-chasing, bogus class-action lawsuits. I would have to navigate through them. Of course, a merger would require approval from the shareholders. That was not a problem because the shareholders also wanted a simplified structure. The process was going to be even more complicated and treacherous for BFC because the NYSE had refused to relist BFC because of the ongoing SEC lawsuit. After all, the NYSE's regulator was none other than the SEC.

My first step was to work with Alison Miller to prepare a proxy so we could propose an offering document.

In 2009 we proposed a stock-for-stock transaction with BFC to acquire Woodbridge. It was approved by the shareholders and we were able to consummate the transaction because neither Woodbridge nor BFC were now on the NYSE.

Next up was Bluegreen.

Initially, we proposed a stock for stock transaction for it as well. It was approved by the shareholders, but the NYSE continued to refuse to list BFC and the merger had to be aborted. We came back with a cash transaction that again was approved by the shareholders. This time, because it was cash, it skirted the NYSE requirements.

Of course, both the stock and cash proposals, though approved by the shareholders, had class-action litigation. Fortunately, Gene Stearns and his legal team were able to defeat them and we were able to consummate the mergers.

BFC now owned 100 percent of Woodbridge and Bluegreen. The prize that remained was merging BFC and BBX Capital.

Tying the Knot Part II

I never lost interest in trying to put BFC and BBX Capital together. In 2016, I attempted it again. BFC proposed to acquire BBX Capital early that year. This was going to be a stock-for-stock transaction, and it was heartily approved by the shareholders.

I was finally about to realize a dream that had begun nearly three decades earlier. Unfortunately, we still could not list BFC on the NYSE. I had unrealistically believed that this time the NYSE would waive the issue with the SEC lawsuit but it didn't. So the deal could not be consummated. Again, we had to abort, regroup, and circle back to try it another way.

After we won the SEC lawsuit, the NYSE immediately embraced BFC and offered a listing. We again proposed a merger to the shareholders. Again, it was approved and this time consummated.

We were finally one single public company that had combined the assets of several disparate entities: Woodbridge, Bluegreen, and BBX Capital. Since BBX's name was better known than Woodbridge or BFC, in 2017 BFC adopted the BBX Capital name. We left Bluegreen with its name.

In 2015, Ray Lopez, former controller, Chief Accounting Officer, and Senior Vice President of Bluegreen, became BBX Capital's new executive vice president and chief financial officer.

Vacation Nation

Growing Bluegreen Corp. was an important component of our agenda. Bluegreen was in the timeshare industry, and we knew we had a tiger by the tail. Its size and achievements were exciting: it has sixty-six vacation club and club associate resorts, six thousand employees, and more than 210,000 Bluegreen Vacation Club owners.

Sugar High

Jarett felt we needed to venture into middle-market operating companies. Our new strategy included the 2013 acquisition of Ontario, Canada-based, $75 million revenue Renin Corporation, which specializes in building supply and home improvement products, which it sells to retailers like Home Depot and Lowe's. Shawn Pearson joined Renin as CEO with a mission to restructure the company to profitability. In 2017, he became CEO of Bluegreen.

We also acquired numerous companies in the confectionary space, under wholly owned subsidiary BBX Sweet Holdings. These included Hoffman's Chocolates, which came on board in 2013. In 2014 we acquired Jer's Chocolates, a purveyor of gourmet luxury chocolates with wholesale distribution and licensing agreements. Helen Grace Chocolates, Toffee Box, Anastasia Confections, and Williams and Bennett followed in 2014. Over time, BBX Capital was selling confections in Costco, Sam's Club, Williams Sonoma, and in hundreds of locations, including many Fifth Avenue stores.

In 2017, we acquired IT'SUGAR, the largest specialty candy retailer in the US with about a hundred locations across the United States and abroad.

Also in 2017, we became the franchisee for MOD Pizza for the state of Florida.

It was an incredible five years. The recession, the stock market decline, and the negative publicity from the SEC litigation reduced the affiliated stock prices to attractive levels. It gave me the ability to achieve a twenty-nine-year dream of putting these companies together. Thank you SEC! This was one crisis we didn't waste. With one united company, we were able to grow our existing businesses and acquire others.

Okay…I won't mention the wrought iron gates again.

LIFE LESSONS LEARNED

- There is no substitute for patience and perseverance. If they don't come naturally to you, take the time to cultivate them. Separately or together, they can yield powerful results.
- Opportunities come to those who are prepared for them (can't say it enough).
- Never let a good crisis go to waste.

BBX Capital

BFC Financial Changes Name to BBX Capital Corporation

BBX Capital Executive Team

Alan B. Levan	John E. Abdo	Jarett Levan	Seth Wise	Ray Lopez
Chairman & CEO	Vice Chairman	President	BBX Capital Real Estate President	Chief Financial Officer

➤ *Led by an entrepreneurial team focused on creating value over the long-term*

BBX's Corporate Strategy

Goal ➤ **Build long-term shareholder value** as opposed to focusing on quarterly or annual earnings

Since many of BBX Capital's assets do not generate income on a regular or predictable basis, our objective is to:

Objective ➤ **Achieve long-term growth** as measured by increases in **book value and intrinsic value** over time

Four Strategic Segments*

①	②	③	④
bluegreen vacations	**≡BBX Capital** REAL ESTATE	≡BBX *Sweet* HOLDINGS	▌RENIN

• NYSE: BXG
• 90% ownership interest
• 69 Resorts
• 219,000+ Vacation Club Owners [1]
	Acquisition, Ownership, and Management of:
	• Developments
	• Joint Ventures
	• Investments
		• Owner of IT'SUGAR, one of the largest candy retailers in North America
		  *100 Locations
		  *> 25 states
		• Operator of a collection of award winning wholesale candy brands
			• Designer, manufacturer and distributor of specialty doors, hardware, and home décor products

(1) Data as of 12/31/19			

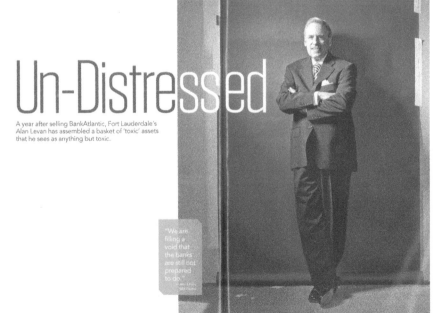

Florida Trend

≡BBX Capital
R E A L   E S T A T E

Acquisition, ownership and
management of joint ventures and
investments in real estate and real estate
development projects.

*Seth Wise, President, BBX Capital
Real Estate, Sun Sentinel*

BBX Capital Real Estate blossoms

Spinoff loaded with key projects

BY PAUL OWERS
Staff writer

When BB&T Corp. bought BankAtlantic in 2012, BB&T had no interest in roughly $500 million in "scratch and dent" assets owned by the Fort Lauderdale-based lender.

"BB&T didn't want them, but we looked at them through a different lens and realized these are fabulous assets that could be turned into a significant profit opportunity," said Seth Wise, an official with BankAtlantic's holding company.

COURTESY/
BBX CAPITAL REAL ESTATE

Seth Wise, president of BBX Capital Real Estate, is busy with several joint ventures.

L to R: Bruce Parker, Seth Wise, Jarett Levan, Jack Abdo, Mayor Jack Seiler, Alan; Breaking ground in Victoria Park, Fort Lauderdale

Droga Chocolates is one of five chocolate wholesalers acquired in 2014

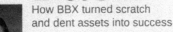

Bouncing Back

How BBX turned scratch and dent assets into success

Editor's note: SFBW's July cover story discussed the legal saga of banker Alan Levan. This article covers how he's found success after the recession.

BY KEVIN GALE

Alan Levan

Chairman and CEO Alan Levan had two key reasons to celebrate at the annual shareholder meeting of BBX Capital in May. One was being fully cleared after 10 years of litigation surrounding BankAtlantic Bancorp. The other was celebrating the five-year anniversary of BBX Capital, which had just seen its shares hit a new peak.

On July 6, BBX hit another milestone when it announced its class A shares would start trading on the New York Stock Exchange under the symbol BBX. BBX's legacy companies, Bluegreen Corporation, Levitt Corporation and BankAtlantic Bancorp, once all traded on the NYSE.

While many banks failed during the Great Recession, Levan in 2012 sold BankAtlantic's 68 branches, $3.3 billion in deposits and $2.1 billion in loans to BB&T. BankAtlantic Bancorp, which changed its name to BBX Capital, realized a gain

of $307 million and kept $600 million in what he calls scratch-and-dent assets.

"The regulators did not like the banks having nonperforming loans on their books. We kept insisting to the regulators that these issues were market-driven, not loan-specific-driven, so all we had to do was wait until the market turned and all this real estate would be golden," says Levan, who turned out to be right.

Some investors stood by the company and bought millions of shares for 35 cents a share in 2009, Levan said at the meeting. The day before the meeting, shares were trading at $7.38. Those who bought a million shares for $350,000 during the dark days of the recession had a $7 million profit.

To realize value from the $600 million in assets, BBX commenced 92 commercial foreclosures and lawsuits and collected more than $100 million in

South Florida Business & Wealth

How sweet it is? BBX swallows up IT'SUGAR

■ With a growing sweet tooth for the candy business, BBX Capital Corp. announced Monday it has acquired the majority stake in South Florida-based candy retailer IT'SUGAR in a $57 million transaction.

Miami Herald

BBX Capital gets Deerfield candy chain

It'Sugar sold
for $57 million

Sun Sentinel

June 19, 2017

BBX Capital buys IT'SUGAR for $57M

South Florida Business Journal

BBX Capital acquires IT'SUGAR for $57 million

IT'SUGAR ceo Jeff Rubin will remain as ceo.

June 19, 2017

Alyse Thompson

Candy Industry

Jeff Rubin—CEO of IT'SUGAR

SEEING AROUND CORNERS

IT'SUGAR Las Vegas
Opened May 2019

IT'SUGAR American Dream Rendering
Opening November 2019

IT'SUGAR Current Footprint

~100 locations in over 25 states and Washington, DC

The New York Times

FOOD

Coconut Brittle Takes Top Prize at Fancy Food Show

SEEING AROUND CORNERS

($ in thousands)		2014 [3]	2015 [3]	2016 [1][3]	2017 [1][3]	2018 [3]
Total Revenues	$	57,839	56,461	65,068	68,935	68,417
Adjusted EBITDA [2]	$	(174)	(68)	1,852	4,595	4,984
Book Value	$	7,155	6,132	10,807	12,698	13,114

Designer, distributor, and manufacturer of:

International Distribution
Canada, United States, and Europe

- Specialty Doors
- Hardware
- Home Décor Products

Lean Management
Focused on Improving Sales and Margin

Balanced Sales Mix
50% of Sales from Big Box Retail

Barn Door Systems
Driving Growth

 Millwork Vendor of the Year - 2016

CHAPTER 25

REFLECTIONS ON A LIFE WELL LIVED

"Men who have attained things worth having in this world have worked while others have idled, have persevered when others gave up in despair, have practiced early in life the valuable habits of self-denial, industry, and singleness of purpose. As a result, they enjoy in later life the success so often erroneously attributed to good luck."
—Grenville Kleiser

After we won the SEC case an abundance of riches in the form of awards, recognition, and honors rolled in. It became quite obvious that much of this had been on hold waiting to see how the SEC case turned out.

There were major multipage feature stories in *The Miami Herald*, *Ft. Lauderdale Sun Sentinel*, *South Florida Business and Wealth*, and *South Florida Business Journal*. *Florida Trend* named me one of the most influential business leaders in Florida. The *SFBJ* recognized BBX Capital as the Business of the Year. Separately the *SFBJ* recognized me as Chairman of the Year.

Bluegreen was recognized by the Boca Raton Chamber of Commerce as the Business of the Year.

We sold Benihana at a large profit.

Nova Southeastern University elected me chairman of the Board of Trustees.

The Association of Fundraising Professionals named Susie and me as Philanthropists of the Year.

Nova Southeastern University asked me to deliver the commencement speech to the graduating MBA class of 2019. They awarded me an honorary Doctorate in Business. I finally received my advanced degree in business!

Our products had great success:

Renin was named Millwork Vendor of the Year at Lowes.

Anastasia's Coconut Cashew Crunch, under our Sweet Holdings umbrella, won the top awards at the Specialty Food Association's Summer Fancy Show.

BBX successfully sold 10 percent of Bluegreen in the public market by doing an IPO. BBX Capital retained 90 percent. Bluegreen was again listed on the NYSE. Shawn Pearson became CEO of Bluegreen and I remained chairman. Bluegreen had become the fourth largest public timeshare company in America after Wyndham Destinations, Hilton Grand Vacations, and Marriott Vacations.

The NYSE invited BBX Capital to ring the opening bell on January 12, 2018, and Bluegreen Vacations to ring the closing bell on the same day. Since I am chairman of both companies, this was a historical moment as I am believed to be the only business person to ring the opening and closing bell on the same day in the 225-year history of the New York Stock Exchange.

As I reflect back upon the recurring themes of my life—family, luck, persistence, determination, optimism, seeing around corners—I have been blessed and am extremely grateful.

Taking Stock

Our announced objective for BBX Capital was to build long-term shareholder value. At the time we announced we were selling

BankAtlantic to BB&T in November of 2011, our stock had plunged to just thirty-five cents a share. By the end of 2012 it was $1.26—it had gone up 260 percent. By the end of the following year, our stock was $2.89—up about 129 percent from 2012. By December 31, 2014, it had risen to $3.20, up another 11 percent. By the following year it was $3.39, up 6 percent. By December 31, 2016, BBX Capital's stock was $4.88, up another 44 percent. And by the end of 2017 it closed at $7.97, up again another 63 percent.

BBX Capital was $10.01 on the NYSE on April 18, 2018 and had crossed the $1 billion market capitalization mark. It was the highest price and market capitalization in BBX's 46-year history. That would be an increase of 2,800 percent since December 31, 2011, the year before we sold the bank. A $10,000 investment in BBX Capital on December 31, 2011 would have grown to $280,000. Bluegreen, 90 percent owned by BBX, hit its market high of $1.8 billion shortly thereafter.

I was sitting in a Bluegreen meeting in Boca Raton on April 18, 2018 when the market closed at 4:00 p.m. I noted that the BBX Capital stock had closed at over a billion dollars. I made a mental note and went back to focusing on the meeting.

An hour later I was in the car driving on I-95. Emotion over-whelmed me. Tears started to pour down my cheeks. I was reflecting on the fact that I.R.E. Financial Corporation, the company I formed in 1972 when I was twenty-eight years old with $20,000 from my family, which ultimately became BFC Financial Corporation, BFC, and finally BBX Capital, was now worth a billion dollars. I was overwhelmed by the enormity of it.

I called Susie and could hardly get the words out. She had been there from the beginning in 1972 and all the way through. I called Alison and Gene, Jack, Jarett, and Seth.

How could our little company be worth a billion dollars on the NYSE? We'd had so many successes, which we more or less took in stride, noted them, and quickly moved on. We had never stopped to celebrate. Now, at this moment I wanted to cherish it more than anything. It was a wonderful forty-six-year ride.

Postscript

As I reflect back on the recurring themes of my life—family, hard work, luck, optimism, perseverance, seeing around corners, and grit—I realize I have been blessed and am extremely grateful.

I miss my father and mother every day, and probably not a day passes when I don't thank them in one way or another for my life.

From my mother I learned about organization, efficiency, tolerance, responsibility, and selflessness. From my father I learned persistence, determination, resourcefulness, what it means to have a good work ethic, creativity, independence, self-reliance, and to stand up for myself.

From each I learned about unconditional love, which I hope I have given to my own children and grandchildren.

As this book goes to print, I am reminded that in 2017 I had a premonition that another recession was just around the corner. Conventional wisdom suggested otherwise, especially since the Dow Jones was in record high territory. We decided we wanted to be flush with cash in the next recession so we could take advantage of opportunities as opposed to being cash constrained. So we started to hoard cash by not reinvesting, eliminating dividends, and building a cash war chest. Of course we had no idea when a recession might hit and what would be the catalyst for a downturn.

Now, in 2020, the world is fighting the coronavirus, unemployment is skyrocketing, businesses are closing, and the future is uncertain. Fortunately, BBX Capital has managed to reserve $125 million in cash and Bluegreen $220 million.

Some might call that "Seeing Around Corners" or Levan's "Luck" again!

The following is a list of titles, positions, and honors I have been fortunate to achieve:

Titles and Positions: Business

Chairman and CEO of BBX Capital (NYSE)
(Formerly I.R.E. Financial and BFC Financial)

Chairman and CEO of BankAtlantic Bancorp (NYSE)

Chairman and CEO of BankAtlantic

Chairman and CEO of Bluegreen Vacations (NYSE)

Chairman and CEO of Levitt Corporation (NYSE)

Board Member: Benihana (Nasdaq)

Titles and Positions: Community Nonprofits

Chairman of NSU Board of Trustees

Finance Chairman: NSU Board of Trustees

Trustee: NSU Board of Trustees

NSU Entrepreneur Hall of Fame: 2002

Chairman of BBX Capital Foundation

Chairman of BankAtlantic Foundation

Member of Broward Workshop

Chairman of Broward College Foundation: 1998–2000

Dedicated Sixty Habitat for Humanity Homes

Member of Young Presidents Organization (Now YPO Gold):
    November 1, 1984–Present

Moderator of YPO Forum: 1991–Present

Moderator of Harvard Business School YPO Education:
    1994–2019

Co-Founder and Co-Chair of Susie and Alan B. Levan NSU Ambassadors Board

Co-Founder and Chair of NSU Fellows Society

Member of Alexis de Tocqueville Society, United Way, Broward County

Honors

Rang the bell on the NYSE seven times as Chairman of BBX Capital Corp., BankAtlantic Bancorp, Bluegreen Vacations, BFC Financial Corporation, Levitt Corporation.

Only businessperson in the 225-year history of the NYSE to ring the opening and closing bell on the same day.

Florida Trend – "One of the Most Influential Leaders in the State of Florida"

Commencement Speaker Nova Southeastern University MBA and MIBA graduating class of 2019, H. Wayne Huizenga School of Business – June 7, 2019

Honorary Doctorate Degree in Business Administration from Nova Southern University – June 7, 2019

Chairman of the Year 2018 – *South Florida Business Journal*

Company of the Year (BBX Capital Corp.) 2018 – *South Florida Business Journal*

Apogee Award 2018 – *South Florida Business & Wealth*

Philanthropists of the Year (Susie and Alan Levan) – National Association of Fundraising Professionals – Broward County 2017

Tulane University Distinguished Alumni of the Year award 2007

South Florida Sun Sentinel Excalibur Award 2006

Florida Atlantic University College of Business, Business Leader of the Year 2006

Jr. Achievement Hall of Fame, Broward County 2005

South Florida CEO Magazine – CEO of the Year, December 2005

Miami Chamber of Commerce Cutting Edge Award 2004

Ernst & Young Entrepreneur of the Year Award for Florida 2003

NSU Entrepreneur Hall of Fame 2002

Habitat for Humanity Spirit of Humanity Award 2000

Miami Herald Silver Knight Award in Citizenship – North Miami HS 1966

Education

Tulane University – Bachelor's degree in Philosophy and English, 1966

President of Tulane Honor Board 1965–1966

President of Tulane College of Arts and Sciences 1966

President of Tulane Chapter of AEPi Fraternity

Business Manager of Tulane Newspaper (*Hullabaloo*), Tulane Yearbook (*Jambalaya*), Tulane Student Directory, Tulane Radio Station (WTUL) 1964–1966

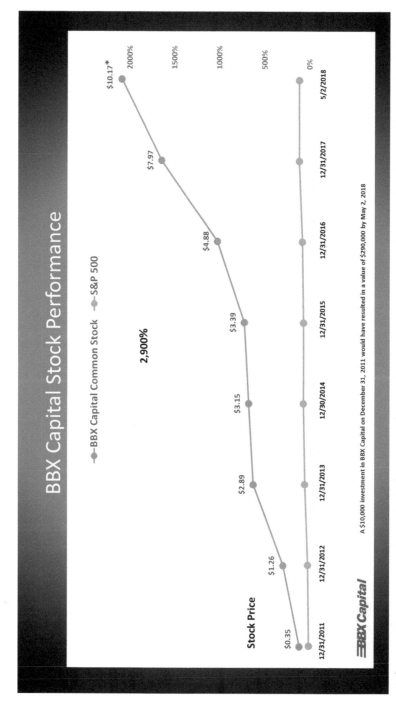

BBX Capital Stock Performance

A $10,000 investment in BBX Capital on December 31, 2011 would have resulted in a value of $290,000 by May 2, 2018.

A $10,000 investment in BBX Capital on December 31, 2011 would have resulted in a value of $290,000 by May 2, 2018.

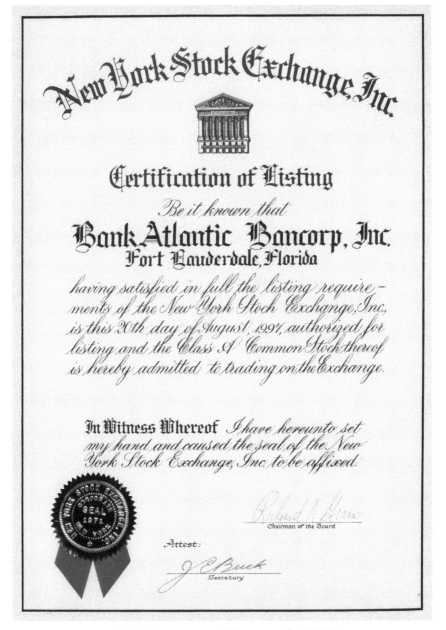

BankAtlantic original listing on the NYSE

We had the honor of ringing the bell multiple times for each of our companies.

Alan and Jack   Alan and Jarett

Alan and Seth   Alan and Ray

Susie and Alan   Jarett, Alan, Jack and Seth

Bell ringing medallion mementos

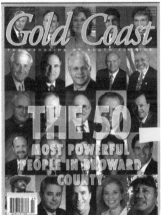

Magazine and newspaper covers

Alan B. Levan, LAUREATE

Alan B. Levan is Chairman & CEO of BankAtlantic Bancorp, a diversified financial services holding company whose common stock is listed on the New York Stock Exchange under the symbol "BBX".

Junior Achievement

*Ernst and Young Entrepreneur
of the Year*

NSU Hall of Fame

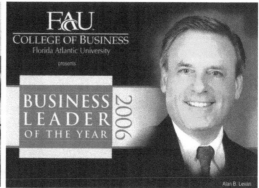

Sun Sentinel Excalibur Award

FAU Business Leader of the Year

Humanitarian of the Year

Tulane University Alumni Award

Philanthropist of the Year

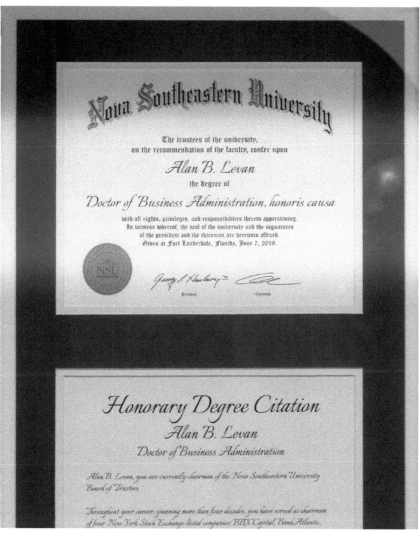

Alan B. Levan – Honory Doctor of Business Administration

CHAPTER 26

MY SWEETEST LP

"I love you every day. And now I will miss you every day."
—Mitch Albom

The year 2018 ended in tragedy. My youngest daughter, Lauren, thirty-six, known to us and her friends as LP, died on September 17, 2018. Diagnosed nine months earlier with non-Hodgkin's lymphoma, she fought a relentless battle but eventually lost.

I've often said I have the ability to remember the good things and shut out the bad, but that only worked until that day. My heart aches every day and I will miss her forever.

Among his many loving, indelible lessons, my father always taught me that we have to move on. But from this tragedy, I don't see how I ever will.

Losing Lauren to non-Hodgkin's lymphoma is an indescribable pain. I ache for her. Sometimes I think it must be the worst pain anyone can feel, and there are days when you have to wonder how the pain doesn't kill you. There is a hole that can never again be filled. Days seem out of sequence. At times the thought of going along like this to the end of my own life seems overwhelming. I must admit I have questioned how I will do it.

When someone passes, I've sometimes found that people tend to enshrine them. That is not my intention with Lauren, but at the same time her extreme kindness, generosity, and many passions and accomplishments—the special daughter, sister, granddaughter, aunt, and fiancée she was—made her a most impressive human being. The thing is, because of her deep sense of humility, Lauren wasn't the least bit interested in impressing anyone. It was never her goal. She was simply comfortable in her own skin.

Lauren was my moral compass. She was unafraid to offer her counsel if she thought I was about to do something that was out of character, or would not serve me or others in the way I thought it would.

"What do you mean?" she would say. "You'll regret this decision; it isn't the right thing for you," she would say quite candidly—which is how we were with one another, perhaps both of us seeing around corners the way I prided myself in doing and the way my mother had before me. Though Lauren didn't share the same DNA, more times than not she shared the same kind of vision.

I can never stop loving LP, as we called her. I go to bed loving her and wake up loving her even more, if that's possible. But it is not only because she is gone and I am grieving. I felt that way when she was here…each day I got to love her and my other children more than I did the day before. The difference is that now I can no longer tell her.

LP was our youngest—an avowed vegetarian before it was fashionable, and a steadfast supporter of animal rights and environmental causes. She was just seven years old when I married Susie, and she survived the kidnapping and all the hours in the sweltering trunk with her mother. Because of the way Susie handled the situation, with Lauren wrapped in her arms and making it into a game they were supposedly playing together, LP never showed any signs of delayed stress or had any psychological scars whatsoever. She went on growing up and living her life with joy and a sense of freedom. She went about things with an infectious abandon. She lived for and in the moment, rushing headlong into every experience as if it were her last day on Earth. I can't help wondering if she somehow knew her life would be cut so short.

There was definitely a dichotomy in Lauren's personality: She was as responsible as she was free-spirited. Though the latter is often associated with a lack of maturity and accountability, it didn't apply to Lauren. She always took care of business and certainly people.

You may recall my talking about our housekeeper, Petrona. Dear Petrona played a pivotal role in Lauren's upbringing from the time she was a few months old until Lauren was twenty-five. She played a key role in our family during and after the kidnapping, spending that terrifying night with us on the floor upstairs, and being tied to the shower door in the downstairs bathroom when I was taken to the bank and Susie and Lauren were forced into the trunk. After Petrona's retirement at age eighty-eight, Lauren took care of her for five years. She found her an apartment, bought her food, took her to doctors' visits, and handled her money until her beloved Petrona's passing. If you subscribe to this kind of thing, now they are together again.

My daughter was an adventurer not only in the realm of traveling the world, which she did solo, with friends, and eventually with her beloved fiancé Travis, but also in her appreciation of restaurants, shows, festivals, concerts, sporting events like Miami Heat and Dolphin games. She was the most "out there" of all of our five kids, yet she had a strong sense of right and wrong. She also cherished family and friends above everything. If you were her friend, you knew you were her friend. LP would do anything for you, and the same thing with family. She was the one that remembered every single birthday and every special event. She may have been immersed in her job, or in some environmental or animal welfare pursuit, or somewhere in the world doing her thing, but she never missed a birthday or anniversary or forgot about any other important occasion—even if we did.

It bears saying again I never stopped learning about humility from LP. It was one of the many things that defined her. She taught me more about that all the time, and certainly how to live a fuller life. As much as I thought I knew and had accomplished in my life, LP found a way to show me how much more there was out there to explore. We had an extraordinary relationship, and in fact all of her relationships—many cultivated as an adult and some even retained from elementary school days—transcended differences. She just didn't see them, choosing to focus on what united people rather than what divided them.

When She Came

Susie always called Lauren her miracle baby, born at a time when, because of health reasons, she'd been told she'd have no more children. She always believed she'd survived being in the trunk of the car because of Lauren, knowing that rather than succumb to a terrible fate, she had to focus all her thoughts and energy on saving this child's life. And it likely saved hers.

As a child, teenager, and certainly as an adult, for LP it was brakes off and high beams on. Her passion for music began early, and in fact because I can't even identify a Beatles song on the radio, she'd quiz me in the car on the way to school in her tireless efforts to educate me—aghast at my music mindlessness (I just didn't get it). Later she channeled her mad love of music into a career doing music public relations and managing various bands and musicians. Wearing her entrepreneur's hat, she founded South Florida Music Obsessed, which produced a website to shine a bigger light on the music scene, providing information that included a blog, reviews, and event listings for the contemporary regional music scene. It was voted South Florida's Best Music Blog by *New Times* magazine.

Lauren was always vitally interested in what I was doing with regard to my own business, though she stopped short of wanting to do the same thing. That she didn't follow me the way Shelley did, initially running the BankAtlantic Foundation, or the way Jarett did when he channeled his law and business degrees into BankAtlantic, really didn't matter. We had a powerful bond and were always there for one another.

When she was thirty-two, Lauren met Travis, her soulmate, and together they acquired two canine companions: Jaco and Fela. Following her diagnosis and throughout exhausting treatments and procedures, Lauren never complained and in fact was a beacon of optimism. She held us up. Travis loved and cared for her—never letting go—both of them deciding not to let her illness deter them from preparing for their January 19, 2019 wedding. Her wedding dress still hangs in Susie's closet, absent my luminous daughter who never got to wear it.

My LP texted or called me every day and would always text me "goodnight." While I miss her terribly and have no idea how I will ever fill the space she occupied in my heart and in my life, I must say somehow I am very much at peace with her passing. I don't have a single element of guilt, or "what if," or "I could have," or "we should have." I am sure that comes from the way she and I navigated the world together.

Though my daughter is gone, her light will never be extinguished. It shines brightly in me and in everyone who ever knew her.

Rest in Peace, Sweet LP

October 18, 1981 – September 17, 2018

Gina and Lauren

Don and Lauren

Jarett and Lauren

Shelley and Lauren

Lauren with her grandparents, Pearl and Zit Levan.

Lauren with friends and cousin Paris (top left)

Wedding Invitation

Lauren and Travis

In Loving Memory

Lauren loved capturing these breath taking sunrises from her balcony.
No matter what – she cherished each new day.

20 IDEAS FOR A SUCCESSFUL LIFE

I think *a lot* of people are quick to offer advice about how to live in the world and that is not my intention. It's not one size fits all.

The following ideas have worked for me, and if you choose to apply all or some of them, I believe they may help you on your own path.

While they may have been mentioned in one form or another at the end of various chapters, under **Life Lessons Learned**, they are consolidated here for easier reference.

1. Persistence and determination are omnipotent.

2. Learn to evaluate the downside on every issue.

3. Be an optimist. If it doesn't come naturally, practice optimism every day and it will soon become second nature.

4. Train yourself to see around corners. This, again, may not come naturally but working at it will sharpen the skill.

5. Bring at least one or two people into your life who don't always agree with you and are capable of telling you things you don't necessarily want to hear, as long as those things are factual and objective.

6. You will always want the best and brightest on your team; look for people smarter than you.

7. Every parent wants their children to love them. If you add reasonable discipline and insist on competency, in addition to loving them unconditionally, you will have a better chance at this.

8. The unique and complex relationship between your child and you is known only by you. Don't substitute someone else's child-rearing recipe for your own experience and good judgment.

9. Luck and opportunity come to those who are ready for it.

10. Work hard with high energy. Outwork everyone. It will pay off.

11. Be confident but not arrogant.

12. Honor your commitments.

13. Live with integrity and high ethics.

14. Adopt a healthy lifestyle and stick with it.

15. Be a student of business and life—read, read, read about what are others doing.

16. Learn to compartmentalize. It will give you an advantage and get you through crises.

17. Sorry for the cliché but think outside the box. Creativity can be your salvation.

18. There is no substitute for kindness.

19. Lead a balanced life.

20. Give back to improve society at all levels.

IN APPRECIATION

There are people who come into our lives for all of it, or for a few decades, a year, a month, or even less. Everyone leaves their mark—some responsible for a pivotal direction we take, others for a new way of thinking, still others for their love, warmth, generosity, and encouragement when we are at our best and our worst.

Many people have made the stories in this book possible. I am forever indebted to those who have impacted and changed the trajectory of my life. I wish I could thank them all, but time and space allow me to only acknowledge some of them here.

My amazing wife Susie: my love, my champion, my reason. I don't remember my life without you. Thank you for always being there for me. You are and have always been my confidant, constant cheerleader, and advisor. You give me strength, courage, joy, and happiness. Thank you for being my angel. Susie and I celebrated our thirty-second wedding anniversary in September 2020. She has not just been the love of my life, but my rock. We've worked together since 1972—forty-seven years. She's been part of my every decision, my ups and downs, my successes and failures. She's Type A as I am and every bit as successful in her own right. We work well as a team—with each other, our children, each other's business, and our day-to-day life. It's a beautiful thing and we don't take it for granted. It requires constant nourishment, hard work and communication, and often time, one-on-one Good and Welfare sessions.

My parents, Zit and Pearl (in memoriam). Thank you for loving me unconditionally and for raising me in a wonderful and happy home. You instilled in me so many important values, for always trusting in me and your continuing encouragement. I could not have asked for better parents and role models. You gave me the foundation for all that was about to come.

My children: Don, Shelley, Jarett, Gina, and Lauren. You have, and continue to, inspire me, even when you don't know you're doing it. You have all been a constant source of joy and pride and the energy of my soul.

Special thanks to Jarett, who as president of our companies created the special culture with our associates. He is credited with BankAtlantic winning the highly coveted J.D. Power award for customer service in the depth of the recession.

My twelve grandchildren: Todd, Tobi, Madeline, Jordan, Tyler, Jacob, Joaquin, Benjamin, Sydney, Timo, Julia, and Andy. I've loved you—even the promise of you—since before you were born. Thank you for bringing such joy, laughter, and sunshine into my life.

My older brother Jay: remember when you would swing with me on the wrought iron gates? Together we were free. I will always treasure our many special memories.

Jack Abdo, partner, trusted friend, and confidante. Thank you for your love, support, and for our game-changing thirty-five-year partnership. You are clearly a brother in arms and also of the heart.

Seth Wise, partner, president of our real estate division, is like family and has been friends with Jarett and our other children since high school. Because of Seth, our reputation for real estate expertise sets us apart.

Ray Lopez, our consummate chief financial officer, has brought a level of sophistication and financial discipline to our organizations. He is now also serving as chief operating officer of Bluegreen Vacations Corporation.

Eugene (Gene) Stearns and Alison Miller: nearly a fifty-year-long love affair. Without you it wouldn't be much of a story to tell because you were, and continue to be, a significant part of all of it. I want you to know how much I value your friendship, advocacy, and support. You protected me, won my legal battles, provided constant strategic guidance, and always had my back. I couldn't have done it without you. I am forever grateful.

Alan Fein introduced us to Benihana and also handled and won the libel suit against the behemoth ABC Capital Cities/*2020*. Alan is steady, methodical, and confident; I've learned a great deal from our interactions.

Grace Mead and the entire Stearns Weaver Miller corporate and litigation teams have been extraordinary advocates. They provide unbelievable backup for Gene and Alison in all of our endeavors.

Terri Levan (in memoriam). You were my college sweetheart, first wife, and the mother of three of our wonderful children.

Norman Silber: My right hand in college and with me at the beginnings of I.R.E. Financial Corporation.

Steve Arky, friend (in memoriam) and my first lawyer. Steve did our original SEC registrations for I.R.E. Financial. His untimely passing in his forties was truly tragic.

Stan Linnick, amazing friend from Tulane University for fifty-eight years, and with me at Levitt, BankAtlantic, and now executive director of the Susie and Alan B. Levan NSU Ambassadors Board. Steady, incredibly loyal, and highly competent.

Frank Grieco, the first professional to join I.R.E. in the early 1970s. Later became the senior finance executive at BankAtlantic in the late 1980s and 1990s.

Dr. Robert Cornfeld: dear friend of forty-seven years. Bob and I have done dozens of real estate transactions. In a world of increasing documentation and lawyers, Bob and I never needed a contract. Our handshake was our bond. Truly one of a kind.

Carolyn Dellapelle and (posthumously) her mother, Jean Carvalho, have played such important roles: My right and left hands, and even at times my brain, for so many years I've lost count. Always going above and beyond, I humbly thank you.

Linda Drapos, our corporate secretary for all of our companies for thirty-seven years. A wonderful person. A blessing.

Julie DeVito and Jen Lewis handle all my personal matters. Without them I would have no records, money, or files.

BankAtlantic's executive management team, the powerful engine competing against the major banks and winning: Lloyd DeVaux, Marcia Snyder, Lew Sarrica, Susan McGregor, Valerie Toalson, Jay McClung, Jeff Mindling, Jim White, Anne Chervony, and of course, Jarett Levan, and Jack Abdo.

My special thanks to Susan McGregor, BankAtlantic's human relations manager and much more. Susan has always provided valuable guidance to me and encouraged me to write this book. Today she's an entrepreneur and businesswoman. I am very proud of her.

The Independent members of the board of directors of BFC Financial Corporation, BankAtlantic, BBX Capital, Levitt Corporation and Bluegreen Vacations Corporation: James Allmand, Norman Becker, Andrew Cagnetta, Lawrence Cirillo, Steven Coldren, Darwin Dornbush, Gregory Haile, Willis Holcombe, Oscar Holzmann, Alan Levy, Joel Levy, William Nicholson, Anthony Segreto, Arnold Sevell, Orlando Sharpe, Neil Sterling, Charlie Winningham. Your advice, counsel and support during incredible periods of growth and despair will always be remembered.

Directors in memoriam: Governor LeRoy Collins, Bruno DiGiulian, Lib Ginestra, AJ Harris, Lawrence Kahn, Philip Morgaman, Earl Pertnoy, Lee Ruwitch, Irvin Shapiro.

Ben Plotkin, friend and investment banker extraordinaire. Ben and his companies have raised hundreds of millions of growth capital for my companies.

Donna Ackerly was on the front line for thirty-nine years of every major merger and shareholder proposal as our proxy solicitor. With her and her team's expertise, we never lost a proxy contest.

My YPO forum. My "guys," all presidents of their own companies, have been the fabric of our social life, business education, advisors, and confidants. We meet once a month and are still together after thirty years. The eight of us traveled around the world on educational and bonding trips. All of us are very different: I'm the most risk-averse but we get along famously as opposites. Wonderful, wonderful memories: Leonard Abess Jr., Joel Altman, Phil Bakes (in memoriam), Mark Begelman, John Guarino, Phil McKnight (in memoriam), and Stephen Riemer.

A special shout out for Joel Altman, brother by a different mother. As close to love as two heterosexual men can get.

George Hanbury, president of Nova Southeast University: a true leader. Passionate about students and acute business acumen, a dual skill not enjoyed by most college presidents. I've enjoyed being on the Board of Trustees and then chairman of the Board at NSU.

Beth Herman, my writing partner and an incredible person. For two-and-a-half years she interviewed, researched, prodded, cross-examined, wrote, and preliminarily edited this book as she did for my wife Susie's book, *Getting to Forgiveness: What A Near-Death Experience Can Teach Us About Loss, Resilience and Love.* How fortunate we were to find Beth. In addition to writing she has become a dear friend.

Lastly, to the more than 15,000 associates of I.R. E. Financial, BankAtlantic, Bluegreen Vacations, Levitt Corporation, Benihana, BBX Capital, BBX Capital Real Estate, Renin Corporation, IT'SUGAR, Anastasia and Hoffman's. Without them none of this would have been possible.

CPSIA information can be obtained
at www.ICGtesting.com
Printed in the USA
JSHW021916031222
33950JS00003B/8/J